EDINB[URGH]
GRANTON, HAYMARKET & LEITH

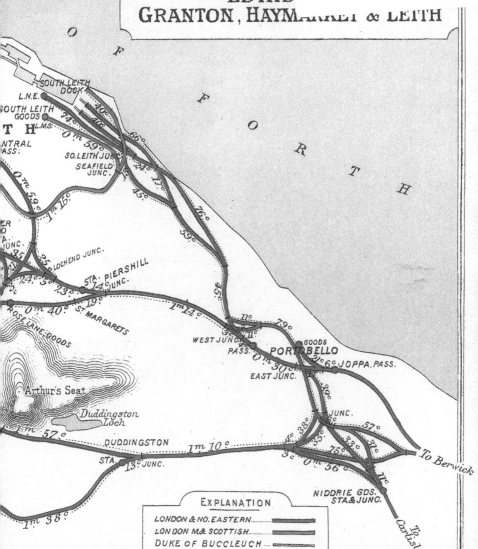

EXPLANATION

LONDON & NO. EASTERN ....
LONDON M.& SCOTTISH ....
DUKE OF BUCCLEUCH ....

The Edinburgh Suburban
and
South Side Junction
Railway

by
A.A. Maclean

THE OAKWOOD PRESS

© Oakwood Press & A.A. Maclean 2006

British Library Cataloguing in Publication Data
A Record for this book is available from the British Library
ISBN 0 85361 645 0

Typeset by Oakwood Graphics.
Repro by PKmediaworks, Cranborne, Dorset.
Printed by Cambrian Printers, Aberystwyth, Ceredigion.

Dedication

To my wife Hermione and son Douglas for their forbearance over the years, and also to John Smith of Bearsden for his continuous pressure on me to keep working on the book.

Title page: Tranquillity of the Edinburgh suburbs in the summer sunshine is caught in this study of 'Glen' class 4-4-0 locomotive No. 62487 *Glen Arklet* at the head of three LNER suburban coaches on the 2.20 pm Gorgie to Duddingston Inner Circle train on 23rd July, 1955. *Author*

Published by The Oakwood Press (Usk), P.O. Box 13, Usk, Mon., NP15 1YS.
E-mail: sales@oakwoodpress.co.uk
Website: www.oakwoodpress.co.uk

Contents

The Line in Detail

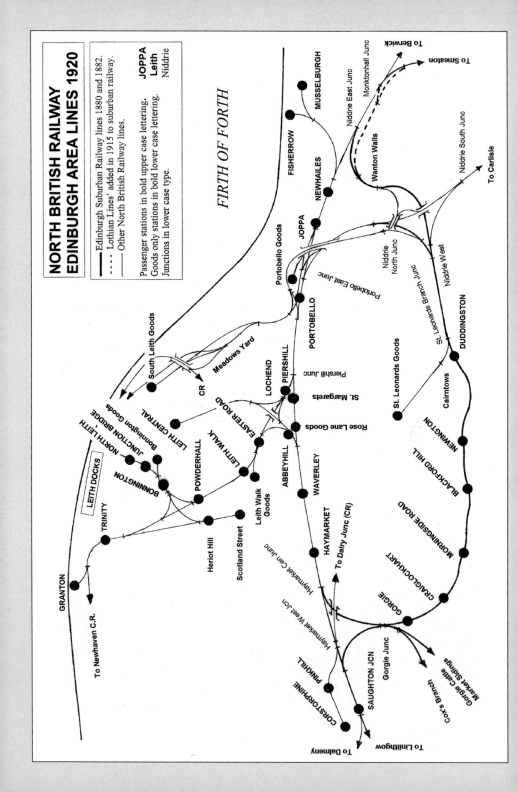

NORTH BRITISH RAILWAY
EDINBURGH AREA LINES 1920

— Edinburgh Suburban Railway lines 1880 and 1882.
- - - - Lothian Lines' added in 1915 to suburban railway.
— Other North British Railway lines.

Passenger stations in bold upper case lettering.
Goods only stations in bold lower case lettering.
Junctions in lower case type.

JOPPA
Leith
Niddrie

FIRTH OF FORTH

Introduction

The compilation of a history of a major suburban railway is fraught with problems. How much did the railway affect the local environment and vice versa? How did urban development affect the line? What was the impact of road competition?

Statistical pundits will find themselves disappointed in this work - for a very good reason. The Edinburgh Suburban & South Side Junction Railway cannot accurately be assessed either by tickets sold or revenue generated. The stations were both local booking offices and railway 'town office' and passenger tickets sold covered both local journeys and from main line termini, the latter having no bearing on the station where the journey was booked. There were also a large numbers of season ticket holders - particularly weekly 'zones' after their introduction in the early 1900s - to and from other suburban stations, but which included destinations on other routes. Season ticket journeys could be made two, four or more times per day according to individual requirements and service suitability and there was a deal of staff residential and duty travel with the railway headquarters being in or near Waverley station. Computerised statistical analysis systems to allocate journeys and revenue - at best estimates - were not available when the line was open. Measurements of journeys were at best taken by head counts of passengers twice or more per annum.

Decline of goods traffic over the railway network as a whole with the development of road transport and the repressive restrictions placed by government on rail in favour of road, particularly in the inter-war years, inevitably led to a decline in freight working. Latterly, most goods wagons in the suburban line yards arrived underload, usually with coal and other minerals, and were dispatched empty. Originating traffic, from most stations, apart from Gorgie and Duddingston where there were significant private sidings, declined until it became virtually non existent. Again, no discrete revenue or vehicle statistics appear to have survived along with records of demurrage, siding rents, etc. relative to the Edinburgh suburban goods stations.

The core objective of this work has been to consider the operating aspects which have now passed into the annals of history, although much of the line still remains open as a significant element of transport strategy in the capital, albeit *sans* sidings, *sans* stations, *sans* signal boxes, virtually as 'plain line'.

The last timetabled suburban passenger train, formed of a Gloucester RCW twin unit No. SC50343/56098 prepares to leave Duddingston on the Outer Circle service to Waverley on Saturday 8th September, 1962. *Author*

5

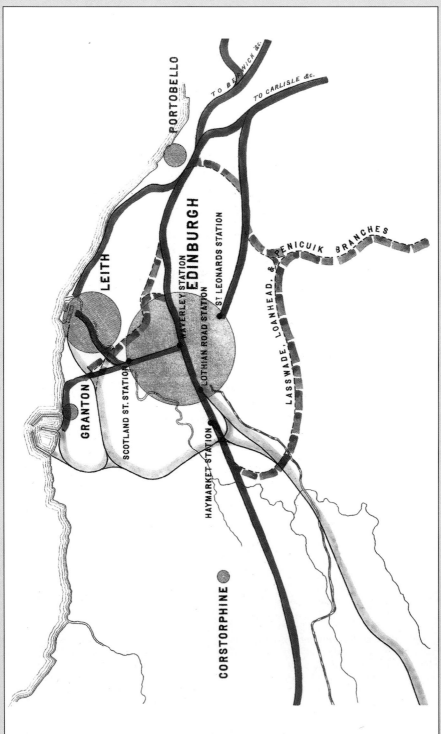

Extract from a November 1865 map of the North British Railway which indicated, by a dotted line, the planned original course of the Edinburgh suburban railway (albeit as part of the line to Lasswade, Loanhead, and Penicuik) and also the deviation line from Waverley to Granton via Abbeyhill. The latter opened in 1868, but it was to be years until the first Act for the suburban railway came to fruition.

North British Railway

Chapter One

Background and Southern Suburbs

In 1865, the North British and Caledonian railways promoted similar lines to that of the later Edinburgh Suburban & South Side Junction Railway (ESSSJR) but after what contemporary sources described as a 'pretty keen fight', the Caledonian Bill was thrown out, but the North British (NBR) one passed. A NBR map of 30th November, 1865 shows the route of the proposed line from Waverley leaving the Glasgow line after passing under the Caledonian Railway's Granton branch and heading for Gorgie before passing under the Caledonian Railway's main line and Granton branch near Slateford. Running close to Edinburgh's then municipal boundary, it joined the old Edinburgh & Dalkeith Railway (E&DR) route east of Duddingston. Both ran parallel for a short distance before the NB line passed under the E&DR and curved north to join the NB main line at the east end of the then Portobello station, thus enabling trains to return to Waverley. There was no spur from Gorgie to the later Haymarket West Junction, but a triangular junction between Cameron Toll and Duddingston, headed south to Roslin and Penicuik, and appeared as the 'Lasswade, Loanhead and Penicuik Branches'. The NBR 1865 schemes were abandoned at that time after the discovery of financial irregularities at Board level.

NB branch lines in the Edinburgh area increased in number after 1865, and although Waverley expanded in the following decade, burgeoning services meant that the railway was always chasing space. All traffic, both goods and passenger, passed through Waverley, and as volume increased, so did congestion. To paraphrase Goldsmith, '... and still they gazed and still the wonder grew, that one small station could carry all that grew'. A radical solution was required and in modern parlance, a 'ring road' was seen as the only solution, also enabling the NB to tap into passenger potential from the capital's expanding southern suburbs. Although circuitous, the railway offered shorter transit times - Waverley congestion and tailbacks permitting!

Following the success of the Tay Bridge, a scheme was put forward to bridge the Firth of Forth at Queensferry. It was conceded that this would result in Fife traffic flows from the east and south, hitherto routed by Granton and the Burntisland ferry, passing through Waverley and the city by-pass line became essential. A survey was undertaken by Sir Thomas Bouch, the eminent engineer (and former traffic manager of the Edinburgh & Northern Railway) who was responsible for many other major civil engineering projects and in the 1870s was in private practice as a consulting engineer based in Edinburgh. A Bill was prepared and put before Parliament, receiving the Royal Assent in August 1880. However, the findings of the report into the collapse of his Tay Bridge in December 1879 halted public confidence in Bouch but the bridges and Edinburgh suburban railway were still considered essential and new engineers and contractors engaged.

The new Forth Bridge Railway Act was passed on 12th July, 1882, that for a revised Edinburgh Suburban & South Side Junction Railway being authorised 12 days later, concurrently with separate legislation for extending the municipal (and police) boundaries of the City of Edinburgh. It is perhaps now pertinent to consider the wider canvas of Edinburgh at that that time and the other forms of public transport that had a bearing on the railway's future passenger traffic prospects.

Municipal Boundaries

The Edinburgh Municipal and Police Extension Act of 1882, took effect from 15th May, 1883 when the suburban line was under construction, and meant that stretches of the line hitherto outwith the city boundary now came within. It crossed the Edinburgh & Glasgow Railway line at right angles and passed through the fork at Gorgie between the lines to Haymarket West and Haymarket Central Junctions, the former being outside (as was Gorgie Junction). The boundary then passed along the east of the railway to the road bridge over the line at Myreside. Stations at Gorgie (and Craiglockhart when it opened in 1887) were outside the city limits, but if one was pedantic in interpreting the Act, their Inner Circle station buildings were in Edinburgh but those on the Outer Circle platforms were not!

At the Myreside Road bridge, the boundary crossed the railway and headed south, embracing the very up-market Morningside College (during its brief existence) but excluded the City Poorhouse a few yards away. Turning east, it brought the developing Morningside to Newington areas within the city, but at Cameron Bridge Toll it crossed the railway heading towards Duddingston Loch. The loch then became part of Edinburgh, although the nearby village of that name was not absorbed until 1901. In the 1920s, the Edinburgh boundary expanded to embrace the south side villages of Craigmillar, Niddrie, and Newcraighall, all of which bordered the suburban railway and expanded considerably in later years, but never had a railway station.

Public Road Transport to 1884

Edinburgh's public road transport was largely unregulated until the 'Edinburgh Provisional Order' of 1867 authorised magistrates to license public transport for routes, stances, timetables, drivers, conductors, etc., and make relevant by-laws. Indeed it was claimed that Britain came into line with Edinburgh with the 1930 Road Transport Act! At first, the horse bus was the main public transport medium in and around the city with regular services operating between the High Street and Leith, Newington and Haymarket; and to Stockbridge. An hourly circular service from Princes Street went via Newington and Morningside. Further afield, some 'country' operators ran services into Edinburgh. Keen competition resulted in many route and timetable changes, although sometimes the operators regulated themselves. As the city expanded, so did the horse bus network.

Under the 1870 'Act to facilitate the construction and to regulate the working of Tramways', Edinburgh Corporation could build and own the tramway infrastructure, but was not allowed to run the services and two groups of promoters emerged. The 'Edinburgh Street Tramways Company' (EST) (with which Thomas Bouch was associated) found more favour than the alternative 'Edinburgh and Leith Tramway Company' and the latter then withdrew. Edinburgh and Leith councillors supported the EST scheme, but when enquiries were made into why the North British Railway did not oppose this apparently competitive scheme, it emerged that the railway had thoughts on using the tram rails for its goods wagons, albeit probably horse hauled. Protective clauses were inserted to prevent this and the Bill was passed unopposed. Under one Schedule, the Corporation agreed to widen the road over the North Bridge within two years, although not necessary the bridge itself, the tram company contributing £2,500 to the cost.

The Edinburgh Street Tramways Company was incorporated on 29th June, 1871 and its Act authorised construction in certain streets, but 'motive power' was restricted to animals. Work proceeded quickly, the first service (Haymarket - Princes Street - Leith) opening quietly on Monday 6th November, 1871. The Post Office at the east end of Princes Street was linked to the foot of Minto Street in Newington on 29th May, 1872 and on 6th July another service started from the Post Office via the West End, Tollcross, Churchhill, Clinton Road, Hope Terrace and Kilgraston Road to the top of Marchmont Road, extending on 11th November, 1872 via Grange Road and the Bridges to form a circular route. The Haymarket and Leith service extended west to Coltbridge in June 1873.

The horse trams had a serious effect on horse bus revenues, some being withdrawn or curtailed. Croall, the major bus operator, 'diversified' by contracting his redundant horses to the Edinburgh Street Tramway Company but as the trams were heavier than the buses, there was dissatisfaction with the types of horses supplied (and the way they were treated). Croall's contract was terminated in 1874 and the tramway company thereafter provided its own animals.

North Bridge road widening started on 11th September, 1873, but as the original completion date had passed, it needed a fresh Act, which also included other uncompleted 1870 schemes. Although receiving the Royal Assent on 30th June, 1874, nothing was included to deal with the bridge arches that hindered railway operations below.

When the first Edinburgh Suburban & South Side Junction Railway Act was passed on 26th August, 1880, Gorgie and Craiglockhart had no trams or buses, (and also, be it said, no potential customers). Morningside had nothing south of Churchhill and Blackford had a short-lived horse bus. However, at Newington, arguably then the most prosperous of Edinburgh's southern suburbs, the tram terminus was next to land that would be the site of the railway station. Duddingston was a self-contained village outwith Edinburgh, with no local public transport (or potential).

The 1881 'Edinburgh Street Tramways Act' authorised an extension from Haymarket by Ardmillan Terrace (east end of Gorgie Road) and today's Harrison Road to the junction of Polwarth Terrace and Colinton Road, some 200 yards short of the future Craiglockhart station. A line from the top of Harrison Road ran via Gilmour Place to join the Church Hill line near Tollcross. A new route opened from Tollcross via Lauriston Place, George IV Bridge and the High Street joined the Newington line at the Tron, yards from the North Bridge and all opened in 1882. An 1882 Act authorised a single track from Church Hill down the then severally named, but continuous streets that now form Morningside Road, passing the Toll Bar and site of the proposed new station, to Morningside Drive and this opened by May 1883. The road at Morningside crossroads was raised when the bridge over the railway was built, trams temporarily terminating at the toll bar. However, Section 34 of that Act allowed the Tramway Company to acquire, build and operate omnibuses, subject to magistrates' licensing conditions.

The new tram routes authorised in 1881 and 1882 were in operation before the suburban railway opened, but although the trams had a more direct route into the city, they had a low average speed and did not seriously trouble the railway for some years. When opened in December 1884, most stations were served by, or were within a short walk, of horse trams or buses. Road transport concentrated on direct services to and from the city centre, whereas the railway circled the southern suburbs before heading towards the city centre. In January 1884, one John Pitcairn made a career move from the Traffic Department of the North British Railway to be General Manager of the Edinburgh Street Tramway Company, where he became well respected by both staff and public alike.

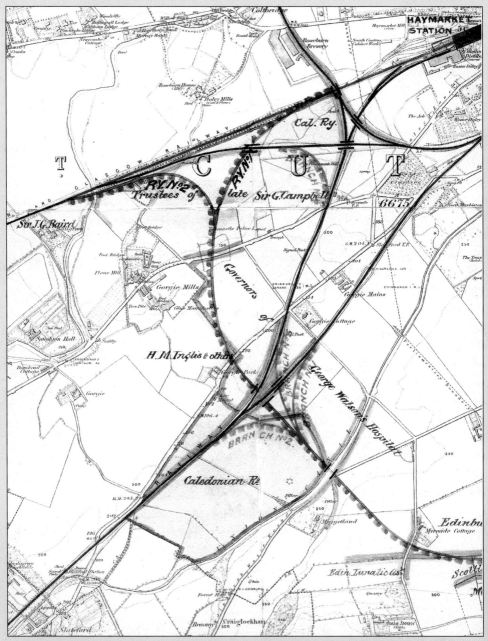

Suburban railway Haymarket and Gorgie proposed junctions 1880-1882. Map drawn up by the North British Railway using the 1855 Ordnance Survey, showing its proposed 1880 and 1882 suburban lines and the projected connections to the Caledonian Railway. The existing lines at 1880 are shown in heavy continuous lines and the proposed suburban railway and the connections in broken lines. Lighter grey continuous lines indicate land ownership boundaries.

Reproduced from the 25" Ordnance Survey Map amended by the NBR

Chapter Two

The Edinburgh 'Suburban' Acts and Actions

When the Edinburgh Suburban & South Side Junction Railway was promoted, there was very limited passenger potential. Apart from the glue works, Gorgie was largely agricultural, Craiglockhart was in open country, Blackford Hill was being considered for purchase by the city as a public park, and the proposed station sites at Morningside and Newington were outside the then Municipal and Parliamentary boundary. However, passenger traffic was not the main objective, which was confirmed in a letter that the railway sent to the Railway Department of the Board of Trade in London on 25th October, 1884, shortly before the line opened. This stated, 'Keeping in mind that the primary objective of the suburban railway was to relieve the main lines between Haymarket West and Portobello of all through goods, mineral and livestock trains, it will be many years until suburban passenger traffic be at all considerable'.

Goods traffic from east and south going north was at that time centralised on Portobello, moving directly from there to Granton (for the train ferry), but westbound traffic passed through Waverley. If the suburban line was not built, when the (Bouch) Forth Bridge opened, all that traffic would pass through Waverley station, even then vastly overcrowded, but there was simply no alternative. The proposed new suburban line would absorb that traffic, relieving the main station, and also carry passengers from the south and east directly through to the Edinburgh & Glasgow (E&G) section or the northern lines of the North British. The new railway was therefore seen to be of great public advantage.

After the Tay Bridge fell, Bouch continued with his contracts, including the suburban railway but the criticism of him in the ensuing report undoubtedly brought about his premature death. Work on his Forth Bridge ceased, with only one pier extant, the design for a new structure being prepared by John Fowler and Benjamin Blake, and being built by Messrs Arrol & Company. Similarly, engineering responsibility for the Edinburgh suburban line passed to Messrs Trimble and Peddie, Civil Engineers of Edinburgh, under whom the scheme was completed. Actually, George Trimble had previously been one of Bouch's assistants. The contractor for the work was Messrs John Waddell & Sons of Edinburgh, one of the main contractors used by Bouch's firm.

The Bill

There is little doubt that the initial Bill for the Edinburgh Suburban & South Side Junction Railway, although legally independent, was prepared by the North British Railway as a NB prodigy. As expected, one of four main objectors was the Caledonian Railway, which expressed its views at the subsequent Parliamentary evidence hearings, perhaps recalling the defeat of its own Bill in the 1860s. The Edinburgh Asylum at Morningside also objected as some of its ground was to be taken by the railway, but this was later withdrawn. Both the others were also over land and were suitably dealt with.

The authors of the Bill expressed the view that there had long been a need for railway communication between the western and southern suburbs of the city and its centre. Indeed, when the Bill was promoted, travel by public transport between Princes Street and either Morningside or Newington took about half an hour. A

11

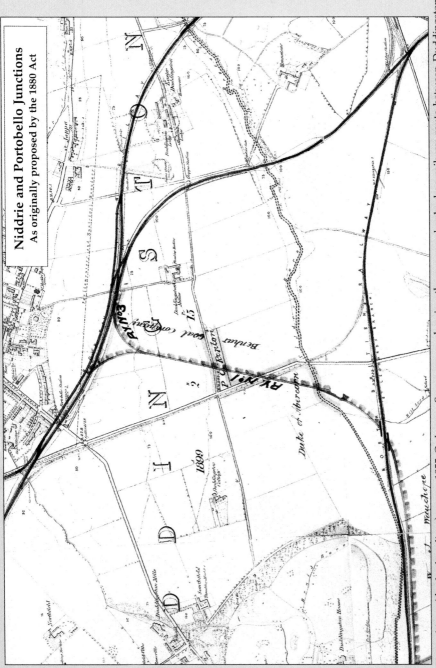

Niddrie and Portobello Junctions
As originally proposed by the 1880 Act

NBR 1880 markings (the broken lines) on an 1855 Ordnance Survey map showing the proposed suburban railway route between Duddingston and Portobello. 'Railway No. 1' was to be the main line from Haymarket Central Junction, 'Railway No. 2' (not shown above) linked Haymarket West and Gorgie junctions and 'Railway No. 3' curved from 'Railway No. 1' towards the Waverley Route junction at Portobello East. A completely reprinted 'simplifier' was later produced showing the original 1880 Act lines and those authorised under the 1882 Act, but this also included the long-lifted Leith branch from Niddrie!

number of prosperous Leith merchants resided in the growing southern suburbs around Newington and claimed that the time taken between their place of work and residence - a distance of about four miles in a virtual straight line - was about an hour.

It was considered at that time that the line would be of considerable importance when completed, not only in changes to the working of the North British in Edinburgh, but also for benefits that it was expected to confer upon the residents of the southern suburbs, particularly with an eye to the future expansion of the city. The proposed line was laid out to meet the perceived passenger requirements of the districts served. It was also proposed to give communication with districts then claimed to be without facilities and a circular train service envisaged to enable the public to travel and join trains to other parts of the country either at Haymarket, Waverley or Portobello, naturally by North British! The planned passenger train service was claimed to give the best possible service to the districts and also stimulate house building along its route, generating new business. Edinburgh Town Council initially requested passenger stations at Gorgie Road, Merchiston Road, Morningside, Blackford Road, Mayfield Street, and Cameron Toll, but Duddingston was not mentioned, as it was not part of Edinburgh until 1901. Despite the circuitous route, the line could provide direct access to the city centre, in competition with slow and not too comfortable horse trams and horse buses.

It seems strange that in seeking to relieve the congestion at Waverley from the north and west, the overall plan would potentially create a new bottleneck at Portobello. The curvature of the connecting spurs would have imposed speed restrictions which was likely to have an adverse effect on both East Coast and Hawick routes with freight trains waiting access to the Suburban over the double track section between the Suburban and Hawick line junctions. The main Edinburgh marshalling yard was also then at Portobello. Paralleling instead of combining with the St Leonards branch was also strange but may have originated in the independent concept of the Edinburgh Suburban & South Side Junction and the North British railways.

The Suburban Board

The Edinburgh Suburban & South Side Junction Railway Company proposed raising its £225,000 capital in 22,500 shares of £10 each. The 1880 Act provided for three Directors, the qualification being a personal holding of not less than 50 shares and the first three were specified in the Act as Sir James Falshaw, Bart, The Rt Hon. John McLaren, and John Weir, who were to remain in office until the first ordinary meeting after the Act was passed. Sir James Falshaw was a Yorkshire-born civil engineer, one-time Lord Provost of Edinburgh and a Director of the North British Railway and the Rt Hon. John MacLaren was the Lord Advocate for Scotland. Powerful people indeed!

The first ordinary half-yearly General Meeting of the Edinburgh Suburban & South Side Junction Railway Company took place in the chambers of the legal firm of Messrs Millar, Robson and Innes at 8 Bank Street, Edinburgh on 27th October, 1880. Present were Sir James Falshaw, the Rt Hon. John McLaren, and Mr W. White Millar, a solicitor before the Supreme Courts of Scotland and prominent Edinburgh lawyer. An apology was read from Mr Weir. The meeting commenced when the Act of Parliament incorporating the company was laid on the table and it was decided to continue with the Directors appointed in the Act. Sir James Falshaw was appointed Chairman, and George B. Wieland, Secretary of the NBR since 1874, was appointed Secretary, in his absence. Sir James and Mr Weir were remitted to see Wieland regarding his remuneration, the tone indicating a refusal to serve was not countenanced!

On 28th February, 1881, John McLaren tendered his resignation from the Board, claiming that his public duties as Lord Advocate prevented him acting as a Director of any company and this was accepted with regret. In his place, the meeting elected Mr Thomas Laudale of 4 Mayfield Terrace, Edinburgh. A month later, Mr White Millar was appointed as the company solicitor and Mr Robert Paterson as land valuator.

Sir James Falshaw had been a North British Director for some years, under the Chairmanship of John Stirling of Kippendavie. In 1881, while remaining Chairman of the Edinburgh Suburban & South Side Junction Railway, he also became NBR Deputy Chairman, the previous incumbent, John Beaumont, stepping down to become an ordinary Board member. In 1882, Stirling, the NBR Chairman for 15 years died, and was succeeded by Falshaw, Beaumont being re-appointed Deputy Chairman. Falshaw remained as Chairman until standing down at his own request in the latter part of 1886, although continuing as Deputy Chairman, Beaumont voluntarily vacating that post again in his favour. The new Chairman was The Marquis of Tweeddale, but unfortunately the expertise of both Falshaw and Beaumont was lost when both died in the first half of 1889. Wieland resigned due to ill health on 3rd March 1892, but was granted a seat on the Board, becoming Chairman in 1901 until he died in office on 26th March 1905, being succeeded by the Earl of Dalkeith.

The Suburban Acts and Actions

The initial Act of Parliament for the Edinburgh Suburban & South Side Junction Railway line was passed on 26th August, 1880. The description of the line divided the proposed route into three separate railways. These were:

Railway No. 1 - Six miles 1,507 yards, approximately, from a junction with the NBR (E&G Section) at or near the bridge carrying the Caledonian Railway Granton and Leith branches over the NB at Haymarket, and terminating at a junction with the NBR some 200 yards south-east of the west corner of the westmost booking office at Portobello Station.

Railway No. 2 - 913 yards, approximately, from a junction with the NB (E&G Section) some 150 yards west of the west end of the bridge carrying the line over the Water of Leith, and terminating at a junction with Railway No. 1, about 185 yards north-east of the north-east corner of Gorgie Public School.

Railway No. 3 - 402 yards, approximately, from a junction with Railway No. 1, some 385 yards south-west of the west corner of the southmost abutment of the bridge carrying the road from Portobello by Duddingston Mains Farmsteading, to, and joining the road from Duddingston to Easter Duddingston, over the NB and terminating by a junction with the NB at or near the bridge over the railway.

The North British Engineers superimposed the route of the new railway on a 25 inch 1853 Ordnance Survey map and this showed 'Railway No. 1' leaving the double track Edinburgh and Glasgow main line by a facing double junction immediately after passing under the Caledonian Railway Granton branch. After running parallel with the E&G line for about 150 yards (a condition imposed by the Act to avoid disturbing Caledonian assets), 'Railway No. 1' then turned south under the Caledonian's Wester Dalry branch, the level of the suburban line being lowered to obtain clearance. A short distance beyond, near the one-time 'Tynecastle Police Depot' at Gorgie, the 'Sub' made a trailing double line junction with 'Railway No. 2', from the E&G line a few yards west of the Wester Dalry branch link at Haymarket West Junction.

Beyond the junction at Gorgie, 'Railway No. 1' passed around the southern suburbs of Edinburgh to meet and parallel the then single track Edinburgh & Dalkeith Railway from Duddingston to Niddrie where it passed under the E&D before heading north to Portobello. This latter section was to cross the abandoned Portobello and Niddrie route of the E&DR, then cross land owned by the Benhar Coal Company (now Portobello Golf Course) and connect with the NBR Edinburgh and Berwick main line in a triangular junction east of Portobello station. The west side of the triangle let trains return to Waverley and the east line ('Railway No. 3' in the 1880 Act) headed east, joining the main line near the Hawick line junction, enabling trains from the south and east to run by the Suburban to Haymarket West Junction, avoiding Waverley.

A clause in the 1880 Act stated that when the line passed under the Caledonian Railway, the width should be not less than 26 ft measured on the square between parapets. If the Caledonian later laid down two additional tracks over these bridges, the NBR was to enlarge the bridge so that parapets would be not less than 50 ft apart. Other clauses in the Act provided for a private siding for Morningside Asylum, the course of the Jordan Burn between Morningside and Blackford Hill, and the road approach to Newington Cemetery.

The Caledonian Railway proposed connecting lines, although these were not progressed. Three severely-curved spurs would leave the 'Sub' about mid-way between the Union Canal tunnel and the bridge carrying the Caledonian Railway main line. All were double junctions, facing to trains from Duddingston and would have been of interest with three divergences almost simultaneously from the 1 in 80 downhill suburban gradient. The four proposed Caledonian connections were:

'Branch No. 1' after turning east, would pass over land belonging to George Watson's Hospital and connect into the Lothian Road (Princes Street) line near the future site of Merchiston station (opened July 1882) by a relatively sharp curve on a rising grade. After 1880, the hitherto open farm land developed into the Shandon housing scheme and, by 1883, the Governors of the hospital had sold 10 acres south of the Caledonian Railway to the Edinburgh Co-operative Building Company for 'lower middle class' domestic housing.

'Branch No. 2' headed west entirely on Caledonian land and linking into its main line between its Granton Branch Junction and Slateford station. The intentions behind this scheme did not come to fruition until 27th November, 1960 (officially 18th December) with the opening of the Craiglockhart - Slateford spur under British Railways, but on a less demanding curvature from the mouth of the tunnel under the Union Canal.

'Branch No. 3' was the most complex and perhaps the most unlikely, given the topography of the area. This was to leave the Edinburgh Suburban line, pass under the Caledonian main line and then climb to connect into their Granton branch just before that passed under Slateford Road. As with Branch 1, this land was also then owned by George Watson's Hospital.

'Branch No. 4' was not directly concerned with the suburban line but linked the Caledonian's Granton branch immediately north of its bridge over Gorgie Road with its Wester Dalry branch a short distance east of where it passed over the Suburban line between Haymarket Central and Gorgie Junction. This spur would have given the Caledonian a direct line from the south via Haymarket West Junction to Polmont and the north, bypassing Edinburgh! None of these schemes came to fruition except eventually Branch No. 2.

Before the Suburban line could start, it had to negotiate land purchase from several proprietors. Considering the normal high cost of suburban land, the actual cost was low, but it was planned to pass through what would today be classified as mostly 'green field' sites outwith the city boundary. However, engineering works over much of the route involved cuttings, tunnels and embankments and a pumping station above the cutting near Myreside Road bridge. The line reached its summit at Morningside Road, just outside the then city boundary. At Blackford, a small cluster of buildings surrounded the proposed station site, but the creation of a public leisure park following the purchase of the hill by Edinburgh Town Council was still being deliberated. Creating a goods yard between Blackford Hill and Newington required realignment of the Pow Burn (the extension of the Jordan Burn) – then the city boundary! At Newington, the most built-up area to be traversed, the line passed between the city boundary and Craigmillar Park developments but, unfortunately, required excavation of the roads leading to Newington Cemetery and the Royal Blind Asylum, and negotiations over making alternative accesses took longer than expected. Duddingston village dated from the 12th century but the line was to pass to the south, through open country. It then ran parallel to, but separate from, the St Leonards branch of the former Edinburgh & Dalkeith Railway before crossing the open land west of Duddingston Mains.

The spur from the junction with the Edinburgh & Glasgow line at Haymarket Central to the bridge under the Caledonian Railway's Wester Dalry branch bridge was on Caledonian Railway land; thence to Gorgie Road was owned by the Trustees of Sir G. Campbell. Land on the east side of the suburban from Gorgie Road to Myreside (between Craiglockhart and Morningside) belonged to the Merchant Company of Edinburgh (Governors, *inter alia*, of George Watson's Hospital). Land on the west side between the Caledonian main line overbridge and the Union Canal was owned by the Caledonian Railway. After passing under Myreside Road, the line briefly entered the land of the Edinburgh Lunatic Asylum Company, thence that of the Scottish Heritages Company east to Morningside crossroads. Beyond Morningside Road, the line, in cutting, passed through the property of the Trustees of the late John Gordon, which, halfway to Blackford Road, yielded to the land of Henry Trotter. From here to Dalkeith Road, the landowner was Sir I.N. Dick Lauder and onward to St Leonards Junction, Mr W.J. Little Gilmour. W.J. Wauchope owned land beyond Cairntows and in the Niddrie area the line headed north-east crossing the lands of the Duke of Abecorn and the Benhar Coal Company before reaching its proposed junction with the North British. As it was to remain separate, the old E&DR from St Leonards via Niddrie to the Hawick line was not included in the 1880 Act.

Under the original Bill and the 1880 Act, for the first six months after the Board of Trade sanctioned opening, the railways, works, stations, offices, conveniences, permanent way and other aspects of the line were to be maintained by, and at the cost of, the Edinburgh Suburban & South Side Junction Railway, to the reasonable satisfaction of the Engineer of the North British Railway. The line was thereafter to be maintained, renewed and updated by the North British Railway.

Anomalies were addressed in the second Edinburgh Suburban Act, passed on 24th July, 1882. This sought to abandon the planned 'Railway No. 1' between Duddingston and Portobello, and all of 'Railway No. 3' (the eastern curve of the main line triangle near Portobello) of the 1880 Act and to build four new lines at the eastern end. 'Railway No. 1' of the 1880 Act was terminated in a field 5 miles 220 yards from Haymarket Central Junction, about 1 mile 1,287 yards short of its original destination. Unfortunately, the same 'Railway No.' terminology was used in both Acts but these related to different lines under the same railway title. For clarity, the 1882 Act lines are suffixed '(1882)' here:

The new 250 yards-long 'Railway No. 1 (1882)', or extension of the curtailed Railway No. 1 in the 1880 Act, connected the Suburban with the Edinburgh & Dalkeith Railway some 425 yards east of the crossing keeper's house at Cairntows level crossing. The original 'Railway No. 2' (Haymarket West Junction to Gorgie Junction) was unaltered, but 'Railway No. 2 (1882)' absorbed the then single Dalkeith line for 1 mile 223 yards, with an additional line laid alongside, connecting at its west end with 'Railway No. 1 (1882)' and reinstating double track between Duddingston and Niddrie South Junction. 'Widening of the St Leonards line' was claimed between St Leonards and Niddrie West Junction, but was in fact only from Duddingston. The newly-formed Duddingston and Niddrie double track had a connection some 370 yards east of the bridge that carried the line over the turnpike road (now Duddingston Park South) from Niddry Mill to Portobello with a new 900 yards-long double track 'Railway No. 3' (1882) which at its northern end connected into the North British Railway's Hawick branch some 30 yards south of the bridge over the Niddry Burn at Niddry North Junction, now the site of Brunstane station. 'Railway No. 4 (1882)' was a double line 1 mile 605 yards long starting some 500 yards east of the bridge over the Niddrie Mill - Portobello turnpike between the spurs to Niddrie North and South Junctions. The path of this railway was a short distance south of the single Edinburgh & Dalkeith Railway Fisherrow branch of 1831, which was closed and lifted after the Musselburgh deviation line at Newhailes opened in 1859. Niddrie station remained in operation (as a goods office without rails, dealing with mineral traffic documentation) and the earthworks of the old line remained intact, although slightly realigned to pass under the 'Waverley Route' instead of across it. At the eastern end, it connected into the main East Coast route, 650 yards east of the Musselburgh branch junction at Newhailes. Actually, the only 'brand new railway' in Railway No. 4 (1882) was the link from near Wanton Walls farm on the original E&DR route to the Berwick line at the new 'Niddrie East Junction'.

The Edinburgh Suburban & South Side Junction Railway 'proper' was just under 5¼ route miles long between Haymarket Central Junction and the junction with the St Leonards branch at Duddingston. The spur between Haymarket West Junction and Gorgie Junction added a further 880 yards and from Duddingston (St Leonards Branch Junction) to Niddrie North Junction, 1 mile 1,100 yards. Niddrie West to Niddrie South on the Waverley Route accounted for just over ½ mile. In summary, the adjustments from the 1882 Act increased total length of the line, from that of 1880 by a mere 86 yards, with new Railway No. 4 adding a further 1 mile 605 yards to its junction with the East Coast Main Line.

Briefly, the tabular comparison between the original and the 1882 revisions are as under:

Railway No. 1 (original)	6 miles	1,507 yards	
Railway No. 1 (1882 revision)	*5 miles*	*220 yards*	
Total loss	*1 mile*	*1,287 yards*	
New extension for Railway No. 1		250 yards	(Duddingston to St Leonards Branch Junction)
New Railway No. 2	1 mile	223 yards	(St Leonards Branch Junction to Niddrie North)
New Railway No. 3		*900 yards*	(Niddrie West to Niddrie North Junction)
Gain from new lines	*1 mile*	*1,373 yards*	
Total gain		*86 yards*	
'New' Railway No.4	*1 mile*	*605 yards*	(Niddrie West - Niddrie East on East Coast Main Line)

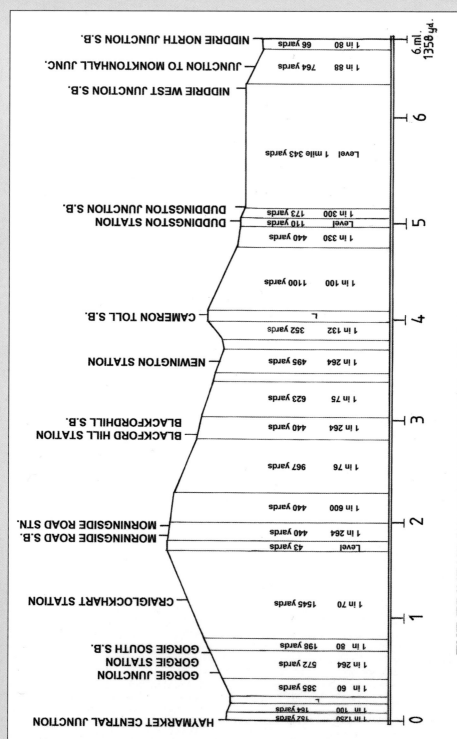

THE EDINBURGH SUBURBAN AND SOUTH SIDE JUNCTION RAILWAY

A plan was prepared as a 'simplifier' for the changes. In its heading, it refers to an increase in the length of the line over the original as being '1,556 yards, or fully ⅞th of a mile'. Perhaps surprisingly, the new plan also showed the Niddrie and Leith branch of the Edinburgh & Dalkeith Railway, and its later junction near Craigentinny with the NB main line which by that time had long been lifted.

The Line in the Making

With the Board in position and the Engineers and Contractors appointed, the Directors held their second meeting in Edinburgh on 1st December, 1880. Trimble and Peddie, Engineers, at 111 George Street, Edinburgh had written to Mr White Millar on 24th November, suggesting remuneration terms to build the line, which the Board accepted. This read:

Referring to the conversation that Mr Peddie and myself had the favour of having had with you yesterday regarding the engineering of the Edinburgh Suburban Railway, I have to state that we have fully considered the question and are prepared to undertake (in partnership) the construction and engineering of the railway at a rate of 2.5% on the cost of the works and stations: this rate of percentage to include the preparation of the working plans and sections, land plans for notices and drains and specifications of all bridges and works, station buildings, sidings, etc. and all engineering superintendence, but exclusive of inspectors wages which we would expect to be paid by the company. In the event of the company furnishing the permanent way materials, there will be of course no percentage charged on the materials furnished, nor percentage on land. Any claim by Sir Thomas Bouch's Executors for work done by me preparing the working plans and sections prior to his death will form a deduction from the above. Trusting the terms will receive your favourable consideration, I remain yours most respectfully, George Trimble.

At Haymarket West, the suburban railway arrived on the south side of the Caledonian Railway's Wester Dalry branch and the Board had hoped that they could avoid purchasing any of the adjacent Damhead Farmstead that bordered the line to provide space. Consequently, the solicitor entered into negotiations for an easement order over the Caledonian's line. Meetings were also arranged with the Merchant Company, owners of a sizeable amount of land that the railway required on the east side of its line between Gorgie Junction and Myreside resulting in some hard bargaining. Land was acquired from the Edinburgh Lunatic Asylum near the Myreside Road bridge and notices to the Scottish Heritages Company specified the area for the railway, but not the station. At Newington, where the land was already largely built over, negotiations were required for that to be excavated for the railway and this resulted in the removal of road access and the tree-lined approach to Newington Cemetery. Here, the solicitor negotiated and got agreement to an alternative roadway, which the railway provided, and also over alterations to the path of the Pow Burn. A similar arrangement was applied for the realignment of the approach drive to the Royal Blind Asylum alongside the site of the proposed railway station.

Delays were experienced in starting work, there being a difference of opinion between the Board and contractor regarding the contract terms. Waddell raised this in correspondence but the Board decided on 23rd March to tell him that either he started work without delay or negotiations would be terminated. The loss of time was deemed so important that the Board convened a special meeting on 28th March to sort out the disputed points. Waddell protested that although initially there were

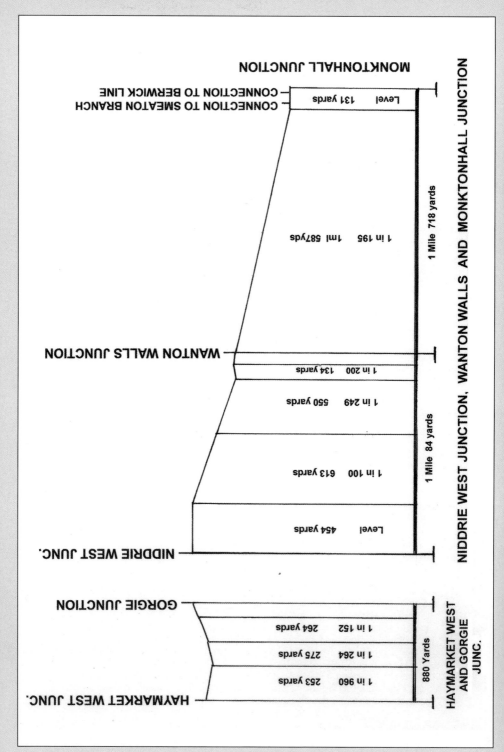

NIDDRIE WEST JUNCTION, WANTON WALLS AND MONKTONHALL JUNCTION

MONKTONHALL JUNCTION

CONNECTION TO BERWICK LINE
CONNECTION TO SMEATON BRANCH

Level 131 yards

1 in 195   1ml 587yds

1 Mile 718 yards

WANTON WALLS JUNCTION

1 in 200   134 yards

1 in 249   550 yards

1 in 100   613 yards

1 Mile 84 yards

Level   454 yards

NIDDRIE WEST JUNC.

GORGIE JUNCTION

1 in 152   264 yards

1 in 264   275 yards

1 in 960   253 yards

880 Yards

HAYMARKET WEST JUNC.

HAYMARKET WEST AND GORGIE JUNC.

only to be four stations, viz. Gorgie, Morningside, Newington and Duddingston, a further two (Craiglockhart and Blackford) had been added after the Parliamentary estimates had been made. Mr White Millar pointed out that all parties had agreed that if there were to be more stations, their cost would be additional to the original contract price in Debentures of the company, interest on which would be deferred to a dividend of 5 per cent per annum on the Ordinary Shares. Waddell claimed that under his agreement with the railway, he was also required to provide £76,695 for the purchase and otherwise of the land and that he should have the benefit of any cost reductions. However, if land costs exceeded this, the company agreed that it would give Debentures for such additional sums and with this arrangement, the company might, by acquiring less land, actually increase the cost of the work.

On 4th April, 1881, Mr Waddell suggested that he would provide the capital of the company if 95 per cent was allotted to him, subject to the option of the North British Railway acquiring the undertaking at 105 per cent plus interest at 5 per cent from the date of payment of the respective calls. However, the Board considered that if Mr Waddell's proposal was accepted, the Caledonian Railway could also be in a position financially to obtain control of the company, and it was thus declined. Ten days later, the Board reached an agreement with Messrs Renton Brothers & Co. and Messrs Brunton Bourke & Co. to provide the capital. The solicitor also prepared an agreement with Mr Waddell for the construction of the railway and it was agreed that the Secretary be paid at a salary of £2,000 during this period.

The Directors considered relationships with the North British Railway and on 2nd May, 1881 the Secretary submitted a draft proposal for an agreement regarding the annual payment made to the latter in respect of through traffic and its option to acquire the Suburban undertaking. Adjustments were made before the Draft was approved.

On 14th July, 1881, the Secretary reported placing all the capital of the company at 95 per cent with 1 per cent commission, subject to the provisions of the agreement between the NBR and the ESSSJR, which was approved. The Board also authorised acquisition of land for the line, requesting the 'utmost despatch' in achievement. An account was opened with the British Linen Bank (the North British Railway's bankers) with one Director and the Secretary authorised to sign cheques.

Mr Waddell and the Chairman signed the contract and the contractor was told to start work immediately. This was done without ceremony from the western (Gorgie) end in August 1881. The construction of the line was finally under way.

Land settlements were discussed during September 1881 and Mr White Millar reported that:

1. He had taken possession of the required Merchant Company ground without any deposit and this was then made available to Mr Waddell.
2. Mr Waddell had asked for possession of a small piece of ground at Gorgie Park belonging to Harry Maxwell Inglis and others, and this had been arranged for £1,000.
3. Correspondence was exchanged with the Caledonian Railway solicitor regarding ground given to the suburban railway under its Act, and although considered as 'very trifling', the Caledonian had nominated a Mr Waterstone as arbiter.
4. Notice had been served on the Royal Morningside Asylum regarding the land to be taken from them.
5. Notices had also been served on the Scottish Heritages Company and their tenants with a view to getting possession of their land, application being made to the Board of Trade to appoint a valuator.

6. The properties of Braid, Colonel Trotter and Sir Thomas Lauder were to be dealt with in the same Session as the Scottish Heritages Company.
7. One difficulty was still unadjusted, namely whether a deviation was required for the line at Duddingston Station and the north line of the St Leonards Branch which would used as part of the suburban line. Mr Walker, the NBR General Manager, had raised an objection, but Mr Carswell, the recently appointed NBR Engineer-in-Chief, claimed that as the engineers had not at that time seen the plans, they had not spoken with Mr Walker.

The formal half-yearly meeting of the Edinburgh Suburban & South Side Junction Railway Company was held in the North British Railway Company offices at 4 Princes Street, Edinburgh on Tuesday 16th August, 1881 in the presence of Sir James Falshaw (Chairman), Mr Thomas Laudale, John Weir, W. White Millar, John Waddell and G.B. Wieland (Secretary). Following the death of Sir Thomas Bouch, the Chairman stated that Messrs Trimble and Peddie had been appointed as the Engineers at a fixed remuneration. An arrangement had also been made with Mr John Waddell to build the railway for £220,000 and the cost of the land, with full payment on completion of the entire works. Steps were being taken to raise the capital and Mr Francis A. Bringloe and Mr James Jobson Dickson were appointed auditors.

Later in the year, correspondence passed between Trimble and Peddie, and the North British Railway's Chief Engineer, regarding the approach of the line to Portobello, and there was joint agreement for a proposed deviation, the Board approving in October 1881 that Parliamentary Powers be obtained, resulting in the 1882 Act. It was also agreed to have a 30 feet-wide bridge at the foot of Blackford Avenue, the landowner providing the land for its approaches. The solicitor arranged for conveyance of the ground for the road to be used by the railway staff and passengers, dispensing with plans for the occupation bridge and road originally proposed through Blackford Estate. The arrangement with Gordon's Trustees regarding the ground required from Braid Estate to dispense with two bridges was adjusted.

Another deviation was agreed in October 1881 for the proposed Blackford station, diverting the line 60 to 70 feet further south and to obtain additional ground east of the station for mineral sidings, isolating about an acre of Colonel Trotter's Estate. To avoid compensation, it was agreed that this ground would be purchased outright. The company also agreed to install bridge abutments on Colonel Trotter's property in Oswald Road, but defer the girders until requested.

Pow Burn Toll House stood in the path of the railway at Newington, and notice was served to obtain immediate possession. However, the service of notice on houses on the east side of the road was delayed until 2nd February. Notice was also served on the Water Trust for the tail of banking resting on the pipe ranks and on Sir Thomas Dick Lauder for ground required for mineral sidings at Blackford, and the deviation of the line through Mr Gilmour's ground there.

At the beginning of December 1881, contracts were let for permanent way materials to the undernoted firms:

Rails	Moss Bay Company, Workington
Chairs	Head Wrightson and Company, Stockton
Fishplates & spikes	P. & W. McLellan, Glasgow
Bolts and Nuts	A.S. Nelson and Company, Glasgow
Sleepers and Keys	Calder Dickson Stewart and Company, Glasgow

Inspection of rails, sleepers and keys was undertaken by the North British Railway Company's inspector.

In January 1882, Messrs Pearson, Robertson and Finlay threatened opposition to the ESSSJR Bill, claiming that power was being sought to delay completing the line for a further three years and to close up Tipperlin Road at Morningside. Residents of South Lauder Road also took umbrage at the proposal to build the coal depot at the end of their road, but their alternative suggestion to build the depot at Causewayside was not practical as this was some distance from the line.

The first earthworks were concentrated in the cuttings between Gorgie and Blackford. Bridge abutments at Gorgie Road were ready for the malleable girders then being built and half of the bridge under Slateford Road was open to road traffic. Work was in progress on the Oswald Road bridge foundations and east abutment of the Haymarket West spur road bridge.

At the end of January, it was agreed at a Special General Meeting in the NBR offices in Princes Street that the Bill authorising the ESSSJR to make new railways and abandon part of their authorised railways, etc., be introduced into Parliament. The Act was passed on 24th July, 1882, 12 days after the Act to enable the Forth Bridge Railway Company to construct a railway across the Firth of Forth.

On 3rd July, 1882 an Act enabled the Edinburgh Street Tramways Company to make more tramways, including one from Churchill to Morningside. This was single line, 910 yards long heading down Morningside Road and over the suburban railway to terminate at Morningside Drive. This included a 77 yards loop line, 11 yards south of the toll bar and a few yards from the proposed railway station. The railway defined the road levels where the tramway passed above it.

In July 1882, a letter was received from Mr Cox, who owned the Gorgie Mill Lade into which the railway proposed to introduce surface drainage from its Gorgie to Myreside cutting. Cox stipulated conditions that were considered impracticable, but this was further complicated by Messrs Tate and Crichton, solicitors for Sir George Campbell's Trustees, requesting permission to connect drainage from their fue with the proposed railway culvert. Consequently, the railway decided to carry its culvert under Cox's Mill Lade directly into the Water of Leith and Campbell's Trustees could connect their fue drain to the culvert, if they paid ⅓ of the pipe maintenance and exonerated the railway from way-leave.

By 14th September, 1882, all land required for the railway had been acquired, apart for some near Newington station. The Newington (Roseburn) Cemetery access road would disappear with the railway excavations, there were problems with Royal Blind Asylum access and the Pow Burn alignment required adjusting between the site of the Powburn Toll Bar and the west gate for Newington Cemetery. Under the Act, as the burn was also the municipal boundary, the City authorities had to approve plans for the burn, and requested an additional culvert be built at joint expense. This affected the accesses and caused delay, but was later resolved when the Council agreed to pay the whole cost of the culvert.

Work then went ahead between Blackford and Duddingston, that between Blackford and Gorgie being well advanced. Restricted width at Newington required the adoption of an island platform instead of the two platforms used elsewhere. The Engineer was told to prepare plans of all the stations, which the Board approved on 2nd October, 1882 with, it was claimed, 'only minor alterations'. However, comparing plans with actual buildings show more than 'minor' changes.

Drawings for three of the four stations (Gorgie, Morningside, and Duddingston) show separate booking offices on each platform, the platforms being linked by a footbridge close to the station buildings. This was changed before opening to apply only at Gorgie and Duddingston. Morningside had its booking offices moved to a single building (which also included a waiting room) on the road bridge at street level, the Inner Circle booking office being deleted and the building shortened. The Outer Circle office had its door repositioned to enter from the platform, becoming designated for the porters. Platforms were linked by a stone stairway with covered glazed canopy link behind the booking office. At Newington, the booking and parcel office was combined at the east end of the station building below street level. Blackford Hill, a late entrant before the line opened, originally had its booking office on the top storey of the Inner Circle building, linked to both platforms by a footbridge. Blackford Hill was the only station with a two-storey station building.

Station buildings, goods offices and weighbridges were of red brick with doors and windows picked out in white, under a slate grey 'hipped' roof, with glazed sash-operated wooden window frames. General waiting rooms had timber frontages with fixed glazing. Buildings were in the then standard NBR style of the day, blending brick with pitch pine, although each was individual in style and layout. There was little attempt at ornamentation, yet they had a pleasing and cheerful aspect. Booking offices also dealt with passenger-rated parcel traffics.

In late 1882 litigation surrounded the boundary wall at the rear of Morningside Asylum, claimed to be the property of the Scottish Heritages Company. The Engineer examined the property title and was authorised to get as much ground as had been sold by the Scottish Heritages Company to the Asylum for sidings at the west end of Maxwell Street

Completion of the Blackford goods yard and its access road was delayed until the Corporation defined plans to divert the Pow Burn, then the city boundary. At that time the stream meandered across the middle of the proposed goods yard.

In January 1883, an application from the Post Office to place a box for the collection of letters on the wall of the railway bridge at Morningside was approved and, 13 months later, they were authorised to install a similar pillar / letter box on the wall of the railway bridge at Mayfield (Newington) station.

On 22nd January, 1883, Mr Cox agreed to sell the ground for the proposed road to Gorgie station and consented to drainage pipes being laid below his Mill Lade, if the railway company agreed to him diverting the water from the Gorgie cutting into his works for his use, should he wish. The question of access to the Royal Blind Asylum at Newington dragged on into March 1883, one suggestion attempting to try for temporary access through the adjacent church property. A small iron trough was placed in the Union Canal before work started to pass boat traffic during construction of the tunnel underneath. The bridge under Myreside Road was the only one not started at that time.

Arrangements for the new wide access driveway to the west end of Newington Cemetery was finalised in June 1883, the railway's contractor replanting as many trees as required to be replaced to restore its original peaceful surroundings.

As the distances from the two 'doubtful' passenger stations at Colinton Road and Blackford to the nearest alternative station were considered relatively small with high construction costs, especially the excavations at Colinton Road on an adverse gradient (1 in 70), it was decided that neither station would be built meantime. However, in October 1883, the Engineers reported that a retaining wall required to be built at the site of the proposed Craiglockhart (referred to as Colinton) station as the solum proved to be clay and not rock as originally thought. The walls on either side of the line were then built 10 feet further back than on the original plan, facilitating the construction of Craiglockhart station in 1887.

Construction work progressed so well that on 9th June, 1883 the Board optimistically informed the North British that the suburban line might open on 1st July 1884, but problems conspired against this when, on 13th November 1883, the roof of the tunnel which carried the line under the Union Canal gave way. The Engineer disclaimed liability and the matter was referred to arbitration under the contract. On 20th December, the North British, through its Chief Engineer, James Carswell, insisted that the reconstruction work had to be to its satisfaction and thus the Suburban Engineer and contractor had to comply with whatever Carswell might require.

Although an area had been identified for the sidings at Morningside, this was not specifically defined, and on 29th June, 1883 it was proposed to provide for this by diverting the historic Tipperlinn Road. The southern part of the road was to become a pedestrian path, and on a new route around the rear of the goods yard, being carried over the station platforms by a metal footbridge. The railway agreed to build a wall on the asylum side of the Jordan Burn and this (and the site of the proposed asylum siding) was approved by the asylum manager. He also agreed not to object to the stream and sewer diversion at the west end of Maxwell Street, and to join fellow managers in an effort to close or divert Tipperlinn Road.

Meantime, between Duddingston and Niddrie, on the route of the old Edinburgh & Dalkeith Railway, since the 1882 Act part of the suburban railway, two elderly bridges awaited new malleable iron girders but otherwise most refurbished and new permanent way on this 1½ mile section was complete apart from ballasting.

Four new bridges were required between Niddrie West and Niddrie East. One took the line under the Waverley Route, slightly south of the original E&DR alignment to Fisherrow and the second, on which work had then started, passed over today's Newcraighall Road. The other two were over occupation roads. Posts for fencing the new double track line between Niddrie West and Niddrie North were in position, and work on that section progressed without incident.

In October 1883, the Suburban's solicitor served notice for the land at Niddrie that the company had powers to take for sidings under the 1882 Act, and which were to evolve over the years into the substantial Niddrie West marshalling yards.

On 13th February, 1884, a memorandum arrived from Major Marindin about a proposed level crossing at Newhailes and also the signal arrangements at Gorgie, Morningside and Duddingston. The Newhailes level crossing was dispensed with after ground was acquired to construct a service road to the existing road bridge and, in respect of the signalling work, the letter was passed to the Engineer to arrange in line with Board of Trade requirements.

On 22nd March, development of the Niddrie sidings was delayed to consider a North British proposed plan and by 9th April the Suburban company had only agreed to land for the sidings on the NBR plan as were in the ESSSJR Parliamentary estimate. For capital or other powers to acquire other land for the Suburban, an option would be taken to enable the NBR to acquire a portion of the adjoining land at the same price as paid by the Suburban valid for five years.

On 9th April, it was agreed to allow the Scottish Heritages Company to form a siding connecting with the suburban line at Morningside provided that the siding was approved by the company's Engineer and sited with as little as possible on railway land. The connection was only to be retained during the pleasure of the Directors and a similar rental charged as for coal offices. It is not clear if or where this siding was actually laid.

On 16th September, 1884, near Gorgie station, the Clerk to the St Cuthbert's Parochial Board requested permission to link drainage from Gorgie School to the railway's drains and this was agreed, but again only during the pleasure of the Directors. Permission was also granted to a Mr Duncan McLaren to lay a water pipe through his property to Newington station, provided that he or his successors later removed it.

The Board of Trade were advised on 1st October, 1884 that it was proposed to open the line to goods and passenger traffic concurrently, but on 27th October it was agreed to open for goods traffic only on 1st November. Local goods yards and sidings for freight traffic were provided at Gorgie, Morningside Road, Newington and Duddingston, although access to Duddingston Goods was achieved from the St Leonards branch. Newington Goods had rail access from points outside Blackford Hill signal box, but the goods weighbridge office and main road entrance was on Mayfield Road, across the road from a footpath leading to Newington passenger station. As the years passed, further sidings, public, private and branches were added, many being later closed in the face of road competition. At Gorgie, an early branch laid from the goods yard to the Glue Works formed the starting point for a private branch to Gorgie Cattle Market opened in 1910. Sidings along the suburban line served several traders, breweries and a distillery. Duddingston was famous for its breweries and private sidings were added for those and lesser traffics as demand dictated. Other than brewery, distillery and cattle traffics, most goods dealt with at yards on the suburban lines were 'inward'.

On 11th December, 1884, a letter of 15th November was received from the Board of Trade enclosing a copy of Major Marindin's second inspection report of the suburban railway and works which authorised its opening for passenger traffic. In accord with previous agreements, the Secretary was authorised to seal the Bill to be introduced into the next Parliamentary Session providing for the amalgamation of the Edinburgh Suburban & South Side Junction Railway Company with the North British Railway.

The last General Meeting of the independent Edinburgh Suburban & South Side Junction Railway Company was held on 11th March, 1885. There it was noted that the line opened for goods traffic on 31st October, 1884 and passenger traffic on 1st December, after which the maintenance and working was in the hands of the North British Railway. The last report by the railway's Engineer on 23rd February, 1885 noted outstanding work consisted mainly of finishing some goods yards and stations and erection of a goods shed at Gorgie. By 11th March these were complete apart from minor work such as painting.

The last Directorial meeting took place on 28th May, 1885, in accordance with the Standing Orders of Parliament. This referred to,

An Act to authorise the North British Railway Company to make several railways in connection with their undertaking, to extend the time for purchase of lands and completion of works, to purchase additional lands, to amalgamate with the companies the undertakings of the Edinburgh Suburban and South Side Junction and Kelvin Valley Railway companies, to consolidate certain stocks within the consolidated line stock of the company, to access the companies Acts in various particulars and for other purposes.

The notice was signed by James Falshaw, as Chairman (by this time also of the North British Railway) and on the motion of Thomas Laudale, Esq., a vote of thanks was accorded to the Chairman. This was signed by George Wieland who was the company (and also North British Railway) Secretary.

The Edinburgh Suburban & South Side Junction Railway then ceased to be an independent company and after 22nd July, 1885 became part of the North British Railway. Other lines were later added at the eastern end, such as connections with the 'Lothian Lines' authorised, *inter alia*, under the North British Railway Act of 15th August, 1913, and which opened in 1915. A by-product of this was the alteration of the line between Niddrie East Junction and Wanton Walls into buffer-ended sidings and the opening of a new double line from Wanton Walls to Monktonhall Junction in lieu.

Opening Day

On the afternoon of Thursday 16th October, 1884, the first fully equipped passenger train (albeit a special) ran over the Edinburgh Suburban & South Side Junction Railway line. This train, the actual timings of which are not recorded, comprised of the locomotive, a saloon carriage, a composite carriage and a luggage brake van. The train was occupied by an inspection party comprising of Mr Walker, General Manager of the NBR; Mr McLaren, general superintendent; Mr Carswell, Engineer; Mr McDougall, goods manager; Mr Rutherford, assistant goods manager; Mr Holmes, locomotive superintendent and Mr George Waddell, representing the construction contractors. None of the party were on the Board of the Edinburgh Suburban & South Side Junction Railway, all being North British Railway men.

The inspection found that the works were so well advanced that there seemed little doubt that the line would open for traffic on Saturday 1st November, 1884. It was estimated that the remaining works would be completed within a few more days. The line, bridges, most sidings, all ancillary structures (with the exception of the internal appointments of station buildings) were complete and ready for traffic. On the following day, Friday 17th October, 1884, the works were inspected and tested by Major Marindin on behalf of the Board of Trade

The 1st November general target was not achieved, but the line did open for goods trains on Friday 31st October, 1884. Passenger services started on Monday 1st December, 1884, although, contrary to previous expectations, some contracted work was still incomplete. On the opening day, the first 'outer circle' train (via Duddingston and Gorgie) left Waverley at 8.15 am and then at hourly intervals until 7.15 pm, connecting with main line services from Edinburgh to Glasgow.

According to the *Edinburgh Courant* newspaper, on Tuesday 2nd December, 1884, the Edinburgh suburban railway opened to the public on the previous morning, and the weather was clear and frosty. A large number of passengers travelled by the first train although several made the journey more from curiosity rather than from any business interest, but it was the general view that the railway would prove 'of great public convenience'. The service was planned to provide trains every half-hour, one train going round the system via Portobello starting at quarter past each hour, the next train going by way of Haymarket and starting at a quarter before the hour, the time taken to perform the circuit of 12¾ miles being 40 minutes.

The *Courant* stated,

On the 'Outer Circle 'line, via Portobello, the trains leave the Waverley Station and call at all the stations on the way, namely Portobello, Duddingston, Newington, Blackford, Morningside, Gorgie, Haymarket and so on to the Waverley. The stations on the line have all been fully equipped with officials, and are remarkable for their convenience and comfort. Special attention seems to have been paid to the erection of commodious

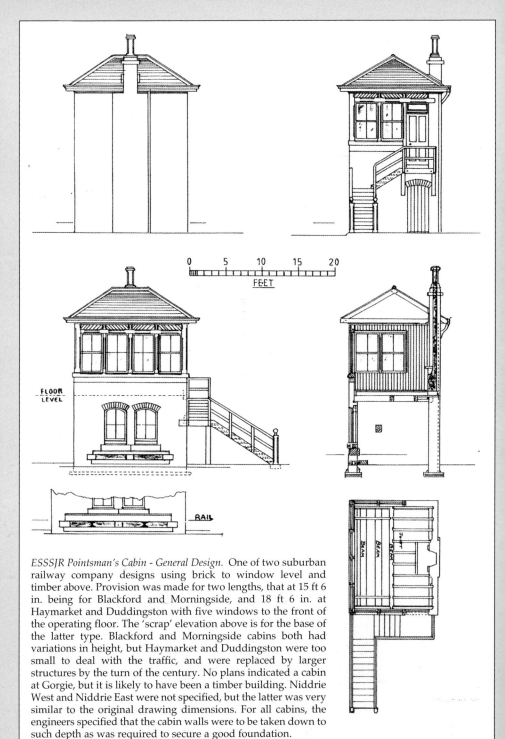

ESSSJR Pointsman's Cabin - General Design. One of two suburban railway company designs using brick to window level and timber above. Provision was made for two lengths, that at 15 ft 6 in. being for Blackford and Morningside, and 18 ft 6 in. at Haymarket and Duddingston with five windows to the front of the operating floor. The 'scrap' elevation above is for the base of the latter type. Blackford and Morningside cabins both had variations in height, but Haymarket and Duddingston were too small to deal with the traffic, and were replaced by larger structures by the turn of the century. No plans indicated a cabin at Gorgie, but it is likely to have been a timber building. Niddrie West and Niddrie East were not specified, but the latter was very similar to the original drawing dimensions. For all cabins, the engineers specified that the cabin walls were to be taken down to such depth as was required to secure a good foundation.

waiting rooms which contrast very favourably with those of any other railway system in Scotland. The two trains which are employed in working the traffic consist of newly constructed carriages of large and comfortable dimensions and are well furnished. The cross bridge at the Waverley Station will be fitted up as quickly as possible, and will probably be finished in the course of a fortnight. It may be added that the return fare to the intermediate stations, Duddingston, Newington, Blackford Hill and Morningside allowing the passengers to come or go either way, are 7*d*. (first class) and 4*d*. (third class) while to Gorgie by Haymarket they are 6*d*. and 3*d*. For the round, the fares are 5*d*. and 3*d*.

Although second class accommodation was still being provided on some North British trains, those on the Edinburgh Suburban line never had this facility.

The opening of the line was also reported in the *Scotsman* of 2nd December, 1884, which stated,

The Edinburgh Suburban & South Side Junction Railway was opened for passenger traffic yesterday morning. As was to be expected, the inauguration of the new enterprise produced a large amount of traffic, especially in the morning and the evening, but indeed, throughout the whole day the trains were well patronised. Taken as a whole, the service was conducted well, up to time and everything for a start was found to work smoothly and satisfactorily. The trains are composed of first and third class carriages, the latter being very comfortable and are fitted with the Westinghouse brake. Considerable disappointment seemed to be expressed by the passengers of the train timed to arrive at Waverley station at 9.57 am on account of the delay which was occasioned at Haymarket where the train was kept standing for fully ten minutes, probably the result of a west going train making a late start from Waverley station, outside which the line in the new station branches off the main line. Up till about 2 o'clock in the afternoon, nearly 200 passengers, exclusive of season ticket holders, were booked at the suburban Waverley station. In the course of the day, the total number of holders of ordinary tickets that travelled from the same point to one or other of the stations on the circuit was 450. Up to 6 o'clock, 125 tickets had been taken out at Morningside station, and for the full day, 150. As already announced, there are two train services, one on the Outer Circle, the line via Portobello commencing at 8.15 am and continuing hourly until 7.15 pm, and the other on the Inner Circle line via Haymarket, beginning at 9.45 am and continuing hourly until 10.45 pm. 40 minutes are allowed for the round the whole of which time was not required by some of the trains yesterday.

Signalling Equipment and Arrangements

Two drawings for signal boxes (termed as 'Pointsmen's Cabins') were produced for the Edinburgh Suburban & South Side Junction Railway. One, which was undated, had brickwork between ground level and the frame of the operating floor windows, with timber above. Two boxes had a length of 15 ft 6 in., width of 12 ft 4 in. and a roof height of 25 ft 0 in. and were intended for Blackford and Morningside. Longer boxes of 18 ft 6 in. length but to the same width and height were envisaged for Haymarket and Duddingston and 'part elevations' for this variation were shown on the main drawing.

The second drawing, dated February 1884, was for an 18 ft 6 in.-long all-wood structure to a similar width and height. There is no indication of intended location, but it was depicted on an embankment. It appears that this box may have been for Gorgie, where there was a slight embankment and may have been planned to have a short operational life as plans for a replacement were drawn up in 1892 with the prospect of an additional branch line to Cox's Glue Works as well as sidings expansion and other layout changes.

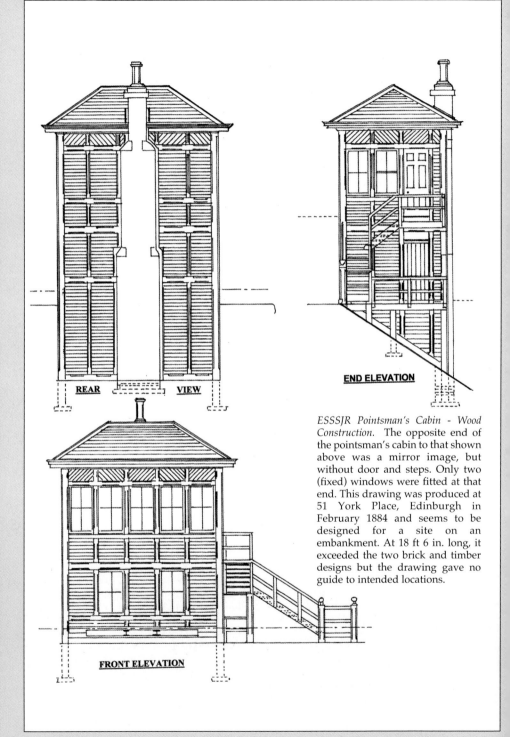

REAR — VIEW

END ELEVATION

FRONT ELEVATION

ESSSJR Pointsman's Cabin - Wood Construction. The opposite end of the pointsman's cabin to that shown above was a mirror image, but without door and steps. Only two (fixed) windows were fitted at that end. This drawing was produced at 51 York Place, Edinburgh in February 1884 and seems to be designed for a site on an embankment. At 18 ft 6 in. long, it exceeded the two brick and timber designs but the drawing gave no guide to intended locations.

In practice the design of the boxes was changed in minor ways between drawing and construction. An external shelf was provided below the window frames and a handrail fitted across the centre of the operating floor windows to enable the windows to be kept clean by the signalmen. In the front elevation, only the end windows could be opened to allow hand signals to be displayed outside the box in accordance with the rules and regulations.

As Duddingston and Gorgie expanded with additional sidings and connections, the original boxes were replaced by larger or more suitably positioned structures. At Duddingston, additional sidings, particularly for the breweries, required a much larger box to replace the original in the fork of the St Leonards branch. At Gorgie, rail traffic expansion in the goods yard and projected private sidings led to the replacement of the original box by two separate cabins, one in the fork at the junction and another on the outer circle approach from Craiglockhart. At Haymarket Central Junction, the North British and Suburban boxes operated within yards of each other until the new Central Junction box displaced both when it opened with the 1890s main line quadrupling between Edinburgh and Saughton. At Haymarket West, the box opened for the Caledonian junction undertook the suburban branch for a time, before being replaced by the new larger 'quadrupling' box.

Over the years, other refinements were made to the box architecture, such as the fitting of end porches to reduce draughts, lamps for locomotive identification, and replacement of wooden steps by brick or stone. Small vitreous enamelled NBR nameboards were also replaced by the wooden LNER types with individual letters that lasted until the end.

Relative to the gradients and traffic density, signal boxes between Niddrie West and Haymarket West/Central (when Cameron Toll was open) were evenly spaced, as the following distances in miles and chains taken from North British Appendices indicate:

	miles	chains					
Niddrie West Jn	0	00	on Inner Circle	Monktonhall Jn	0.00 0.00		
Duddingston	1	12	on Inner Circle	Niddrie East	1.05 1.05		
Cameron Toll	1	06	on Outer Circle	(Newhailes Jn	0.25)		
Blackford Hill	1	05	on Outer Circle	Wanton Walls*		1.31 0.00	
Morningside Road	1	09	on Inner Circle	Niddrie West		1.03	0.00
Gorgie South	1	10	on Outer Circle	Brunstane Park*			0.59
Gorgie Jn	0	28	in Junction fork	Niddrie South			0.59
Haymarket West Jn	0	28	in Junction fork				
Haymarket Central Jn	0	37	south of the line				

Cameron Toll (1900 to 1921) functioned as an 'intermediate block post', to increase line capacity, and Block Telegraph regulations for traffic on double lines of railway applied throughout. Boxes with an asterisk dated from 1915.

Semaphore signal posts were lattice, surmounted by one of two 'Stevens' type finials. As was normal NBR practice, signal lamps on single posts were initially mounted on a windlass arrangement, enabling them to be serviced at ground level, although ladders were latterly fitted. Ground signals were of the distinctive curved top Stevens flap type. The flaps fell forward when 'cleared' removing the inset red glass from the front of the lens. After 1895, the green (or yellow) indication was given by a small coloured glass spectacle plate, moving across the front of the lens when the 'flap' was lowered. Some of these signals were mounted on separate lattice or wooden posts, or gantries to aid visibility.

Original main line suburban signal arms were lower quadrants of the then North British 'standard', based on a Stevens pattern with a single spectacle plate containing a red glass. When the signal was 'cleared', the lowering of the arm removed this glass from the front of the lens, giving a white aspect, or as white as the signal oil would

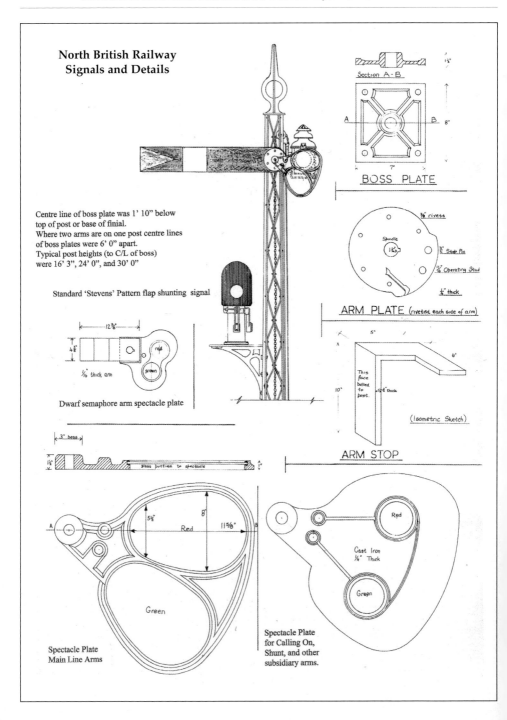

**North British Railway
Signals and Details**

Section A - B

BOSS PLATE

Centre line of boss plate was 1' 10" below
top of post or base of finial.
Where two arms are on one post centre lines
of boss plates were 6' 0" apart.
Typical post heights (to C/L of boss)
were 16' 3", 24' 0", and 30' 0"

Standard 'Stevens' Pattern flap shunting signal

ARM PLATE (riveted each side of arm)

⅜" thick arm

Dwarf semaphore arm spectacle plate

This
face
bolted
to
post.

(Isometric Sketch)

ARM STOP

glass puttied to spectacle

Red

Green

Spectacle Plate
Main Line Arms

Red

Cast Iron
¼" Thick

Green

Spectacle Plate
for Calling On,
Shunt, and other
subsidiary arms.

permit, for 'all clear'. On 18th November, 1895, as part of a NBR wide scheme, Suburban signal aspects were changed from white to green for 'clear', the new colour being claimed as of 'Admiralty standard' and when coupled with the yellowish paraffin lamp flame, produced a very distinctive shade. This change required new two-aspect spectacle plates and glass to be fitted to all main line arms, but the front face of both stop and distant signals continued to be painted red with a white vertical stripe, distant signals being identified only by a fishtail 'V' cut into the end. Reverse sides were white with black vertical stripe. Reliance was placed on the route knowledge of the driver to distinguish 'stop' from 'distant' signals, particularly after dusk. Subsidiary semaphore signal arms (e.g. 'Calling on', 'Warning', 'Shunt Ahead' or 'Back Shunt') and their spectacle plates varied according to function, but after dark the same colours were displayed as main line arms, although some types continued to use white as the 'clear' indication in accordance with rules and regulations.

Signal cabin lever frames and ground frames had mechanical interlocking. Most ground frames connecting sidings and main running lines some distance from signal boxes were controlled by 'Annett's Lock' on the ground frame's control lever. This key was obtained from the signal box (where it was interlocked with the protecting main line signals). Ground frames levers were mechanically interlocked within each frame if required. Signal arm changes well into the LNER period had NBR pattern lower quadrant spectacle plates, the castings lettering indicated that they were made in the railway's own workshops.

The block instruments were also used for 'routeing' in the manner of telegraphs. The needles used the 'Line Clear' and 'Train on Line' positions as 'left' and 'right' respectively, the number of beats in each direction being transmitted and acknowledged before the instruments were finally 'pegged' for the train concerned. Different routes had different numbers of 'left' and 'right' beats. Boxes also had a 'block switch' to enable it to be switched out if required, and 'long section working' instituted. In addition to block instruments, telephones and telegraph equipment, hand lamps, flags, and wire tensioning stirrups, each box had a varnished card showing the line gradient profile. Gradients varied according to the production date. Some boxes also had mechanical detonator placer stirrups or levers.

In 1916, the former Great Central Railway introduced three aspect semaphore signals and a yellow glass for the 'cautionary' indication, although other semaphore arms remained red with a white vertical band and red and green spectacle glasses. After Grouping, the red glass in distant signals was replaced by yellow and arms were repainted yellow with a black chevron. Reverse sides of all signals were painted white with corresponding black band or chevron. On the Edinburgh suburban, signal arms (as well as flags and hand lamps) of the individual boxes were changed on :

Mon. 8th Nov. 1926	Haymarket West, Haymarket Central, Gorgie Jn and Gorgie South
Tue. 9th Nov. 1926	Morningside Road and Blackford Hill
Wed. 10th Nov. 1926	Duddingston (and Cairntows crossing)
Thu. 11th Nov. 1926	Niddrie West
Fri. 12th Nov. 1926	Niddrie North and Niddrie South
2nd Mar. 1927	Monktonhall Jn, Wanton Walls Jn and Niddrie North Jn

Two significant signalling practice changes took place on the line after 1930. Hitherto, track circuits were indicated on signal posts by a white six-sided 'diamond' plate mounted vertically with a central lens showing a purple light after dark. The lamp was dispensed with after 3rd November, 1930 and replaced by a plain plate or

Two 'Absolute Block' instruments that once adorned the block shelf at Morningside Road signal box. The 'Up' line instrument on the right had its armature 'pinned' into either 'Line Clear' or 'Train on Line' position but that on the left had a trigger catch on the handle. To give 'Line Clear', the pin at the bottom left had to be depressed when operating the handle. Both units therefore required two hands to operate. *Author*

LIST OF TELEPHONE CIRCUITS

18TH MARCH 1907.

Superintendent of Line, Edinburgh (1) ...
  ,, ,, ,, (2) ...
Station Superintendent ,, ...
Goods Shunter's Cabin, ,, ...
Sack Superintendent's Office, Edinburgh
Sack Store, Edinburgh ... ...
Waverley East Box ... ...
Abbeyhill Junction Box ... ...
 ,, Booking Office ... ...
London Road Junction Box ... ...
Hydraulic Engine House, London Road...
 Easter Road ... ...
 Lochend North Box ... ...
 ,, South Box ... ...
Piershill Box ... ...
Leith Central Box ... ...
 ,, Booking Office ... ...
St Margarets Night Office ... ...
 ,, Locomotive Office ... ...
 ,, Box ... ...
Craigentinny Box ... ...
Portobello East Watchman's Box... ...
 ,, West Watchman's Box
 ,, West Box ... ...
 ,, (South Leith Junction Box) ...
 ,, Telegraph Office ... ...
 ,, Locomotive Office ... ...
 ,, East Box ... ...
Joppa Box ... ...
Niddrie North Box ... ...
 ,, South Box ... ...
 ,, West Junction Box ...
 ,, West Office ... ...
 ,, West Locomotive Office ...
 ,, East ... ...
Duddingston Box ... ...
Cameron Toll Box ... ...
Newington Booking Office ... ...
 ,, Goods Office ... ...
Blackford Hill Box ... ...
Morningside Road Box ... ...
 ,, Booking Office... ...
Gorgie South Box ... ...
 ,, Booking Office ... ...
 ,, Yardsman's Cabin ... ...
 ,, Junction Box ... ...
Haymarket West Junction Box ... ...
 ,, Central Box ... ...
 ,, Locomotive Office ... ...
 ,, East Box ... ...
 ,, Booking Office ... ...
Waverley West Box... ... ...
Edinburgh Locomotive Office ... ...
Waverley South Central Box ... ...
 ,, Suburban Box ... ...
 ,, North Central Box ... ...
Haymarket Yard ... ...

This chart depicts telephone arrangements in operation between signal boxes and headquarters before the advent of the control systems. Vertical lines show the extent of each separate circuit and black dots the locations along its route which had telephones.

Above: Morningside Road signal box had a typical North British interior. Levers were of the Stevens' pattern and woe betide anyone who pulled them without protecting the polished tops with a cloth. Here, signalman Alexander Forbes is in charge - complete with ubiquitous cigarette!
Author

Right: NBR 'Stevens' pattern signal arms. Originally these had only a single spectacle plate containing a red glass with the white light of the uncovered lens indicating 'all clear', but later, spectacle plates with red and green glasses were fitted. In the mid-1920s, red glass in red-painted distant signal arms (with white vertical band) was changed to yellow, the arms, also painted yellow, having a black chevron matching the cut out 'V'. *W.A.C. Smith*

Above: Restricted space adjacent to steps required a very short arm at Morningside Road. The original lower quadrant arms were changed in the early 1950s to the upper quadrant style, the new arms requiring a piece to be removed from the end for clearance. *Author*

Left: For years, the repeating signal arm for setting back into Morningside goods yard was an 'open scissors' type, but before the yard closed, it was replaced by this electrically-operated banner repeater signal. The signal carried the identification plate RM26 (Repeater Morningside Road lever 26). *Author*

a new 'D' plate indicating a Fireman's Call Plunger that was used to advise the signalman that a train was standing at the signal. Other changes were the gradual replacement of lower quadrant signal arms by those working in the upper quadrant after 17th November, 1931. Main line junctions such as Haymarket, Niddrie and Monktonhall were soon equipped, but the first purely 'suburban line' box to be changed over was Gorgie Junction on 24th November, 1940. At first, existing shunting signals were unchanged, but disc signals with a painted red bar on a white disc operating in the 'upper quadrant' appeared from 3rd May, 1935.

World War II enforced some changes. Nameboards were removed if the letters exceeded six inches in height and each evening the windows had to be blocked up with close fitting frames of wire mesh combined with wood or Essex board. A peephole was officially allowed at each end, but unofficially, the signalmen made extra holes. When showing lamps to trainmen in compliance with Block Regulation 5, all signal box lights had to be dimmed and entries made in Train Register Books by the light of oil hand lamps.

Colour light signals came to the Suburban in 1942 with automatic signals at Cameron Toll breaking up the section between Duddingston and Blackford Hill, once controlled by Cameron Toll box. Conforming with Air Raid Precaution regulations, Duddingston and Blackford Hill signal boxes had dimming switches that remained until 17th July, 1945. Dimming of oil lit signal lamps was achieved somewhat automatically with the reduction in the quality of the oil supplied to lamp rooms. Indeed, it was not unknown for signal lamps to extinguish themselves!

After 24th April, 1945, signal post telephones linked directly to signal box diagrams or block shelves had plates with diagonal black and white stripes fixed to the telephone box cover. Other lineside phones to signal boxes had a black 'St Andrew's cross' on a white ground.

Gorgie was resignalled with upper quadrants in 1940, but it was not until after the war that other suburban box signals were dealt with, including replacement of the Stevens 'flap' type ground signals by upper quadrant discs. A lower quadrant 'scissors' arm repeater for the 'back shunt' at Morningside Road, remained for some more years but was rarely used.

For the 1956 spur connecting Craiglockhart with Slateford, mechanical signalling was temporarily introduced from a signal box (actually a large wooden garden shed) sited where a runaway down the grade would have been diverted by the catch points into the end of the box! The scheme involved changing other Morningside Road Outer Circle signals to colour lights, the Inner Circle remaining semaphore (with extra signals to increase line capacity). Some had electric lighting.

Major signalling changes occurred in 1976 with the transfer of Gorgie Junction and Niddrie to panels at Haymarket and Portobello respectively, before final concentration in the Waverley Power Box. This was followed by the elimination of Duddingston junctions and the Niddrie yard connections, replacing mechanical by colour light signals on both Inner and Outer Circles, closure and removal of goods yard sidings and elimination of mechanical signal boxes. The suburban line was thus reduced to plain line with junctions only at Haymarket (West and Central), Craiglockhart and Niddrie.

Chapter Three

Operating the Suburban

The main objective of the Edinburgh Suburban & South Side Junction Railway (the 'Sub') was, by providing an alternative route for freight around Edinburgh, to ease the extremely serious congestion at Waverley. Although engineered to take the heaviest locomotives and loads of the day, sidings and yards along its route were not, and local permanent way staff remedied this as the need arose.

It was the normal operating practice, at least on the North British, for lines to be described as 'up' and 'down' depending on whether they were going to, or coming from, the London direction respectively. Here, the Edinburgh Suburban & South Side Junction Railway presented an anomaly. Inner Circle trains from Waverley to Haymarket Central Junction were on the down line, but this became the up line to Niddrie North Junction, and thereafter, the down line again to Waverley. Conversely, Outer Circle trains were up trains from Waverley to Niddrie North Junction and down trains from there to Haymarket Central (or West) Junctions, becoming up trains again for the run into Waverley. In addition, between Newington and Morningside Road, the down line went uphill and the up line went downhill! Perhaps it is easier to consider the lines in local terminology as the Outer and Inner circles. Through trains from the South were easier to describe as from Niddrie East Junction (later Monktonhall Junction) to Haymarket West Junction they were down trains, and in the reverse direction, up trains.

East Coast and 'Waverley Route' freights joined and left the suburban line at Niddrie East (later Monktonhall) and Niddrie South Junctions respectively, and significant marshalling yards evolved at Niddrie West. Through freight trains between the North and West of Scotland and the South and East traversed the Suburban via the Haymarket junctions, avoiding Waverley. Some of these through trains also served intermediate yards and yards on the Suburban, supplementing the local 'trip' workings.

Although the line was conceived, opened and operated for a few months by the legally independent 'Edinburgh Suburban & South Side Junction Railway Company', there is no evidence that any rules, regulations and working instructions other than those which applied on the North British Railway. The NBR issued a new edition of its Rule Book in 1884, the year the line opened, but the earliest surviving Appendix to the Book of Rules and Regulations and Working Time Tables in the Suburban period was issued in May 1896. New Rule Books were issued in 1891, 1898, 1914 and 1921 and its Appendices, which included the train signalling arrangements in 1898, 1901, 1907, 1914 and 1921. Appendix 29 appeared on 18th March, 1907 and claimed to have 'considerable and important alterations to the methods of block working' apparently relating to Block working using the Sykes' Electrical Interlocking Apparatus. This applied to parts of the suburban railway route, but had no impact on the suburban line proper. The 1914 Rule Book highlighted variations between NBR and Railway Clearing House instructions in bold type, Appendix No. 30 appearing the same year. The final NBR Rule Book was issued on 1st January, 1921 and remained operational until 1st January, 1933, the NBR Appendix (No. 31) of 1st October, 1922 extending to 1st March, 1937, with supplements keeping both up to date. The 1933 Rule Book was reprinted with amendments included in 1945, and the final London & North Eastern Railway

Timetable July 1900

Inner Circle Service

	1	2	3	4	5	6	7	8	9	10	11	12	13	14	15	16	17	18	19
	am	am	am	am	am	am	pm	pm	pm	pm	pm	pm	pm	pm	pm	pm	pm	pm	pm
Edinburgh Waverley	5.45	8.15	8.45	9.45	10.45	11.45	12.45	1.15	1.45	2.45	3.45	4.45	5.15	5.45	6.45	7.45	8.45	9.45	10.45
Haymarket	5.49	8.19	8.49	9.49	10.49	11.49	12.49	1.19	1.49	2.49	3.49	4.49	5.19	5.49	6.49	7.49	8.49	9.49	10.49
Gorgie	5.52	8.22	8.52	9.52	10.52	11.52	12.52	1.22	1.52	2.52	3.52	4.52	5.22	5.52	6.52	7.52	8.52	9.52	10.52
Craiglockhart	5.55	8.25	8.55	9.55	10.55	11.55	12.55	1.25	1.55	2.55	3.55	4.55	5.25	5.55	6.55	7.55	8.55	9.55	10.55
Morningside Road	5.58	8.28	8.58	9.58	10.58	11.58	12.58	1.28	1.58	2.58	3.58	4.58	5.28	5.58	6.58	7.58	8.58	9.58	10.58
Blackford Hill	6.01	8.31	9.01	10.01	11.01	12.01	1.01	1.31	2.01	3.01	4.01	5.01	5.31	6.01	7.01	8.01	9.01	10.01	11.01
Newington	6.03	..	9.03	10.03	11.03	12.03	1.03	..	2.03	3.03	4.03	5.03	..	6.03	7.03	8.03	9.03	10.03	11.03
Duddingston & Craigmillar	6.07	..	9.07	10.07	11.07	12.07	1.07	..	2.07	3.07	4.07	5.07	..	6.07	7.07	8.07	9.07	10.07	11.07
Portobello (arr.)	6.13	..	9.16	10.13	11.15	12.13	1.13	..	2.13	3.13	4.13	5.13	..	6.17	7.13	8.13	9.13	10.13	11.14
Portobello (dep.)	6.14	..	9.17	10.14	11.16	12.14	1.14	..	2.14	3.14	4.14	5.14	..	6.18	7.14	8.14	9.14	10.14	11.14
Piershill	6.18	..	9.21	10.18	11.20	12.18	1.18	..	2.18	3.18	4.18	5.18	..	6.22	7.18	8.18	9.18	10.18	11.18
Abbeyhill	6.22	..	9.24	10.22	11.24	12.22	1.22	..	2.22	3.22	4.24	5.22	..	6.28	7.23	8.23	9.22	10.22	11.22
Edinburgh Waverley	6.28	..	9.29	10.26	11.26	12.26	1.26	..	2.26	3.26	4.28	5.26	..	6.32	7.27	8.27	9.26	10.26	11.26

Outer Circle Service

	20	21	22	23	24	25	26	27	28	29	30	31	32	33	34	35	36	37	38	39
	am	am	am	am	am	am	am	pm	pm	pm	pm	pm	pm	pm	pm	pm	pm	pm	pm	pm
Edinburgh Waverley	6.45	7.15	8.15	..	9.05	10.17	11.15	12.17	1.15	..	2.17	3.15	4.15	5.17	..	6.15	7.15	8.17	9.15	10.15
Abbeyhill	6.48	7.18	8.18	..	9.08	10.20	11.18	12.20	1.18	..	2.20	3.18	4.18	5.20	..	6.18	7.18	8.20	9.18	10.18
Piershill	6.51	7.21	8.21	..	..	10.24	11.21	12.24	1.21	..	2.23	3.21	4.21	5.23	..	6.21	7.21	8.23	9.21	10.21
Portobello (arr.)	6.54	7.24	8.24	..	9.13	10.27	11.24	12.27	1.24	..	2.26	3.24	4.24	5.26	..	6.24	7.24	8.26	9.24	10.24
Portobello (dep.)	6.55	7.25	8.25	..	9.14	10.28	11.25	12.28	1.25	..	2.27	3.25	4.25	5.27	..	6.25	7.25	8.27	9.25	10.25
Duddingston & C'millar	7.02	7.32	8.32	..	9.21	10.35	11.32	12.35	1.32	..	2.34	3.32	4.32	5.34	..	6.32	7.32	8.34	9.32	10.32
Newington	7.06	7.36	8.36	..	9.25	10.39	11.36	12.39	1.36	..	2.38	3.36	4.36	5.38	..	6.36	7.36	8.38	9.36	10.36
Blackford Hill	7.08	7.38	8.38	9.03	9.27	10.41	11.38	12.41	1.38	2.08	2.40	3.38	4.38	5.40	6.13	6.38	7.38	8.40	9.38	10.38
Morningside Road	7.12	7.42	8.42	9.07	9.31	10.45	11.42	12.45	1.42	2.12	2.44	3.42	4.42	5.44	6.17	6.42	7.42	8.44	9.42	10.42
Craiglockhart	7.14	7.44	8.44	9.09	9.33	10.47	11.44	12.47	1.44	2.14	2.46	3.44	4.44	5.46	6.19	6.44	7.44	8.46	9.44	10.44
Gorgie	7.17	7.47	8.47	9.12	9.36	10.50	11.47	12.50	1.47	2.17	2.49	3.47	4.47	5.49	6.22	6.47	7.47	8.49	9.47	10.47
Haymarket	7.21	7.51	8.51	9.16	9.40	10.54	11.51	12.54	1.51	2.21	2.53	3.51	4.51	5.53	6.26	6.51	7.51	8.53	9.51	10.51
Edinburgh Waverley	7.25	7.55	8.55	9.20	9.44	10.58	11.55	12.58	1.55	2.25	2.57	3.55	4.55	5.57	6.30	6.55	7.55	8.57	9.55	10.55

All trains connected at Abbeyhill with the North Leith Service (sometimes with very long waits) Also 3, 4, 6, 7, 9, 11 and 12 with South Leith services from Portobello. In the reverse direction, 22, 24, 25, 28, 30, 32, 33, and 34 connected at Portobello with trains from South Leith.

(LNER) Appendix appeared on 1st November, 1947, remaining in operation (with amendments) until 1960 when separate Sectional Appendices were published for the three Scottish Region Divisions, a separate 'General' section covering the whole Region. The first British Railways (BR) Rule Book dated from 1st January, 1950, being updated in January 1962, but later issues appeared in loose-leaf format. The Appendix was later reissued in 1969, before it too became a loose-leaf document.

The first suburban passenger service was a circular one, based on Waverley. An island platform was built on the south side of the station to accommodate the service and a more comprehensive facility was provided in the 1890s Waverley rebuilding with all the facilities of a self-contained station and these were used by other services as required. The 'circle' trains called at Haymarket, Gorgie (renamed Gorgie East in 1952), Morningside (Morningside Road from July 1885 to avoid duplication with 'Morningside' on a branch from Bathgate), Blackford (renamed Blackford Hill after opening), Newington, Duddingston & Craigmillar (intermittently during its career shortened to Duddingston) and Portobello. Craiglockhart joined the suburban line on 1st June, 1887 in almost open country, although suburbia was slowly extending in its direction. This station was closed briefly from 1st May, 1890 when a temporary station opened on the other side of the Union Canal tunnel to serve the Edinburgh Exhibition of that year and it did not reopen until 1st January, 1891, some months after the exhibition closed. The sharp curve at London Road, Abbeyhill linked the Piershill and Easter Road line with Waverley in 1886 and enabled suburban trains to add Abbeyhill to their route, and Piershill opened on 1st May, 1891. In the late 19th century, the suburban service fell foul of the morality of the day, because it was alleged to provide an opportunity for young unchaperoned couples to meet in compartments on the trains and for the cost of a return ticket could conduct their affairs while the trains circled the city! On 1st July, 1903, the opening of the Leith Central branch switched most trains to that terminus, until it closed on 7th April, 1952, when passenger services returned to the pre-1903 position although the station remained open for carriage storage and servicing into the diesel age.

From about 1885, in addition to the carriage roof boards, North British passenger train destinations were shown on the front of locomotives by curved boards fitted into brackets above the engine smokebox door, or on the rear of bunkers or tenders. The boards were flat iron plates, $\frac{1}{8}$ in. thick, tapered fixing spigots being fixed at 18 in. centres, although sometimes, particularly latterly, the board had a bracket fitted to go over a lamp iron. Boards were mounted clear of the headlamps, some engines having the lamp bracket above the board. Originally maroon with hand-painted white or cream lettering, with some having black shading in the NBR period, this changed to black letters on a white ground in the LNER era, the white usually becoming cream with atmospheric exposure. Both Outer and Inner Circle trains used the single word 'Suburban'. After 1923, some 'imported' engines had brackets on the smokebox door and bunker rear for rectangular carriage-type boards and some NBR boards had their lower corners cut to fit. New 'V1' tank engines built after 1930 had mounting brackets above the smokebox door and on the bunker coal rails for the original NBR curved pattern. Although few headboards were still used in the late 1930s in Edinburgh, they were still in use in the Glasgow area into the 1950s.

Suburban line goods yards were diagrammed to be served by some through freight trains as well as local 'trip' workings, but most related to livestock traffic for Gorgie, and / or Morningside Road, Blackford Hill and Duddingston. The 'Stone Lye' at Morningside Road was served by short distance West Lothian working in 1897 and the October 1899 working timetable showed a Glasgow (College) to Portobello freight calling at Duddingston at 7.20 pm daily for two vans of locally made margarine - one for Glasgow via Portobello, the other to be detached at Niddrie West for Dundee. Plans were drawn up in 1906 to convert the site of the Portobello marshalling yard into a fully mechanised goods depot, similar to High Street in Glasgow, to serve all Edinburgh suburbs, but this never materialised.

Local suburban freight trains timetabled to serve the suburban yards in October 1901 were as follows:

		Outer Circle			
Train Number		28	53	60DP	71
		am	*am*	*pm*	*pm*
Portobello			11.40		3.28
Niddrie West	*arr.*		11.48		3.36
Niddrie West	*dep.*	8.00	12.00 *noon*		3.50
Duddingston		8.10	12.25 *pm*	1.57	4.02
Drybroughs Sdg				2.20	4.10
Blackford Hill		8.20	1.01	2.30	4.45
Morningside Road		8.48	1.10		4.55
Gorgie		8.58	1.17		5.09
Haymarket		9.03	1.24		5.12

DP Duddingston Pilot.
53 Shunts Duddingston and Blackford Hill for passenger and goods trains.
71 Shunts Stone Lye at Morningside Road. Calls Drybroughs if required. Shunts Blackford Hill and Gorgie for passenger trains.

Some trains lifted traffic at Morningside Road and space was to be left at Niddrie to take these wagons.

		Inner Circle		
Train Number		40	57	82
		am	*pm*	*pm*
Haymarket		10.00	1.30	6.56
Gorgie		10.10	1.40	7.25
Morningside Road		10.20	1.50	7.33
Blackford Hill		10.35	2.08	7.45
Duddingston		10.45	2.15	
Niddrie West	*arr.*	10.55	2.20	8.00
Niddrie West	*dep.*	11.12	2.35	8.15
Portobello		11.18	2.40	8.20

40 Conveys livestock on train.
64 In addition to local freights above, No. 64, a through train from Perth, also called at Morningside Road or Blackford Hill to set down livestock.

Local train identification to and from the east end of Waverley after the quadrupling, station rebuilding and resignalling of the 1890s was by a combination of a unique electro-mechanical dial type instrument above the lever frames in Waverley and Abbeyhill Junction signal boxes and unique locomotive headcodes. As well as normal lamp irons above each buffer, main coupling and below the chimney, the engines had an additional lamp bracket over the buffers at both ends and, of the 18 codes in the 1907 Appendix, seven were local to Edinburgh. The suburban trains carried two white discs or lamps over the left-hand buffer, regardless of whether on Inner or Outer Circle services. The extra lamp irons were fitted to some 'imported' engines after Grouping, such as the GNR 'N2' and LNER 'V1' tanks, but by 1930, when the 'V1s' appeared, local headcodes had been abolished! However, the extra brackets continued to be fitted to new 'V1' (and later 'V3') engines up to 1939. Of course, many other NBR headcodes did not necessarily conform to later standard arrangements.

Rule 174(b) stated that side chains of coaching stock had to be coupled, but on 29th January, 1907 NBR staff were instructed that this arrangement was suspended and that side chains were to be uncoupled and hooked up and used only for failures of the main coupling. However, the actual Rule remained unaltered in both 1914 and 1921 Rule Books.

Money was remitted to the bank centrally, and specified trains carried a numbered security box in the brake van into which stations deposited their padlocked leather cash bags. Trains were identified to stations by a circular which varied according to the timetables, and taking a 1907 Suburban example, Cash Box No. 38 was in the van of the train due at Waverley at 9.54 am with bags from Leith Central, and all suburban stations between Duddingston and Gorgie. A messenger then took the cash to the British Linen Bank (BLB) Headquarters in Edinburgh (the North British used this bank for its business). Later, most stations banked at their local BLB branch, Craiglockhart staff carrying their cash bag to Morningside Road.

The first of the Reid six-coupled goods engines (later LNER class 'J35') had been built in July 1906, but it was not until 17th October, 1907 that their maximum permissible train loads were published. At that time, maximum loads appeared in the Sectional portion of the General Appendix, with all locomotives divided into seven categories. These covered the 18 inch six-coupled engines, with all the other locomotives being grouped into First, Second or Third class, each being further divided into four- and six-wheeled types. Loadings were specified only in numbers of loaded goods wagons, with some amplifications such as one loaded bulk grain wagon counting as two loaded ordinary wagons. This rather crude system lasted until 1913 when a more definitive system was introduced.

In 1912, the North British started planning a freight traffic control system based on the North Eastern Railway scheme at Middlesbrough. Opened in August 1913 using the former Leith branch passenger station in Portobello yard, redundant after that service was withdrawn in 1905, it initially dealt mainly with Lothians mineral traffic, including the Niddrie yards. The system worked quite well, but was considered as unsuitable for major development on its original site, although in October 1914 it was extended to include the Edinburgh suburban line.

In conjunction with the new system, separate route headcodes were introduced in 1913 for local Edinburgh goods trains, replacing normal classifications and using a dark blue disc with a white upright cross by day and a purple light by night. Included in the 16 local freight codes were trains to St Leonards, over the suburban line and to Haymarket via Gorgie. These carried a disc or lamp over the left-hand buffer and above the centre of the buffer beam, a normal white lamp being placed over the right-hand buffer. Eastbound trains to Niddrie West had discs over the right-hand buffer, the centre of the buffer beam, and a white lamp over the left-hand buffer. It is not clear how long these headcodes survived, but they do not appear to have had a long innings. It may have been too unwieldy to operate, with some goods trains requiring to change headcodes more than once *en route* or simply due to

SEASON TICKETS.

These Tickets are folded in book form, and a specimen is shewn below. On portions of the Line, where traffic is considerable, the limits between which the Tickets are available will be printed thereon, both inside and outside; but, where traffic is light, these particulars will be written on the Tickets.

SPECIMEN OF SEASON TICKET.

First Class—Outside, YELLOW; Inside, WHITE.
Third   „   „   GREEN;   „   GREEN.

INSIDE.   OUTSIDE.

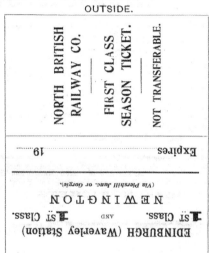

Season Tickets issued to Scholars, Apprentices, and others, under 18 years of age (except such Tickets as are available only between Stations on the Forth and Clyde Section), are distinguished by being stamped in the following manner, viz. :—

Tickets issued to Scholars, &c., under 14 years of age, at One-third Fare (stamped in red) - - - - - - - - - - (UNDER FOURTEEN YEARS OF AGE.)

Over 14 and under 18 years of age, at Half-Fare (stamped in blue) - - - - (OVER FOURTEEN AND UNDER EIGHTEEN Years of Age.)

Tickets available only between Stations on the Forth and Clyde Section, under 17 years of age, at Half-Fare (stamped in blue) - - - - (N. B. R. (FORTH AND CLYDE SECTION) Half-Ticket UNDER Seventeen Years of Age.)

Circular issued in 1913 regarding season tickets on the NBR related only to periods of a month or more. This specimen in the document referred to services between Newington and Waverley and also included details of the endorsements which were required to be made before the tickets were issued.

depleted manpower and increased traffic created by World War I. Unlike passenger train headcodes, the freight ones never made it to the Rule Books and Working Time Tables Appendices.

On 1st September, 1913 the new NBR 'Maximum Loads of Engines' book was introduced in line with the new control system. Locomotives were classified for power by a letter in one of two groups, A to G being for freight engines and H to R for passenger, 'A' and 'H' being the most powerful in their groups. When the final NBR 0-6-0 tender locomotives appeared, they were classified 'B', but with a later increase in boiler pressure and thus power they were accorded 'S', after the passenger locomotives. The LNER classified them 'J37'. From June 1919, the power class appeared on cab sides of tender engines, and bunker sides of tank locomotives as 4 in. square brass plates with raised letters and borders. An ever-decreasing number of these plates remained in position until the engines were scrapped many years later.

In May 1916, Portobello Control moved to an upper floor at Waverley station where there was room for expansion, and contributed to the division of the former 'Traffic' Department into separate District Operating and Commercial functions. Wagon control and distribution, based on reports from yards, depots and sidings at least once per day was undertaken in an adjacent room. Unfortunately, communications were by a cumbersome internal railway telephone system based, not on telephone numbers, but a series of coded rings which rang out on all signal box, station and depot telephones on the particular circuit. The need to listen for one's own code could distract signalmen, and others within earshot, particularly when the 'ten o'clock time signal' of an unspecified number of short rings was sent out! There were also many times when depots were told to send wagons 'all speed' to a destination, after the last train had already departed!

In the Control office, goods trains were indicated on a large line diagram pin board by a colour coded pin bearing the departure depot, time and destination, pushed through a second plate with the engine number, home depot and power class. Every running line, refuge siding and capacity, signal box, crossover, and station (passenger and goods) was shown and positive locomotive identification was needed 24 hours per day. Through trains were only reported by certain signal boxes, but local trains at every calling point, quoting wagons attached and detached, arrival and departure times, minutes late, etc. The Suburban (and other) boxes acquired oil, gas or (sometimes) electric lamps on their fronts to read engine numbers after dusk (with varying degrees of success).

Despite the 'reserved occupation' status available to railway staff in essential positions, many had joined the colours and as the demand for trains increased, passenger services reductions were implemented after February 1915. By 1917, the number of NBR passenger trains had actually reduced by 45 per cent over that of 1914. Locomotive and manpower shortages were further complicated by increases in military traffics, and on 1st January, 1917, Craiglockhart and Blackford Hill were temporarily closed, as it was considered that alternative services were available by tramways or motor buses. The closure lasted until 1st February, 1919. Piershill, on the north side of Edinburgh served by suburban circle trains also closed on the same day, but did not reopen until 1st April, 1919. Employment of women in clerical and operational grades increased, but was not always welcomed by the men!

All traffic vastly increased during World War I and was exacerbated when the United States of America eventually joined the war in 1917 and their personnel and equipment had to be catered for. Troops arrived at Clyde ports and many of their trains were routed via Glasgow, the Edinburgh Suburban line and then via the Waverley or East Coast routes to the South. Each train carried about 25 officers, 440 men, six nurses and some 10 tons of baggage. One locomotive worked each train from the port to Niddrie West, but two locomotives were provided at Niddrie for Waverley Route gradients.

Warnings at the start of temporary speed restrictions were indicated to trainmen by circulars and by flagmen at the site, but by June 1917, perhaps resulting from manpower shortages, this changed to the familiar circular 'C' (commencement) and square 'T' (termination) boards. Advance warning of the restriction (at that time without the actual speed restriction) was by a large yellow 'arrow' shaped board with inset green and white lamps.

As the war continued, the Suburban hosted the unwelcome sight of ambulance trains with their grim cargoes moving from ports to inland hospitals. By the end of 1918, it was estimated that the then suburban service terminal of Leith Central had dealt with 210 trains and Craigentinny (where there were no practical platforms and few facilities) with 110.

The coal shortage arising from the 1920 miners' strike affected train services and from 25th October, three Outer Circle (2.20, 3.36, and 7.15 pm) and three Inner Circle (11.33 am, 2.36, and 3.33 pm) trains from Leith Central, together with the 8.16 pm Outer and 10.20 pm Inner Circle trains from Waverley were temporarily withdrawn.

A new 'Maximum Loads of Engines' book came into operation on 20th October 1920 on the 1913 pattern. Lines were divided into sections and the ruling gradients for each were shown as 'rising' or 'falling'. Loads for the five freight locomotive classes (A-E) were shown in numbers of wagons, sub-divided into Goods, Mineral, Empties and Live Stock, but passenger engine (H-R) loads were indicated by tonnage. The classification 'S' (LNER 'J37') introduced in 1919 was not shown and even the largest passenger engines when on goods trains had maximum loads equal to an 18 in. goods (LNER class 'J36'). Conversely, six-coupled goods engines of class 'B' ('J35' and 'J37') could take the same passenger train loadings as the large 4-4-0 and 4-4-2 tender engines, but only on slow trains! After Grouping, locomotives transferred into the NB area and which also worked over the Suburban acquired load classifications (but not plates) under the NB system. These were 'J9' and 'J24' (C), 'D11' (J), 'C7' (K), 'D1' (M) and 'K2' (S). These lasted until 1928 when a new load book was published with LNER locomotive type codes and which also covered freight and passenger stock trains.

The weekday suburban passenger train service in the last summer of the North British Railway comprised of 12 trains on both Outer and Inner Circles completing the round trip, with other trains serving the suburbs between Waverley and Duddingston. In all, 19 Outer and 21 Inner Circle trains were provided, mostly to meet commuter, factory and brewery requirements although not all stopped at every station. The 7.25 am Inner Circle train from Leith Central terminated at Blackford Hill, returning as the 8.30 am Outer Circle local to Waverley. The last two trains from Leith Central were the 7.18 pm Outer and 7.56 pm Inner circles, later trains starting and terminating at Waverley.

In the first LNER time tables, several through freight trains continued to call at the intermediate suburban yards. On an average weekday the suburban goods train timetable was:

Inner Circle

Train No.		23	26	44	85	101	107	115
					WO			
		am	*am*	*am*	*pm*	*pm*	*pm*	*pm*
Cowlairs		5.20						
Bathgate						7.40		
Portobello							5.52	8.08
Haymarket			6.55	11.20			9.00	11.20
Gorgie CMS					5.25			
Gorgie		7.16	7.15	11.35	5.40	8.45+	9.40	11.35
Craiglockhart		7.21						
Morningside Road		7.29	7.30	12.04 *pm*		9.15+	10.00	11.50
Blackford Hill		7.34	7.50	12.25		9.37+	10.25	12.10 *am*
Newington		7.37						
Duddingston	*arr.*		8.05	12.45				
	dep.	7.45	8.12	12.50		10.03+	10.50	12.25
Niddrie West	*arr.*	7.50			6.00	10.12	10.58	12.32
	dep.	8.02			6.13	10.35	11.20	12.50
Portobello	*arr.*	8.07				10.50	11.35	1.05
	dep.	8.09						
Piershill		8.42						
North Leith		9.02						
Hardengreen								2.12
Berwick						11.36		
Haymarket			10.31	2.35				
		Granton						
		& Carlisle						

No. 23   Stores train. Booked to run on 24th October, 28th November and 26th December, 1922. (Note conflicting timings with No. 26 on these dates.)

No. 85   Cattle train from Gorgie Cattle Market Sidings, reversing at Gorgie. WO = runs Wednesdays only.

No. 101   + indicates calls to set down traffic only. Through goods train from Bathgate.

No. 107   Lifts perishable East Coast traffic from Haymarket and Gorgie also traffic for Newcastle (Forth). Also shunts McKenzie and Moncur siding at Morningside Road and lifts any important perishable traffic at Blackford Hill.

Outer Circle

Train No.	35	88	103
	am	*pm*	*pm*
Portobello		5.47	8.08
Niddrie West	9.15	6.01	8.19
		6.25	8.55
Duddingston	9.45	6.37	9.05
Blackford Hill	10.00	6.53	10.00
Morningside Road	10.15	7.52	10.25
Gorgie	10.25	8.15	10.55
Haymarket	10.31	8.25	11.00
Niddrie West	12.50 *pm*		
Portobello		11.35	12.55 *am*

No. 35   Conveys the 'Road Van' for small loads from Leith Walk on the previous night's 12.15 am Stirling freight.

No. 88   Uplifts Glasgow traffic from Blackford Hill for Haymarket as required.

Timetable July 1922 – The last summer before electric trams in the street

Inner Circle Line

Station	am	am	am	am	am	am	pm	pm	pm	pm	pm	pm	pm	pm (SX)	pm (SX)	pm	pm	pm	pm (A)	pm
Leith Central	5.30	7.25	8.07	8.25	9.31	11.37	12.29		12.55	1.32	2.32	3.32	4.31		5.05	5.31	6.38	7.56		10.20
Abbeyhill	5.33	7.28	8.10	8.28	9.34	11.40	12.32		12.58	1.35	2.35	3.35	4.34		5.08	5.34	6.41	7.59		10.24
Edinburgh Waverley (arr.)	5.37	7.32	8.14	8.32	9.38	11.44	12.36		1.02	1.39	2.39	3.39	4.38		5.12	5.38	6.48	8.03		10.28
Edinburgh Waverley (dep.)	5.46	7.35	8.20	8.37	9.45	11.46	12.40	12.55	1.10	1.42	2.42	3.45	4.46	5.10	5.20	5.42	6.58	8.12	9.20	10.31
Haymarket	5.50	7.39	8.24	8.41	9.49	11.50	12.44	12.59	1.14	1.46	2.46	3.49	4.50	5.14	5.24	5.46	6.54	8.16	9.24	10.34
Gorgie	5.54	7.43	8.28	8.45	9.54	11.54	12.48	1.03	1.18	1.50	2.50	3.53	4.54	5.18	5.28	5.50	7.02	8.20	9.28	10.37
Craiglockhart	5.57	7.46	8.31	8.48	9.57	11.57	12.51	..	1.21	1.53	2.53	3.56	4.57	5.21	5.31	5.53	7.01	8.23	9.31	10.39
Morningside Road	6.00	7.49	8.34	8.51	10.00	12.00	12.54	1.08	1.24	1.56	2.56	3.59	5.00	5.21	5.34	5.56	7.04	8.26	9.34	10.44
Blackford Hill	6.03	7.52	8.37	8.54	10.03	12.03	12.57	1.11	1.27	1.59	2.59	4.02	5.03	5.24	5.37	5.59	7.07	8.29	9.37	10.52
Newington	6.05		8.39	8.56	10.05	12.05	12.59	1.13	1.29	2.01	3.02	4.04	5.05	5.26	5.39	6.01	7.09	8.31	9.39	10.58
Duddingston & Craigmillar	6.10		8.43	9.01	10.13	12.10	1.04	1.19	1.33	2.06	3.08	4.09	5.10	5.31	5.43	6.06	7.14	8.37	9.44	
Portobello	6.18			9.09	10.18	1.04	1.12	1.32	2.14	3.16	4.17	5.18	5.39	5.48	6.14	7.22	8.45	9.52		
Edinburgh Waverley (arr.)*	6.44	8.24	8.38	9.26	10.31	1.15	1.32	2.24	3.35	4.28	5.33	5.48	6.00	6.41	7.48	8.55	10.01			
Piershill	6.21	8.27	9.12	10.24	12.21	1.15	2.17	3.19	4.20	5.21	5.39	5.52	6.17	7.25	8.48					
Leith Central	6.25	8.31	9.16	10.28	12.25	1.19	2.21	3.23	4.24	5.25	5.45	5.55	6.21	7.29	8.52					

Outer Circle line

Station	am	am	am	am	am	am	am	am	pm	pm	pm	pm (SO)	pm (SX)	pm (SO)	pm (SX)	pm	pm	pm	pm	pm
Leith Central	6.46	7.29	8.14	9.16	10.55	12.05	1.10	1.17	1.56	1.59	2.26	3.47	4.56	6.22	7.18	9.04				
Piershill	6.50	7.33	8.18	9.20	10.59	12.09	1.14	1.21	2.00	2.30	3.51	5.00	6.26	7.22	9.10					
Edinburgh Waverley (dep.)*	6.10	7.24	7.50	8.08	9.05	11.38	1.07	2.13	3.45	4.45	6.12	7.10	9.04							
Portobello	6.54	7.37	8.06	8.22	9.25	10.02	11.38	12.13	1.18	1.25	2.03	2.34	3.55	5.04	6.30	7.26	9.10			
Duddingston & Craigmillar	7.03	7.45	8.15	8.33	8.59	9.37	11.11	12.26	1.29	1.33	2.07	2.42	4.03	5.12	6.38	7.34	9.20			
Newington	7.07	7.49	8.19	8.37	9.03	9.41	11.15	12.30	1.33	1.37	2.00	2.11	2.46	4.07	5.16	6.42	7.38	9.24		
Blackford Hill	7.10	7.52	8.30	9.06	9.44	11.18	12.33	1.36	1.40	2.03	2.49	4.10	5.19	6.45	7.41	9.27				
Morningside Road	7.14	7.55	8.24	8.43	9.10	9.48	11.22	12.37	1.40	1.44	2.07	2.05	2.53	4.14	5.23	6.49	7.45	9.31		
Craiglockhart	7.16	7.57	8.27	8.35	9.12	9.50	11.24	12.39	1.42	1.46	2.10	2.16	2.55	4.16	5.25	6.51	7.47	9.33		
Gorgie	7.19	8.00	8.30	8.38	9.15	9.54	11.27	12.43	1.45	1.49	2.13	2.58	4.19	5.28	6.54	7.50	9.36			
Haymarket	7.23	8.04	8.34	8.42	9.19	9.58	11.31	12.47	1.49	1.53	2.17	2.13	3.02	4.23	5.32	6.58	7.54	9.40		
Edinburgh Waverley (arr.)	7.27	8.08	8.38	8.46	9.23	10.02	11.35	12.51	1.53	1.57	2.21	2.17	3.06	4.27	5.36	7.02	7.58	9.44		
Edinburgh Waverley (dep.)	7.34	8.11	8.53	9.28	10.10	11.42	1.00	1.57	2.03	2.21	2.32	3.08	4.33	5.41	6.33	8.07				
Abbeyhill	7.37	8.14	8.55	9.31	10.13	11.45	1.03	2.00	2.06	2.35	3.11	4.36	5.44	7.06	8.10					
Leith Central	7.40	8.17	9.01	8.58	9.34	10.16	11.48	1.06	2.03	2.09	2.38	3.14	4.39	5.47	7.09	8.13				

Notes: SX = Saturdays Excepted. SO = Saturdays Only. * = Change at Portobello. f = Arrives 12.28 on Saturdays A = Calls at Piershill 9.55 pm and Abbeyhill 9.58 pm.

Over the next few years, locomotives and rolling stock acquired new liveries, those of the old North British fading into memory, although the new colours were no less pleasing. Operational and engineering staff received new uniforms, but clerical staff continued wearing their own clothes. Stations and other buildings remained in NB colours for some time.

Through staff reports, suggestions and statistics, services continued to be reviewed to ensure maximum value for expenditure and the lightly loaded 11.14 am Outer Circle train from Duddingston and an Inner Circle (via Gorgie) service that arrived at Duddingston at 3.06 pm were both withdrawn in 1924. This provoked an angry response from Drybrough's Brewery management who claimed that both trains formed an important part of their operation as the 11.14 am was used by staff connecting at Waverley with trains to other parts of the country, particularly the Borders. They reminded the LNER that there was now no outward service between 9.35 am and 12.17 pm, and that the incoming train brought shift and other workers to the brewery, including those returning from lunch. The brewery also obliquely referred to the amount of their beer traffic that passed over the LNER which they might reconsider if the trains were permanently withdrawn. The LNER enquired and found that the withdrawal of the trains gave no savings in train crews or engines, but if the trains were restored it might have ramifications from other organisations which had also lost services. Thus it was agreed that the 2.42 pm from Waverley (3.06 pm at Duddingston) would be reinstated from 10th October, 1924, but the superintendent of the line resisted reinstatement of the 11.14. This incident perhaps illustrates the power of the Duddingston breweries, although after a few years the hastily restored train was again withdrawn - permanently!

Hitherto, side lamps on the rearmost vehicles showed red to the rear and white forwards indicating to drivers that their trains were intact, but as all coaching stock trains then had continuous brakes this was now no longer relevant and thus side lamps were discontinued after 5th May, 1924. Sidelights on freight trains fitted throughout with continuous automatic brakes continued until 3rd November, 1930.

By 1926, there were only two surviving Edinburgh twin headlamp codes - over the right-hand buffer for North Leith and Corstorphine and left-hand buffer for Suburbans. North Leith had four- and six-wheel stock (and a Railcar on and off after 1929) and Corstorphine trains operated west of Waverley whereas Suburban sets were programmed for six modern bogie vehicles. Both codes were withdrawn in the 1st January, 1930 Appendix Supplement. Two other local codes involved single lamps above the centre of the buffer beam and over the right-hand buffer for Dalkeith/Polton/Glencorse/Penicuik (merged earlier from separate codes) and left buffer for Musselburgh but these also gradually disappeared.

The February 1928 revision of the NBR 'Maximum Loads of Engines' book incorporated locomotive types added since 1922, and also increased load limits for many existing designs. Some types still in service were omitted, notably the (then) LNER classes 'J31', 'J88' and 'Y9'. Circulars and supplements regularly updated the document.

As before, freight train loads were defined by the number of wagons in the formation but now only as 'Goods' or 'Mineral'. A 'ready reckoner' table was provided for other types, passenger trains continuing to be calculated by tare weight tonnage.

Other LNER areas' engines authorised to traverse the Suburban had goods load limits equal to local NB engines.

C12, J22, J69, D17, D20, D23, & N1	= J33	B13, C6, C7, J9, J21 & J24. J26, J27, J39	= J37
J25	= J35	J50 & K2	= N14

The following table shows the passenger train loads (tons) for the locomotives specified:

Outer Circle		D11, D29, D30/2/3/4,	N2	C16 D36	C15, G9, D1, D31	D25	G7	D51	
From	To								Notes
Monktonhall Jn	Haymarket West	420	410	400	380	350	320	300	TL AT
or Niddrie South		370	310	295	265	230	200	160	TL ADMR
		255	250	240	210	180	160	120	TL UA
Leith Central ⎫ Monktonhall Jn ⎬ Niddrie South ⎭	Morningside Rd	200	180	180	168	144	128	96	
Morningside Rd	Haymarket West Edinburgh	296	252	240	212	184	160	124	

Inner Circle									
Haymarket West	Niddrie South or	420	410	400	380	350	320	300	TL AT
	Monktonhall Jn	315	294	280	235	220	200	160	TL AGMR
		220	189	180	160	130	120	90	TL UA
Haymarket West Edinburgh Wav.	Morningside Rd ⎱ Morningside Rd ⎰	176	147	140	128	104	96	72	
Morningside Rd	Niddrie South	252	242	230	204	176	160	128	
Morningside Rd Morningside Rd	Monktonhall Jn ⎱ Leith Central ⎰	296	252	240	212	184	160	128	

TL= Through load (express trains). AT = Assisted throughout. UA = Unassisted.
ADMR = Assisted Duddingston to Morningside Road. AGMR = Assisted Gorgie to Morningside Rd.

Pacific and Atlantic types were not listed for local suburban passenger work. The tare weights of 'standard' LNER suburban carriages were quoted in the book as first class = 28 T. 4 cwt; third class = 29 T.; brake third = 26 T. 5 cwt, a five-coach formation being 138 tons 14 cwt but larger NBR suburban stock built after 1906 was slightly longer and heavier. Later supplements equated the 'V1' 2-6-2 tanks and 'Shire' 4-4-0s to an 'N2', and the 'A1', 'A3' and 'A4' Pacifics and 'V2' 2-6-2s were restricted to through empty coaching stock trains between Haymarket West and Niddrie South or Monktonhall Junctions. These had a 25 miles per hour maximum speed in either direction and loading was restricted to 375 and 425 tons for up and down directions respectively. 'D49' 4-4-0s were also heavily restricted.

Interestingly, the largest passenger locomotives, such as the 'A4s', when working goods trains were only considered as being of equal power to the class 'J36' goods engines! During the 1930s, the booked formations of suburban circle trains were reduced from six to five vehicles with the loss of a full first class carriage.

A feature for many years was the 'Road Van' conveying small freight consignments in otherwise 'Wagon load' services. Although largely supplanted by the motor lorry, in June 1931 the Edinburgh Suburban still had its own timetabled vehicle. Leaving Leith Walk Goods station at 10.10 pm daily, it was tripped over to Niddrie West Yard where it lay until 9.00 am on the following morning. It then served Duddingston, Newington, Morningside Road, and Gorgie before terminating at Haymarket, the 'back working' leaving at 10.35 am, with traffic for intermediate points to Newington, thence to Leith Walk for the next run. Station staff had documents to let them gauge traffic routeing to make the best connections for onward consignment movements. Road Vans were loaded according to the destinations of the contents. Documentation (such as invoices) accompanied the Road Vans in the custody of the train guard.

On 1st March, 1937, a new Appendix issued for the Southern Scottish Area replaced that of the October 1922 North British Railway edition. Instructions were continued for banking on the gradients up to Morningside Road from both sides. Passenger trains required to have the banking engine coupled to the rear of the train and the trains stopped at the summit for detaching but arrangements for goods trains differed. Between Lochend South, Niddrie and Morningside Road bank engines could join and leave the parent train at any intermediate signal box (usually Duddingston Junction). The fireman coupled the banker to the train, but uncoupling was done by the guard while the train was in motion using a coupling pole through the opening window at the rear of his van after passing Morningside Road down distant signal. Open verandas on the first LNER standard 20 ton brake vans simplified this, but the later LNER 'Queen Mary' vans presented problems! From Haymarket West or Central Junctions (via Gorgie), the assisting engine was not coupled to the train. Passenger train guards need not remove the tail lamp when a banker was added, but goods train guards had to remove their tail lamps. The instructions continued in the 1960 Appendix but by 1969 goods trains were in line with passenger trains.

The Suburban was a useful alternative route for out of gauge loads, particularly at weekends. An example from 1937 was a 90 ton stator which although only some 15 ft 0 in. in length was some 11 ft 10 in. in both height and width. The journey from Parsons of Newcastle to Glasgow Corporation at Dalmarnock took three successive Sundays. The stator was loaded on LNER transformer set 158253 with two pairs of girders on rollers to enable transverse movement to clear platforms *en route* and, on 18th July, left Newcastle for Berwick where it lay for a week before reaching Blackford Hill yard where it was staged for a further week before going on to Glasgow. The *LNER Magazine* claimed that this was the largest ever load conveyed over the Southern Scottish Area, the engine used over the Suburban being class 'V1' 2-6-2 tank No. 2919.

After 12th October, 1937, outer casings of passenger train tail lamps began to be painted white in place of red, bringing them into line with freight train tail lamps and also greatly increasing their visibility to signalmen.

War was declared on 3rd September, 1939, but the LNER continued to run its summer timetable for a few more days but from 11th September a drastically curtailed emergency service was implemented.

An 'Emergency Timetable' of 2nd October was superseded on 4th December when the nine Outer and 10 Inner Circle trains were respectively raised to 12 and 14 (Saturdays excepted) and 11 and 12 on Saturdays respectively. During the war, the passenger trains retained their five-coach formations, but were frequently supplemented by non passenger carrying coaching stock vehicles such as milk tanks, etc, and being 'conditional' these did not appear in marshalling documents.

The first report of the LNER Post-War Development Committee of September 1943 again raised the question of a major goods marshalling yard in the Edinburgh Area. By that time, the land envisaged for the schemes of 1922/3 and 1929/30 had been lost, but anyway, the basic marshalling yard concept had been reappraised and estimated to cost some £900,000 apart from land, legal expenses and compensation. It was considered that marshalling LNER traffic at Portobello, Meadows, Niddrie West, Hardengreen and South Leith Yards was unsatisfactory and uneconomical and providing a central well-placed modern marshalling yard was deemed essential to make the most of Edinburgh's central position for east central Scotland. Once again, the economic situation, this time in the post-war period, defeated this plan, which was shelved until investment became available in the 1950s, when new yards were conceived, and this time implemented at Millerhill on the city's southern

Edinburgh Suburban Line, Leith (Central), Etc.

Mls. from Edinburgh	OUTER CIRCLE		a.m	a.m	a.m	a.m.	p.m	Ex Sats p.m	p.m	p.m	Ex Sats p.m
	Leith (Central)	lev.	6 45	7 15	8 3	—	1212	1241	1 13	—	5 2
	Piershill		6 49	7 20	8 7	.	1216	1245	1 17	.	5 6
	(a) Edinburgh (Waverley)	lev.	6 40	7 10	8 1	—	12*5	—	1 3	—	4 44
3¼	Portobello		6 52	7 25	8 11	.	1219	.	1 20	.	5 9
5¾	Duddingston		6 59	7 30	8 18	8 32	1228	—	1 30	2 5	5 16
7¼	Newington		7 3	7 34	8 22	8 36	1232	.	1 34	2 9	5 20
8	Blackford Hill		7 5	7 36	8 24	8 38	1234	—	1 37	2 11	5 22
8¾	Morningside Road		7 8	7 39	8 27	8 41	1237	.	1 40	2 14	5 25
9½	Craiglockhart		7 10	7 41	8 29	8 43	1239	—	1 42	2 16	5 27
10	Gorgie		7 12	7 43	8 31	8 45	1241	.	1 44	2 18	5 31
11¼	Haymarket		7 16	7 47	8 35	8 49	1245	—	1 48	2 22	5 35
12½	Edinburgh (Waverley)	arr.	7 20	7 51	8 39	8 53	1249	.	1 52	2 26	5 39
	Edinburgh (Waverley)	lev.	7 21	7 56	8 42	8 55	1253	—	1 53	2 29	5 42
	Abbeyhill		7 24	7 59	8 45	8 58	1256	.	1 56	2 32	5 45
	Leith (Central)	arr.	7 27	8 2	8 48	9 1	1259	—	1 59	2 35	5 48

Miles from Edinburgh	INNER CIRCLE		a.m	a.m	a.m	a.m	p.m	p.m	Ex Sats p.m	Ex Sats p.m	Ex Sats p.m	Ex Sats p.m	Ex Sats p.m
	Leith (Central)	lev.	5 41	7 23	—	8 17	1228	1258	1 30	4 32	5 5	5 42	6 5
	Abbeyhill		5 44	7 26	.	8 20	1231	1 1	1 33	4 35	5 8	5 46	6 8
	Edinburgh (Waverley)	arr.	5 48	7 30	—	8 24	1235	1 5	1 37	4 39	5 12	5 50	6 12
	Edinburgh (Waverley)	lev.	5 53	7 40	Leave Polton at 8-3 a.m.	8 25	1240	1 10	1 40	4 44	5 19	5 53	6 17
1¼	Haymarket		5 56	7 43		8 28	1243	1 13	1 43	4 47	5 22	5 56	6 20
2½	Gorgie		6 0	7 46		8 32	1247	1 17	1 47	4 51	5 27	6 0	6 24
3	Craiglockhart		—	7 49		8 34	1249	1 19	1 49	4 53	5 29	6 2	6 26
3¾	Morningside Road		6 5	7 52		8 37	1252	1 22	1 52	4 56	5 32	6 5	6 29
4½	Blackford Hill		6 8	7 55		8 40	1255	1 25	1 55	4 59	5 35	6 8	6 32
5¼	Newington		6 10	7 57		8 42	1257	1 27	1 57	5 1	5 37	6 10	6 34
6¾	Duddingston		6 16	8 0		8 52	1 1	1 30	2 2	5 7	5 46	6 17	6 40
9¼	Portobello		6 23	.	8 23	8 58	1 8	.	2 9	5 14	5 53	6 24	6 47
12½	(b) Edinburgh (Waverley)	arr.	6 53	—	8 40	9 11	1 28	—	2 26	5 26	—	6 36	7 8
10¾	Piershill	lev.	6 26	.	8 26	9 2	1 12	.	2 13	5 18	5 56	6 28	6 51
12¼	Leith (Central)	arr	6 29	—	8 30	9 5	1 15	—	2 16	5 21	5 59	6 31	6 55

Edinburgh (Waverley) and Leith (Central).

(Trains arrive about 7 minutes after departure times).

b All Trains stop at Abbeyhill 3 minutes later, except those marked *b*

Leave Edinburgh (Waverley)—7-21, 7-56, 8-42, 8-55 a.m ; 12-53, 1-53, 2-29, †5-42 p.m.
Leave Leith (Central)—5-41, 7-23, 8-17 a.m.; 12-28, *b*12-45, 12-58, †1-30, †4-32, †5-5, †5-42, †6-5 p.m.

* Saturdays only † Except Saturdays ‡ Except Mondays § Mondays only

a Passengers from Edinburgh for Duddingston and other Stations change at Portobello

b Passengers for Edinburgh from Duddingston and other Stations change at Portobello

The last LNER timetable, 6th October, 1947.

outskirts. Unfortunately, traffic handling concepts and the outputs from the Lothian coalfield were about to change forever.

On 17th January, 1946, the LNER introduced new nomenclature for additional running lines, such as loops, etc., throughout the system where entry and exit was controlled by different signal boxes. Suburban lines affected were:

Niddrie West and Duddingston	Up Goods Loop	became	Up Goods Independent.
	Down Goods Loop	became	Down Goods Independent.
Portobello East and Niddrie West	Down Loop Line	became	Down Goods Independent.
Haymarket Central and Haymarket West	Goods Loop	became	Goods Independent (2 way signalled).

The new nomenclature appeared in the November 1947 issue of the LNER Scottish Area Appendix, but on 23rd December, 1948, standardisation over British Railways meant that the 'Independent' became 'Line', remaining thus until the reissue of the Appendix in October 1960. It is doubtful if the 1946 names were much used by staff on the ground.

In late 1946, the Suburban was included in a new Train Control telephone system for Edinburgh District Control, replacing the antiquated system installed in 1916. Controllers now dialled the number on an automatic telephone for the signal box or office with which they wished to communicate, and the bell only rang at that location. In reverse, each place on any of the 19 circuits could call the Control Office by pushing a button on the side of their dedicated 'Control Phone' which brought up a light on the Controller's panel, considerably reducing Control Room noise. The wall-mounted pinboard control diagram was replaced by desktop rolls of custom-designed graph paper which took cognisance of gradients and timings to achieve a straight line, easily highlighting anything requiring attention. Desks with telephone consoles were placed along the centre of the room and could accommodate 11 controllers, the deputy chief controller and his clerks sitting at a desk transversely across one end. Lighting was now fluorescent.

In the immediate post-war period, railway operation severely suffered from poor locomotive and rolling stock availability, a combination of advancing years and minimal wartime maintenance. Locomotive availability fell to 75 per cent, and for some larger engines was as low as 67 per cent. Traffic build-ups were inevitable and wartime problems did not end with the peace.

In November 1947, the LNER issued its 'Route Availability' categories giving numbers between 1 and 9 (the highest number being the most restrictive) to individual routes. The Suburban was accorded RA9, although locomotives of RA8 and RA9 were limited to speeds of 25 mph, with former Great Northern class 'N2' 0-6-2 tank locomotives (RA6) being restricted to 40 mph to protect the track. Up to four RA9 engines could run coupled together, but were limited to 30 mph, oddly 5 mph higher than if they were on their own!

All sections of line were classified according to the classes of locomotives permitted to work over them, the criteria being axle load. The Edinburgh Suburban line was allocated RA9, meaning that any LNER locomotive could work between Monktonhall/Niddrie North/Niddrie South junctions and Haymarket Central/West junctions, but engines in Groups 8 and 9 were restricted to 25 mph and 'N2' tanks (RA6) to 40 mph. The scheme did not cover former LMS engines.

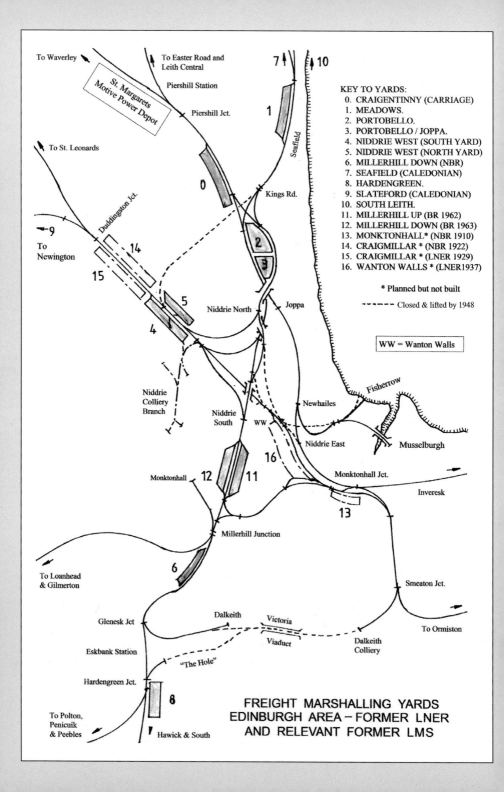

To Waverley

To Easter Road and
Leith Central

7 ↑   ↑ 10

St. Margarets
Motive Power Depot

Piershill Station

Piershill Jct.

1

Seafield

To St. Leonards

0

Kings Rd.

Duddingston Jct.

9

To
Newington

14

15

5

Niddrie North

Joppa

2

3

4

Niddrie
Colliery
Branch

Niddrie
South

WW

Newhailes

Fisherrow

Niddrie East

Musselburgh

Monktonhall

12   11

16

Monktonhall Jct.

Inveresk

13

Millerhill Junction

To Loanhead
& Gilmerton

6

Smeaton Jct.

To Ormiston

Glenesk Jct

Dalkeith

Victoria

Viaduct

Dalkeith
Colliery

Eskbank Station

"The Hole"

Hardengreen Jct.

8

To Polton,
Penicuik
& Peebles

Hawick & South

KEY TO YARDS:

0. CRAIGENTINNY (CARRIAGE)
1. MEADOWS.
2. PORTOBELLO.
3. PORTOBELLO / JOPPA.
4. NIDDRIE WEST (SOUTH YARD)
5. NIDDRIE WEST (NORTH YARD)
6. MILLERHILL DOWN (NBR)
7. SEAFIELD (CALEDONIAN)
8. HARDENGREEN.
9. SLATEFORD (CALEDONIAN)
10. SOUTH LEITH.
11. MILLERHILL UP (BR 1962)
12. MILLERHILL DOWN (BR 1963)
13. MONKTONHALL* (NBR 1910)
14. CRAIGMILLAR * (NBR 1922)
15. CRAIGMILLAR * (LNER 1929)
16. WANTON WALLS * (LNER1937)

* Planned but not built

------ Closed & lifted by 1948

WW = Wanton Walls

FREIGHT MARSHALLING YARDS
EDINBURGH AREA – FORMER LNER
AND RELEVANT FORMER LMS

A new British Railways 'Freight Train Loads Book' covering the former Scottish Area lines was issued on 31st May, 1948, with LNER locomotives shown in line with former London Midland & Scottish Railway (LMS) power classifications style in place of the former alpha-numeric codes, and divided into tender and tank engines. However, LNER men continued to refer to their engines in the LNER style until the end of steam. The passenger train loads book of 1928 as amended remained in use. Several adjustments were made before being finalised in 1953.

The suburban line came under threat in 1949 with the publication of a substantial tome entitled *The Civic Survey and Plan for Edinburgh*, produced at the instigation of the former Edinburgh Town Council. Together with proposals for road and air transport in the capital, it recommended a drastic reshaping of railways in the Lothians, including the reduction of Waverley to a passing station. This plan included an (over)ambitious scheme to make a new double track railway from the St Leonards branch (which was also to be doubled) near Duddingston Loch, tunnel under the Meadows and emerge at a new two level railway station at Morrison Street near Haymarket where there would be interchange with other forms of transport. With the immediate post-war economic climate, most recommendations, including the passenger service aspects, were not implemented, but coal traffic flows changed after the Scottish Region of British Railways enabled merging of the old LNER and LMS within the city. Westbound traffic from Lothian coalfields that had hitherto traversed the suburban line would pass via Granton to Crew Junction, the new starting point for several Dalry Road mineral trains. Leith and Granton pilots were recast, with LMS engines allocated to LNER lines and vice versa. This was a laborious and roundabout route but perhaps the best available with the infrastructure of the day.

Drastic changes in handling suburban freight are illustrated in Working Time Tables for the immediate post-nationalisation period. Gone were the famous 'stores train', and calls at suburban yards by goods trains were replaced by just two. One, known as the 'Sub Goods' and usually headed by a Haymarket 'N15' engine, left Haymarket Goods about 8.55 am and called at intermediate sidings only to set down wagons. The other used a St Margarets-based 0-6-0 (or whatever else was available) from Duddingston, known as 'The Shunt' and which ran to Morningside Road and back shunting Newington and Morningside Road yards and private sidings, placing any wagons left by the 'Sub Goods' into the appropriate trader's lyes. Provision existed for this trip train to go forward to Gorgie and Haymarket if required, but it rarely, if ever, did, with the back working of the 'Sub Goods' providing this service. All the work of 'The Shunt' was done on the outward journey, the return to base usually, but not always, being 'non-stop', taking particular care through the Newington station 'dog leg' and the curve and grade to Cameron Toll. The locomotive returned tender first, the non-stop portion being welcomed by the crew, apart from during the winter weather.

One non-passenger duty of (usually) Haymarket 'V1' or 'V3' locomotives used part of the Suburban to turn mail vans from Kings Cross each weekday morning. The vans, with net apparatus on one side only, were hauled from Waverley to Gorgie Junction, propelled to Haymarket West Junction and hauled from there to Waverley just after 8.00 am. On Sundays, this was a St Margarets turn, also with a 'V1' or a 'V3', which later worked a Cowdenbeath service.

On 8th June, 1953, the LNER 'Route Availability' booklet was reissued, and now included several LMS and BR Standard locomotive classes although the former did not carry the coding on the locomotive. RA9 and RA8 locomotives, which included classes 'D49', 'J37', 'J38' and 'K3', were still restricted to 25 mph and the 'N2' tanks to 40 mph, but as the line speed for the Suburban was 40 mph anyway, this had little effect. Rebuilding the 'V1s' as 'V3s' raised their RA number from 3 to 4, but this had no practical effect!

DIESEL TRAIN SERVICES

EDINBURGH (Waverley)— SUBURBAN STATIONS and MUSSELBURGH

CORSTORPHINE — NORTH BERWICK

EDINBURGH (Waverley)— PEEBLES — GALASHIELS

9th JUNE until 14th SEPTEMBER, 1958
(or until further notice)

Leaflet giving full details of above services can be obtained at Ticket Offices and accredited Rail Ticket Agencies

Published by British Railways (Scottish Region) B.R. 350 4—8/2450—8—May, 1958.   Printed in Great Britain by McCorquodale, Glasgow.

Poster issued by British Railways regarding the introduction of diesel multiple units (dmus) to the suburban (and other) local lines in September 1958. A Gloucester twin appears in the heading.

The British Railways Modernisation Plan of the mid-1950s facilitated a review of freight operations in Edinburgh. £700,000 was authorised to provide a double line connection between the Suburban and former LMS at Slateford to simplify Lothian collieries movements to west Scotland. At that time traffic could be exchanged at Granton, Camps and Seafield, but these had single tracks, hampering operations. The new connection also provided access from Slateford via the Suburban to the Niddrie yards and work started in 1957. South-east of Niddrie, a new marshalling yard scheme was being developed for Millerhill, with centralised goods train marshalling, rather than the rather tedious, time consuming and labour intensive inter-yard tripping then in use.

On 1st June 1957, a new 'Loads of Passenger Trains' booklet became operational, using the power classification system of the old LMS and was simpler than that of the former LNER. In the new document, maximum tonnage permitted for locomotive-hauled passenger trains on the suburban (and Leith Central) lines were:

Section of Line		Class of Passenger engine						
	Line	*2*	*3*	*4*	*5*	*6*	*7*	*8*
Edinburgh Inner Circle	–	160	220	250	270	375	375	375
Edinburgh Outer Circle	–	220	250	300	320	425	425	425
Edinburgh & Leith Central or	Down	220	225	250	270	350	350	350
Piershill (via Abbeyhill)	Up	280	345	375	390	500	500	500

Power class '2' included the 'C15', 'C16' and 'N15s'; class '3' the 'D11', 'D49', 'V1', 'N2' and NB 4-4-0s and class '4' the 'V3'.

On 17th June, 1957, Scottish Region adopted the trip and shunting engines reporting system which had been operating in the Edinburgh area for two or three years using an 'E' prefix and number on an oval 'target' over an engine lamp bracket.

Gloucester twin diesel multiple units based on Leith Central Diesel Depot took over suburban passenger services on Monday 9th June, 1958 working the former steam timetable with minor timing increases to allow for engineering work on the new Craiglockhart-Slateford Junction spur. Concurrently, services to Musselburgh, Rosewell and Hawthornden, and the Caledonian line between Edinburgh (Princes Street) and Leith (North) were also dieselised. On the Suburban, destination screens indicated 'EDINBURGH' above slightly smaller text of either 'INNER CIRCLE' or 'OUTER CIRCLE'. All passenger trains were classed 'B' on the left-hand panel below the centre driving cab window, the right-hand panel being white. Tail lamps could be electrically lit but as these had single filaments, paraffin tail lamps remained supreme!

The Craiglockhart and Slateford spur opened in 1959, increasing the number of trains between Niddrie and Craiglockhart Junction over the suburban line. The ex-LMS locomotives were no more immune from failures on the gradients than indigenous breeds.

On 8th September 1961, a report was published in the *Scotsman* newspaper that closure of some of the Edinburgh Suburban stations was being contemplated. This apparently alerted two of the city's MPs; Mr J.A. Stoddart, the MP for West Edinburgh quoted from a Select Committee report of 1960 that in the first year of diesel operation the receipts from the suburban railway went up by between 23 per cent and 30 per cent. Mr Michael Clark Hutchison, MP for South Edinburgh expressed the view that the nature of railway accounting was such that the railways themselves did not know which lines were paying their way and which were not. It was noted that the general policy appeared to use the yardstick of profitability or at least non-loss as the basis for reprieve. He expressed the view that this was misleading in that the result of closing the stations

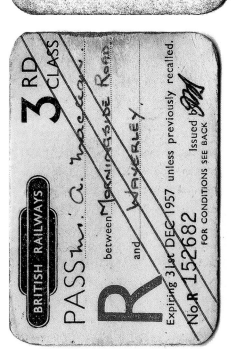

A selection of season tickets used on the line.

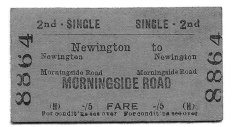

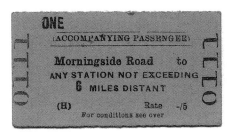

A selection of single and return tickets used on the line.

Timetable February 1961

Inner Circle Service

From	1	2	3	4	5	6	7	8	9	10	11	12	13	14	15	16	17	18	19	20
			SX M		SX M	R	SX M	M	R	SX	SO	SX M	SX R	SX	SX M	SX M	SX	SX M	SX C	SX
	am	am	am	am	am	am	am	pm	pm	pm	pm	pm	pm	pm	pm	pm	pm	pm	pm	pm
Edinburgh Waverley dep.	5.53	6.48	7.09	7.30	7.45	8.25	8.45	12.22	12.35	1.05	1.15	1.27	1.45		4.26	4.55	5.10	5.22	5.45	6.12
Haymarket	5.57	6.52	7.13	7.34	7.49	8.29	8.49	12.26	12.39	1.09	1.19	1.31	1.49		4.29	4.59	5.14	5.26	5.49	6.16
Gorgie (East)	6.01	6.56	7.17	7.38	7.53	8.33	8.53	12.30	12.43	1.13	1.23	1.35	1.53	2.19	4.33	5.03	5.18	5.30	5.53	6.20
Craiglockhart	..	..	7.20	7.41	7.56	8.36	8.56	12.33	12.46	1.16	1.26	1.38	1.56	2.22	4.36	5.06	5.21	5.33	5.56	6.23
Morningside Road	6.06	7.01	7.23	7.44	7.59	8.39	8.59	12.36	12.49	1.19	1.29	1.41	1.59	2.25	4.39	5.09	5.24	5.36	5.59	6.26
Blackford Hill	..				8.02	8.42	9.02	12.39	12.52	1.22	1.32	1.44	2.02	2.28	4.42	5.12	5.27	5.39	6.02	6.29
Newington	6.13	..	7.28	7.48	8.04	8.44	9.04	12.41	12.54	1.24	1.34	1.46	2.04	2.30	4.44	5.14	5.29	5.41	6.04	6.31
Duddingston	6.20	7.09	7.36	7.51	8.08	8.47	9.08	12.45	12.58	1.32	1.37	1.49	2.08	2.34	4.49	5.21	5.36	5.49	6.08	6.34
Portobello	6.23	7.16	7.43		8.15		9.15	12.52	1.05	1.39			2.15	2.41	4.56	5.28	5.43	5.56	6.15	
Piershill	..	7.19	7.46		8.18		9.18	12.55	1.08	1.42			2.18		4.59	5.31	..	5.59	..	
Abbeyhill	6.26	7.23	7.49		8.21		9.21	12.58	1.11	1.45			2.21	..	5.02	5.35	..	6.02	..	
Edinburgh Waverley arr.	6.29	7.26	7.52		8.24		9.24	1.01	1.14	1.48			2.24	2.47	5.05	5.38	5.49	6.05	6.21	

Outer Circle Service

	21	22	23	24	25	26	27	28	29	30	31	32	33	34	35	36	37	38	39	40
								SX	SX	SX	SO	SO	SX		SX	SX	SX			
	am	am	am	am	am	am	am	pm	pm	pm	pm	pm	pm		pm	pm	pm			
Edinburgh Waverley	6.30	6.55		7.56	8.12			12.10	12.49	1.11	1.11				4.59	5.23	6.02			
Abbeyhill	6.33	6.58		7.59	..			12.13	12.52	1.14	1.14				..	5.26	6.05			
Piershill	6.36	7.01		8.02	..			12.16	12.55	1.17	1.17				5.04	5.29	6.08			
Portobello	6.39	7.04		8.05	8.18			12.19	12.58	1.20	1.20				5.07	5.32	6.11			
Duddingston	6.50	7.15	8.00	8.12	8.28	8.55		12.25	1.04	1.27	1.27	2.00	2.05		5.16	5.39	6.17			
Newington	6.54	7.19	8.04	8.16	8.32	8.59		12.29	1.08	1.31	1.31	2.04	2.09		5.20	5.43	6.21			
Blackford Hill	..	..	8.06	8.18	8.34	9.01		12.31	1.10	1.33	1.33	2.06	2.11		5.22	5.45	6.23			
Morningside Road	6.59	7.24	8.09	8.21	8.37	9.04		12.34	1.13	1.36	1.36	2.09	2.14		5.25	5.48	6.26			
Craiglockhart	..	7.27	8.12	8.24	8.40	9.07		12.37	1.16	1.39	1.39	2.12	2.17		5.28	5.51	6.29			
Gorgie (East)	7.05	7.31	8.16	8.28	8.43	9.10		12.40	1.18	1.42	1.41	2.15	2.20		5.31	6.00	6.37			
Haymarket	7.08	7.34	8.19	8.31	8.46	9.13		12.43		1.45		2.18	2.23		5.34	6.04	6.40			
Edinburgh Waverley arr	7.12	7.38	8.23	8.35	8.50	9.17		12.47		1.49		2.22	2.27		5.38	6.07	6.44			
To	R	R	M	M		M				R					M	M	R			

C = From 5.10 pm ex-Edinburgh Waverley Inner Circle Train.   M = To or from Musselburgh.   R = To or from Rosewell & Hawthornden.

would be to load traffic on to already overcrowded roads and that not enough had been done to attract passengers to the suburban line.

As a result of the threat of closure, a council of Edinburgh citizens were formed to fight any further rail closures in the city and the support was sought of Lord John Hope, Minister for Works and also MP for the local Pentlands constituency, as well as Messrs Stoddart and Clark Hutchison. The committee was led by Mr William Geddes a Musselburgh solicitor. Statistics produced by British Railways indicated that at Duddingston an average of 140 joined and 130 alighted there each day. Respective figures for the other suburban stations were Newington 130/130; Blackford Hill 160/160; Morningside Road 280/330; Craiglockhart 120/150 and Gorgie East 380/410. These proved to be of no avail and the closure of the suburban line progressed. Closure notices were posted, and after the Town Council refused to intervene, on the casting vote of a committee chairman, passenger trains ceased between Gorgie and Duddingston (both inclusive) on Monday 10th September, 1962. This closure was before the 'Reshaping of British Railways' Report of 1963 and, contrary to subsequent local newspaper items, responsibility did not rest with Doctor Beeching! Notwithstanding, the line continued to be maintained to passenger train standards for diversions, etc.

Meantime, Edinburgh (Princes Street) closed on Sundays after 20th May, 1962, its services diverting via the Slateford-Craiglockhart spur and around the suburban line via Portobello, increasing the journey time by about 15 minutes. On the first day, all trains were hauled by former LMS class '5MT' 4-6-0 locomotives, apart from a solitary Carlisle 'Jubilee'.

In March 1963, a survey by the Edinburgh Suburban Travellers Association and the then recently formed Scottish Railway Development Association claimed that most people who had used the suburban line before closure were worse off in almost all aspects of local travel. Apparently, 92 per cent of the respondents to a questionnaire were formerly daily travellers and included those that made four journeys per day and 80 per cent stated that they now travelled by bus. Complainants stated that they had experienced an increase in the length of their working day and increased expenditure.

The opening of the new marshalling yards and locomotive servicing facilities at Millerhill in June 1962 (up yard) and May 1963 (down yard) had a profound effect on freight workings in Edinburgh. Several old flat yards in the area closed and its geographical position meant that freight trains could now run from Millerhill through Waverley as well as from Niddrie and around the Suburban. Additional daytime paths were available with the virtual annihilation of Edinburgh local passenger services and the decline in output from the Lothian coalfield was in tandem with that in traditional heavy engineering. Traffic patterns were recast, and the Suburban became a mere shadow of that a few years before. Gone were the days (and particularly nights) of the application of Absolute Block Regulation 5 ('Section Clear but Station or Junction Blocked') on the Outer Circle when north- and west-bound trains followed each other in fairly close succession.

In 1964, Scottish Region management decided on the basis of a rating structure for small consignments that in two out of three Traffic Divisions, livestock conveyance, other than in train loads from ports to inland destinations, would be discontinued. This affected Gorgie Cattle Market sidings, although traffic levels were generally low anyway by then.

Upgrading the freight-only Granton branch from Slateford to Granton Junction, refurbishing the double line from there to the Caledonian Distillery Siding points and connecting that to the Edinburgh and Glasgow Main line at Haymarket started in 1964. When opened, Sunday trains over the Slateford - Craiglockhart link and

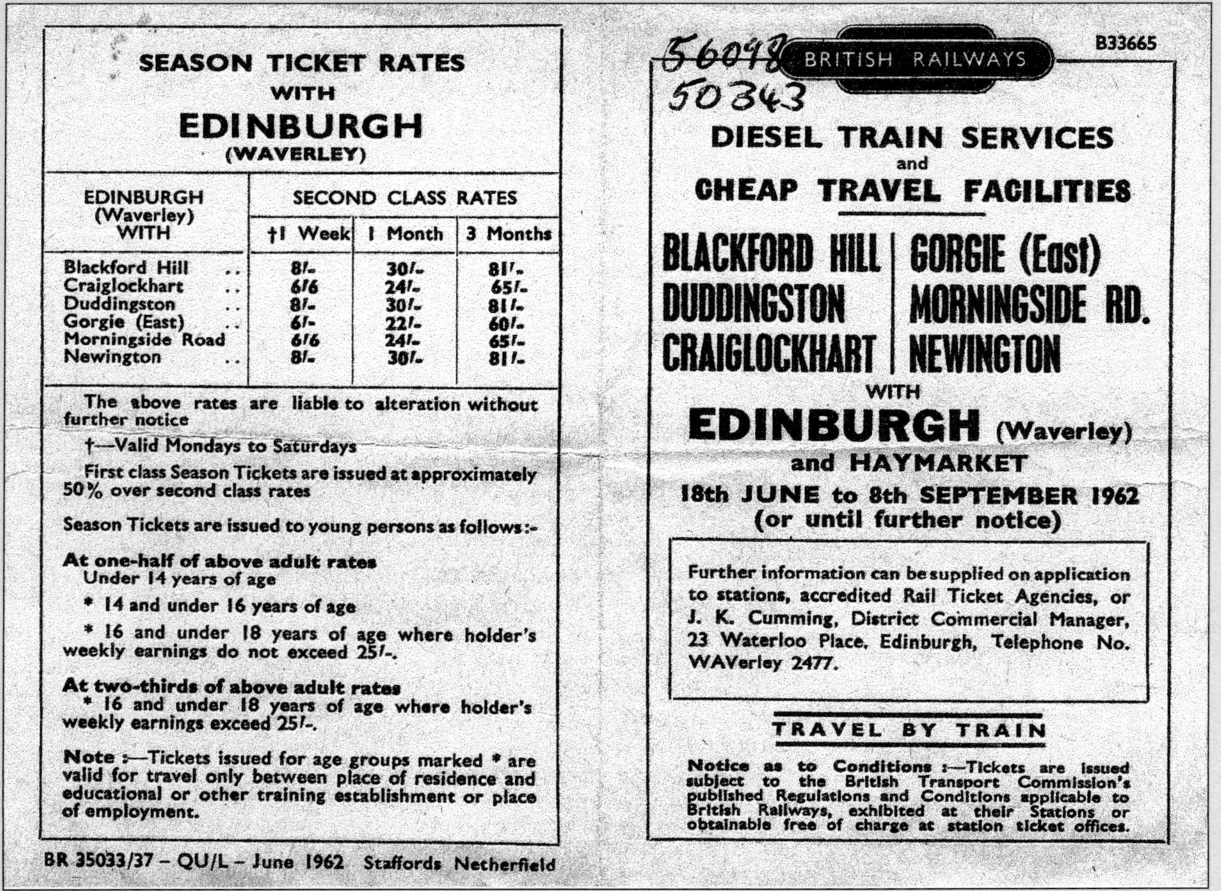

B33665

BRITISH RAILWAYS

56090
50343

DIESEL TRAIN SERVICES
and
CHEAP TRAVEL FACILITIES

BLACKFORD HILL | GORGIE (East)
DUDDINGSTON | MORNINGSIDE RD.
CRAIGLOCKHART | NEWINGTON

WITH

EDINBURGH (Waverley)
and HAYMARKET

18th JUNE to 8th SEPTEMBER 1962
(or until further notice)

Further information can be supplied on application to stations, accredited Rail Ticket Agencies, or J. K. Cumming, District Commercial Manager, 23 Waterloo Place, Edinburgh, Telephone No. WAVerley 2477.

TRAVEL BY TRAIN

Notice as to Conditions :—Tickets are issued subject to the British Transport Commission's published Regulations and Conditions applicable to British Railways, exhibited at their Stations or obtainable free of charge at station ticket offices.

SEASON TICKET RATES
WITH
EDINBURGH
(WAVERLEY)

EDINBURGH (Waverley) WITH	SECOND CLASS RATES		
	† 1 Week	1 Month	3 Months
Blackford Hill ...	8/-	30/-	81/-
Craiglockhart ...	6/6	24/-	65/-
Duddingston ...	8/-	30/-	81/-
Gorgie (East) ...	6/-	22/-	60/-
Morningside Road ...	6/6	24/-	65/-
Newington ...	8/-	30/-	81/-

The above rates are liable to alteration without further notice

†—Valid Mondays to Saturdays

First class Season Tickets are issued at approximately 50% over second class rates

Season Tickets are issued to young persons as follows:—

At one-half of above adult rates
  Under 14 years of age
  * 14 and under 16 years of age
  * 16 and under 18 years of age where holder's weekly earnings do not exceed 25/-.

At two-thirds of above adult rates
  * 16 and under 18 years of age where holder's weekly earnings exceed 25/-.

Note :—Tickets issued for age groups marked * are valid for travel only between place of residence and educational or other training establishment or place of employment.

BR 35033/37 — QU/L — June 1962   Staffords Netherfield

To EDINBURGH (Waverley) — DAILY (except Sundays)

	am	am	am			pm SX		pm SX	pm SX	pm SX
Edinburgh (Waverley) leave	6 35	7 0	8 14	12 10				4 57	5 23	6 2
Duddingston	6 50	7 15	8 28	12 25		2 5		5 16	5 39	6 17
Newington	6 54	7 19	8 32	12 29		2 9		5 20	5 43	6 21
Blackford Hill		7 21	8 34	12 31		2 11		5 22	5 45	6 23
Morningside Road	6 59	7 24	8 37	12 34		2 14		5 25	5 48	6 26
Craiglockhart		7 27	8 40	12 37		2 17		5 28	5 51	6 29
Gorgie (East)	7 5	7 31	8 43	12 40		2 20		5 33	6 0	6 37
Haymarket	7 8	7 34	8 46	12 43		2 23		5 36	6 3	6 40
Edinburgh (Waverley) arrive	7 12	7 38	8 50	12 47		2 27		5 40	6 7	6 44

From EDINBURGH (Waverley) — DAILY (except Sundays)

	am	am	am		SO pm	SX pm				pm SX	pm SX
Edinburgh (Waverley) leave	5 56	6 6	6 46							5 24	6 10
Haymarket	6	6 9	6 49							5 45	6 14
Gorgie (East)										5 49	6 18
Craiglockhart										5 53	6 21
Morningside Road										5 59	6 24
Blackford Hill											6 27
Newington	6 16										6 29
Duddingston	6 27										6 32
Edinburgh (Waverley) arrive	6 32										6 47

SO—Saturdays only   SX—Saturdays excepted

CHEAP TICKETS — TO EDINBURGH
BY ANY TRAIN - ANY DAY (where train service permits)

From

**BLACKFORD HILL,   CRAIGLOCKHART,   DUDDINGSTON,
GORGIE (EAST),   MORNINGSIDE ROAD   and   NEWINGTON**

Second Class Single	Second Class Return
8d.	**1/3**

The above fares are liable to alteration without further notice

First class tickets are issued at approximately 50% over second class fares.

The tickets are valid on the date for which issued and passengers can alight at any intermediate station on surrender of tickets

The final passenger train timetable, 19th June to 8th September, 1962.

WITHDRAWAL OF PASSENGER TRAIN SERVICE

FROM THE

EDINBURGH (Waverley) OUTER & INNER CIRCLE LINE

On and from
MONDAY, 10th SEPTEMBER, 1962

With the approval of the Transport Users' Consultative Committee for Scotland the passenger train service will be withdrawn from the above-mentioned line and the following passenger stations will be closed.

BLACKFORD HILL	GORGIE (EAST)
CRAIGLOCKHART	MORNINGSIDE ROAD
DUDDINGSTON &	NEWINGTON
CRAIGMILLAR	

Thereafter the following arrangements will apply.

PASSENGERS

Edinburgh Corporation Transport Department operate frequent bus services in the districts served by the stations to be closed. Passengers travelling by rail to or from places outwith these districts can travel from or to Edinburgh (Waverley) or Edinburgh (Princes Street) stations.

PARCELS AND OTHER MERCHANDISE TRAFFIC BY PASSENGER TRAIN

Alternative facilities for above-mentioned traffic in less than truck loads, also traffic in full truck loads requiring collection or delivery by railway road service, will be available at Edinburgh (Waverley) or Edinburgh (Princes Street) stations.
Traffic in less than truck loads will be accepted for despatch at Duddingston & Craigmillar and Gorgie (East) goods stations.
For Traffic in full truck loads not requiring collection or delivery by railway road service, facilities will be available at Duddingston & Craigmillar and Gorgie (East) goods stations and similar facilities will also be available at Morningside Road and Newington goods stations which will become unstaffed public sidings under the supervision of the Station Masters, Gorgie (East) and Duddingston & Craigmillar stations respectively.

FREIGHT TRAIN TRAFFIC

Alternative facilities for above mentioned traffic in less than truck loads, also traffic in full truck loads requiring collection and delivery by railway road service are available at Edinburgh (Waverley) and Edinburgh (Lothian Road) goods stations.
Facilities for traffic in full truck loads not requiring collection or delivery by railway road service will be available at Morningside Road and Newington unstaffed public sidings.
The facilities available at Duddingston & Craigmillar and Gorgie (East) goods stations will continue as at present.

BRITISH RAILWAYS

British Railways poster intimating withdrawal of the suburban passenger train service and arrangements for other facilities.

Suburban line ran direct into Waverley. Some West Coast portion trains and a postal train also used this route, but other Princes Street traffic continued pending Ministry of Transport approval to the closure of Merchiston station, between Slateford and Princes Street which had opened at the same time as the Suburban. Freight dealt with at Lothian Road goods station was transferred to the former NB station at Leith Walk East, via the new spur and Waverley, or by the suburban line. Morrison Street mineral depot briefly remained operational pending transfer of traders to a new site, and closed to make room for an ubiquitous car park.

Despite the increasing dieselisation, diesel-hauled passenger trains over the suburban line were still rare, apart from occasional main line diversions, specials, excursions and charters.

Duddingston, once a teeming hive of activity and junction for the St Leonards branch declined as breweries succumbed to improvements in production techniques elsewhere, and/or merged with other brewing giants and gradually ran down as production closed or distribution switched to road. The St Leonards branch also felt the dead hand of closure descend upon it and its final train ran on Saturday 3rd August, 1968. The track bed is now a public walkway.

Newington Goods closed on 2nd January, 1967 and the goods yards at Gorgie, Morningside Road and Duddingston closed in January 1968, mostly as a result of coal concentration schemes. Under these, small domestic coal merchants were (often unwillingly) removed to new locations dedicated to dealing with bulk coal traffic, and railway management policy led a decline in wagonload traffic in favour of full trainloads. Although ideal for accountancy, this led many firms to switch to road haulage. There were fewer trains but more powerful diesel locomotives could haul heavier trains of shorter lengths more economically. Siding connections were reduced or removed, those remaining being increasingly under remotely controlled local ground frames.

Most locomotives normally using the Suburban were based on Haymarket, although engines from all over Britain gradually appeared. Traffic continued to fall and, from early September 1968, the line closed from 6 am on Saturdays, but not before a flurry of movements took place, with light engines heading for Haymarket. Sometimes, these were in multiple or tandem, producing some interesting combinations! Trains that hitherto used the line on Saturdays ran via Waverley until the Suburban boxes reopened at 6 am on Mondays. One unusual visitor in September 1968 was a 'Freightliner' service from Glasgow via Newcastle to Sheffield, but by next summer this went via Haymarket East Junction and Waverley.

The value of retaining the suburban line as a diversionary route was often amply demonstrated and not just for purely railway purposes. For example, when an electricity authority placed new 275kv overhead power lines over the Waverley Route between Niddrie North and Portobello East junctions on 22nd and 29th December, 1968, 'Waverley Route' trains left from the west end of Waverley and ran via Haymarket Central, the suburban line and Niddrie South.

New business continued to be won to rail, and used the suburban line to by-pass Edinburgh. Trains of new motor cars from the BMC factory in Bathgate passed through Waverley, thence by the Outer Circle to Craiglockhart, Slateford and the West Coast Main Line. When the suburban line was closed, this train ran through Waverley to Craigentinny, propelled back to Easter Road, then went back through Waverley and the Duff Street connection to Slateford. Motive power was usually the by then ubiquitous class '47'.

The Inner Circle platform at Gorgie East, closed to passengers in September 1962 but still intact, was reinstated for a day on 21st May, 1969 when it was used by a special for the Household Cavalry attending a Royal visit to Edinburgh. The train comprised of a class '40' diesel, BSK, CK, CCT and about 20 horseboxes of British Railways standard design in mixed green and maroon liveries. With the blue CCT and blue and grey passenger carriages, it made a colourful spectacle.

Duddingston Junction and Blackford Hill signal boxes closed on 15th June, 1969, signalling equipment being quickly removed from the former. The suburban line was thus reduced to just two block sections, between Niddrie West and Morningside Road, and Morningside Road and Gorgie Junction. Craiglockhart Junction was controlled from Morningside Road's panel. Duddingston Junction box was demolished on the 12th April, 1970 and Blackford Hill on the next day.

There were some brief nostalgic flashes. In August 1970 Morningside Road yard held old Great Western Railway tank wagons with road works tar. An electrical transformer was also loaded there for Beauly under 'Out of Gauge' conditions.

A charter train was organised by the prestigious Cockburn Association on 18th November, 1973 in an attempt to show the public how proposals for railway development in the city would work. The train, which unusually ran on a Sunday, left Haymarket station platform 1 (the north arrival platform) and passed through Waverley, Portobello, Niddrie, Craigmillar, Newington, Morningside and Craiglockhart to the Caledonian line at Slateford before heading west to Midcalder. The train was patronised by some 500 people and the nine-coach train was formed of three triple sets.

Morningside Road, the last Suburban box, closed on 26th June, 1977, although shown as a 'ground frame' in the October 1977 Sectional Appendix, pending removal of its yard connections. Edinburgh Signalling Centre concurrently absorbed Morningside Road and Portobello relay room, which had absorbed Niddrie West. The simplified signalling with multiple aspect colour lights was now controlled from Edinburgh signalling centre who decided routeing though Waverley or via the 'sub' as suitable, the latter now being plain line from Niddrie West to Craiglockhart, then Gorgie Junctions.

The 1st October, 1977 Appendix included a subtle change from that of January 1969 as mileages which had hitherto been shown as between signal boxes was changed to refer to lineside mileposts, but by then all suburban line signal boxes had been closed. It also contained little detail on the suburban line.

By the summer of 1981, most freight by-passed Waverley and used the suburban line, apart from when crew changing was involved.

Wanton Walls Junction ceased to exist in 1963 with the closure of the single Lothian Lines spur from Niddrie North (originally Brunstane Park) and the signal box closed in January 1967. The name was reused for a short time for the junction between the original Lothian Lines and the 1962 spur to Millerhill Yard. The line from here through Wanton Walls to Niddrie West was closed in the autumn of 1984 and lifted, but trains could still pass over the spur line and through the yard complex to and from the Suburban or Waverley.

A special train was chartered by the Morningside Association on 2nd June, 1984 and about 200 people took the opportunity of travel around the Suburban for a fare of £2. Apparently the tour had been sold out for some weeks beforehand and a three-coach Metropolitan Cammell diesel multiple unit (dmu) (101 330) was supplied for the event. The train left Waverley at 6.40 pm and ran by the Inner Circle, returning to Waverley at 7.24 pm. Naturally, the train called at the overgrown platform at Morningside Road. A second charter left at 7.29 pm and returned at 8.06 pm and an excursion brochure was supplied to passengers giving a brief history of the line. A retired SMT bus conductor on the train recalled that every second week of his late shift, he would buy a first class weekly season ticket which gave him unlimited travel around the suburban, and one year, during his winter holiday, he managed an estimated 200 miles, surely a record!

Another scheme to reopen the Suburban to passengers was put to Edinburgh councillors two months later, but, as was becoming normal, nothing further happened.

The centenary of the opening of the suburban line was celebrated on 4th December, 1984 when the preserved North British Railway 0-6-0 *Maude* hauled two packed excursion trains, each of four coaches around the circle. Resulting from the miners' strike, the coal supplied for the journey came from an opencast mine.

New permanent speed restriction boards were introduced from early 1986 replacing the traditional style with separate cut out white or cream painted numbers on a black horizontal bar and supporting frame. The new signs were similar to road signs being circular with a red reflective edge and the speed in black on a reflective white background and worked well in conjunction with the new electric locomotive headlights.

In October 1986, a report appeared in the *Scotsman* of a proposal to re-open the Suburban circle to passenger trains with new platforms at Bingham, Cameron Toll, and the Jewel (Niddrie North), and stations at Gorgie, Craiglockhart, Morningside Road, Meadowbank and Niddrie. An estimated capital outlay of some £4.3m was claimed to be repayable in about 5 years, but as with several previous schemes, it headed into obscurity.

In late 1987, freight was increasing over the suburban line with bulk commodity trains of motor cars in covered double-deck car transporters, cement, and permanent way materials. On 5th October, the Abbeyhill-Easter Road-Lochend triangle closed and coaching stock that used it to reverse for return working or pass to Craigentinny for maintenance, then used the Haymarket West-Gorgie Junction-Haymarket Central, or the Niddrie triangles.

Derailment of a class '37' diesel on the Suburban in early 1987 led to a temporary ban on this class over the line and for a time their trains passed through Waverley.

Track remodelling at Waverley in late 1988 deprived trains arriving at Platform 20 of a direct exit to Craigentinny. Thus another locomotive was attached at the rear and took the stock out via Gorgie and the Inner Circle. Newhailes bridge works in February 1989 had some eastbound dmu services starting from the west end of Waverley and following the same route

In January 1989 a scheme was proposed to incorporate the suburban as part of a local rapid transport network, but Lothian Regional Transport, showed no interest in the scheme. A year later, Lothian Regional Council discussed proposals for an Edinburgh Light Railway with a predicted completion before the end of that decade but this also came to nought.

Haymarket South tunnel was planned to close during the summer timetable of 1989 to permit engineering work for the Carstairs and Edinburgh electrification. West Coast Main Line (WCML) trains ran via Portobello and the Suburban to Slateford, extending journey times, the local Shotts line dmus working to and from Haymarket. Department of Transport approval for the electrification was not announced until 13th September, 1989, by which time much of the work, which was supported by both Inter-City and Railfreight, was well in hand. The tunnel opening was delayed until 16th October, 1989 due, it was claimed, to a fault in the tunnel inherited from the original construction. Railfreight considered electrification from Slateford to Millerhill via the Suburban, with line singling to increase bridge clearances, but this was not developed.

An accident on the Slateford - Haymarket line early on 22nd August, 1990 caused west coast trains to be re-routed via the suburban line into Waverley, but the Shotts Line dmus reversed at Craiglockhart and ran via Gorgie East to Waverley.

The Scottish Region of British Railways became the first geographical Profit Centre on 27th May, 1991 under the British Railways Board 'O for Q' (Organisation for Quality) organisation. ScotRail became responsible for most internal passenger services and the freight business owned all Scottish non-passenger lines including the Suburban from Monktonhall, Millerhill and Portobello East to Slateford, Haymarket Central and West junctions.

Speculation regarding the Suburban reopening to passengers was rekindled on 9th March, 1992, when 'Sprinter' unit 150 245 conveyed Edinburgh councillors (with on-board refreshment trolley) around the Inner Circle line, leaving Waverley at 2.36 pm and returning about 3.25 pm. Unfortunately, as had happened so often before, no further action was taken.

For a time in the summer of 1992, the Outer Circle suburban line was intermittently closed, trains in both directions using the Inner Circle and being accompanied by a pilotman. Westbound trains to Millerhill reversed at Niddrie West on the curve to Portobello before running 'wrong line'. At that time, class '60s' worked coal traffic around the Suburban daily.

In April 1993, refurbishment of some London underground stock at Rosyth Dockyard brought tube trains to the suburban line and at least one train from the Carstairs line passed around the Inner Circle through Waverley and by the Forth Bridge.

Whenever the Engineer took possession of the south lines through Princes Street Gardens, there was no direct link between Waverley and Slateford. For example, in October 1993, Glasgow-bound East Coast Main Line (ECML) electric-hauled trains terminated at Waverley, dmu 'Sprinters' making forward connections by Portobello and the Suburban to Slateford and Glasgow. This route was also followed by the steam-hauled 'Queen of Scots' specials between Waverley and Haymarket West.

On 29th January, 1994, unit 158 703 stood in Edinburgh Waverley with a destination indication of 'Bingham'. A station between Nottingham and Grantham, it was also the name of the terminus of an Edinburgh bus service a stone's throw from the suburban line, frequently proposed without success to reopen to passengers. Six years later, the *Edinburgh Evening News* announced that 'Crossrail', the brand name for reopening selected railway lines in Edinburgh, had plans for new stations - and passenger service - to Bingham (later named Brunstane) and beyond to Newcraighall on 3rd June, 2002.

On 23rd May, 1994, a signal fault in Haymarket relay room created major disruptions. The Slateford *to* Haymarket line was closed, trains diverting via Craiglockhart and the Inner Circle, adding some 30 minutes to the journey. Initially, a dmu 'shuttle' between Carstairs and Waverley was provided by stock ranging from HSTs to 'Sprinter' twins. East Coast services to Glasgow Central and westbound North Berwick trains terminated at Waverley. Other trains passing through the Haymarket area had 3 minutes added for a 20 mph blanket speed restriction on all lines.

The Emergency Working Timetable of 6th June, 1994, brought timetabled passenger trains back to the Inner Circle suburban line (albeit non-stop). Electric-hauled WCML trains from the South called at Carstairs where a diesel was attached in the rear to haul the train to Edinburgh, the electric locomotive (with lowered pantographs) trailing in the rear like a humble goods brake van! Extra 'paths' returned the diesels (almost invariably class '47/8s') to Carstairs for their next turn. Electrical haulage from Edinburgh to Carstairs and the dmu trains via Shotts ran normally, but with speed restrictions. The Slateford to Haymarket line reopened on 22nd August, through East Coast workings resuming two days later.

Lines between Craiglockhart Junction and Haymarket Central and West Junctions and the Haymarket junctions crossover roads initially remained closed, trains which had used these routes to and from the Suburban continuing through Waverley, enabling this section of line to be available for drainage work. Rails were lifted and ballast removed on the Inner Circle line in September 1995, track panels being laid on top of the Outer Circle. Later that year, the Haymarket triangle was reopened as far as the Gorgie East station site, but beyond to Craiglockhart Junction remained lifted.

In late January 1997 a Haymarket-based class '117' dmu was used for route learning between Dalmeny and Slateford via Portobello and the Suburban before the massive civil and signal engineering work of 8th and 9th February, 1997 to reinstate junctions put out of action in 1994. West and south trains between Waverley and Slateford ran via Portobello and the suburban line. Electric ECML services west of Edinburgh were replaced by HST or 'sprinter' links via the Suburban, Slateford and Motherwell. Junctions and signalling were restored to pre-1994 condition on 4th March, 1997, but a limited amount of single line working remained near Duddingston and some freight continued to run through Waverley.

A separate scheme was claimed as being costed and claimed as feasible in the latter part of 2002 using a private consortium to reopen the full Edinburgh suburban line, also became stillborn. An alternative scheme involved the North Berwick service extending to Newcraighall via the suburban line to Waverley to reduce congestion.

Route Availability codes, pioneered by the LNER in 1947 and subsequently slightly modified, still enable the line to take the latest and heaviest diesel locomotives. Although the LNER had engines in RA9, their RA8 was equivalent to the present RA7, the latest diesels (up to class '67') falling into that category.

Ironically, the Craiglockhart spur built to take Lothian coal traffic to the west, now moved coal from the west into the Lothians. Most of the traffic was coal for power stations, although Freightliner sets, other block trainloads and empty stock for prestige passenger trains such as the 'Royal Scotsman' are frequent visitors (the latter in the summer season).

Most freight trains today are headed by modern heavy duty locomotives, and although in the past the term 'foreign' related to a locomotive from a separate motive power district of British Railways, today this can mean having been built in a foreign country, be it England, Canada or Spain.

The Operations Control office may have moved from the upper floor at Waverley station to Glasgow many years ago, and computers may mean more effective working disciplines, but the essence of the suburban line still remains undimmed despite the bumbling and cumbersome bureaucracy inherent with the incompetent politics of privatisation. It remains to be seen that if the expected growth in passenger traffic at Waverley exceeds the handling capacity of the station, the Suburban will again offer an avoiding line around the city of Edinburgh, for which it was originally conceived 120 years ago. Local passenger trains may return, although currently this appears unlikely, but it will be secondary to the freights. History appears to be about to repeat itself.

A splendid array of Victorian railwaymen surround this domeless locomotive, former Edinburgh & Glasgow Railway 0-4-2 tender engine by then NBR No. 331 and fitted with a Stroudley single window cab. Rebuilt by Drummond and Reid, it became an Edinburgh suburban line passenger train regular until displaced by Reid 4-4-2 tanks after 1911. It was withdrawn in 1913 as NBR No. 1032.

Author's Collection

Chapter Four

Motive Power and Rolling Stock

Suburban Motive Power

Most North British and London & North Eastern Railway engines that visited Edinburgh put in an appearance at some time or another. Topography also required locomotives to be provided at Gorgie and Duddingston to assist goods trains up the hill towards Morningside Road and these were usually large yard pilot or shunting types. Sometimes, locomotives being delivered from Glasgow locomotive works were 'birds of passage', often 'dead' in goods trains, and engines on trial from manufacturers were not unknown. After 1923, locomotives returning to home depots from English works also appeared. The Suburban had been engineered for the largest locomotives of the time, and this proved a wise investment.

When the Edinburgh Suburban & South Side Junction Railway opened, the North British, who provided the motive power, possessed some 585 locomotives, in stock or under construction, a few of which had origins in the 1840s. The largest class comprised of 101 general service six-coupled tender types to the designs of Dugald Drummond built between 1879 and 1883, the rebuilt survivors becoming LNER class 'J34', the last being withdrawn in 1928. Essentially for freight, 26 acquired air brakes and a further three were dual braked for coaching stock work and supplemented 88 Wheatley engines built between 1867 and 1875 which became LNER class 'J31', the last surviving until 1937. Thirty-two heavy main line goods engines had also been built in 1876/77, rebuilt survivors becoming LNER class 'J32'. Matthew Holmes took over as locomotive superintendent in 1883, and 18 of his first main line goods engines were in service by the end of 1884, a further 18 being added before 1887. The last of this class was withdrawn in 1932 as LNER class 'J33'. In 1888, the first of Holmes 18 in. goods engines entered service, and by December 1900 168 of these were in service. Given power classification 'C' by the NBR in 1913 and 'J36' by the LNER, withdrawals started in 1931, but the final withdrawals were in 1968, the last Scottish-allocated British Railways steam locomotives. Holmes was succeeded in 1903 by W.P. Reid who introduced larger six-coupled goods engines in 1906 that were built up to 1913 and became NBR class 'B' and LNER 'J35'. Between 1914 and 1921 the final NBR 0-6-0 freight design appeared as power class 'B' but later, with increased boiler pressure, they were uprated as class 'S' and LNER class 'J37'. British Railways classed them as '4F' but uprated to '5F' in May 1953. Several of this rugged class survived into the last days of steam in Scotland.

As new locomotives entered service, former stalwarts 'cascaded' to lesser duties, several Edinburgh-based engines becoming very familiar on suburban duties, such as local trip work, banking and shunting. In the early 1900s, light suburban goods trains between Haymarket and Duddingston and incline banking duties were entrusted to old six-coupled tender engines from a batch of 62 built to a Willam Hurst design between 1860 and 1867. Rebuilt during their careers (some several times) they were latterly classed as 'Third Class Six Wheeled Coupled', but all had gone by 1914. Wheatley 0-6-0 tender engine, No. 43, built at Cowlairs in 1871, regularly worked a local goods turn in late Edwardian days from Portobello to Haymarket, shunting yards and sidings *en route*. It was one of 38 built at Cowlairs between 1867 and 1873 for Fife and Lanarkshire coal traffic using materials from

Thomas Wheatley introduced a 'standard' 0-6-0 and 88 were built between 1867 and 1875. No. 363 came from Dübs & Co. in March 1869 with Naylor's (somewhat unreliable) safety valves. The class was rebuilt between 1883 and 1900 with 4 ft 9 in. boilers, dome safety valves and round cabs. No. 363 also acquired a Wheatley stovepipe chimney. Renumbered 1148 in October 1912 and latterly part of LNER class 'J31' it was withdrawn in December 1924, still in NBR livery.

Author's Collection

condemned engines where suitable, but had distinctive 10 spoke driving wheels. Rebuilt under Holmes, No. 43 became 1187 in 1913, but was condemned in 1914. The final 20 of the type (430-449) were rebuilt as saddle tanks and used for shunting, eight working at Portobello. In tender form, the class was extinct by 1920 but three saddle tanks lasted until 1924 as LNER class 'J84'. Two other six-coupled goods saddle tank engines associated with the Suburban in 1914 were old Wheatley 0-6-0s Nos. 1204 and 1215. Built in 1872 as Nos. 39 and 405 respectively, they were latterly Haymarket goods yard pilots, but foraged further afield on local trip and special goods work, becoming class 'E' in 1913 and being withdrawn in 1922. In 1923, the sole survivor became LNER 'J81'.

One type which worked early passenger services were Wheatley six-coupled saddle tanks of the 1870s, several lasting into the 20th century and also used were small tender locomotives, such as a Wheatley 4-4-0 of 1873. Displaced from 'Waverley Route' expresses by Drummond's 'Abbotsford' class, the class of four gravitated to these less arduous duties. No. 422 of St Margarets, heavily rebuilt under Holmes in 1890 but retaining its solid bogie wheels and small Wheatley tender, worked suburban circle passenger trains during that decade. A 'Second Class Four Wheeled Passenger Engine' in 1907, it became class 'P' in 1913 and renumbered 1214 in 1914, lasted until 1918.

Five former Edinburgh & Glasgow Railway (E&GR) 0-4-2 tender locomotives with 5 ft 1 in. driving wheels also regularly worked the passenger service. Beyer, Peacock in Manchester and Cowlairs in Glasgow built 18 between them for mixed traffic purposes, but graduated largely to passenger work. Four (317/21/30/31) became regular Edinburgh suburban engines later being renumbered 1058, 1062, 1031 and 1032. No. 1066 (ex-E&G 97 and NBR 325) was also used for a time before moving to East Lothian in mid-Edwardian days and was withdrawn in 1911. Summarising, these were:

E&GR	Built	Builders	NBR	Rebuilt	Duplicated	Number	Withdrawn
84	1864	Cowlairs	330	1892	1906	1031	1913
85	1864	Cowlairs	331	1888	1909	1032	1913
89	1859	Beyer, Peacock	317	1871	1903	1058	1915
93	1861	Beyer, Peacock	321	1882	1903	1062	1915

After July 1903, most suburban trains operated into and out of the then newly-opened Leith Central, the reversal in the terminus requiring altered locomotive working arrangements.

Between December 1911 and December 1913, the North British introduced 4-4-2 tank locomotives built by the Yorkshire Engine Company (thus known as 'Yorkies') and some became familiar suburban engines. Initially four (6, 12, 48 and 53) allocated to St Margarets were diagrammed to work over the Suburban and Nos. 6 and 15 (in 1946 LNER 7464 and 7466) became regular Suburban passenger engines. In 1913 the NBR rated the class as power class 'M' and by 1923, suburban passenger trains were also being worked by sister engines Nos. 133 and 134 from the eight then allocated to St Margarets. The Haymarket trio (Nos. 1, 25 and 141) mainly worked to Fife and Queensferry, but one diagram also included suburban forays. Between 1923 and 1925 the LNER added 9000 to their NB numbers and classified them as 'C15', Nos. 9043 and 9135 getting their first LNER liveries at St Margarets. Some of the larger later NB 4-4-2 tanks (class 'L' – LNER class 'C16') were allocated to St Margarets but were not regularly on suburban trains.

No. 9572 of LNER class 'J33' had been built at Cowlairs in January 1884, the first freight design of Matthew Holmes retaining Drummond-style cab and tender. Power classification 'D' in 1914, Duddingston breweries are being shunted by this veteran on 19th August, 1926. She was finally withdrawn in May 1932.

No. 369 was built in 1866 to a Hurst design by Dübs & Company in Glasgow, with a weatherboard with a bent top for a cab and sandboxes incorporated into the leading splashers. Classified after 1872 as a 'Third Class Six Wheeled Coupled' engine it was rebuilt over the years with a more modern boiler, round cab, new chimney and fittings. This veteran had been equipped with Westinghouse brake equipment but retained its four-wheel tender when in Morningside goods yard on a local trip working, its proud crew posing in front. Renumbered 1109 in 1909 it was condemned in 1914, one of the last four of the class.

J.F. McEwan Collection/Kirkintilloch Library

No. 463 was built by Neilson to a Drummond design in 1876, one of a class for heavy long distance freight work, particularly over the Hawick line, but the class was rebuilt by Holmes with rounded cab and altered wheelbase, making them very similar to his later 18 in. goods engines which became LNER class 'J36'. Power class 'C' (the same as the 'J36') after 1914 and renumbered 1317 in 1917, No. 463 was withdrawn in 1922. Survivors became LNER class 'J32' but all had been withdrawn by 1925.

Author's Collection

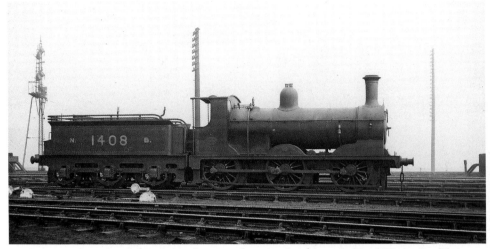

Drummond produced this design for general service freight work, No. 1408 starting life at Cowlairs in 1879 as NBR No. 175. Rebuilt in 1904, classed 'D' in 1914 and renumbered in 1920, it was withdrawn in 1923 as LNER class 'J34', the last one of which was withdrawn in 1928.
Author's Collection

No. 85 was an 1885 Cowlairs product for secondary main line goods work with a more conventional tender. On local goods work by 1923, No. 85 worked as Duddingston pilot and on suburban freights. Withdrawn in January 1929 in NBR livery, it was the last unrenumbered NBR engine, but by then part of LNER class 'J33'. With crude tender cab and heading a single cattle wagon and NBR passenger brake van, it has the through goods headcode perhaps bound for Gorgie cattle market.   *Author's Collection*

NBR No. 648 was built at Cowlairs in February 1891 for long distance goods work, but over the years was increasingly used for general purposes. Classified 'C' in 1914 and rebuilt in December 1915, it was sent abroad from October 1917 to May 1919 and acquired the name *Mons* on its return. As LNER class 'J36', it was very familiar on the Edinburgh suburban line, being withdrawn as BR No. 65224 in June 1963. *Author's Collection*

The penultimate North British freight locomotive class was the class 'B' (LNER class 'J35'), represented here by No. 365 in early LNER lined-black livery as 9365. A St Margarets engine, it would have been no stranger to the Suburban in roles ranging from express freight and occasional passenger, to yard shunting. Built in 1909 and superheated in 1926, it lost its Westinghouse brake in 1947 and was withdrawn as BR No. 64495 in 1958. *Author's Collection*

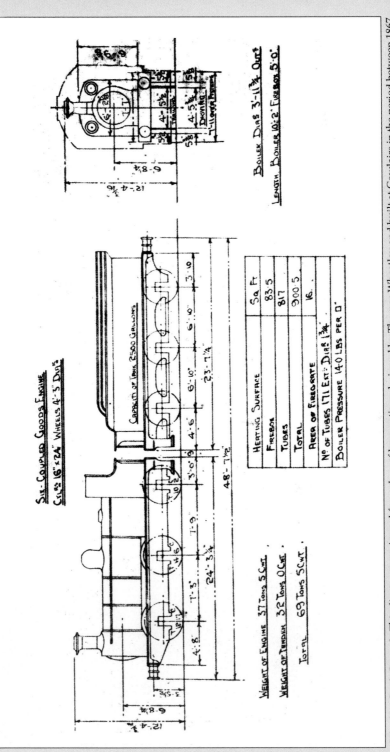

Suburban Goods Power I. This diagram was issued for a class of locomotives designed by Thomas Wheatley and built at Cowlairs in the period between 1867 and 1873 to cater for coal traffic from Fife and Lanarkshire. There were 38 locomotives in the class, but the use of old materials meant that there could be variations in appearance from engine to engine. However, their 10 spoke driving wheels were distinctive. Displaced over the years by more up to date machines, they gravitated to lesser duties and found employment on local inter-yard and trip train working. The final 20 to be built were rebuilt as saddle tanks and put to work on yard shunting duties before their ultimate demise.

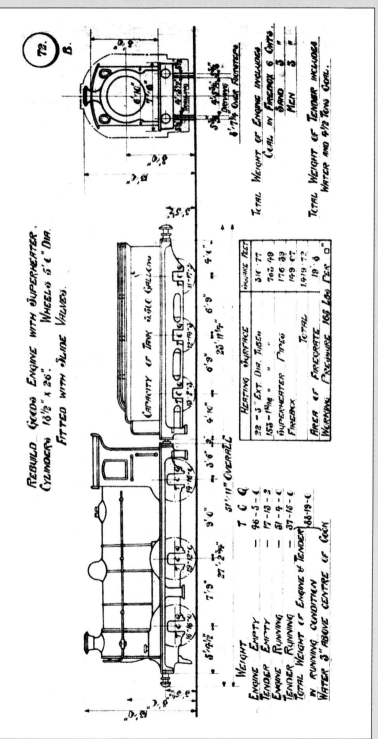

72.

B.

REBUILD GOODS ENGINE WITH SUPERHEATER.
CYLINDERS 18½" x 26". WHEELS 5'6" DIA.
FITTED WITH SLIDE VALVES.

CAPACITY OF TANK 3,500 GALLONS

HEATING SURFACE	SQUARE FEET
22 – 5" EXT. DIA. TUBES	316·77
153 – 1¾ig " "	702·49
SUPERHEATER FLUES	176·39
FIREBOX	149·07
TOTAL	1419·72
AREA OF FIREGRATE	19'·6
WORKING PRESSURE 165 LBS PER ☐

	T	C	Q
WEIGHT			
ENGINE EMPTY	96	5	0
TENDER EMPTY	17	13	2
ENGINE RUNNING	51	4	0
TENDER RUNNING	37	16	0
TOTAL WEIGHT OF ENGINE & TENDER	88·19	0

IN RUNNING CONDITION
WATER 3" ABOVE CENTRE OF COCK

TOTAL WEIGHT OF ENGINE INCLUDES
(COAL IN FIREBOX 6 CWTS
SAND 3 "
MEN 3 "

TOTAL WEIGHT OF TENDER INCLUDES
WATER AND 4½ TONS COAL.

Suburban Goods Power II. This diagram represents class 'B' locomotives which dated from 1906, and were the penultimate heavy goods engines of the North British being built up to 1914. 'Top Link' machines in their prime, they also 'cascaded' to lesser duties when their work was taken over by more modern engines in their final years. Common on many of the St Margarets workings which moved local minerals and other freight, sometimes suitable engines were employed on passenger trains. All bar three of the class survived the LNER who classified them as 'J35'. In the British Railways period, they were rated as '3F', the last of the class in service being withdrawn in October 1962.

Originally built by Beyer, Peacock in 1859 as Edinburgh & Glasgow Railway No. 89 this locomotive was renumbered 317 by the North British when taken over in 1865. Rebuilt with a short cab in 1871 and named *Jamestown* in 1880, it lost its name in the post-Drummond era and was renumbered 1058 in 1903, becoming a regular Edinburgh Suburban engine before the arrival of the Reid 4-4-2 tanks in 1911. Photographed at the west end of Waverley about 1900, it remained in service until 1915 and when withdrawn was the last of its class.

P.M. Westwater Collection

NBR No. 330 started life as Edinburgh & Glasgow Railway No. 84 at Cowlairs in 1864 and was rebuilt in 1892 although retaining open-fronted brass-beaded splashers. One of the '329' class, it was renumbered 1031 in 1906 and was a regular Suburban performer until 1911 being finally withdrawn in 1913. *Author's Collection*

With the introduction of the 1913 control system, locomotive liveries changed for the third time since 1900. At first the lettering had been 'N B R' with a metal numberplate on cabside or tank engine bunker. About 1908 this changed to 'N B' with the company crest between the letters, but retaining the numberplate. Identification for post-1913 control reporting by signal boxes resulted in a large number (18 in. overall height) replacing the crest, those still lettered 'NBR' having the 'B' replacing the 'R' with the number placed between. Tank engines identification was not such a problem, but tender engines numbers were on the tender, the numberplate remaining on the cab side and tenders could be changed. As an experiment, one engine (class 'C' No. 749) had a large number on the cabside, but this was not developed. Incidentally, company initial letters could be of 7½, 9 or 12 in. overall height. A separate problem was that when locomotives were 'duplicated', the original numberplate sometimes remained in position with the new painted number carried between 'N' and 'B'.

After 1915, freight locomotive livery changed from bronze green (in its multitude of shades) to black with double yellow or chrome lining which may have had relevance to the availability of materials and manpower at the time. It was, however, a gradual process and only undertaken if repainting was deemed necessary. This livery was attributed to Walter Chalmers who superseded Reid in 1919 and remained until the North British lost its separate identity in 1923.

In March 1924, a new 0-6-2 tank locomotive arrived at Haymarket from Cowlairs, and became inextricably linked with the Suburban until condemned 34 years on. LNER class 'N15' No. 125B and then 9125, it became 9220 in 1946 and 69220 under British Railways. It was the regular engine for the morning 'Sub Goods' trip train between Haymarket and Niddrie.

St Margarets continued to provide most suburban passenger motive power, including NBR 'Intermediate' type 4-4-0s, but better locomotive diagrams led to other types, not just from St Margarets, making an appearance on passenger trains.

The reign of the 'Yorkies' on suburban trains declined when Great Northern Railway 0-6-2 tanks, LNER class 'N2', arrived in the spring of 1925. Employed on transfer freights and similar work to the indigenous 'N15' 0-6-2 tanks for a year or so, two (Nos. 2586 and 2587), started working suburban passenger trains, being joined later in 1925 by another (894) which became the regular Musselburgh branch engine. They were powerful enough, but not overtly popular with enginemen or permanent way staff and their reign was relatively short, being displaced in 1930 by the first Gresley class 'V1' 2-6-2 tank locomotives, the engines which became most closely associated with Suburban passenger work until the end of steam. Nos. 2586 and 2587 went south in the early 1930s, and 894 moved to Glasgow.

In the early Grouping period, still active elderly Wheatley and Drummond goods engines were replaced by surplus slightly younger six-coupled engines from other LNER areas and those allocated to St Margarets and Haymarket undertook light freight trip and shunting work. Haymarket engines could be seen at Gorgie, and St Margarets engines at Duddingston and Niddrie where one duty from both ends included banking trains up the hill to Morningside Road.

The first Gresley LNER Group Standard 0-6-0 to traverse the Suburban was class 'J38', which arrived in 1926, gradually taking over long haul and heavy mineral workings from the 'J37s'. British Railways classified the 'J38s' as '6F' and this exclusively Scottish class was supplemented in 1929 with the first tranche of class 'J39' (BR '5F') for similar work. 'J38' and 'J39' class engines were regular Suburban performers into the 1960s, vacuum-fitted 'J39s' working some passenger trains. A few

Originally Edinburgh & Glasgow Railway 0-4-2 mixed traffic locomotive No. 91, NBR No. 319 was built by Beyer, Peacock in December 1859. Rebuilt by Holmes in 1887 into the condition shown and renumbered 1060 in 1903, it was withdrawn in 1913. Sister engine No. 1058 was a regular Suburban passenger locomotive. *Author's Collection*

Wheatley introduced a large passenger tank engine class in 1870 and provided the crew with front and rear weatherboard, but no roof! Some were later fitted with Westinghouse brakes that were removed when they were relegated to trip work and shunting, the last survivor becoming LNER class 'J81'. No. 62 was built in 1873 at Cowlairs, rebuilt in 1901 (*as seen here*), renumbered 1231 in 1914, and withdrawn in 1921. Two sister engines, Nos. 1204 and 1215 (formerly Nos. 39 and 405) latterly shunted Haymarket Goods, with trips around the Suburban to Niddrie. *Author's Collection*

No. 221 was a Cowlairs product of 1871 for local passenger work. Rebuilt in 1895 and 'duplicated' in 1913 as 1210, by 1914 she was engaged on freight and shunting work in power class 'E'. One of a 15 strong class, all bar one were withdrawn between 1920 and 1922, the survivor briefly becoming LNER class 'J81'. Despite the headcode, she appears to be the Waverley West End pilot sometime between 1895 and 1913. *Author's Collection*

No. 844, built in 1905 at Cowlairs, was one of 35 short wheelbase tanks used for shunting yards with sharp curves. 1914 power classification 'E' and later LNER 'J88', she was condemned in March 1958, latterly as BR No. 68328. At Gorgie in June 1921, this Haymarket engine shunted the Cattle Market sidings. *Author's Collection*

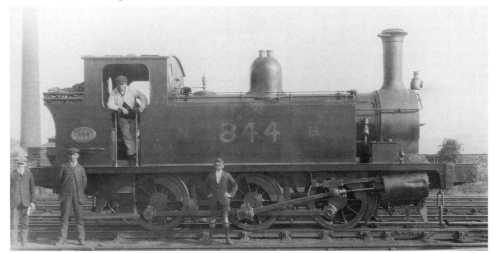

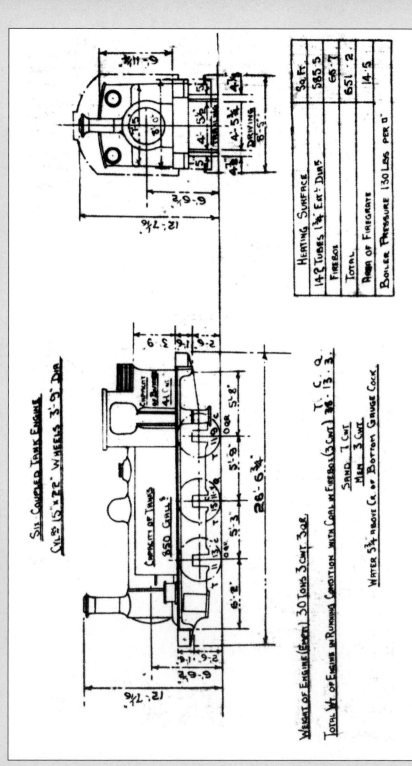

NBR Suburban Goods, Trip and Shunting Tank Locomotives I. Most commonly used for yard shunting, local inter-yard trip working or, on occasions, banking operations in the late NBR, LNER or British Railways era. The class 'F' (LNER class J88) 0-6-0 tank engine provided from Haymarket shed, was found in the distillery and cattle market sidings at Gorgie where sharp track curvature favoured engines with a short wheelbase. Introduced in 1904, the last survivor of the class was not taken from service until October 1962.

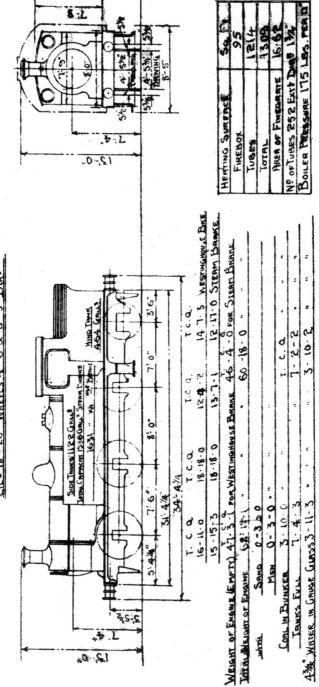

SIX COUPLED SIDE TANK ENGINE WITH RADIAL WHEEL

CYLS 18" × 26" WHEELS 4'-6" & 3'-9" DIAR

HEATING SURFACE	Sq ft
FIREBOX	95
TUBES	1214
TOTAL	1309
AREA OF FIREGRATE	16.62
Nº OF TUBES 252 EXT DIAR 1¾"	
BOILER PRESSURE 175 LBS. PER □"	

NBR Suburban Goods, Trip and Shunting Tank Locomotives II. The class 'A' (LNER class 'N15') 0-6-2 radial tank were provided by either the St Margarets or Haymarket depots and were widely used for local inter-yard trip working, shunting Suburban goods or marshalling yards or the provision of banking assistance from Gorgie up to Morningside Road on the Inner Circle line. Developed from a design of 1909 intended for assisting trains up the gradient from Glasgow Queen Street to Cowlairs, the last survivor was not withdrawn until October 1962.

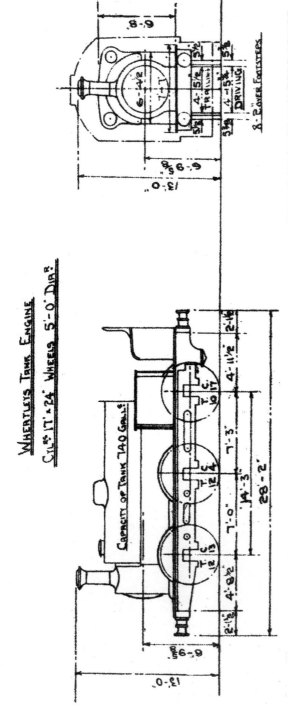

WHEATLEYS TANK ENGINE

CYLS 17" × 24" WHEELS 5'-0" DIAR.

CAPACITY OF TANK 740 GALLS

TOTAL WEIGHT OF ENGINE 35 TONS 14 CWT

HEATING SURFACE	SQ. FT.
FIREBOX	83.7
TUBES	775.66
TOTAL	859.36
AREA OF FIREGRATE	16
Nº OF TUBES 171 EXTᴰ DIA 1¾"	
BOILER PRESSURE 140 LBS+ER □"	

NBR Suburban Passenger Tank Engines I. A Thomas Wheatley design introduced in 1870.

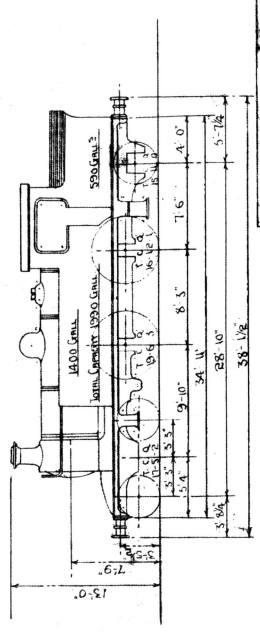

FOUR COUPLED BOGIE SIDE TANK WITH RADIAL WHEEL

CYLRS 18" × 26" WHEELS (COUPLED) 5'-9" (BOGIE) 3'-6" & (RADIAL) 3'-9" DIAR

590 GALLS

1400 GALL

TOTAL CAPACITY 1990 GALL

HEATING SURFACE		SQ. FT.
FIREBOX		95
TUBES		1214
	TOTAL	1309
AREA OF FIREGRATE		16' 6"
NO. OF TUBES 252	EXTL DIAR	1¾"
BOILER PRESSURE 175 LBS PER □"		

TOTAL WT OF ENGINE 68-15-2 WITH COAL IN FIREBOX 6 CWT.

SAND 2.6 CWT MEN 3 CWT. BRICK ARCH 5 CWT 2.9 RS

COAL IN BUNKER 4 TONS

WATER IN BOILER 6" ABOVE CENTRE OF BOTTOM COCK

WEIGHT OF ENGINE (EMPTY) 52-4-0

NBR Suburban Passenger Tank Engines II. The W.P. Reid 4-4-2 tank design known as 'Yorkies' which dated from 1911.

Approaching the Mound tunnels on an Outer Circle working, 'C15' class 4-4-2 tank engine No. 133 bears its North British number but LNER lettering. The leading vehicle in the train is a four-wheel, three-compartment passenger brake van still in NBR livery and bearing the large destination board 'Suburban and Leith Central' which did not fit the brackets on LNER bogie carriages. Renumbered 9133 in May 1925 and 7481 in July 1946, the engine survived until February 1956. The carriage had a much earlier demise. *R.W. Lynn Collection*

'C15' locomotives shared Suburban workings with other types as availability and diagrams dictated, but in 1925, the arrival of the 'N2' 0-6-2 tanks to Great Northern design marked the eclipse of the 'Yorkies'. No. 2586 (later BR No. 69553) stands at Gorgie on an Inner Circle service about 1927. Despite the extra lamp brackets for Edinburgh local code, the engine carries the standard 'Stopping Passenger' indication. The leading vehicle (No. 3158) is a five-compartment bogie brake third of 1914 which lasted until 25th December, 1954. *R.W. Lynn Collection*

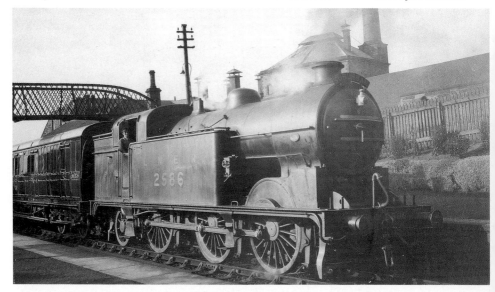

2-8-0 Great Central Railway locomotives (LNER class 'O4') came to Scotland for mineral work, but were at first prohibited over the suburban line, working from Fife through Waverley to Portobello. Fourteen GNR class 'K2' 2-6-0 locomotives (Nos. 4691-4704) modified to the NB loading gauge came north in 1925. Equivalent in power to the 'J37', five went to St Margarets in 1926/27 and were used on express freights, such as the Duddingston - Newcastle (Forth) beer train. More 'K2s' later came north and when Cowlairs assumed responsibility for maintenance of the whole class from 1943, every 'K2' appeared on the Suburban at one time or another. Other GNR pattern moguls heading freights over the suburban line were the more powerful class 'K3', the first arriving in 1926, three more in 1930, and another eight between 1935 and 1938. Some others were later transferred in from the North Eastern Area.

The LNER 1928 Loads Book included class 'J69' 0-6-0 tanks imported from the Great Eastern section in 1927 and 1928. Twenty engines were shown, 10 with Westinghouse and vacuum brakes and 10 with steam brake only. Five initially went to St Margarets but although acknowledged as powerful they were not too popular with footplatemen and mostly worked as yard shunters. Used mainly at Leith Docks, and sometimes as Waverley Pilots, they were also loaned to Haymarket, for yard shunting at Gorgie or Haymarket. Although the class 'J50' was also listed, and one was tried out at Niddrie West in 1925, it was not until 1946 that two others moved briefly from Glasgow to St Margarets for trip and pilot duties.

By April 1932 St Margarets had eight class 'V1' locomotives (Nos. 2905-9/17/18/24) and Haymarket four (2910/15/16/20). Between them, they worked the majority of suburban services in and around Edinburgh. However they did not have an exclusive monopoly and various other locomotives, passenger, mixed traffic and freight, tender and tank, were also used as economic diagramming (or motive power availability) dictated. Indeed, some 'temporary' 'V1' replacements lasted a long time. The original batch were supplemented in 1935 by three more (Nos. 2929/30 and 2897) and in 1936 by No. 2899, resulting in 12 of the class being allocated to St Margarets. A further two (425 and 467) were added in 1938 making a depot allocation of 14 at the outbreak of World War II. The Haymarket 'V1' allocation remained at four.

In October 1939, the former Musselburgh 'N2' locomotive No. 894 returned to St Margarets and worked the Suburban trains for a spell. Returned to Parkhead during the war, it became 9564 in May 1946, and was withdrawn at Carlisle in June 1961.

Wartime brought unusual locomotives to the Suburban passenger trains such as a green class 'B12' 4-6-0 (No. 8526) on 31st January, 1940. This Aberdeen-based locomotive had gone south with the 1939 Christmas traffic and was returning to its home depot, having strayed as far south as Tyneside. 'V1' class 2-6-2 tank locomotive No. 465 (later 7659), displaced in 1939 from the North Eastern Area by new 'V3' tanks, also regularly worked Suburban trains. Edinburgh 'V1' tanks capably handled freight as well as passengers and wartime traffic creating an unprecedented demand for their services. A familiar type on Suburban trains in February 1940 was 'C15' 4-4-2 tank 9131 returned to the city from the Borders. Shortages of 'V1s' in early 1941 brought a return of other 4-4-2 tanks and Haymarket 'V1' diagrams were even being covered by Great Northern 4-4-0s. Vacuum-braked 'J36s' worked some suburban line passenger trains and 'C16' No. 9451 replaced No. 465 in St Margarets Suburban link for a time.

Cover for Haymarket-based 'N15' 0-6-2 tanks undergoing Cowlairs shopping was provided, in the absence of an Eastfield engine, by St Margarets, and these undertook Gorgie Pilot duties. Sometimes these engines had vacuum brakes and screw couplings and to help the shunters, a three-link coupling was placed on the coupling hook.

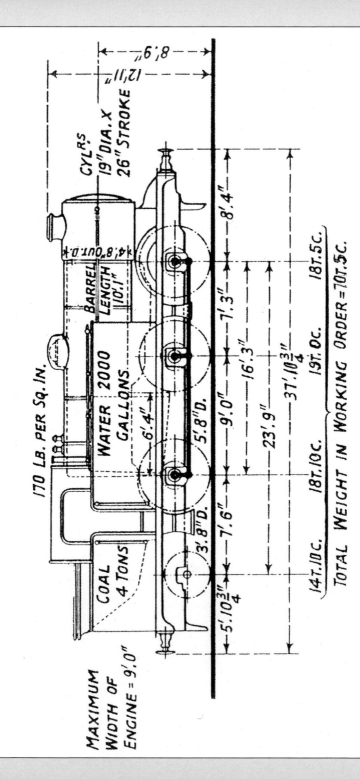

LNER Suburban Passenger Steam Motive Power I. The first locomotives introduced to the Edinburgh suburban line by the LNER in 1925 were some of the former Great Northern 'N2' type adapted for the Southern Scottish Area loading gauge. Although powerful, they were not to the liking of the Civil Engineer and lasted in Edinburgh only until the advent of the 'V1' type in 1930.

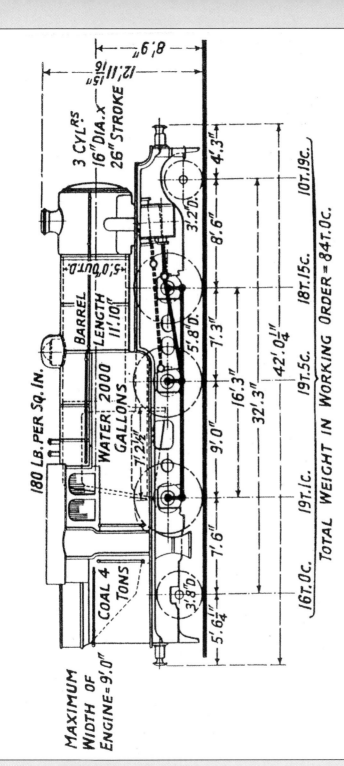

LNER Suburban Passenger Steam Motive Power II. Perhaps the locomotive type most associated with Edinburgh suburban line were the 2-6-2 tanks which were introduced in 1930 as class 'V1'. A development was introduced in 1938 with a higher boiler pressure and classified as 'V3' - to which some of the 'V1s' were later converted. There was a technical difference in route availability coding when this scheme came into operation after the war, but this was generally ignored and both types were interchanged freely. The 'V1s' and 'V3s' remained dominant on the suburban line services until they succumbed to the diesel multiple unit in 1957.

In 1942, St Margarets Depot got a 70 feet turntable at the rear of the main shed that was brought into use in October. Shortage of space during the installation meant six Suburban engines, four 'V1s' (Nos. 467, 2906-8), and two 'C16s' (Nos. 9448 and 9452) were temporarily moved to Haymarket. 'C15' class No. 9131, by then at Haymarket, became a Suburban regular.

Duddingston Pilots were briefly graced in mid-1942 by the handsome North Eastern Railway 'D17' class 4-4-0 No. 1921 (from Carlisle) and the newcomer shared the work with two other NER locomotives, 'J24' 0-6-0s Nos. 1852 and 1858. Unfortunately, the active life of the old stalwart, which had at one time graced East Coast expresses, was extremely short, as it was laid up at St Margarets after a week!

Locomotives from other railways also worked freights over the suburban line from late 1942, the most striking being 10 Southern Railway (former London & South Western Railway) 'N15' 'King Arthur' class 4-6-0s (Nos. 739/40/42/44/ 47-9/50/51/54) loaned to the LNER at Newcastle. Generally liked by the North British men, with haulage power akin to the LNER 'K2', they went back to the Southern in September 1943 when the LNER motive power situation eased with the influx of Ministry of Supply locomotives. Other suburban line strangers included LNER engines which had rarely ventured north of the border such as a Great Central 0-8-0 of class 'Q4', Great Northern 2-8-0s of class 'O2' and Great Northern Atlantic No. 4453.

In February 1943, Haymarket exchanged three 'B12' 4-6-0s (Nos. 8500/03/21) for three 'D49s' (Nos. 265, 277 and 311) from St Margarets. The 'B12s' failed to impress and were relegated to freight, being joined by No. 8511 in March. Since 1940, St Margarets already had No. 8526, but, unimpressive on suburban line passenger work, it was also mainly used on freights. Two other Great North of Scotland (GNS) engines moved from Kittybrewster to St Margarets in March 1943 ('D41' 4-4-0s Nos. 6880/98) but with a low power rating (BR later classed them '2P') they were confined to local yard trips and freight between Niddrie West and Bathgate Junction over the Suburban. All 'B12s' and 'D41s' returned to the GNS area at the end of the year.

The LMS '8F' 2-8-0 design was chosen as the War Department 'standard' early in the war, but in 1943 'Austerity' 2-8-0 tender locomotives of both British and American builds and larger War Department's 2-10-0 machines appeared. Although the stay of the American engines was brief, the British types became heavily engaged on freight work, making regular suburban line appearances.

In May 1945, the Royal Train arrived from Waverley at Gorgie's Inner Circle platform double-headed by Haymarket 'B1' class 4-6-0s Nos. 8308 *Klipspringer* and 8303 *Impala*. After detaching, both B1s moved forward to the platform end. Meantime, Haymarket class 'V1' 2-6-2 tank No. 2915 coupled on the rear and drew the train across to the Outer Circle and along to Haymarket West Junction where No. 2915 was uncoupled and LMS 'Coronation' class Pacific No. 6241 *City of Edinburgh* (borrowed for the occasion) coupled on at the opposite end and took the train up the Wester Dalry branch to Edinburgh (Princes Street), probably trying to give the impression it had been there since leaving London!

The 'J24' 0-6-0s at Duddingston were replaced by North British class 'J35' or 'J36' locomotives from St Margarets after the war and four treble-shifted pilots formed a single link of 12 crews based on Duddingston with the same as yard pilots. Besides shunting local breweries, trips were also made to Niddrie, Morningside Road and Gorgie, and freights assisted to Morningside Road. One diagram also included an 8.35 am cattle train on Tuesdays from Gifford to Gorgie. However, maintenance backlog and poor coal quality hampered performance, so banking requirements stayed high.

Painted numbers of the 17 Edinburgh-based 'V1' suburban engines changed under the 1946 LNER renumbering:

St Margarets Nos. 2905-09/18/24, 2929/30, 2897, 425, 465, 467 became Nos. 7605-9/18/24, 7629/30, 7649, 7666/59/70 and
Haymarket's Nos. 2910/15/17/20 became Nos. 7610/15/17/20 (No. 2916 had gone to Dunfermline in January 1945).

At Nationalisation, St Margarets had 13 'V1' tanks, comprised of 7605-9/17/24/29/30/49/59/66/70 and Haymarket three (7610/15/20). No. 2917 (7617) had moved from Haymarket to St Margarets releasing No. 7618 to Stirling in late 1946. Westinghouse-fitted 'V1' No. 7668 arrived from the Great Eastern Area, in March 1949, its air brake equipment remaining until converted from 'V1' to 'V3' in May 1954.

LMS '2P' 4-4-0, then No. M666, was transferred from Carstairs to St Margarets on 7th December, 1948. Initially working the Berwick local goods and banking from Dunbar to Grantshouse, it had a slip coupling fitted, which it retained (unused) after moving to Duddingston for banking. It was not popular, and its sojourn at St Margarets was brief.

During early 1949 some LMS 4-6-0s were transferred to St Margarets - nine workworn and tired old Caledonian Railway '60' class, others having already been withdrawn on their parent line. They were unpopular at first and were used, *inter alia*, on long haul freights such as over the Waverley route to Carlisle and the odd one appeared on the suburban line. One was condemned while at St Margarets, but the others returned whence they came before the end of the year.

Arguably one of the less successful types used on suburban line passenger trains were the small LMS-designed 2-6-0 tender engines, of which three were delivered to St Margarets, brand new in 1950 (Nos. 46460-46462). Classified '2P', they had difficulty on the gradients, with five coaches, especially starting away from Craiglockhart. Within a few years, two had gravitated to the Great North of Scotland area, the other (No. 46462) making occasional Suburban forays on lighter three-coach sets or officers' saloons.

The early nationalisation period generally maintained the LNER atmosphere, with the reappearance of some types that had been used on the line in the past. 'N2' 0-6-2 tanks made occasional outings on suburban line trains, reliving the late 1920s period. Shortage of 'V1' tanks produced a variety of alternatives from North British 4-4-2 tanks to tender engines from 'Glens', and 'Directors' to 'B1s'. Vacuum-braked North British 0-6-0s were also pressed into service, some from sheds remote from Edinburgh. As the 1950s progressed, other LNER engines appeared, as did LMS-designed 2-6-0s of the '431XX' series allocated to LNER sheds.

Power classifications for several LNER types changed during 1952 as conversions to the LMS classification settled down. 'V1' tanks reduced from '4MT' to '3MT'. Between 1952 and 1961, some V1s were uprated to 'V3' ('4MT') with increased boiler pressures and tractive effort, but increased axle weight raised the Route Availability from RA6 to RA7, although this did not get much practical attention. Only Nos. 67610/29/30/49/59 were still class 'V1' when condemned.

The April 1955 *Railway Observer* noted that of the North British tank engines allocated to Haymarket, 'N15' class No. 69169 and 'J88' No. 68339 were Gorgie No. 1 and 2 pilots respectively, with old faithful No. 69220 still working the Suburban Goods Trip. The 'J88', also a regular on the Haymarket shed pilot, sported a 1909 boiler with lock-up safety valves on the dome.

Arguably the classes most closely associated with the Edinburgh suburban line in the LNER period were the Gresley 'V1' and 'V3' introduced in 1930. St Margarets-allocated No. 2908 was withdrawn in the December 1962 as British Railways No. 67608, having been displaced from the east of Scotland by dieselisation.   *Author's Collection*

LMS 2-6-2 tank No. 40159 of Dawsholm, which was unsuccessfully tried out from St Margarets for a few months from the summer of 1957. It is seen on Outer Circle work at Morningside Road on a rake of corridor vehicles.   *Author*

Hill-climbing problems to Morningside Road continued into the autumn. Freight failures were not infrequent, some having a 'domino' effect on the local passenger services and resulting in some strange workings. The *Railway Observer* reported that at the end of October 1955 No. 62488 *Glen Aladale* stalled on a freight and was helped up the hill by 'J83' 0-6-0 tank No. 68473 at 4.20 am. An hour later, 'J38' 0-6-0 No. 65928 also stuck, delaying the 5.52 am Inner Circle passenger. No. 68473 was again pressed into service with two corridor carriages to form the balancing 6.44 am Outer Circle train while the 8.28 am Inner Circle service got LMS class '5MT' locomotive No. 44700 on another spare rake. Two days later, 'D11' No. 62692 *Allan-Bane* deputising for No. 69220 failed on the 'Sub Goods', and was replaced by 'B1' 4-6-0 No. 61102. On 3rd November, the absence of a pilot resulted in 'J35' 0-6-0 No. 64553 dividing its train on the hill.

Although most problems were on the Inner Circle, the Outer Circle was not immune. Perhaps being autumn, trains were affected by the 'wrong kind of leaves'. Class 'C16' No. 67492 was used to head some suburban line passenger trains, but on 25th October, 1955 it was pressed into service banking freights from Duddingston, bunker first!

The first recorded BR Standard class '2MT' 2-6-0 locomotive on the line was No. 78048 of St Margarets at the head of the 12.10 pm Outer Circle on 18th November, 1955, having arrived at the depot only a few days before. This type only rarely put in appearances and usually on three-coach formations on 'off peak' workings.

In May 1957, two of Dawsholm's small former LMS taper-boilered 2-6-2 tank locomotives (Nos. 40159/86) came to St Margarets. Tried on the Edinburgh Suburban, their power was inadequate and although No. 40186 stayed in Edinburgh, No. 40159 moved up to Elgin for assessment. It returned to St Margarets but both went back to Dawsholm in March 1958.

Saturday 7th June, 1958 saw the passing of the last booked steam-hauled Edinburgh Suburban train, the 2.05 pm Outer Circle service from Duddingston to Waverley headed by St Margarets class 'V1' 2-6-2 tank locomotive No. 67649. After arrival at Waverley, the train continued as empty coaching stock to Leith Central. After diesel railcars were introduced on Monday 9th June, 1958, some 'V1' and 'V3' tanks left for pastures new in the west of Scotland, starting in July with Nos. 67605, 67608 and 67609. In January 1959, Nos. 67629 and 67630 went to Parkhead, partially offset by No. 67606 returning from Hawick, where it had worked the Kelso branch since 1956.

Banking engines from Duddingston continued to feature 'strangers', such as Polmont 'J36' No. 65306, but some of the other engines used on this duty were quite unsuitable, such as the 'Shire' class 4-4-0s including No. 62711 *Dumbartonshire*. On the Inner Circle, No. 62718 *Kinross-shire* helped 'Hunt' class No. 62743 *The Cleveland* on the 'sub goods' from Gorgie one November morning in 1958, the 'Hunt' having replaced 'N15' No. 69220 which had been condemned two weeks before.

After the opening of the Craiglockhart-Slateford spur on 16th March, 1959, former Caledonian and LMS engines appeared regularly but the first 'passenger' train over the spur was a Craven dmu twin-set carrying the Scottish Area Board of the British Transport Commission on a tour of Edinburgh lines on 19th March, 1959.

The first Scottish-allocated Birmingham RCW type '2' (later class '26') main line diesel locomotives (Nos. D5320-22) arrived in April 1959. Intended for an accelerated Edinburgh and Aberdeen passenger service in the 1959 winter timetable, they were kept away from public gaze by using them on freights between Niddrie, Dundee and Perth via the Suburban and were maintained at Leith Central as Haymarket's diesel facilities were not then ready.

A touch of colour appeared when the blue prototype English Electric 'Deltic' locomotive undertook trials in Edinburgh between 8th and 12th June, having arrived via Carlisle and Hawick. The engine made a round trip each day from Craigentinny via the Outer Circle and Waverley to Berwick-upon-Tweed, returning via Waverley and the Inner Circle line. Using the Hallade Track Recording Car in the formation, loads of up to 18 bogies were successfully dealt with.

The last purely steam Suburban working, the Duddingston No. 2 Pilot that shunted Newington and Morningside Road, became diesel hauled with 350 hp 0-6-0 locomotives from 17th August, 1959, the last steam working being with class 'J35' 0-6-0 No. 64515. Unfortunately, although economical and more comfortable for the crew, the new machines lacked speed, particularly returning to base at the end of a shift! However, Duddingston No. 1 Pilot, which worked the St Leonards branch goods traffic, continued with steam, a fairly regular engine being another St Margarets 'J35' No. 64535.

In September 1960, No. 67624 became the first Edinburgh 2-6-2 tank to be condemned. A St Margarets Suburban stalwart, it had arrived new as class 'V1' No. 2924 and been converted to 'V3' in November 1952. No. 67670, the once immaculate North Berwick branch engine, was next in August 1961 although it had only been reboilered as a 'V3' in July 1959. Heavy expenditure seemed to mean little in the drive for the elimination of steam (and ascendancy of the accountant). Other displaced 'V1' and 'V3' tanks were used on parcels and freight working. No. 67666 had a slip coupling for assisting trains from Duddingston to Morningside Road, the pulley set-up differing from that on the 'V1' and 'V3' Cowlairs Incline pilots.

Steam to diesel transition on freight trains did not mean an end to the unplanned use of the Gorgie Pilot, and an upturn in trade during 1960 increased calls on its time. For example on 26th December, 1960, a Craiginches (Aberdeen) to Niddrie freight, double-headed by two 1,180 hp diesels, stalled at Craiglockhart and No. 69211, transferred to Haymarket in February 1959 to replace the condemned No. 69169, rendered assistance. No. 69211 only survived until 27th October, 1962.

The zenith of Suburban local passenger motive power occurred on the afternoon of 26th February, 1961. To cater for the Scotland - Ireland rugby match at Murrayfield, the twin railcar on the 1.11 pm Outer Circle was replaced by class 'A4' Pacific No. 60024 *Kingfisher* on a rake of locomotive-hauled stock, but a less suitable engine for local suburban traffic would be hard to imagine. The Craiglockhart gradient was steeper than anything on the East Coast Main Line and Cowlairs at least had the advantage of a running start and banking engine!

The first revenue earning passenger train passed over the Slateford - Craiglockhart connection on 27th May, 1961. It was a special excursion from Law Junction to Edinburgh Waverley, headed by class '5MT' 4-6-0 No. 45008 of Hamilton and was one of several such specials, some of which called at Portobello *en route* to Waverley.

The Edinburgh Suburban line closure was agreed by the Transport Users' Consultative Committee, but there was a delay in getting Ministry of Transport clearance and the 'last day' was set for Saturday 8th September, 1962. The last passenger train was the 2.00 pm 'Outer Circle' from Duddingston to Musselburgh, comprised of Gloucester twin dmu Nos. SC50343/56098 and although there was much photographic activity at stations, there was no cacophony of fog signal detonations.

Reduction in the requirement for the 'V1' and 'V3' tanks resulted in several being stored. Seafield hosted Nos. 67605/6/49 in mid-1962 until the shed closed on 13th October and No. 67607 was stored at Hurlford in Ayrshire.

West Highland line LNER 'K4' class 2-6-0 locomotives, displaced from their native heath by diesels, gravitated to Thornton and became regular suburban line visitors. No. 61994 *The Great Marquis* was privately purchased by Viscount Garnock and restored to its original LNER livery as No. 3442 at Cowlairs before heading for the Middleton Railway. It traversed the Suburban *en route* on 27th April, 1963 with an open wagon and goods brake van, then 'worked its passage' with 30 vacuum-braked mineral wagons from Millerhill to Heaton. Former express steam appeared on some through freights, such as 'A1' Pacific No. 60157 *Great Eastern* in June 1963 on a northbound trainload of esparto grass from Granton.

In mid-September 1963, the first class 17 'Clayton' Bo-Bo diesel No. D8545 arrived at Haymarket. Their diagrams included freight work over the Suburban and their arrival fuelled press speculation that the demise of St Margarets was imminent (no doubt delighting local residents) and led to suggestions that the Suburban might reopen for passengers. Edinburgh Town Council was said to be pressing the Secretary of State, but the same council had agreed its closure two years before!

Bulk grain vans still provided traffic for distilleries and on 18th June, 1964 a York 'V2' class 2-6-2 (No. 60963) traversed the Outer Circle with a train of these heading for the North British Distillery at Gorgie.

During the reconstruction of Haymarket Depot from 1964, the depot's steam allocation, including several 'Pacifics', were transferred to St Margarets for freight and parcels duties - and were kept well employed, frequently traversing the suburban line. However, steam became rarer and the arrival of further batches of types '1' and '2' diesels heralded the end.

By 22nd April, 1967 only 30 steam locomotives survived in the Scottish locomotive fleet, and their final day was set to be May Day (1st May) 1967. Two elderly Scottish engines survived this cull in class 'J36' 0-6-0s Nos. 65288 and 65345 of Dunfermline and Thornton respectively. Their survival was not due to sentiment, but to having being set aside 'stored serviceable' pending commercial filming work which never materialised. Withdrawn on 5th June, 1967, they were the last North British Railway locomotives; the last representatives from pre-Grouping Scottish railways; the last Scottish-allocated pre-nationalisation steam locomotives; the last Scottish Region-allocated steam locomotives and in No. 65288, the last 19th century British Railways locomotive. Before No. 65288 had been transferred to Thornton in December 1963, it had often worked 'The Shunt', between Duddingston and Morningside Road. A few engines remained in steam after the two 'J36s' had been withdrawn, but this was as stationary boilers or for carriage heating.

English-based steam engines appeared on occasional workings into Millerhill and were serviced in the small facility that had been included in the original plan, and turned on the triangles at Niddrie, Lochend-London Road-Craigentinny or Haymarket Central-Gorgie-Haymarket West. Meantime, diesel locomotive diagrams were securing better use of resources, and greater attention to loadings reduced hill climbing failures on both sides of Morningside Road.

It was the practice at certain rugby internationals at Murrayfield for a dining car special to run from Glasgow to Murrayfield, but as this station closed in 1962 alternative arrangements were made. In late 1967, the special (hauled by Brush type '4' diesel No. D1767) was routed around the Suburban and then through Waverley to Balgreen Halt on the Corstorphine branch, the then nearest station to the ground, to allow time for meal service.

After the withdrawal of British Railways standard gauge steam locomotives in 1968, diesel locomotives gradually lost their 'D' prefix to the number, but this took time to fully implement and some went straight to the 1971 Total Operations Processing System (TOPS) numbering.

Suburban line motive power observations between August and November 1968 were reported in the *Railway Observer*. The percentages of the total represented by the various types in the sample period were:

Class	%	Class	%	Class	%	Class	%
17	18	24	6	37	8	47	13
20	3	25	16	40	15		
21	½	26	16	45/46	2		

All other classes contributed less than one per cent each and were mostly from classes '27', '50' and '55'. Of the local engines Nos. D7602-7608 from class '25' were the most frequent, with Nos. D5300-5306 of class '26' a close second. Only 13 different class '25s' were seen, but there were 93 class '47' engines in the 13 per cent total. The days of varied locomotive types were past.

Diesel locomotives were renumbered from 1971, a two digit class code prefixing a three digit number in blocks from '001'. This was to aid the introduction of the computerised TOPS control of freight rolling stock, pioneered in Scotland at Millerhill two years later.

Two familiar main line diesel locomotive classes were withdrawn by the end of 1971. One was the 900 hp Clayton class '17', introduced in 1962 before the implementation of the 'Reshaping of British Railways' Plan and intended for light goods and branch line work. Never really successful, with branch line closures and wagonload traffic decline, their end was not unexpected but one (No. D8568) has been preserved. The other class was the North British Locomotive Company class '29' diesel-hydraulics dating from 1959 which also failed to live up to expectations despite refurbishing (and reclassification from class '21').

As the 1970s progressed, private and public sidings and their connections were lifted and the old marshalling yards and crossovers removed. After 1976, the signalling centre in the former Waverley Goods Yard controlled signals that were not automatic. Some double line sections, such as in the Niddrie Area and between Gorgie and Haymarket Central were singled. The Suburban became plain line between the Niddrie West and Gorgie, apart from Craiglockhart.

Steam continued to make rare appearances on charters, excursions, tours or special workings. From the mid-1980s until 1991, well patronised public 'Santa Specials' circled the city using mostly Mark I carriages, often privately-owned but with steam heating in working order! With the relentless expansion of multiple units, even Santa was not immune and later steam yielded this last suburban line monopoly, said to be due to falling bookings.

Passenger steam appeared on the line in September 1980 on a Falkirk - Dundee charter. The Winchburgh-Dalmeny spur was unavailable, and the train, headed by LNER 'D49' class 4-4-0 No. 246 *Morayshire* ran via Waverley, Portobello, the Outer Circle to Haymarket West and thence to the north. Next Spring, the preserved 'J36' *Maude* double-headed *Morayshire* on a Pullman special from Larbert to Edinburgh via Haymarket West and the Inner Circle line and Portobello. On 19th May, 1990, *Osprey* (then renamed *Union of South Africa*) headed two steam trips via Portobello, suburban line, Haymarket West, then over the Forth Bridge for a tour via Cowdenbeath and Kirkcaldy returning direct to Waverley.

On 7th July, 1989, the 0800 from Kings Cross arrived in Waverley with No. 43070 leading, the rear power car having no protective cover over its right-hand side head and tail lights. The train departed towards Haymarket as the 1330 to Kings Cross and, just after 1400, passed through Waverley again without stopping with No. 43070 still leading, passengers having had an involuntary tour of the Gorgie triangle. The train could have run via the suburban line and Millerhill to the East Coast Main Line, but perhaps the train crew were not 'passed' for the suburban line, or Millerhill was not cleared for passenger trains.

An October 1990 report noted that class '56s' initially allocated to Toton, passed the site of Newington station twice a day with opencast coal, but these trains ceased in March 1991. However, by August/September 1991 they were back, being hauled by a '56' and a class '37' and in the spring of 1992 coal trains over the Suburban were usually double-headed by a variety of locomotives either in tandem or in multiple according to coupling capability.

Class '66' diesels made their appearance in early 1999 on crew training before settling down to regular work on the coal trains in company with class '56' and '60s'. The old stalwarts of classes '37' and '47', now usurped in power capacity (and increasing age) with the later breeds, still remained in evidence.

St Margarets had closed with the end of steam and Millerhill was always predominantly a locomotive servicing depot. The last Haymarket-allocated locomotives, albeit class '08' shunters, were transferred away in 1991, the depot then being only used for the multiple unit maintenance, most locomotive maintenance in Scotland now being dealt with at the Motherwell Depot. Reduction in the number of locomotives and maintenance depots, expansion of multiple units and national diagramming developments in the last part of the 20th century produced much standardisation, and dare one say monotony, other than in liveries. There were only 11 main line general purpose diesel locomotive classes on the former British Rail network at the end of 2002, comprising of classes '20', '31', '33', '37', '47', '56', '57', '58', '60', '66' and '67', most of which were regular suburban line visitors.

Passenger Carriages

I. The North British Railway Period

When the Edinburgh suburban opened, passenger comforts were similar to those on many other contemporary railway operators. Footwarmers, those token gestures to winter climatic conditions and which were present in 16th century Sedan Chairs in the city(!), were only placed under seats in first class compartments. These large flat metal cans filled with hot water from boilers at terminal stations were replaced as necessary. With the draughts in compartments, their effectiveness must be suspect but steam heating was still a decade away. Lighting was ordained to be, as far as possible, by gas, which at least also gave out a small amount of heat from its roof-mounted globes but compared favourably with its oil predecessor.

North British Railway coaching stock had been criticised since 1846 and passenger business growth up to 1875 meant that a good number of veteran cars were still around in a variety of conditions. In February 1867, Thomas Wheatley was appointed as locomotive superintendent and under his tenure the passenger-carrying fleet statistically grew from 963 to 1,175 although some older carriages had been 'paper entries' and never actually existed, others being the NB proportion of Joint Stock fleets. Nevertheless, the growth in numbers reflected a substantial

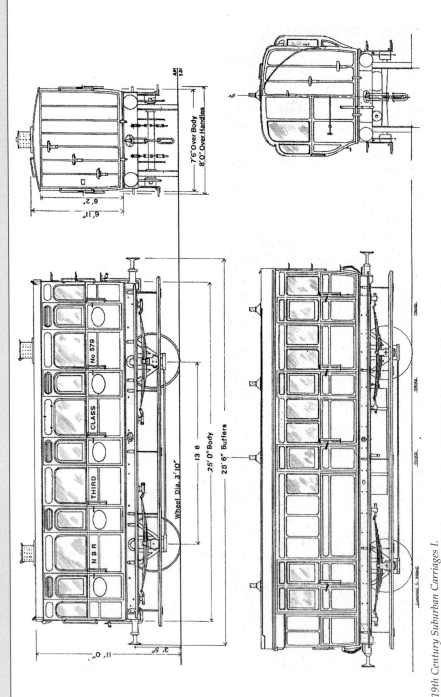

19th Century Suburban Carriages I.
Top: Ashbury-built third class vehicles used until *c.* 1895. 25 ft 0 in. x 7 ft 6 in. over body.
Bottom: 4-wheel brake third built at Cowlairs and used after 1884. 28 ft 6 in. x 7 ft 6 in. (ducket 9 ft 0 in.) over body.

investment in carriages of larger capacities, many of which were built by Messrs Ashbury of Manchester and bought 'off the peg' between 1870 and 1875.

Wheatley resigned almost eight years to the day on which he was appointed, leaving a carriage fleet in much better shape than that he had inherited although still unheated, oil lit on four wheels, with a few six-wheelers. His successor, Dugald Drummond, almost immediately produced prototypes with external styling that remained standard over the remainder of the NBR existence. Initial vehicles were four-wheelers, some with 'domed end' roof' types, but soon the first six-wheelers appeared, virtually a 'stretched' four-wheeler. Initially 7 ft 6 in. wide, in the early 1880s this became 8 ft 0 in., apart from the composite passenger/brakes where the passenger ends remained at 7 ft 6 in. Almost all Drummond's NB stock was built at Cowlairs. Although the NB retained second class until 1892, it declined after 1878, some new Drummond cars being upgraded to second class as required, but not for the Edinburgh Suburban & South Side Junction Railway. Matthew Holmes succeeded Drummond in 1882 and continued the Drummond style.

When the Edinburgh Suburban service opened in December 1884 the initial timetable could have been worked by two sets of stock, one on the Inner and one on the Outer Circle. The vehicles were claimed to have been, at least initially, of the 'latest' four- and six-wheel stock, then being built, although as with any railway, elderly stock gravitated into the workings at various times. Brake vehicles at each end were generally four-wheeled, containing three passenger compartments at one end and a guard's/luggage compartment at the other although some six-wheel carriages were also used. The standard North British passenger vehicle of the time was either the 28 ft 4 in. four-wheeler with four first or five third class compartments or the 35 ft 6½ in. six-wheeler, with either five first or six third class compartments. Four-wheelers remained in production until 1894 and six-wheelers until 1901, with improvements being incorporated over the years, most suburban services' stock operating on the Westinghouse air brake. Oil lamps were placed into holes in the compartment roof (a wooden plug was fitted during daylight), but this later changed to ordinary and then to incandescent gas.

Destinations were painted on large wooden boards, painted black with cream letters, a small projection from the lower edge fitting into brackets on the coach cantrail or bodyside panel between cantrail and glazing. These held the board vertically, useful for stock with the 'Drummond' roof contour where oil or gas lamps were serviced from roof level.

The NBR started building general service bogie stock in 1901, two years before Holmes retired. Initial vehicles were eight-compartment thirds, followed in 1902 by three-compartment brake thirds. First class passengers had to wait until 1903. All were basically 'stretched' six-wheelers with two extra compartments, gas lit - but still unheated. Compartment dimensions were identical with their six-wheeled forerunners. The three-compartment bogie brake third combined the accommodation of a four-wheel brake third and a four-wheel full brake on one underframe, but the five-compartment brake third was still three years away. Bogie coach roof contours were those of the Drummond era. When displaced by later builds, they 'cascaded' downwards, replacing six-wheelers on commercially sensitive services, in turn eliminating 'Ashbury' and other stock from the 1870s.

With a body length of 49 ft 8⅙ in., several of these early bogie carriages were allocated to the Edinburgh area, but used on the equivalent of longer distance routes. Although not intended for suburban services, as public transport competition at that time was either horse bus or slow cable car, some were included in the more

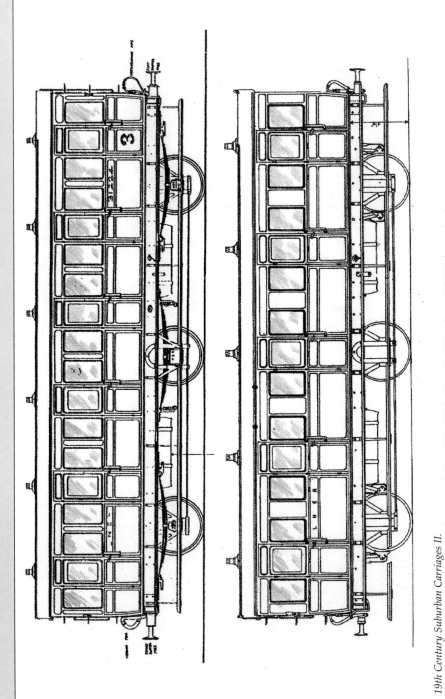

19th Century Suburban Carriages II.
Top: 6-wheel third compartment vehicle used after 1884. 28 ft 6 in. x 7 ft 6 in. (later 8 ft 0 in.) over body.
Bottom: 6-wheel first class compartment vehicle used post-1886. 28 ft 6 in. x 7 ft 6 in. (later 8 ft 0 in.) over body.

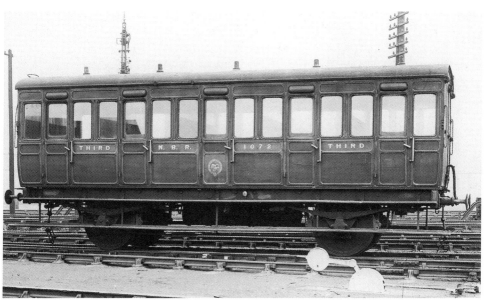

No. 1072 represents the 'standard' four wheel third class vehicles built (in both 7 ft 6 in. and 8 ft 0 in. widths) in the 1880s and 1890s. Westinghouse-braked and gas lit, some survived in traffic until the 1930s. 28 ft 6 in. long over body, a brake third was fashioned by changing two compartments at one end into a guard's and luggage area as shown on page 88.

Author's Collection

For the first 20 years, Suburban passengers were conveyed in either 4- or 6-wheel vehicles, the only evolution being a width increase from 7 ft 6 in. to 8 ft 0 in. and some were still at work in the mid-1930s. This third class example, NBR No. 860, is Westinghouse-braked, gas lit and unheated. Non-sprung return door locks are evident by the variations in handle positions.

Author's Collection

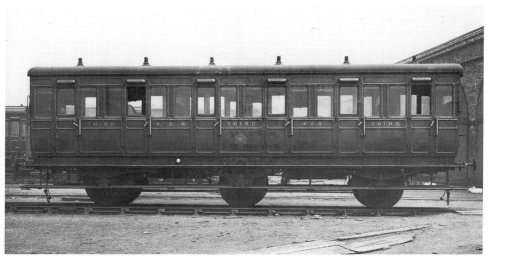

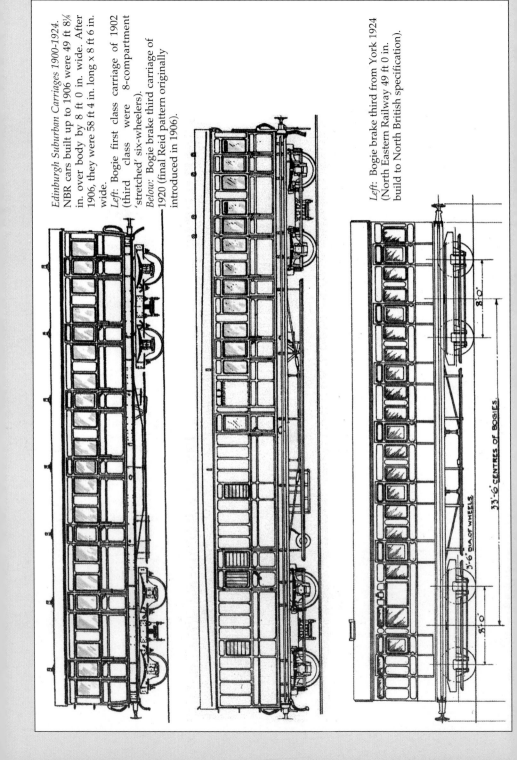

Edinburgh Suburban Carriages 1900-1924. NBR cars built up to 1906 were 49 ft 8⅝ in. over body by 8 ft 0 in. wide. After 1906, they were 58 ft 4 in. long x 8 ft 6 in. wide.

Left: Bogie first class carriage of 1902 (third class were 8-compartment 'stretched' six-wheelers).

Below: Bogie brake third carriage of 1920 (final Reid pattern originally introduced in 1906).

Left: Bogie brake third from York 1924 (North Eastern Railway 49 ft 0 in. build to North British specification).

8'0"

33'-6" CENTRES OF BOGIES.

3'-6" DIA. OF WHEELS.

8'0"

important 'business' trains. The development of a more prosperous, and dare one say voluble, clientele, particularly in Morningside and Newington areas, also spurred the NB into providing greater suburban comfort standards.

W.P. Reid succeeded Holmes as locomotive superintendent during 1903 and started evaluations and experiments for a new carriage roof profile before the final pattern appeared in 1906. Reid's carriages were 58 ft 4 in. long and 8 ft 6 in. wide over body, and although the initial production was of corridor vestibuled stock soon non-corridor variants appeared. These new cars initially replaced stock in services to Carlisle, Glasgow (via Bathgate) and Fife, cascading the earlier bogie stock down to important suburban services, in turn gradually replacing four- and six-wheelers. Suburban ladies found that their secluded 'Ladies Only' compartments became 'general user' after 3rd April, 1906, although the railway conceded that they would label only if specifically requested.

The arrival of the electric tramcar had an immediate effect on travel in Glasgow, but this was not felt in Edinburgh which was wedded to its cable car system until the early 1920s. Consequently, the more modern stock tended to go to the west of Scotland, although the Edinburgh suburban line clientele did benefit. The first Reid vehicles were gas lit, but some were built with electric lighting (and steam heating) although a number were converted to gas before reverting to electricity due to the North British hierarchy indecision, the roof mounted gas pipes being used as conduit for the electric wiring!

In 1912, the North British Railway began changing from Westinghouse (air) to vacuum brakes, dual braking being pre-planned and defined in carriage working diagrams. This was well in hand at the outbreak of World War I, when most Edinburgh suburban line passenger engines had dual brake equipment and most trains had fixed formations.

As new builds increased between 1907 and 1915, Reid stock appeared more regularly on suburban services supplemented by earlier bogie stock and further displacing four- and six-wheelers. First class interiors had relatively luxuriously upholstered seating four-a-side, but the six-a side seating in the third class remained basic, although better equipped than their predecessors. Upholstery was not particularly comfortable, interior woodwork being varnished vertical tongue and groove panelling relieved by a single picture frame on each side below the luggage racks. One frame held a 'landscape format' rectangular mirror, the other, usually, an advertisement for NBR hotels. Concurrently, experiments were made in external lining and lettering styles, although the maroon body colour with white roof and black underframe remained. Regular suburban line sets were supplemented by other stock in 'lie-over' time at Waverley and during heavy user periods such as 'Trades' holidays, Suburban bogie stock was liable to be temporarily withdrawn for more lucrative long distance and excursion work and replaced by up to nine-coach formations of elderly four- and six-wheel vehicles dating from the 1880s, a practice continued into the early LNER period. NBR bogie vehicles had the name of their 'home' depot fixed to the solebars. Vehicles passing to workshops were replaced by one from the works 'pool' which remained in the set until the regular vehicle was returned, when the 'works' vehicle moved on to another set or depot to repeat the process.

In the two or three years before the 1923 Grouping, detailed North British Railway carriage building programmes were produced but put on 'hold', partially to allow construction of stock from earlier programmes delayed by the manpower and material shortages resulting from the Great War, and also uncertainty regarding the policy of the new organisation.

After 1901, four- and six-wheelers were gradually displaced by bogie vehicles that were at first 'stretched' six-wheelers. No. 31620 is one of 70 built between 1902 and 1905, the interior appointments being almost identical to the shorter cars. They were also Westinghouse-braked, gas lit and unheated. *Author's Collection*

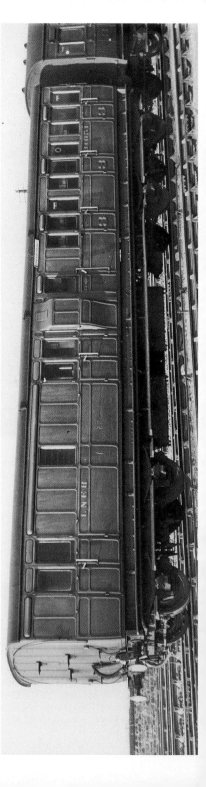

The first 'production' bogie brake thirds had three third class compartments and a large brake/luggage area, equivalent in total to a four-wheel brake third and full brake. No. 31651 is one of 26 built between 1902 and 1904, and which lasted until 1940. Ten five-compartment brake thirds of the same length were built in 1905. *Author's Collection*

By 1922, the 'standard' Suburban cars were 58 ft 4 in. long and 8 ft 6 in. wide over body with nine third class (90 seats) or eight first class compartments (64 seats). There were some with other interior layouts, but these tended to be 'refugees' from other routes. Brake vehicles had either three or five passenger compartments, but in 1920 came the first 'compromise' vehicle with four passenger and one luggage/guard's compartment. Had Grouping not intervened, this would probably have become the 'standard' over the whole North British network.

II. London & North Eastern Railway

The North British carriage building programme for 1922 and 1923 provided for five sets of six standard 58 ft 4 in. long, 8 ft 6 in. wide non-corridor stock for suburban working to answer road competition. In Edinburgh, the new electric tramcars introduced in 1922 were rapidly displacing the old slow and increasingly unreliable cable cars with a serious impact on railway traffic. Each set was to have two brake thirds, two firsts and two thirds, with 26 third and 16 first compartments per set.

A strong plea was made from the North British officers for the modern bogie stock that they had planned and the new LNER management agreed to provide the Edinburgh suburban line with new bogie coaching stock to cater for the perceived importance of its clientele. Meantime, some modern (by North British standards) former North Eastern Railway bogie carriages were transferred in to the area where they were quickly absorbed. The North British request for vehicles of its own design was over-ruled by the new concern, although concessions were made regarding some interior appointments. Dedicated sets of new bogie coaching stock were delivered but the carriages were only 49 ft 0 in. long over body and externally panelled in the old North Eastern Railway style, having been built at York. Niggling criticism was raised from the former NBR hierarchy that internal fittings and notices in the new cars were lettered as for the 'North Eastern Railway', and not 'LNER', and this resulted in pointed inter-area correspondence until compromises were reached.

The new stock was in varnished teak livery, fully lined out, and lettered 'L&NER' in the centre of the bodyside. Numbering was at first in a new 10xxx range at each end of each side, but this was later changed to the former NBR series based on class, but with the LNER Area suffix 'B'. The number of compartments were marginally less first class than the NBR proposal with 28 third and 14 firsts but the new stock was introduced to Suburban passengers in complete six car rakes. Each train had a six-compartment brake third at each end, the two first class cars in the centre being flanked by a third class vehicle on each side. Regardless of their 1924 build, they were considered as 'non standard' and most were displaced to other services after three years by 'LNER Group Standard' 51 ft 0 in. long vehicles under the 1924 Carriage Building Programme. Interestingly, one of these latter types, the five-compartment brake third, had an identical interior layout to a North British predecessor, the guard being at the inner end of the van, nearer the passengers.

LNER carriage boards were mounted in brackets on the cantrail of the LNER Group Standard cars (there was no room on the bodyside panelling) but were of a different length to NBR boards. The number of vehicles in a train determined the number and position of the boards, which were white with hand-painted black letters. A six-car train would have boards on each side of the end vehicles and the two centre cars. Three-car formations had them on end vehicles only.

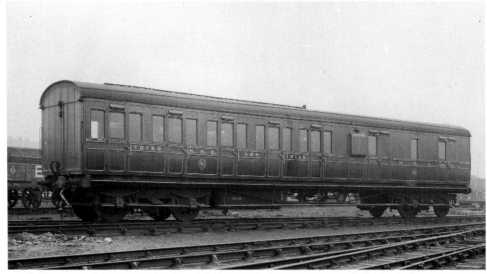

Following roof contour evaluations (which included a clerestory type), the final NBR carriage profile was determined in 1906. Five-compartment brake third No. 508 of 1908 was Westinghouse-braked and gas lit, but later dual-braked and electrically lit, becoming only vacuum-braked in 1933. Officially withdrawn in January 1949, it had actually been broken up in October 1948! Changes were made to the exterior bodysides for some vans built during World War I, but no drawings or diagrams of these were produced.   *Author's Collection*

The first LNER Group Standard carriages arrived in 1925 from York. Third class No. 10292B of this batch is in its original fully lined out teak livery (including ends). Later renumbered 3151 it was withdrawn as No. SC82032E in February 1960 and broken up the following month.
Author's Collection

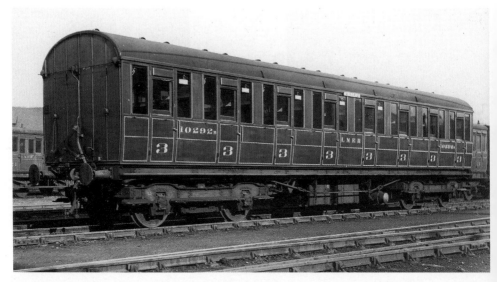

Although GE area 'Quints' had been used briefly in 1925, it was not until 1938 that the LNER produced articulated suburban stock for Scotland. Glasgow-based twins had four passenger compartments in the brake thirds, whereas those for Edinburgh had five, but inter-district working blurred the concept. Edinburgh twin No. SC86918/9E was photographed at Shields Road in Glasgow.   *W.A.C. Smith*

Wooden bodies yielded to steel paneling after World War II, and an example of post-war suburban stock is depicted in five compartment brake third No. SC87197E. Built in 1951 after the formation of British Railways, the vehicle survived until April 1966 and is photographed at Cadder yard shortly after condemnation.   *Author*

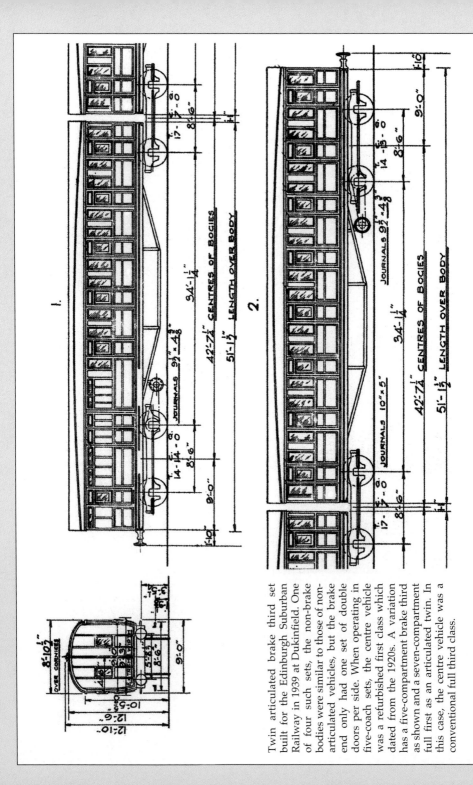

Twin articulated brake third set built for the Edinburgh Suburban Railway in 1939 at Dukinfield. One of four such sets, the non-brake bodies were similar to those of non-articulated vehicles, but the brake end only had one set of double doors per side. When operating in five-coach sets, the centre vehicle was a refurbished first class which dated from the 1920s. A variation has a five-compartment brake third as shown and a seven-compartment full first as an articulated twin. In this case, the centre vehicle was a conventional full third class.

A large number of 'Group Standard' non-vestibuled suburban stock arrived after 1925 and many were formed into complete sets for inter-district and major suburban services, generally in Glasgow, although some worked in sets with the older NBR bogie stock. 'Group Standard' carriages built after 1927 had body widths (over handles) increased from 9 ft 0 in. to 9 ft 3 in., and routes were cleared, one by one, by the Area Civil Engineer before they were allowed into service, displacing the 1924 suburban line stock to other services. Half a century later, BR Mark III coaching stock clearances required some of the then closed suburban line platforms to have the edge coping or in some instances, the entire platform removed.

An agreement with the Imperial Tobacco Company in the early 1930s brought commercial advertising inside carriages, the 'Smoking' labels being increased in depth to refer to certain tobacco products. The LNER provided for the four rectangular panels under each luggage rack to display advertisements in the Scottish Area in 1932 when they took over advertising from Messrs Slaughter & Co. Advert change was facilitated by the hinged bottom frames below the luggage racks on 'Group Standard' vehicles then in use, particularly on diagrams confined to certain depots and diagrams.

The 'Group Standard' vehicle interiors between seat back upholstery and above the luggage rack were of dark varnished wood, but from about 1934 in new builds (and refurbished older stock) lighter pastel colours were used with Bakelite-framed watercolour scenic prints flanking oval mirrors above the seats on both sides of the compartment.

Two complete steel-panelled six-car sets had been delivered from Messrs R. & Y. Pickering of Motherwell in 1938 for the Musselburgh line and these put in occasional appearances as 'filling in' turns around the Suburban and out to Gorebridge. They were not actually diagrammed as complete sets around the Suburban, but appeared as individual twin units. Externally painted in a simulation of varnished teak (complete with imitation beading and lining) they later succumbed to an all-over uniform unlined brown-painted wartime finish. Most were still working in the Edinburgh area 20 years later, although the original sets had long been dissipated.

In 1939, the Edinburgh suburban circle services gained three new twin articulated vehicle sets. They had conventional LNER teak-panelled bodies, and were built at the Dukinfield works of the former Great Central Railway in Manchester. Although similar vehicles had been previously built for the Glasgow suburban services, the Edinburgh and Dundee area stock had five passenger compartments in the brake thirds, the Glasgow district sets having four. Brake compartment door arrangements also differed from that used hitherto. 'Edinburgh Suburban sets' were formed as (Twin) brake-third/first; (Twin) third/brake-third, with a single refurbished 1927 design third (which matched externally) between. In some formations, two brake third/third twins were supplied, the single centre carriage was a matching non-corridor first. One Musselburgh route twin unit had a third/composite layout, but rarely ventured on the suburban line. Where twins were not available, such as during maintenance, similar capacity non-articulated stock was used. Edinburgh suburban circle rakes were maintained at Leith Central, but other Edinburgh area sets were allocated to Craigentinny. Thus, Suburban formations were regularly maintained, but when replacements were unavoidable, stock came from Craigentinny, either as sets or as individual vehicles.

In May 1944, the LNER produced a 'Report on the Design of Passenger Rolling Stock' for post-war implementation when it was estimated more than half the fleet would be over 20 years old. Included were nine 52 ft 4 in. x 9 ft 0 in. over body non-

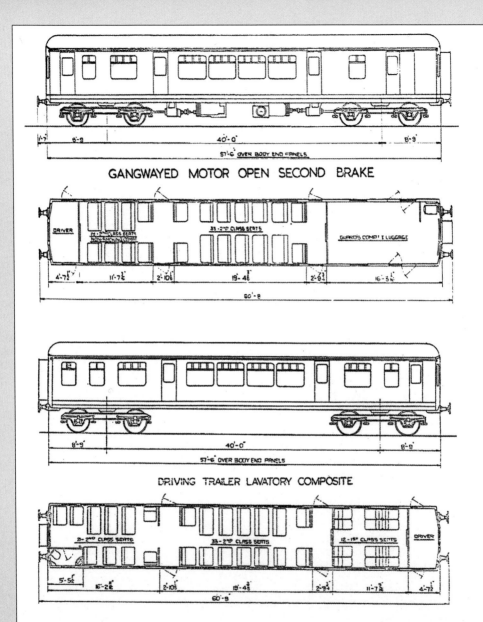

GANGWAYED MOTOR OPEN SECOND BRAKE

DRIVING TRAILER LAVATORY COMPOSITE

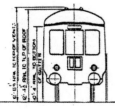

The British Railways modernisation plan of the mid-1950s led to the wholesale introduction of diesel multiple units on local, and not so local services. The Edinburgh suburban line was selected for early dieselisation and the first two-car sets were those built by the Gloucester Carriage & Wagon Co. in 1957. Based on Leith Central, initialy a sub-depot of St Margarets, these twin sets took over from the former five-coach steam sets on virtually the same timetables. Although popular with their passengers, particularly with the view forward through the cab, they were too late to prevent closure and indeed the class had a relatively early demise north of the border.

corridor types. From 1946, three types (third, first and composite with lavatory) were built, and a four-compartment brake third introduced, all with steel exteriors. Three more types were added between 1950 and 1953, two of which, a five-compartment brake third and composite, were in the 1944 plan. There was also a brake composite with two first and four third class compartments with the firsts adjacent to the van, and not as in the 1944 scheme at the outer end of the carriages. Several post-war vehicles entered Edinburgh suburban services, replacing older stock.

In May 1945, the Edinburgh suburban circle service was booked to be operated by three five-car sets, each including two articulated twins. The large influx of post-war all-steel non-corridor designs allowed many older vehicles to 'cascade' to less important routes, but the suburban circle line was only affected by temporary replacements for maintenance. After all, the wooden-bodied twins were only six years old. The five-coach formations remained as standard for the remaining steam traction period, although some off-peak services had three-car sets of brake third, composite lavatory and full third.

III. British Railways Suburban Steam Stock

When Leith Central closed to passengers on 18th March, 1952, suburban circle trains ran from Piershill to Abbeyhill via the Abbeyhill Loop, avoiding terminal reversals and sets were transferred to Craigentinny for maintenance. British Railways standard non-corridor stock first appeared in 1954 and made little impact on former LNER Edinburgh suburban lines apart from replacing the few remaining pre-Grouping cars that occasionally appeared in suburban sets for maintenance purposes but former LMS vehicles were rare.

Two years later, the diesel multiple unit era dawned and thus the total of British Railways standard non-corridor vehicles allocated to the Scottish Region only reached 132. Three BR standard types went into service, a six-compartment brake third, nine-compartment third and a composite (rare in east Scotland) with three first class compartments in the centre. Seat springing in the BR vehicles was much softer than in former LNER types, but this was liable to be a tad wearing! The initial Scottish diesel multiple unit fleet went to the east of Scotland, the displaced LNER and BR stock moving to the west of Scotland, initially to former LNER North Clydeside lines.

IV. The Diesel Multiple Unit Era

On 13th April, 1956, the first diesel railcars arrived at Leith Central on loan from the Eastern Region for staff training and trial passenger operations, although not used on the suburban line. These Metropolitan Cammell twins were motor brake seconds Nos. E79055/56 and trailer composites Nos. 79271/72, which were returned to the Eastern Region in October 1956. The next influx took place in the week ended 28th August, 1957 when the first Scottish-allocated sets arrived at Leith Central, then considered a sub-shed of St Margarets, for the Edinburgh and Glasgow service. Although not used on suburban passenger work, training trips were run over the line.

Diesel multiple units that worked the suburban line up to closure were twins, comprising of a driving motor brake second and driving trailer composite with first class accommodation behind the driver in the non-motorised car. Basically the

The ubiquitous Scottish four-wheel open wagon evolved over the years into this specimen with characteristic 'cupboard' type doors, the RCH standard having drop side doors. No. 15042 was built by R. & Y. Pickering of Wishaw in 1912 with a 16 ton capacity and was withdrawn as LNER No. 715042 in May 1948.   *Author's Collection*

To deal with specified perishable traffics such as used in passenger trains, six wheel fruit and yeast vans, similar to fish vans but without windows in the doors, were built by outside contractors. No. 27610 came from Hurst, Nelson in 1916 and is shown in its first maroon coaching stock livery as allocated to Niddrie West. It was withdrawn from traffic in June 1946.   *Author's Collection*

Gloucester Railway Carriage and Wagon Company build, seating 12 first and 106 second class passengers, were used, although other types appeared from time to time. Dundee-based Metropolitan Cammell twin sets also appeared. Replacement of a five-coach steam set with a twin diesel unit led to complaints particularly from first class travellers on lack of privacy. Once over the initial shock of the transition to open saloons, the Gloucester sets were generally preferred due to their larger glazed area, particularly for forward observation, but were not too popular with maintenance staff. Some Derby and Craven cars also appeared from other areas.

Local dmus could run in multiple with each other but not with 'Inter-City' units on the Edinburgh and Glasgow service due to different wiring arrangement in the inter-unit jumper cables. Dmu flexibility resulted in (unadvertised) through diagrammed workings between Suburban and other local Edinburgh area services. One provided a 'circular tour of Edinburgh' - a feature in steam days - and was quietly advertised (but officially frowned upon) by blackboard announcement to the public outside at least one station.

In the spring of 1959, new 3-car Metropolitan Cammell dmu sets arrived at Dundee (some were initially allocated to Thornton). Consequently, Dundee lost some of its Metro-Cammell twins, those coming to Leith Central working Suburban (and other Edinburgh) services alongside the Gloucester cars. However, for most of the diesel multiple unit era, Gloucester cars predominated and it was perhaps fitting that one of these sets formed the final train in 1962.

Goods Wagons

In the mid-1880s, grease axleboxes and dumb buffers were common on goods wagons, but train speeds were not high. As time passed, first the dumb buffers gave way to sprung types and then grease axleboxes by oil (and in a few cases roller bearing) types.

Initially, Gorgie, Morningside Road and Newington goods stations handled many agricultural elements and it was not unusual to see flocks of sheep and herds of cattle emerging from goods yards and literally 'hoof it' out to their respective farms accompanied by ever attentive sheepdogs. However, as the city expanded and roads improved, traffic was lost to road with the railways penalised by legislation. This was particularly noticeable after World War I when numbers of former army vehicles became available to entrepreneurial members of the public. Railway companies had to publish their rates, which could readily be undercut by the new carriers who could pick and choose their commodities and markets in a way that the railways could not match as common carriers. The railways tried to reduce costs by concentrating general goods at larger depots with delivery from railheads, but this was only partially successful.

From the outset, goods yards played a significant role in the dealing with stone, slates and other building materials for the expanding Edinburgh southern suburbs. Contractors for the new Royal Observatory on Blackford Hill even had their own siding and another stonework siding at Morningside Road was served for many years on a daily basis. Once the suburbs expanded and the 'tinkling of chisels' quoted by Robert Louis Stevenson in his *Picturesque Notes* had faded into the distance, domestic coal from the several Scottish coalfields, mostly from the Lothians, became the main commodity. This usually passed in railway-owned or colliery wagons but there were some local traders' wagons mostly owned or leased by larger coal merchants, such as Bruce Lindsay Brothers and Waldie.

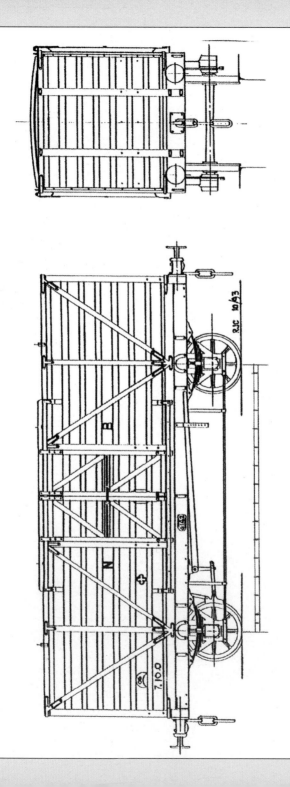

Empty Cask Wagon. One of the variations of this type which were used for the return of empty beer casks to the breweries, this particular type originated in a general arrangement drawing of June 1918, although wagons had been built at Cowlairs since 1905. An earlier similar design for an 8 ton vehicle with hinged doors was dated September 1893. At one time carrying capacities of this type were stated as being 10 and 12 tons, with a tare weight of 7 tons 10 cwt. A right-hand lever brake on each side operated the single brake block on that side only. The wheels of 3 ft 1 in. diameter ran in 8 in. x 3¾in. journals, those of the 12 ton capacity wagons being 10 in. x 4¾ in. No. 7231 of 1895 (by then No. 707231) survived into British Railways era, being withdrawn in August 1952, but most had been withdrawn by the end of 1948.

Special wagons used to return empty casks to breweries and distilleries, several being converted from coke wagons, with their height and light construction, the wagons going to places where full beer barrels were sent, to bring back 'the empties'. NBR No. 3544, was 'custom' built in 1905, becoming No. 703544 in the LNER fleet on 19th September, 1923, but did not survive into the British Railways era.   *Author's Collection*

Livestock traffic over the suburban line was for many years a staple traffic element and is represented here by 1914 Hurst, Nelson-built No. 2435. It was one of 200 with 'Traceur' axleboxes but conventional NBR hand brake rigging and 'Instanter' type couplings, presumably to ease transit shocks to cattle. It had no power brake and was withdrawn before World War II.
Author's Collection

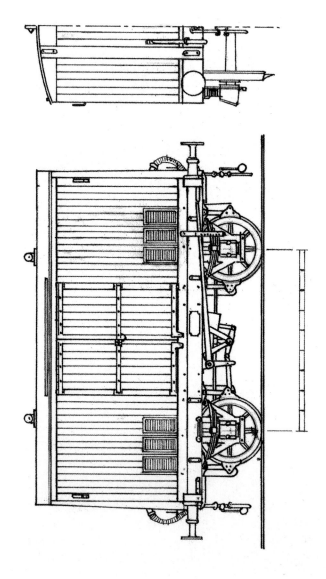

Yeast Van. The North British Railway diagram for this type of vehicle designates them as being for 'fruit, yeast and cheese' but vans used for cheese traffic (painted white) had doors on one side only and those for the fruit traffic had an additional four vertical louvres centrally at floor level at each end. 16 ft 3 in. over body and with a width of 7 ft 5½ in., the yeast vans had a nominal tare weight of 8 tons and were painted in passenger lake with lettering in chrome unshaded yellow as befitted passenger-rated traffic. Originally dual-braked, many of the Westinghouse fittings were removed in the 1930s. A six-wheel variant was added later which shared a number of features with similar fish vans, but unlike the latter, had no windows in the doors.

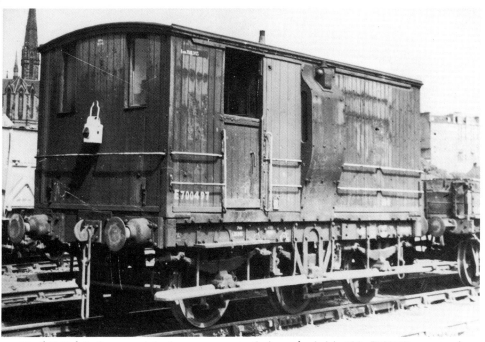

North British Railway goods brake vans were mostly four-wheeled, but No. E700497 was one of a small number of six-wheelers. In the mid-1950s, sister vehicle No. E700158 was used for its last duties in Edinburgh deputising for the usual LNER brake on 'The Shunt', between Duddingston and Morningside Road.   *Authors Collection*

The final development of the NBR four-wheel brake vans was is represented here by No. DE773629 which dates from 1923. A number of this build were acquired (and renumbered) by the Civil Engineer about 1947 this being one. Although not strictly 'revenue earning stock', it was pressed into service on the Duddingston and Morningside 'Shunt' trip, and is seen about to leave the latter yard on its return working about 1955.   *W.S. Sellar*

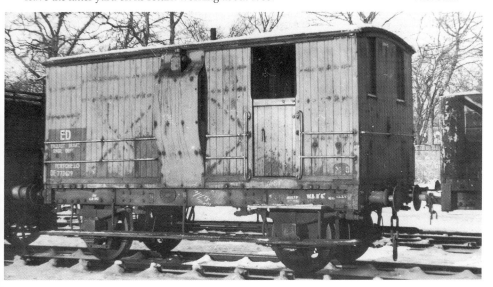

Livestock was extensively handled at all suburban yards until World War I, and facilities existed to deal with these. At Gorgie, cattle market sidings were established in 1910, absorbing work from several other city locations. The sidings, literally along the road from an abattoir, were laid by Edinburgh Corporation from a branch serving a glue factory that used animal hides. The sidings handled large numbers of vehicles which arrived (and occasionally departed) as full train loads, multiple loads, wagonloads, and also for wagon cleaning.

One specific traffic referred to in suburban working time tables in the 1890s was Apple Blossom margarine, dispatched daily in wagonloads from Duddingston to Glasgow and Dundee. Refrigerated vans were probably used for this traffic, but as far as is known, none were specifically lettered.

A constituent of the brewing processes at Gorgie and Duddingston was yeast, but this was extremely vulnerable to wet or damp and railway companies had several vehicle types dedicated to this passenger-rated traffic. Indeed, some NBR four- and six-wheel yeast vans were lettered for return to Niddrie West and Duddingston. Individual painted numbers were listed in the General Appendix to the Rules and Regulations, as were similar vans for fruit and milk churns.

Loaded beer casks were dispatched from local brewery private sidings or in smaller consignments from goods stations in conventional railway open wagons or covered vans. Special high-sided open slatted-side wagons similar to box vans were used to return the empty casks to the breweries, some being specifically lettered for the Duddingston and Niddrie areas. There were five variants of these wagons, comprising an 8 ton capacity wagon with hinged doors (NBR Diagram 23) and others with 3, 8, 10 or 12 ton capacities and sliding doors which were all to Diagram 71. In October 1914, some redundant coke wagons with hinged side doors were converted into cask wagons, these hybrids becoming NBR Diagram 107. Despite their unique style and function, these wagons were not termed as 'Special Wagons', either by the NB or their successors. In the LNER era, those with hinged doors had capacities gradually downrated from 8 to 3 tons (Diagram 65B). The 18 ft 3 in.-long sliding door types with 8 ton capacity became Diagram 66B and the larger 24 ft 0 in. sliding door 10 and 12 ton types were also included in Diagram 66B. The 3 ton variants had gone by 1940, but some others were still in service into the 1950s.

Duddingston was one of very few locations on the North British where wagons were authorised to be shunted within the goods yard by the use of poles, or towed with ropes or chains by a locomotive on an adjacent line.

Traders' Liveried Wagons

Records exist of some firms connected with the suburban line that owned wagons, or more likely leased or rented vehicles in their own liveries and these are summarised below. A number of traders displayed large scale model wagons bearing their liveries in their shop windows, but in many cases, these were 'wish' models rather than actual replicas.

James Waldie & Sons

This was a well-known firm of Edinburgh coal merchants who operated a substantial number of mineral wagons, registered with the North British. Waldie's wagons were mostly based on Haymarket (NB) Coal Yard in which the firm had a sizable lairage and maintenance was undertaken at two Edinburgh locations. Vehicles, lettered as 'Waldie, Leith', were repaired at Leith Walk (East) Goods, but those only branded 'Waldie' were done at Haymarket.

MacKenzie Brothers (Foundry) Ltd
    This appears to relate to Messrs McKenzie & Moncur, an engineering firm in the Slateford (Gorgie) and Balcarres Street (Morningside) areas of Edinburgh, and both works had private siding connections. The solitary vehicle for which details have been located (No. 2) indicate a 10 ton capacity 6-plank open wagon, based on Gorgie.

Andrew Stewart, Gorgie
    At least six vehicles appear to have been owned by this firm, also based in Gorgie. A record shows wagon No. 6 as a 10 ton capacity open 6-plank vehicle, albeit registered with the Caledonian Railway in 1903.

The Niddrie and Benhar Coal Company
    This colliery was connected to the suburban line at Niddrie and a large fleet of open mineral wagons of varying dates and capacities served their various collieries in the central belt including Niddrie, Woolmet and Newcraighall. Some 12 ton capacity 7-plank open wagons were registered with the North British Railway in 1909 and based on Portobello but at least one was allocated to Niddrie (on purely NB territory) and registered with the Caledonian Railway!

David Inglis, Newington
    This firm appears to have had only two vehicles, (Nos. 17 and 22) the second of which was a 4-plank 10 ton capacity open wagon built by R. & Y. Pickering in 1904 and registered with the North British.

Coal was the main commodity handled in Suburban goods yards and some local merchants owned or leased wagons painted in their own livery. One such wagon was No. 22 from David Inglis of Newington. This 10 ton capacity 4-plank vehicle was built by R.Y. Pickering of Wishaw in 1904 and registered by the NBR.   *R. Cockburn Collection*

Leith General Warehouses/Distiller's Company Limited

Perhaps the most striking local traders' vehicles were four variations of peak-roofed grain wagons registered by the NBR and built by Messrs R. & Y. Pickering of Wishaw and Hurst, Nelson of Motherwell between the 1890s and World War I. Best known were those owned by the Leith General Warehousing Company (Messrs Berry, Barclay and Company of South Leith) others carried the liveries of the Distiller's Company at Haymarket and the North British Grain Storage and Transit Company which subsequently sold their wagons to the Leith General Warehouses. Four types were built, the earliest having six boards and a wooden underframe running on grease axleboxes, which after 1907 were restricted to a speed of 15 miles per hour. A further similar design incorporated a higher roof, and two others (10 and 10½ planks) had high roofs and steel underframes. Because of their specific design and purpose, they survived two world wars and nationalisation. The vehicles were distinctive in their individual liveries and very familiar in and around Edinburgh, particularly in the Haymarket and Gorgie areas. After withdrawal, some were sold on and reliveried, such as to Hutchison of Kirkcaldy for similar duties, or simply for grain storage. The final specimens seem to have been scrapped in early 1971. Standard wood or steel bulk grain vans of LNER or BR designs took over the residual grain traffic until the distilleries ceased to use rail transport.

There were, of course, other private-liveried wagons from collieries outwith the Lothians which supplied local coal merchants. These apart, most other wagons dealt with in Suburban yards were owned by the various railway companies.

Other than minerals, most wagons dealt with in Suburban yards and sidings were railway owned, but grain was conveyed from Leith Docks to the Gorgie distilleries in special trader-owned vehicles. Ten ton capacity, Leith General Warehouses No. 97 is at Niddrie in the 1930s with lettering which was later contracted to 'L.G.W.' Grease axle boxes hampered speed, but several lasted into the 1970s on local trip working. *Author's Collection*

Chapter Five

Haymarket to Gorgie

Haymarket West Junction

Until 1873, the North British Railway's main line at the later site of Haymarket West Junction was plain double track. In that year, the NBR agreed to the Caledonian making with 'all due despatch' a junction between the two companies at 'Dalry' (in railway terms entirely in Caledonian territory some distance from the North British). The NBR also consented to 'the powers of the Caledonian Railway Company under the North British and Edinburgh and Glasgow Railway Companies Amalgamation Act 1865 ... being extended and made applicable to traffic via Dalry Junction from stations and places on the Caledonian Railway North of Larbert Junction ... and vice versa'.

The Haymarket West Junction-Dalry Middle Junction branch was made under the Caledonian & NBR Wester Dalry Act of 1874, and may at first have been considered a 'joint line', although the line was a Caledonian preserve. According to the LNER Divisional Accountant's records, the Caledonian paid the North British £573 as the cost of making Haymarket West Junction. The North British maintained the connection and received annually from the Caledonian £57 6s. 0d., being 10 per cent interest on cost to cover renewals and maintenance. The Caledonian also laid a 'down line refuge siding' on its own land on the approach to the junction. The Wester Dalry branch may have formed part of the Caledonian main line to the north, but all their lines at Haymarket West Junction were classified as 'private sidings' by the LNER appearing as such in their Sidings Registers.

Haymarket West Junction signal box officially opened on 1st July, 1876 and NBR minutes of 29th June, 1876 note Board of Trade sanction to open the junction for Caledonian goods traffic on Monday 3rd July, 1876. Passenger trains started later, removing the Caledonian presence from an already overcrowded Waverley, doubtless to the relief of both concerns!

Under the Edinburgh Suburban & South Side Junction Railway Act of 1880, Railway No. 2 was the curve from Haymarket West Junction which joined the Suburban at Gorgie Junction. This was the more significant of the two Haymarket spurs, providing a route for freight (and occasional through passenger) trains to avoid Waverley. The additional connections and signalling required an extension to the existing signal box.

Quadrupling the main NBR lines between Corstorphine Junction (renamed Saughton Junction after 1902) and Waverley required a much larger signal box and this replaced the older box on 28th April, 1895. Between the new north and south main lines a refuge siding from the up south line could accommodate 20 wagons, engine and brake van awaiting transit to the Suburban or Wester Dalry branch. A longer westbound refuge siding for the down line, parallel to the NB main lines east of the Caledonian connection, could hold 66 wagons, engine and van. A short siding was initially laid in from the branch to Gorgie, probably for coal for the signal box, but was removed after about 20 years. Haymarket West also controlled the junction for the double track Corstorphine branch authorised in 1898, and opened on 1st February, 1902 which connected into the north main lines but not into the Suburban.

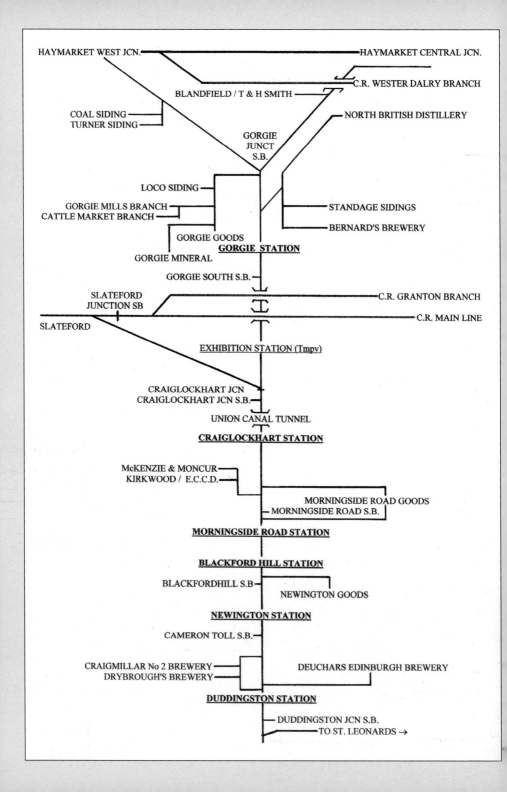

Haymarket West Junction marked the western end of the suburban railway. The signal box dated from April 1895 replacing an 1876 box (extended 1884 for the suburban line) at the junction with the Caledonian Railway's Wester Dalry branch. Part of the rear wall was glazed to give maximum visibility. *Author*

Haymarket Central Junction box opened on 7th October, 1894 as part of the Edinburgh-Saughton widening, replacing an earlier box on the site built for the opening of the suburban line in 1884. At the end of its life, its control area expanded briefly over the final rump of the Caledonian Railway's Granton branch. *N.D. Mundy*

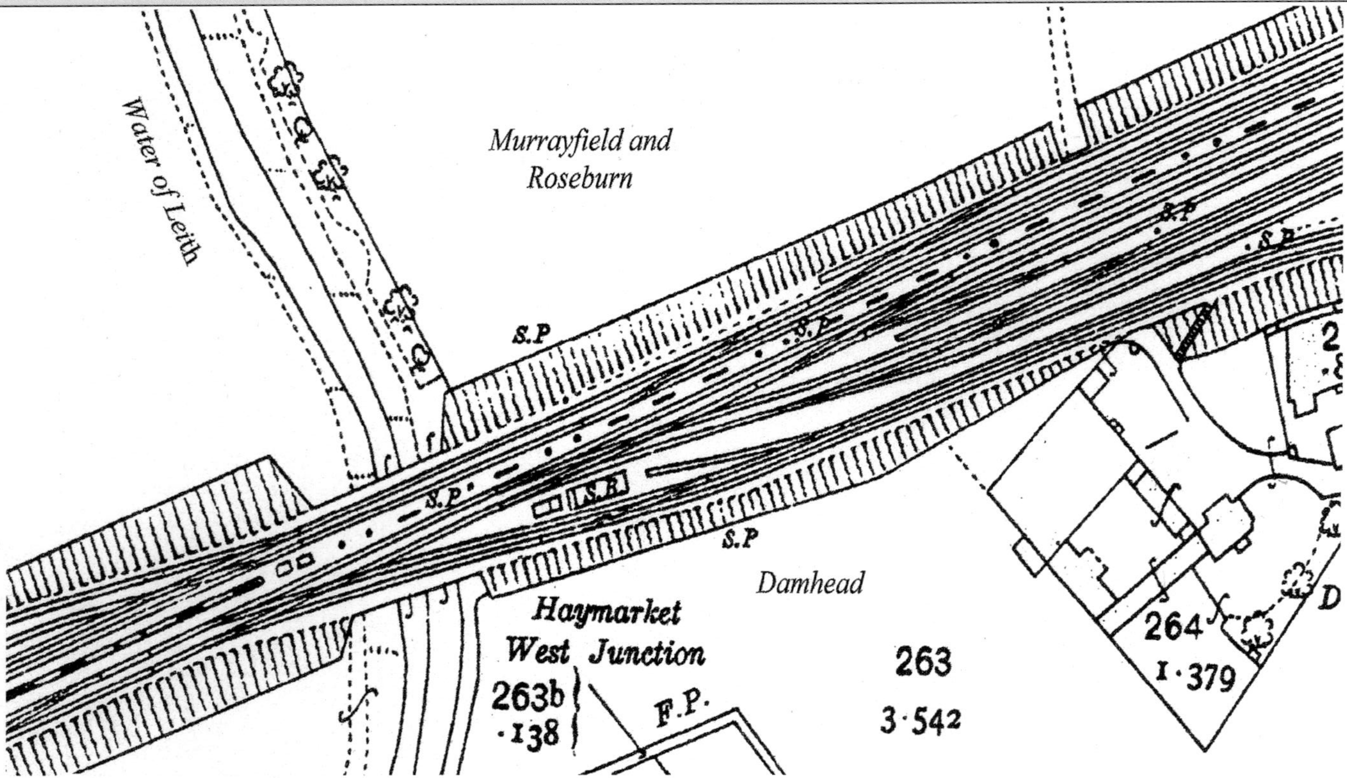
D
E
F
G
H
J
A
B
C
Water of Leith
Murrayfield and Roseburn
S.P
S.P
S.P
S.P
S.P
S.P
S.B.
Damhead
Haymarket West Junction
263b
·138
F.P.
263
3·542
264
1·379
D

Key

A	Corphorstine branch
B	North main lines
C	South main lines
D	Haymarket sheds
E	North main lines
F	South main lines
G	Down line siding
H	Caledonian lines
J	Suburban lines

Haymarket West Junction. *Reproduced from the 25", 1893 Ordnance Survey Map*

In July 1959 before the start of rationalisation, the frame contained 73 levers including four spaces, and eight spares. Thirteen were for the Wester Dalry branch, eight for the Suburban, and eight for the Corstorphine lines. Seven others applied to loops and sidings, the other 25 working main line signals and crossovers.

Passenger trains were withdrawn from the Wester Dalry branch on 2nd March, 1964, freight services following a week later and this branch and connections became available for removal. Corstorphine branch passenger services ceased after 30th December, 1967, freight lasting until 5th February, 1968 when Corstorphine box closed. The branch and Haymarket West connection were removed shortly thereafter.

At first, the Suburban passed behind Haymarket West box, avoiding the Caledonian junction, but under the 1971 track renewal programme, the line to Gorgie Junction was relaid over the solum of the Wester Dalry branch and passed in front of the box. Previous access to the Suburban was direct from the south up main, but now the facing connection led into the south down main before joining the line to Gorgie, the work being completed with appropriate signalling on 23rd April, 1972. The line from Gorgie Junction was not altered meantime, continuing with mechanical signalling, although a new illuminated track diagram was provided. Three position block instruments continued to control the trains. In the spring of 1975 under the Edinburgh resignalling scheme, the junction layout was further altered. New double line 'ladder' crossovers were installed between all lines permitting 40 mph running between north and suburban lines in both directions, enabling Saughton Junction crossovers to be taken out of use.

Haymarket West Junction box closed on 15th December, 1975, its track and signalling arrangements coming under the Haymarket panel until Edinburgh Signalling Centre took full control. The box was demolished, the realigned down Gorgie loop passing over its site, but its name survives. The down south line siding, which had a 5 mph entry speed restriction was retained for a time, but all other sidings and loops were removed.

Haymarket West Junction to Gorgie Junction

This double line spur, also known as the 'Gorgie Loop', did not feature in the 1865 proposals, but formed 'Railway No. 2' under the 1880 Edinburgh Suburban & South Side Junction Railway Act. To minimise intrusion on the Caledonian Railway land, its western end was mentioned in Clause 41 in the 1880 Act as being restricted to 12 chains (264 yards) east of the bridge carrying the Edinburgh and Glasgow Railway over a public road. This required the loop to parallel the Wester Dalry branch, passing to the rear of the Haymarket West Junction boxes before joining the E&G main line just west of its bridge over the Water of Leith. The distance between Gorgie Junction and the (1895) Haymarket West Junction boxes was 604 yards, but the extra length imposed on the 'Gorgie Loop' increased this to 880 yards. From Gorgie, the gradient fell for the first 675 yards by between 1 in 132 and 1 in 236, then rose over the remainder at 1 in 960. There were three bridges in the section, the first carrying the line over a western extension of Wheatfield Road into what was then open country, the second over a public road that evolved, widened and realigned, into Westfield Road. A century later this became part of Edinburgh's West Approach Road, using the former Wester Dalry branch earthworks. The third bridge carried the line over a narrow road to the former Damhead Farm and now leads to Murrayfield playing fields.

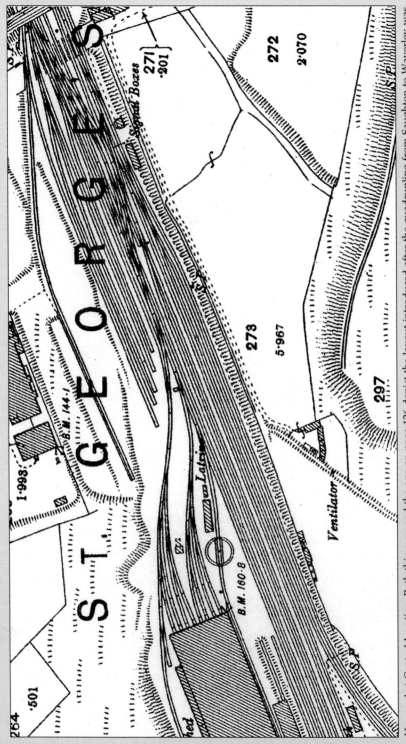

Haymarket Central Junction. Both this map and the one on page 126 depict the layout introduced after the quadrupling from Saughton to Waverley was brought into operation during the 1890s. Subsequently, the junction points at Haymarket Central were moved nearer the divergence of the suburban line and in the mid-1930s, in conjunction with the Waverley power signalling scheme, still further away from the signal box.

Reproduced from the 25″, 1893 Ordnance Survey Map

Although never used for regular passenger services, the Gorgie loop was heavily used (as planned) by freights by-passing Waverley and taking the suburban line to and from Niddrie for the East Coast and Waverley routes. With the main Edinburgh and Glasgow line and the Haymarket Central and Gorgie Junction spur, it also formed a triangle that could turn locomotives when the Haymarket motive power depot turntable was either too short or out of order. It also turned postal vehicles to ensure that traductor nets and arms were on the correct side of their trains out of Edinburgh. Later, the triangle was also used for reversing other coaching stock such as the E&G push-pull sets and Inter-city 125 High Speed Trains.

'Gorgie Loop' Sidings

A private siding connection, shared between two traders with their own sidings, trailed into the westbound loop line, 462 yards from Haymarket West immediately east of the Westfield Road bridge. The connection was protected under Block Telegraph Regulations and until Gorgie Junction box (418 yards away) replaced that at the station in February 1897, had its own signals.

Installed for Messrs James Turner & Co., stone cutters and builders of 11A Wheatfield Street, 100 yards of the original 283 yards single line buffer-ended siding were on North British Railway land. The trader bore the entire cost, which included £225 for the loop connection. The siding descended by a 1 in 135 gradient, crossing the extension of Wheatfield Road on the level. The gradient dictated that that no wagon was to be uncoupled from the engine until both were at a stand and, during shunting, level crossing and gates were controlled by the trader's staff. The siding had a 10 wagon capacity and opened on 20th May, 1896 and at first including a wagon turntable connecting with another turntable to a parallel siding line alongside Turner's premises. At one time, it was intended to make a cart road through to Gorgie Road, eliminating the level crossing and bridge under the Gorgie loop, but this was never carried out.

In 1911, Turner's agreed to share part of their siding from about 40 yards out from the level crossing with the Niddrie & Benhar Coal Company, the latter then creating a small coal yard with four buffer-ended siding lines and coal storage bings* alongside Turners premises. Both firms' lines separately crossed Wheatfield Road, each having their own crossing gates a few yards apart. Later, the gates and the Turner's line served only by the turntable was removed, although the turntable in the original siding initially remained. After 1947, coal yard sidings and staff came under the National Coal Board, but operating instructions remained unchanged until the loop connection and sidings were removed in the 1970s, the area becoming a small business park.

Haymarket Central Junction

Before the Edinburgh Suburban & South Side Junction Railway arrived, signalling in the area was undertaken from a small cabin, 30 yards east of the Caledonian Railway overbridge. This controlled the west exit from the old Haymarket engine shed and goods yard, a main line crossover with a scissors crossing, main line and subsidiary signals. This cabin was about 12 feet long, adequate at that time, but quite inadequate for later developments. When the Suburban was built, it diverged from the main NBR lines on the opposite side of the Caledonian bridge.

---

* A 'bing' is a Scottish universally used word for a heap or pile, normally associated with coal and minerals.

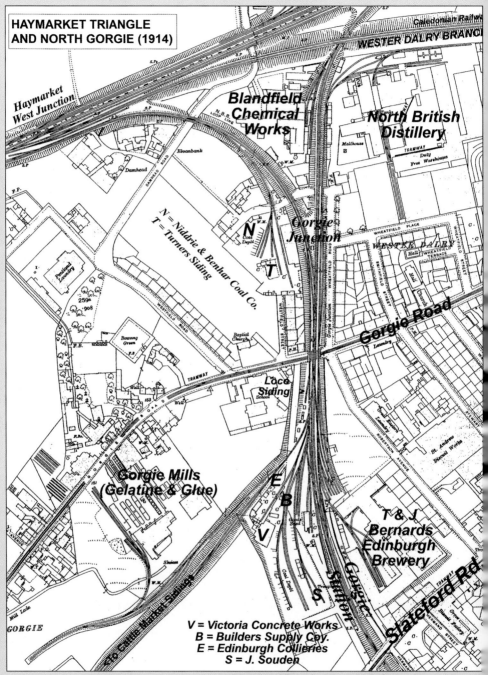

HAYMARKET TRIANGLE
AND NORTH GORGIE (1914)

Reproduced from the 25", 1914 Ordnance Survey Map

To control its junction signals and points, the Edinburgh Suburban & South Side Junction Railway Company, then still legally independent, prepared drawings for a separate 14 ft 0 in.-long signal box near the junction, 80 yards west of the Caledonian bridge and similar in style to the other suburban line boxes. Both boxes were on the south side of the main line, about 140 yards apart. At that time, a quiet meandering 20 feet wide country lane that later became Russell Road passed under the main line and the single goods yard/locomotive depot headshunt 20 yards west of the Caledonian bridge. A small footpath lay along the base of the new embankment that supported the suburban line.

Main line quadrupling under the NBR (Waverley Station) Act of 1891 between Haymarket and Saughton, required a new longer bridge to carry the Caledonian Railway branch over the North British, realigned entrance to Haymarket goods yard and a new Haymarket engine shed. Both small boxes were replaced by a new Haymarket Central signal box that opened on 7th October, 1894 just west of the suburban box, 813 yards from Gorgie Junction, and 1,041 yards from the Haymarket West Junction box that was to open in 1895.

Originally the suburban line connection was a conventional double junction almost outside the suburban box. Suburban trains left the main line and ran alongside for about 250 yards before heading south towards Gorgie. With the 1890s quadrupling, a form of 'ladder crossover' was installed, and the junction location moved west to allow movements from the new main line to the north direct to the Suburban. This reduced the length of parallel line, but it still had to pass under the Wester Dalry branch. On Sunday 23rd September, 1934, the main line junction was relaid 109 yards further west. New distant signals were provided and relevant home signals repositioned, the entire Haymarket Central Junction locking frame being renewed a month later. Following the closure of Haymarket East box (at the west end of the Haymarket station island platform) on 11th October, 1936, under the Waverley West colour light resignalling, the next box to the east was Waverley West, the signalling system becoming 'Train Describer'.

When the Duff Street connection (Haymarket East Junction) opened in 1964, as a temporary measure, Haymarket Central also controlled part of the former Caledonian Railway Granton branch between Granton Junction (between Duff Street Junction and Slateford Junction) and Crew Junction until that line was lifted. At that time, Haymarket Central had a 95 lever frame, but a growing number were being painted white, as they became 'spares'.

Haymarket Central box remained operational for a further week until concurrently with Haymarket West, its work transferred first to a panel in Haymarket Relay Room and then on 3rd October, 1976, to the Edinburgh Signalling Centre.

Haymarket Central Junction to Gorgie Junction

Part of Railway No. 1 in the 1880 Edinburgh Suburban & South Side Junction Railway Act, this could trace ancestry to the 1865 NBR (Loanhead, etc., Branches) Act, promoted to counter a reported Caledonian foray into the Lothian coalfield.

As mentioned, the Suburban originally paralleled the main lines, but the length of this was reduced first by the 1890s quadrupling layout, and again in 1934, before being singled in 1975.

A large locomotive water tank was built in the fork between suburban and main lines, opposite the 1890s Haymarket engine sheds. This had a conventional tank

Between Gorgie Junction and Haymarket Central Junction in July 1962 with a Gloucester Railway Carriage & Wagon Company twin unit on an Inner Circle service. The original 1890s parallel line from a connection at Haymarket Central Junction signal box had been repositioned nearer this site in the 1930s. This was later replaced by a simple double junction with the Glasgow line before today's single line, single lead junction.   *W.A.C. Smith*

This strange locomotive was the experimental Reid-MacLeod turbine built by the North British Locomotive Company in Glasgow under works No. 23141. The engine comprised of a long girder frame on which the boiler and condenser were mounted, all carried on two eight-wheel bogies with the condenser leading and chimney in the rear. The LNER allowed testing over the main Edinburgh and Glasgow line in April 1927 and it is seen traversing the Inner Circle approach to Gorgie where it turned on the triangle.   *Author's Collection*

mounted atop a brick base which contained pipes, valves and from time to time, office or stores accommodation. In the late 1950s the structure was replaced by a new metal tank on a tall metal frame on the opposite side of the main lines and subsequently removed.

A speed restriction of 20 mph was laid down for trains or engines passing over the suburban line junction, and thence to Gorgie Junction was 40 mph, the normal suburban line maximum. However, in the 1960 Sectional Appendix the Haymarket Central to Gorgie Junction line maximum speed was reduced to 30 mph in both directions.

Some 152 yards after leaving the 1 in 1,250 gradient of the main Edinburgh and Glasgow line, the grade increased to 1 in 100 for 161 yards, before levelling out to pass under the Wester Dalry branch. After the Caledonian line closed in March 1964, this bridge was removed, (as was the one to the west over Westfield Road) but replaced by a new road bridge as part of Edinburgh's Western Approach Road. Beyond the bridge, the line rose at 1 in 80 towards Gorgie Junction.

Resignalling and track rationalisation resulted in the closure of the Outer Circle line between Gorgie Junction and Haymarket Central between 30th November and 7th December, 1975. All trains then used the former Inner Circle line, bi-directionally signalled and renamed as the 'Up and Down Haymarket curve'. This led into the simple single line 'ladder' arrangement sequentially across all the main lines eastwards towards Haymarket station.

Daniel Bernard's Brewery (later Blandfield Chemical Works [T. & H. Smith]) Siding

In 1840, Thomas and James Bernard opened their Edinburgh Brewery in the North Back of the Canongate, part of the ground of which was to form the solum of the Waverley reconstruction in the 1870s. Thomas died in 1874 and was succeeded by his two sons, Daniel and John Mackay Bernard. They opened their Edinburgh Brewery in Slateford Road in 1888, but after a family dispute Daniel set up his own brewery in April 1889, a few hundred yards north of his brother's premises. The rail-locked site was cramped, but road access existed from Westfield Road to the north and passing under the suburban line, their main entrance was in Wheatfield Road. The Gorgie loop passed to the west of the brewery and the Suburban to the east. A trailing connection from the Outer Circle line was installed between Haymarket Central Junction and Gorgie Junction, with points on the Gorgie side of the Wester Dalry (Caledonian) branch bridge. Initially, a single buffer-ended siding was provided at the total expense, including maintenance, of the trader, and although not recorded in the NBR Sidings Register, existed before 1893. A second siding was later added, parallel to the first, forming a loop with an intermediate loading bank and later still, a third short buffer-ended siding with its own catch points was added at the Haymarket end before the brewery closed in 1906.

Thomas and Henry Smith, both qualified doctors, founded a pharmaceutical firm in 1836 and in 1847 opened their Blandfield Chemical Works in the Canonmills area of Edinburgh, and became a limited company in 1904. In 1906, they moved some processes to the closed Daniel Bernard's brewery building in Gorgie and used the open ground on the opposite side of the Gorgie loop for cultivating pharmaceutical plants. T. & H. Smith merged with the pharmaceutical firm of Duncan Flockhart & Co. in 1952, and in 1960 with J.F. MacFarlan, forming MacFarlan Smith Ltd. The holding company of Edinburgh Pharmaceutical Industries was bought by Glaxo in 1963, but a 1990 management buy-

An August 1930 aerial view of Daniel Bernard's brewery (by then expanded and owned by the pharmaceutical firm of T. & H. Smith) in the foreground and the North British Distillery and Tynecastle Park of Heart of Midlothian FC above.

John Jones Collection

out acquired MacFarlan Smith from Glaxo and now operates as Meconic plc, retaining MacFarlan's old telegraphic address and trademark, from the old brewery at 10 Wheatfield Road in the fork of embankments bearing Gorgie loop and Haymarket Central lines. The Westfield Road access now links into the Western Approach Road.

The railway siding connection was controlled by an Annett's Key-released ground frame, interlocked with suburban line signals. The signalman withdrew the key from his frame and gave it to the guard or shunter who then showed it to the driver as the authority to pass Gorgie Junction's 'Outer Circle' advanced starting signal at 'Danger'. The ground frame was then unlocked for shunting, no wagons being left on the main line. When finished, points were reset, locked and the key returned to the signalman who replaced it in the frame, to resume normal working. Siding alterations were made in 1908 at the firm's expense when the loop was dispensed with. The siding next to the suburban line was slued, straightened and buffer-ended 4 ft 6 in. from a coalbunker at the south end of the former loop. The loading bank line nearest the brewery was shortened and buffer-ended and thereafter, the firm had three buffer-ended tracks, all on their own land, although the 'sub' points (and protecting trap points) were on railway land. The connection was later removed after the firm's rail traffic ceased.

Gorgie

'Gorgie' dates from the Robert the Bruce era, the name said to derive from the Welsh 'Jorcyn', or a wedge of land between the north of Craiglockhart Hills (the 13th century 'Craggis de Gorgin') and the Water of Leith at Roseburn. Gorgie Mill existed by 1494, the dam or Mill Lade flowing from a water chord below Fords Road, giving Damside and Damhead their names and by 1733 also served Gorgie and Dalry mills. Wester Mains of Gorgie appear on 19th century maps as West Gorgie, a name revived in 1983 for streets built in its fields, although some claim the name is derived from Gorgie Farm. In 1812, Gorgie Park was on Slateford Road, east of Moat Drive, the name 'Gorgie Road' appearing only c.1883.

The original station was of a small wayside type midway along a cobbled road linking Slateford Road with Gorgie Road. The goods yard had five buffer-ended sidings, one with a small goods shed. To the west was Cox's Glue Works and, at a time when social conditions for employees were usually less than desirable, Robert Cox, the then owner, had provided 'model cottage dwellings' of two and three apartments with 'a large closet' for his workforce near the works. His tenants also had a coal yard, bleaching green, a schoolhouse with visiting preacher on Sunday evenings, and the equivalent of today's licensed grocer. This area formed most of the local housing when the railway opened.

The railway formed the Municipal Boundary after 1882, and apart from the Mills there was only agriculture to the west. To the east, T. & J. Bernard's Edinburgh Brewery and to the north the North British Distillery were being built and both wasted little time becoming rail connected. Within 20 years, industrial and domestic premises surrounded the station although dwelling houses were criticised as providing minimum facilities for maximum rent.

When the railway opened, public transport along Gorgie Road was by horse bus, replaced by horse trams under an 1896 Act, extending to the new city boundary after 1897. Cable trams appeared on 14th December, 1900, achieving all of 9½ mph after 1905, and on 22nd October, 1922, the first electric trams rumbled along Gorgie Road to Robertson Avenue next to the railway bridge. In December 1922 a single siding

This bridge carried the suburban line, and branch to the North British Distillery, over Wheatfield Road. On the right beyond the bridge is the former headquarters of Daniel Bernard's Brewery (now McLaggan Smith) and in the background, another bridge carries the line between Gorgie and Haymarket West Junctions (the Gorgie Loop) over the same road.   *Author*

was authorised in Wheatfield Road for tram standage for Heart of Midlothian Football Club matches at nearby Tynecastle Park, but this was changed to be west of the bridge, in 1925 blossoming into a full depot for 70 trams. An open air bus park with basic workshop opened next to this on 3rd June, 1951, six bus routes being garaged there. Closed to trams in April 1953, the bus depot lasted to 1957 when the site was sold. With the tram depot doors bricked up, it became a North British Distillery warehouse with another warehouse alongside.

Slateford Road was at the north end of the station road, but not densely populated. Electric trams started on 8th June, 1910 over the 1¼ mile line between Slateford and Ardmillan Terrace as a cable car link from Gorgie Road would have had ducting problems on the bridge over the railway approach to the then new cattle market. Four cable cars were converted to electric traction with overhead current collection and were operated by the Edinburgh & District Tramways Company as a discrete route from a trailing junction at Ardmillan Terrace outwith their then operating lease. For the next decade, this was the only bit of Edinburgh with electric trams, the rest of the city remaining wedded, with growing public disenchantment, to its cable system. Residential housing along Slateford Road developed after World War I and to provide a better service, the Ardmillan Terrace junction was relaid as a facing double junction from the city, through electric trams starting on 29th April, 1923, the single track with passing loops being doubled throughout in 1926. A bus service from Waverley serving Slateford Road also started in April 1923.

Gorgie (Station) Signal Box

No drawings appear to have survived for the 1884 Gorgie signal box and it is not mentioned in a Board of Trade Inspector's report of February 1884 covering suburban line signalling, although a NBR report of September 1884 stated that the box was being roofed. The box is shown in the 1892 plan for resignalling Gorgie and scaling this indicates dimensions which are in line with the drawing of the wooden 'Pointsman's Cabin' of February 1884. Sited at the Haymarket end of the yard sidings on the down side of the line, it was 275 feet from the bridge over Gorgie Road, its rear overlooking the slope and shallow cutting of the station approach road. Steps to the operating floor were at the Gorgie Road end, and it had two rear structures of indeterminate function. Near the goods yard throat and opposite the connection for the North British Distillery branch, standage sidings, and Bernard's brewery, it was ideally sited for that time, but not for the future.

J. & G. Cox, owners of the nearby glue works had made a provisional agreement with the NBR in 1890 for a branch into their premises. However, although nothing came of this at that time (it took 15 years to come to pass), the siding would have added to the box's role. Meantime, Gorgie was expanding in both residential and industrial terms and the North British Railway appear to have considered that the time was approaching to review the signalling arrangements in the area, resulting in its 1892 resignalling scheme. Under this plan, the original box would be removed and replaced by one in the Gorgie Junction fork but this did not come to fruition until 1897. Meantime, the original box appears without identification on the 1893 Ordnance Survey map, almost as if in limbo.

Gorgie Junction and Signal Box

Initially, this was a plain 'Y' junction immediately north of the bridge over Gorgie Road controlled by Gorgie station box and bearing a 20 mph speed restriction regardless of route or direction but the plans of 22nd January, 1892 showed the new box in the fork of the Haymarket West and Central Junction lines. Sidings on the up (Inner Circle) side, hitherto operated by the station signal box, were to be worked from a dwarf ground frame controlled from the new box, but this evolved into a smaller second cabin opened concurrently off the Craiglockhart end of the Outer Circle platform and which became Gorgie South. Endeavours and agreements made (and unmade) to form the branch to Gorgie Mills, and reshaping the goods yard lines may have delayed implementation.

Scaling up plans, Gorgie Junction box was 23 ft 0 in. (26 ft 0 in. over steps) long by 13 ft 0 in. wide and a typical North British box of the period, differing slightly from the previous designs. The signalman operating the locking frame faced the North British Distillery. Opened at noon on Sunday 14th February, 1897, as well as Haymarket West (604 yards) and Central (813 yards) Junctions, the new box worked at various times to Gorgie South (616 yards), Morningside Road (1 mile 836 yds), and Craiglockhart Junction. Its control area also varied over the years, dictated by signals and pointwork changes.

The bridge over Gorgie Road, which carried three tracks (two suburban main line and the siding for the North British Distillery) was widened and strengthened by 1903 and the former down sidings headshunt extended to form a down loop from Gorgie yard towards Haymarket West Junction. This enabled trains departing from Gorgie yard to leave without fouling the line to Haymarket Central and may have been affected by discussions taking place with Edinburgh Corporation for a branch to the

GORGIE JUNCTION
SIGNAL BOX

10th MAY, 1930

41 WORKING LEVERS
4 SPARE LEVERS
(8 21 42 43)

Down Line Sidings
Ground Frame release
lever 45 in signal box.
Phone at Ground Frame.

1. Haymarket West to up main distant.
2. Haymarket West to up main home.
3. Haymarket West to up main points.
4. Haymarket Central to up main distant.
5. Haymarket Central to up main home.
6. Up main starter.
7. Up main advanced starter.
8. Spare.
9. Stone Lye to Haymarket West points.
10. Stone Lye to Haymarket West signal.
11. Down main to Haymarket West points.
12. Facing point lock bar for No. 11 points.
13. Down main starter to Haymarket Central.
14. Down main junction home to Haymarket Central.
15. Down main intermediate home.
16. Down main inner home.
17. Down main outer home.
18. Haymarket Central down main line inner distant.
19. Haymarket West down main line inner distant.
20. Down main outer distant.
21. Spare.
22. Down main advanced starter.

23. Down main starter to Haymarket West.
24. Down main home to Haymarket West.
25. Down main to up line sidings.
26. Down main to up main line points.
27. Down main to up main line.
28. Down main to up line sidings.
29. Up line sidings to down main.
30. Up line sidings shunting.
31. Up main line to down main line signal.
32. Up main line to up or down line sidings disc.
33. Haymarket Central down main backing signal.
34. Down main line to down sidings.
35. Down sidings to down main points.
36. Down line sidings to down main.
37. Haymarket West to shunting siding signal.
38. Shunting sidings to Haymarket West points.
39. Shunting sidings to Haymarket West signal.
40. Down line sidings shunting.
41. Release for 3-lever ground frame (mechanical).
42. Spare.
43. Spare.
44. Release for 8-lever ground frame (electrical).

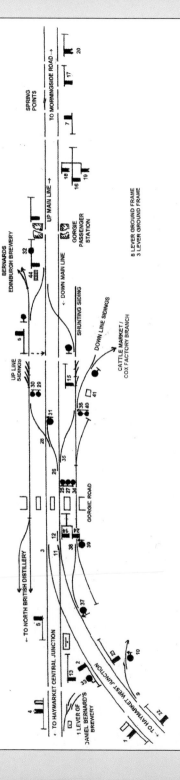

GORGIE JUNCTION

proposed Gorgie slaughterhouse and cattle market. No similar avoiding facility existed for arrivals from the north and west. The opening of the Gorgie Mills branch in May 1905 and the 'branch off the branch' to Gorgie Cattle Market sidings in June 1910 only marginally affect its workload as these were controlled by the yard staff.

On 20th March, 1924, a scheme was drawn up in the quest for operating economies by the LNER in which it was proposed that both Gorgie Junction and Gorgie South boxes, opened concurrently in 1897, be closed and their work transferred to a single new box in Gorgie goods yard near the site of the original Gorgie signal box. This proposed structure was to be no less than 37 ft 6 in. long by 13 ft 0 in. wide, and sited between the down suburban main line and the down line sidings where the points from the up main line joined the down line sidings. Doubtless it would have been built to North British Railway designs, similar to that of 1927 at Berwick-upon-Tweed. The cost of the Gorgie scheme as at 16th February, 1924 was estimated as £7,190 with £4,612 charged to Revenue, but it was decided not to proceed at that time.

In 1931, a minor resignalling scheme was undertaken at Gorgie when a new 44-lever locking frame was installed and arrangements made to close Gorgie South box, involving a degree of additional siding controls by ground frames released from the Gorgie Junction box.

The workload of the box was only marginally reduced with the opening of the Craiglockhart Spur in March 1959 which gave westbound freights direct access to the former Caledonian lines, and the withdrawal of the passenger train service in September 1962 had little effect. However, the opening of Millerhill up yard in 1962 and the down yard in 1963, meant that north and west freights could pass through Waverley, avoiding the Suburban altogether. Local domestic coal traffic was affected by the 1966 Haymarket Coal Concentration scheme and the loss of traffic to road led to a decline in Gorgie as a rail centre, exacerbated by cattle market relocation and

Gorgie Junction signal box opened on 14th December, 1897 concurrent with one south of the station. Originally, Gorgie had a single box between the station and bridge over Gorgie Road, but as operating demands grew, it was unable to cope. Gorgie Junction box reflected the North British architectural styles of the period when it opened and closed on 14th December, 1975, having absorbed Gorgie South in 1931. *Author*

closure of the glue works and brewery. For most of its existence, Gorgie Junction box had been open continuously from 11 pm on Sunday nights to 6.00 am on the following Sunday, but from the late 1960s some weekend shifts were withdrawn. The days when 'down' freights literally followed each other from Niddrie West had gone forever.

Under the Edinburgh resignalling of the 1970s, the double line between the Gorgie and Haymarket Central junctions was singled, the Outer Circle track being taken out of use and then removed on 30th November, 1975. Initially, semaphore signals for trains from Haymarket Central remained operational, there being no connection from the former Outer Circle line to the new single line, but a new facing crossover was installed at Gorgie Junction a month later and colour light signals commissioned. The then bi-directionally signalled former Inner Circle line became the 'Up and Down Haymarket Curve', 'up' referring to trains travelling towards Haymarket Central. Gorgie Junction box survived for a further fortnight but on 15th December, 1975 its remaining work was transferred to a panel in Haymarket Relay Room near Duff Street Junction, and on 3rd October, 1976 to Edinburgh Signalling Centre. Gorgie Junction box was then demolished.

Gorgie Locomotive Workings and Servicing

Initially, a simple headshunt sufficed for Gorgie goods yard on the Outer Circle side. By July 1904, this was extended to form a through loop line after widening and strengthening the bridge over Gorgie Road and extended to make a trailing connection into the 'down' Haymarket West line. Yard connections to and from the Suburban were unchanged. The branch from the goods yard throat to Gorgie Mills opened in 1905 and, in 1910, Edinburgh Corporation opened their City Cattle Market branch, which was taken from the Gorgie Mills branch.

Gorgie pilot engines were supplied from Haymarket depot, and at the start of the 20th century there were two double-shifted engines, one from 6.00 am on Mondays purely for shunting and the other shunting when not giving banking assistance to Morningside Road. Outwith the hours of the latter, providing banking engines was a relatively complicated business. With the communication system then in use, it was laid down that between 6.00 am and 6.00 pm, trains from the north and west requiring assistance called at Dalmeny and Ratho respectively. These stations wired Haymarket West who in turn telephoned Gorgie to telephone Niddrie West to immediately send a pilot engine. Between 6.00 am and 10.00 pm should wagons of livestock arrive at Gorgie, Haymarket Depot was telegraphed to send a pilot to Gorgie to trip the wagon/s to Haymarket where the cattle market was before moving to Gorgie.

With the enlargement of the goods yard, and opening of the two branches, the number of engines working in the area rose. To get the best use, a simple servicing facility was created on a buffer-ended line that made a trailing connection on the site of the original headshunt, now part of the through line to the Gorgie loop. Haymarket engine sheds were only half a mile away, but it saved light engine mileage running to and from the shed by main line engines serving the cattle market sidings and which could also turn on the Gorgie triangle. The facility comprised of only a brick-built water tower and column, engine pit and bothy beside the station cart road on the site of the original 1884 Gorgie signal box.

By 1922, increased workload led to the provision of two treble-shifted shunting pilots, one of which was also used for local trip working and the other for assisting to Morningside Road. An additional engine was provided mainly for livestock traffic and worked from 3 pm on Mondays and 9.00 am on Tuesdays and Wednesdays.

In the summer of 1949, Gorgie had four pilots. No. 1 was treble-shifted from 6.00 am on Mondays until 10.00 pm on Saturdays, to shunt the station and sidings. No. 2 worked from 12.15 am Mondays to 6.00 am Sundays, mainly to assist trains to Morningside Road and shunt at Gorgie as required. No. 3, double-shifted, worked from 9.00 am on Tuesdays and Wednesdays only, making trips on Tuesdays to Dalmeny for livestock, shunting the cattle market and station and making other trips as required. Single-shifted No. 4 did not operate on Tuesdays and Wednesdays, but shunted and assisted as required. Gorgie Pilots were usually six-coupled 0-6-0 tanks (latterly LNER Class 'J88'), the larger 'radial' 0-6-2 tanks (LNER class 'N15') undertaking heavier duties.

Gorgie Mills Branch

Mills had existed in Gorgie since the 13th century. The Cox family, grain millers in Linlithgow since 1725, arrived in 1798 and stayed for 170 years. Initially milling corn on the north side of today's Gorgie Road, Cox diversified into leather tanning and glue manufacturing in 1799 on vacant land on the opposite side of the road. Glue making was highly suited to open air sites, not being the most pleasant treat offered to one's olfactory system.

Animal hides arriving in the factory were stored in dry warehouses before being steeped in open pits for up to three months in a softening mixture of lime and water. Pits were stirred occasionally to ensure proper preparation before removal for washing to remove impurities. The hides were then boiled in large vats inside the factory, producing a jelly like mixture that solidified after cooling which was then sliced, stacked and dried before grinding into powder for bagging and dispatch. Production depended on a good clean water supply, available from spring water piped from reservoirs after the mill lade of the Water of Leith became contaminated. In 1900, the firm entered the domestic culinary market with table jellies in several flavours, although glue production remained its staple industry.

It took 15 years to provide a siding into the works. Agreements made on 13th and 27th March, 1890 between the NBR and Robert Cox failed to produce a siding. Further agreements were concluded with the Trustees of the (by then) late Robert Cox and Harold Bennett Cox on 19th April, 1899 and then with J. & G. Cox Ltd in 1901. These also failed to produce sidings. Eventually agreement was reached in 1904 between trader and railway for the latter to make at its own expense a railway through Gorgie Park (between suburban line and Slateford Road) into the mill. The siding had 143 yards on railway land and 1,367 yards on the trader's, the cost being estimated at £3,013, the railway bearing the cost and retaining ownership of the materials. Cox paid for a wagon weighbridge built under the railway's supervision, but the railway bore the cost of the loop line on which it was installed.

The branch was a single buffer-ended line flanked for much of its length by a long loop to the south and the weighbridge loop to the north. At Gorgie goods yard throat, the branch crossed the station road on the level (without gates) before heading west to the mill in a 'headshunt' arrangement where the wagons reversed, entering the mills by a bridge over the mill lade into a group of buffer-ended sidings. Due to the gradient, wagons had to be brought to a stand before uncoupling from the engine, and none were allowed to stand on the hill, the curvature forbidding the use of six-wheel vehicles. The branch opened on 17th May, 1905 and later that year the trader added a loading bank siding on his land west of the mills on a 1 in 30 falling grade. The points and first 22 yards of this were NBR property and two

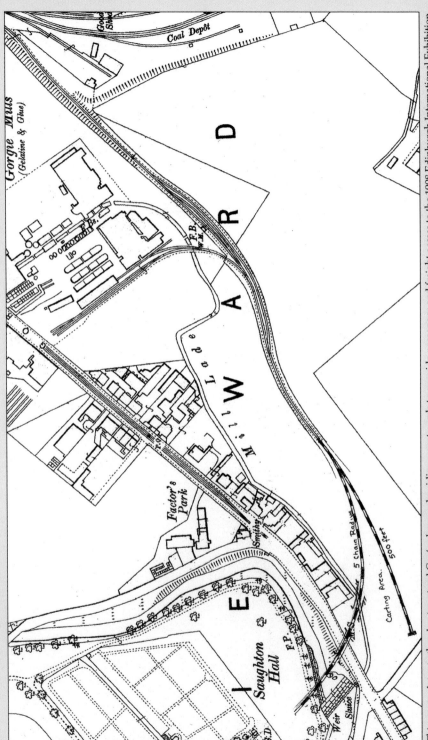

This map relates to the plan to extend Cox's glue works sidings westwards to provide passenger and freight access to the 1908 Edinburgh International Exhibition (later the Scottish National Exhibition) held in the grounds of Saughton Hall Mansion. The projected line, which would have included a bridge over the Mill Lade and a trestle viaduct over Gorgie Road, is shown with a broken line. Passenger access for the exhibition later came from a new temporary station on the Corphorstine branch at the place where the LNER installed Balgreen Halt in 1934. Freight for exhibition was dealt with at the NBR Gorgie Goods station.
Reproduced from the 25″, 1908 Ordnance Survey Map

existing sidings had their points repositioned nearer the branch junction at Gorgie. In June 1906, more changes were made at Cox's expense (£234).

On 19th March, 1907, the NB prepared plans to extend the branch (which was its property) into the Edinburgh (later Scottish) National Exhibition that was open from May to October 1908 in the grounds of nearby Saughton Hall. A new bridge was to carry this extension on a 5 chain radius curve over the mill lade and then by trestle bridge over Gorgie Road. Points on this line provided for a buffer-ended 500 feet-long siding alongside a suggested 'carting yard' with access to a farm road (today's Moss's Road). These plans were not progressed and instead a temporary station was built at Balgreen on the Corstorphine branch (and on the up north main line). This was removed after the exhibition closed, but a new passenger only station, Balgreen Halt, opened on the same site in January 1934 to serve new domestic housing schemes.

On 29th June, 1912, Cox's arranged locally for the use of their siding by Messrs Melville, Dundas and Whitson for off-loading equipment and materials next to the siding that the latter leased from Edinburgh Corporation.

The NBR supplied track for an additional siding, a new gate across the line and relevant signalling in 1921. When complete, the trader covered the railway's costs and took over ownership of the loading bank line south of the Mill Lade.

With the decline in traffic, the sidings closed on 25th May, 1968, the rails being later removed. Latterly an important factory product was a special adhesive for match heads, but after sourcing cheaper materials from abroad, Bryant & May, who had taken over Cox's premises and business, closed the entire Gorgie plant in 1969 with the loss of some 70 jobs. The mills were later demolished and the site occupied by a telephone exchange and new housing, aptly named Coxfield.

Gorgie Cattle Market Sidings

A Charter granted by James III in 1477, stipulated that cattle were not to be brought into Edinburgh, but sold outside the city wall, at sites such as in the Grassmarket and Kings Stables Road in the lee of Edinburgh Castle. In 1843, the market moved to Lauriston Place and new premises east of Lady Lawson Wynd (now Street) and the Edinburgh Slaughterhouses Act of 1850 legislated for standards of hygiene on meat for human consumption. In 1900, part of the 1843 site was taken by the Fire Station building that is still on the site and the rest moved out in 1907 to make way for the College of Art. Cattle auctions were then being held in Tollcross and in a building in Haymarket NBR goods yard that housed Edinburgh Ice Rink after the cattle market closed when a new site at Gorgie opened.

Discussions had taken place for some time on a site for municipal cattle market and slaughterhouse and, after investigating several alternatives, Edinburgh Town Council decided in 1902 to lease 25 acres in a 'green field' site near Gorgie Farm with good railway access potential. The Caledonian Railway main line out of Princes Street passed a few hundred yards south and the NBR suburban line to the east.

The North British Railway produced plans for a branch and sidings to serve the new site, the first being completed on 31st October, 1903, and showed the extent of its projected sidings, connecting lines and the siding that was to be shared with the Caledonian. The slaughterhouse was to the north of the sidings with access from a loading bank that could hold 40 wagons, engine and van on a loop that enabled either Caledonian or North British trains to arrive and engines to 'run round' for return to their respective lines. There were three buffer-ended sidings with a total

An August 1930 aerial view of Gorgie with Cox's Glue Works in the foreground, with the railway goods yard and concrete works at the top of the photograph.
Bill Roberton Collection

capacity of 104 wagons at the Gorgie end of the loading bank for wagon standage. Two more loading bank-equipped sidings each with 35 wagon capacity were south of the 'through' line, accessible only from the NBR Gorgie yard, and with their own reception and departure lines. Before the final arrangement was defined, several other schemes were developed, modified and discarded.

Construction of the new markets started in 1909 and in 1910 the Corporation made an agreement with the North British and Caledonian railways to provide railway facilities, engineers for the branch being Blyth and Westland. The Corporation built and paid the costs of the branch between a new road east of the markets (Chesser Avenue after the then Convenor of the Council Markets Committee) and the North British boundary at Gorgie where it joined the Gorgie Mills branch. The NBR bore the cost of works on its own land and had exclusive rights to work and operate the branch, assuming financial responsibility for maintenance. The Caledonian's Slateford market branch had a similar arrangement.

Sidings provision for this 'Mineral Line', were lavish. At the Gorgie station end, the branch connected with Cox's branch on North British land, and here, the railway supplied the track, which ran adjacent to the Gorgie Mills line, approaching the platforms by three parallel interconnected lines. The north line was for departures and the south for arrivals, the centre road forming a reception siding for incoming trains or rounding, but trains or wagons could be propelled in any direction if required. At the markets end were six main platform lines and four smaller ones to the north and the 3,600 feet total platform frontage could accommodate up to 200 cattle wagons at a time. Trains discharged their cargoes, the beasts being driven along the platforms and under Chesser Avenue to the market wherein was included the slaughterhouse. There were fewer Caledonian sidings but these were geographically better placed. The new markets officially opened on 8th June, 1910, the official party being conveyed along Slateford Road in the first Edinburgh electric tramcars!

In March 1913 under an Agreement between the Corporation and the two railways, the former provided the ground for a line to link the two separate branches. The Caledonian were to build the line, costs being divided between Corporation ($\frac{1}{2}$) and railways ($\frac{1}{2}$) and ran from west of the Caledonian's Slateford station, around the market by a single line under Chesser Avenue. This enabled the Caledonian to have its own loading bank on one side of a loop, reducing its need to proceed to Chesser Avenue and thus to the NB area. The link line was started, but never finished, although two sidings in the NB area, neither of which had a loading bank, were considered as joint Corporation, North British and Caledonian Railway lines. One would have been the link line and the other a siding on the north side of the smaller group. In 1928, the through line from Slateford was raised as technically it was still in abeyance, but after discussions, all concerned agreed to cancel the agreement, abandon the plan for this line and the 'link' siding was lifted. Meantime, the long North British end lines and platforms proved useful to the military during World War I and indeed afterwards, handling troop trains in connection with Redford Barracks and removing pressure from passenger stations of both railways.

The October 1922 North British Appendix specified the working method for the approach lines to the platforms. With no conventional signalling, drivers were cautioned to run at speeds that would enable them to stop short of any obstruction. Before leaving the branch at the Gorgie end, they had to stop clear of the incoming line until signalled forward by the shunter or person in charge. This was changed on 4th July, 1930 when it was agreed that trains could depart from the 'arrival' line, but only with the telephoned consent of the Gorgie yard foreman. By November 1947, departing

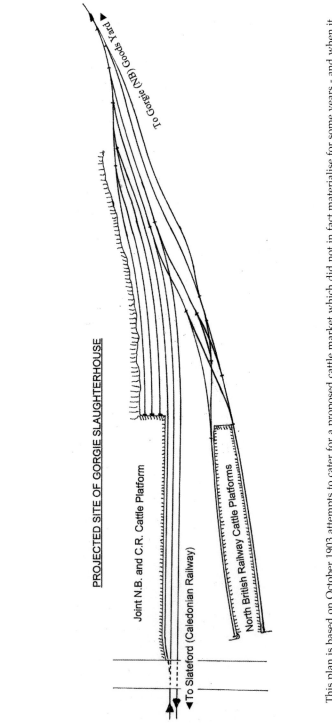

PROJECTED SITE OF GORGIE SLAUGHTERHOUSE

To Gorgie (NB) Goods Yard

Joint N.B. and C.R. Cattle Platform

▲To Slateford (Caledonian Railway)

North British Railway Cattle Platforms

This plan is based on October 1903 attempts to cater for a proposed cattle market which did not in fact materialise for some years - and when it did it was on a more lavish scale than that depicted here. Perhaps the fact the sidings and branch were built by Edinburgh District Council and not the NBR was relevant!

North British Railway

trains faced a fixed stop board (with a red light after dark) at the exit from their line that could only be passed on the authority of the yard foreman or shunter. These arrangements remained until the branch closed.

The presence of the slaughterhouse could lead one to think that cattle arrived in the sidings on a 'one way ticket', but there was a two way flow, auctioned cattle being loaded for an outward journey, sawdust being supplied by the railway free of charge. The farming community were approached in the market by the railway's commercial representative, known (before the days of fancy titles) as the 'canvasser', who had the task of outbidding competing road hauliers and also liaising with clerical staff at the station or in the sidings on traffic secured and vehicles required. Market day was generally a Tuesday, and extra railway staff (where possible from the station's relief complement) were drafted in to meet the demand. Cattle wagons were 'charged' by size, not by overall measurements, but by a moveable internal partition as 'small', 'medium' and 'large', a strange requirement in assessing wagon size being that beasts would be unable to 'go down'. Norrie Munro, a Gorgie relief clerk, recalled occasions when cattle wandered off, entering the narrow office on the platform, leading to very literal interpretations of 'push and pull working' to get it back out. One clerk was at the head pushing, and another at the rear pulling!

A private siding was laid at a cost of £335 for the Edinburgh Water Trust from the southernmost Cattle Market sidings approach line from Gorgie. The LNER carried out the work on 14th December, 1928 and the Corporation paid the costs.

Messrs Munro and Miller feud ground adjoining the Cattle Market sidings in 1942 to build a factory for making mild steel and copper tubes. After considering a jointly owned line, all parties agreed on 30th September, 1942 that the No. 1 loading bank siding of the Corporation would be allocated to the firm as a private siding.

In its heyday, special trains or wagons of cattle had run to and from the sidings from the Lothians and further afield, but cattle traffic by rail had declined in the face of road competition. Perhaps the final blow was the decision in 1964 of Scottish Regional management to consider only block train loads of cattle from ports to inland centres. The branch was cut back to its junction with the Gorgie Mills branch on 4th December, 1967, and removed entirely with the latter's closure on 25th May, 1968, the railway recovering its own track.

Edinburgh District Council inherited the Corporation's rails on the Cattle Market sidings branch and in February 1976 more than 2,000 feet of this was donated to, and lifted by, members of the Strathspey Railway Association, for their line between Aviemore and Boat of Garten. The branch embankment was made from landfill material and had been smouldering for years. As children used the area as a playground after the line closed, Edinburgh District Environmental Health Committee recommended spending £7,100 to remove the danger in September 1977. With all traces of the branch finally removed, domestic, retail and light industrial premises took its place.

North British Distillery Sidings

In 1884, the massive Caledonian Distillery at Haymarket was acquired by the consortium of the Distillers Company Limited (DCL). Seeing this as creating a virtual grain spirit production monopoly, a consortium of blenders and merchants led by Andrew Usher (credited with producing the first blended whisky in 1857) set up an independent grain distillery at Gorgie. This was virtually in a 'green field site' with room for expansion, as Gorgie tenements had not then reached that far west. Smaller than the

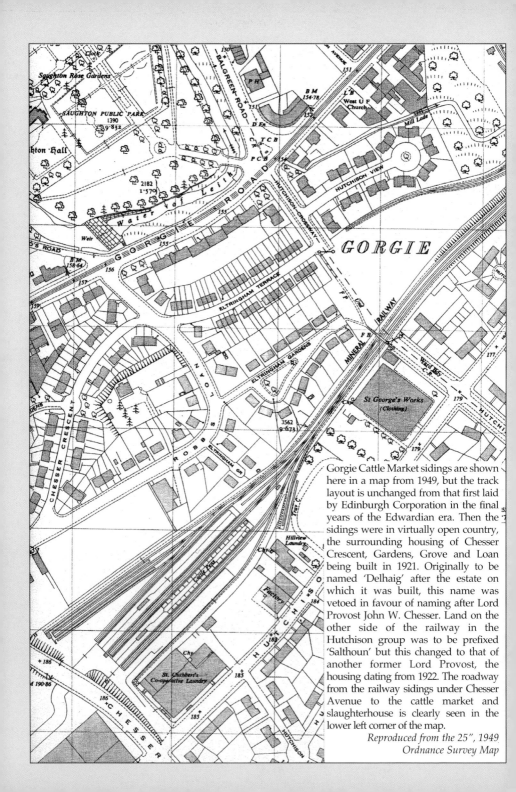

Gorgie Cattle Market sidings are shown here in a map from 1949, but the track layout is unchanged from that first laid by Edinburgh Corporation in the final years of the Edwardian era. Then the sidings were in virtually open country, the surrounding housing of Chesser Crescent, Gardens, Grove and Loan being built in 1921. Originally to be named 'Delhaig' after the estate on which it was built, this name was vetoed in favour of naming after Lord Provost John W. Chesser. Land on the other side of the railway in the Hutchison group was to be prefixed 'Salthoun' but this changed to that of another former Lord Provost, the housing dating from 1922. The roadway from the railway sidings under Chesser Avenue to the cattle market and slaughterhouse is clearly seen in the lower left corner of the map.

Reproduced from the 25", 1949 Ordnance Survey Map

Caledonian Distillery, it had easy potential access to the then new Edinburgh Suburban & South Side Junction Railway. Perhaps in defiance to the Caledonian Distillery at Haymarket, mainly served by the Caledonian Railway (CR), the new consortium's premises were named 'North British Distillery'. Whisky needs several years' storage and barrel standage and this venture was an act of faith created with a view to the future.

In early 1886, when the distillery was being built, the proprietors concluded an agreement with the NBR to form a siding into their premises. Rails, chairs, sleepers and other siding materials would remain the property of the railway who would also be responsible for repair and renewals. The Distillery discharged the Hypothec* over the siding materials on their land and the railway traffic potential was expected to be substantial.

The line into the distillery ran parallel with the suburban line and beyond the bridge over Gorgie Road a small loop was created before going downhill into the distillery in which there was a small internal network of buffer-ended sidings.

The distillery siding opened on 26th August, 1886, the NBR Siding Register noting that a 10 in. diameter water pipe was laid from the NBR-owned Union Canal along the suburban railway free of way-leave to the distillery and permitted a supply of process water, the distillery paying the railway £250 per annum. Two distillery sidings were extended under an agreement of 1889. The one at the foot of the Caledonian Railway's Wester Dalry branch embankment was extended by 44 yards and the distillery 'arrival' headshunt by 20 feet. The NBR Sidings Register also notes two more sidings laid at NBR expense in July 1901. Engines were able to run-round and shunt within the premises.

Whisky production went into abeyance between 1917 and 1920 when the premises were earmarked to produce acetone ammunition explosive for the Great War. Ironically, men returning from the services after the hostilities found the acetone plant in the middle of the distillery - unused. During World War II, the distillery again ceased distilling due to lack of materials and manpower, but diversified into fields such as cattle feed. Whisky production resumed again after the war, later rising to record levels!

In addition to wagons of fuel and other raw materials arriving and sealed vans departing, the sidings hosted distinctive wood wagons, with high sides and sloping roofs but without side or end doors. Grain loaded through roof hatches was discharged through hopper doors under the wagons. These wagons had grease axleboxes which severely restricted their speed but as the distance that they travelled was not great, this was not of real consequence. The final examples of these veterans were withdrawn in 1971 and, until the firm ceased using rail transport in 1973, rail-borne grain entered the distillery in more modern wood or all steel standard grain wagons, often from further afield than Leith Docks.

The distillery had its own engines, the first coming from Neilson & Co. in Glasgow in 1897, a second being added in 1927 from the North British Locomotive Co. at Hyde Park works. Both were later sold to the Shotts Iron Company in Lanarkshire and two Ruston & Hornsby diesel shunters taken into stock in 1945, one of which was scrapped in 1960, and the other in 1970. In 1958, a Ruston & Hornsby 4-wheel diesel mechanical shunter was bought with another in 1965. When the distillery withdrew from rail transport, both were stored before the older passed to the Lochty Railway in Fife in March 1974, and is now stored at Methil under the Kingdom of Fife Railway Preservation Society. The other went to the Scottish Railway Preservation Society on 3rd March, 1974 and ran under its own power at 10 mph along the Edinburgh and Glasgow main line, albeit with stops *en route* at Bathgate and Bo'ness junctions and is now at the Scottish Railway Museum at Bo'ness.

---

* The official legal wording is used here. 'A Hypothec' is a lien or security over goods in respect of a debt due by the owner of goods. In this instance, the NBR laid sidings on distillery land for which the distillery could have raised rent, but this right was discharged (or not used).

Prior to World War I, the cattle market sidings were extremely busy dealing with traffic for the city. Here, cattle wagons have been discharged at the two main island platforms with cattle flakes (a Scottish term for a cattle fence), probably awaiting removal of detritus at the siding group with two small island platforms north of the main yard. *M. Cant Collection*

This aerial view of Gorgie, which included the Cattle Market Sidings, is dated about August 1930 by which time the poaching practices or perhaps sheer convenience of road competition had seriously affected the economics of the cattle traffic by rail. *John Jones Collection*

The distillery sidings and main line connection closed on 1st August, 1973, although the distillery continues to produce grain spirit for blending, since 1993 as part of Lothian Distillers Ltd. It is now the last operating distillery in a city that was once able to boast a number of such establishments - on both sides of the law!

T. & J. Bernard's Edinburgh Brewery Sidings

The brewery officially opened in 1888, the attractive main office on Slateford Road being designed by Messrs Blanc and Gordon in 1887 in mixed Renaissance style with a round corner tower. Road access was from Slateford Road down a road behind the Inner Circle station building parallel to the railway and the footpath to the Inner Circle platform.

Agreement was reached in 1885 between the NBR and Daniel and John Mackay Bernard to provide a siding connection and this opened on 3rd March, 1885 although the plans were dated a month later! It was the first private siding at Gorgie, and its initial use was probably to bring construction materials to the site of the brewery. A goods line was laid alongside the Inner Circle suburban line on the approach to the station, and the connection was taken from the trap points at the Gorgie station end. The first 66 yards were curved left and on railway land before it crossed Bernard's access road before entering the brewery. The railway rented a triangle of ground from Bernard's at £1 per annum from Whitsunday 1891 on which a parallel railway siding was laid, but in 1900 Bernard's bought all siding materials from the NBR for £949 1s. 0d. In March 1895, T. & J. Bernard became a limited company to acquire the business, and survived as such until taken over in early 1960 by the Scottish Brewers consortium in Edinburgh. In April 1960, Scottish Brewers merged with Newcastle Breweries as Scottish & Newcastle Breweries and production at Bernard's Slateford Road brewery ceased.

The siding closed on 3rd May, 1971, and was later removed and many brewery buildings were demolished, the office block in Slateford Road being converted into domestic housing. Three large rectangular utilitarian brick storage bonds for the North British Distillery later occupied much of the brewery site with road access by the brewery lane from Slateford Road, but these were replaced by new bonds outwith the city. The site is currently being developed as domestic housing.

Inner Circle Wagon Standage Sidings

A goods line was laid parallel with the Inner Circle suburban line between the bridge over Gorgie Road and station platform. Bernard's Brewery siding was taken from this line in a 'Y' junction where it entered the suburban line, and the north end was extended across Gorgie Road to form the North British Distillery loop, branch, and sidings in 1886. Near the centre of the goods line, a connection trailed into the Outer Circle line, the Inner Circle being accessed at the station end.

Two long buffer-ended sidings were laid between the loop on the goods line and Outer Circle connection and a further four of differing lengths between the Outer Circle connection and brewery entrance, the latter groups having direct access to the Outer Circle line. The 'headshunt' for both of these groups was the approach line to the North British Distillery and these private siding traffics could be separated from goods yard operations. However, with the brewery closure, loss of the distillery rail traffic in 1973, and diminution of wagonload traffic, the sidings and suburban line connections were removed.

This bridge carried the suburban railway across Gorgie Road. The station entrance was from a slope by the gate on the extreme right and the large billboard was a familiar site for many years. The bridge was widened from two to four tracks, the two flanking the main line being goods lines, a low railing across the top of the girder was later sheeted in. In the immediate left foreground the road led to Gorgie tramway depot. *Author*

Gorgie Goods Yard and Sidings

Gorgie had the smallest goods yard on the Suburban when it opened in 1884, perhaps reflecting its then rural position. Initially, there were six buffer-ended siding lines with a common headshunt at the Haymarket end, rail traffic being confined between the railway and cart road linking Slateford Road with Gorgie Road which also served as the station footpath, its gradient being down from Slateford Road, level past the station buildings, then downwards again to Gorgie Road. The siding next to the suburban railway had a loading bank, and adjacent were two buffer-ended sidings, one of which had an 80 ft 0 in.-long by 26 ft 6 in.-wide goods shed containing a single track and equipped with a canopy on the roadway side. The small separate goods office was some 17 ft 0 in. long by 11 ft 0 in. wide at the buffer-stop end of the goods shed.

As Gorgie expanded, some sidings were extended and new lines added. In 1896, additional engineering work resulted in the goods yard siding accommodation virtually doubling in size, when a new 'raft' of sidings opened on the west side of the station cart road and pedestrian footpath on 29th November. These connected into existing goods yard sidings but as they crossed the station roadways, specific working instructions were brought into operation to ensure safety in working. Shunting over the roadway was restricted to 3 mph, and between 5.30 am and 11.30 pm, working arrangements required two shunters in attendance, where possible, one to ensure the road was safe and the other to shunt.

Working the longer new sidings required the original headshunt to be extended and the bridge over Gorgie Road acquired an additional western portion on its girders to accommodate it, the bridge itself being strengthened in July 1904. One of the two new long yard sidings had two shorter sidings connecting from it, coal traffic storage and distribution occupying most of the area, as with most urban yards. The westernmost original goods yard line was also extended over the cart road, dividing half-way down its extension into two buffer-ended lines. Revised instructions were issued on 26th October, 1904.

Known as 'Gorgie' until May 1952, passenger and goods stations became 'Gorgie East' to differentiate from the former CR goods station, dating from 1890 and slightly east of Slateford station, which became 'Gorgie West'. In the early 1970s, rail traffic decline and concentration of coal business at Haymarket, led to the goods yard closure and the site was cleared, providing a wild life habitat for some years. In 1994 it was redeveloped with 72 residential flats and spaces for eight small businesses, in the wake of traditional industry decline. The site was also used for a housing innovation that opened on 25th November, 1999, hailed as Britain's first car-free urban housing development. A mix of owner-occupier, rented and shared housing, residents in the 120 flat complex had to agree not to keep a car on the premises - there were no car parking spaces anyway - but they could still own one, creating friction in neighbouring streets.

Stone Depots Sidings

Two firms are identifiable as having stone depots within Gorgie goods yard, although not classified as private sidings.

William Forrest & Co. had offices at 21 Comiston Road (near Morningside Road station), and worked the Braehead East Quarry on the Benhar branch, using a rail-connected site in Gorgie yard for stone dressing. The single 233 ft-long, buffer-ended siding opened on 17th August, 1898, connecting with an existing goods yard line. The 65 ft x 30 ft stone works were at the buffer stops, the stone yard having a boundary fence punctuated only by the gate across the siding where it crossed the station cart road. Land and trackwork were the property of the North British Railway. When the new sidings opened in 1904, Forrest's connected to the rear of the new group west of the cart road. With a then 'standard' 8 ton mineral wagon length of 18 ft 3 in., the 233 ft-long siding could accommodate 12 such wagons within the gate.

Before World War I, the siding length was shortened by some 30 feet when a new larger works replaced the original. Now known as 'Victoria (Ordnance Survey states 'Victory') Concrete Works' mechanical handling equipment and more small buildings were gradually added, but these latter had gone by the early 1930s. The NBR 1921 List of Goods Stations shows the siding in use for stone dressing, but an LNER sidings chart shows the same siding also being used by the Builders' Supply Company for concrete work.

By 1930, the rail connection into the Victory Concrete Works had all but gone, the siding being cut back by some 60 feet and new buildings erected across its former trackbed. A new 90 ft loading bank was built at the repositioned buffer stop and the Edinburgh Collieries Company were using the siding. It is perhaps obvious to claim that the siding was used for coal traffic, but a number of collieries had their own brickworks and new domestic housing in the Slateford area was expanding. It is possible that the siding acted as a standage point for bricks arriving in coal company wagons, complementing the stonework, concrete and other building materials.

A contemporary aerial photograph shows eight wagons in the siding - but a 66 yard section of a 135 yard long siding next but one across was used by the Builders Supply Company. It was the same length in the same yard, but in a different position to that previously used by Forrest, and Builders Supply.

Another stone depot was located for a time in the goods yard and operated by Messrs J. Souden. Two buffer-ended sidings were allocated to this trader, adjacent to the west side of the cart road in the '1896' group of sidings.

Gorgie passengers and goods stations were halfway up a gradient between Gorgie Road and Slateford Road. This 1961 view from the latter shows the main entrance with the Outer Circle passenger buildings just visible in the middle distance, and the former cart road, by then resurfaced. *Author's Collection*

Seen from the station footbridge, class 'V3' No. 67605 enters the Inner Circle platform at Gorgie with the 1.45 pm from Edinburgh Waverley on 21st April, 1958. Three months later, the engine was transferred from St Margarets for the first time in its career, but returned in October 1961 to spend its final year at its old depot, being withdrawn in December 1962. This early afternoon service was usually formed of three instead of the usual five vehicles and adequately catered for the traffic on offer. Gorgie goods yard is behind the platform on the left, and on the right is Bernard's Edinburgh Brewery. *G.M. Stadden*

Chapter Six

Gorgie to Craighouse

Gorgie Passenger Station

Two hundred yards south of the bridge over Gorgie Road lay Gorgie passenger station. The Outer Circle platform and buildings had access on the level from the cart road that linked Slateford with Gorgie Roads. The Inner Circle platform had footpath access only from Slateford Road, the footpath being alongside the Edinburgh Brewery access road and a standard NBR iron lattice footbridge at the Craiglockhart end of the station buildings linked both platforms. The passenger station was below the level of Slateford Road and above that of Gorgie Road, and thus separate boards were positioned at both road entrances to highlight the route. Platform buildings contained the usual passenger facilities, and at first there was a booking office on each platform, operated by a booking clerk who changed offices according to the timetables. Latterly, the heaviest passenger loadings were towards Waverley and the Outer Circle booking office was retained, the other becoming an office for the station master.

On 1st May, 1908, the Scottish National Exhibition opened in the grounds of Saughton Hall Mansion, west of Balgreen Road and which today forms the Saughton rose garden and, public park and the NBR built a temporary station at Balgreen on the Corstorphine branch. Such was the public interest, separate facilities were also provided for passengers travelling via the suburban railway to and from Gorgie. For the period of the exhibition, the neat and sedate station became an animated hive of humanity!

Although its prime function was in dealing with commuters, the station was ideally placed for the Heart of Midlothian football club traffic at Tynecastle Park, and from 1925, the home of Scottish Rugby Union at Murrayfield. When 'home' games were being played, the station could be extremely busy, with special trains from the north and west (for football) and south and east (for rugby) and their return workings. The empty coaches were worked away to other locations, often suburban line goods yards, pending their return working.

The station was renamed 'Gorgie East' in May 1952, but there was no urgency to alter ticket stocks (there was never a Gorgie West passenger station) and 'Gorgie' tickets continued to be issued until stocks became exhausted, a process that took several years. However, as with other suburban line stations, it closed to passengers and passenger rated traffic in September 1962. The station master at that time was George Cowie, then nearing retirement, and in his office were two brass torches which he had used as a young railwayman, to light the gas in the carriage compartments. The torches had long wicks that were dipped in methylated spirits before being lit. As the station remained open for goods traffic, when George Cowie retired in February 1963, a former traffic apprentice, R. Henderson, succeeded him.

After a period when the railway tried to tempt a tenant, buildings and platforms were removed. The Outer Circle platform went on 21st September, 1975 but as the buildings had been demolished and the Inner Circle platform had been cut back to provide clearances for the Mark III coaching stock, little remained. Today, no trace of the station exists and the former cart road and footpath from Slateford Road has been considerably upgraded into an access road for the new housing on the site of the firmer goods yard and further down towards Gorgie Road, is reverting to nature.

Gorgie Outer Circle Station Buildings

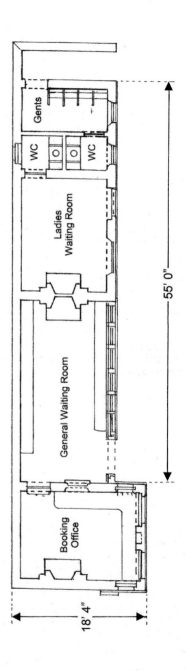

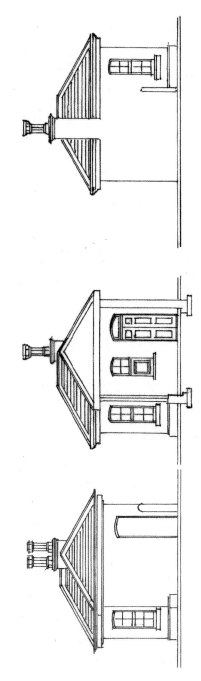

Elevation from Gorgie Road end (omitting 'decency wall').

Section through general waiting room looking towards booking office

End elevation from Slateford Road.

The Inner Circle passenger station buildings at Gorgie were a 'mirror image' of those on the Outer Circle, and including a booking office. As the predominance of passenger traffic was to the city, this latter office was to be reassigned for the use of the station master.

Gorgie station viewed from the south (Slateford Road) end. In the right middle distance is the brewery of T. & J. Bernard, and the station cart road linking Slateford and Gorgie Roads is on the left. Gorgie South signal box was sited at the near end of the left-hand platform between 1897 and 1931.   *J.F. McEwan/East Dumbartonshire Library*

4-4-0 No. 9504 *Glen Aladale* heads an Inner Circle train at Gorgie in the summer of 1924, in the apple green LNER livery and carrying the local headcode for Suburban passenger trains. Bogie coaching stock is of mixed North British Railway vintage. No. 9504 became No. 2488 in 1946 and survived in service until October 1960, latterly working occasional on passenger trains and on 'The Shunt' freight from Duddingston.   *R.W. Lynn Collection*

Gorgie South Signal Box

This was at the Craiglockhart end of the Outer Circle platform. In 1892, when plans were made to close the then single Gorgie signal box and relocate it in the fork of the junction, there was no mention of a second box, but there were references to ground frames being provided to control some siding connections. In the event it was decided to provide a signal box and the new signalling requirements were divided between Gorgie Junction and Gorgie South, both opening on 14th February, 1897. However, the bulk of the signalling fell upon Gorgie Junction, and the smaller Gorgie South operated as little more than an intermediate block post between Gorgie Junction and Morningside Road and led a rather precarious existence, being a ready candidate for closure. Dimensionally, it was 20 ft 0 in. long (23 ft 0 in. over steps) and 13 ft 0 in. wide. In 1924, a resignalling plan was drawn up, but not implemented, to replace both Gorgie boxes by a new larger structure near the site of the original Gorgie box. However, a new scheme was developed and agreed on 10th May, 1930, although not implemented until 12th September, 1931, which resulted in signal box closure at Gorgie South and removal of its crossover road and the mechanical clearance bar on the Inner Circle line siding points. An eight-lever ground frame, electrically controlled from Gorgie Junction, at the Haymarket end of the Inner Circle platform operated connections between Inner Circle and Outer Circle sidings and relevant retained former Gorgie South disc signals and a new semaphore, 60 feet off the end of the up platform. This was an 'outer back shunt signal' for movements from the up line to either the up or down line sidings. The former Gorgie South up home and advanced starter became the Gorgie Junction up starter and advanced starter respectively, its former down home becoming Gorgie Junction's down main inner home with a new down outer home provided 1,129 yards from Gorgie Junction. The Gorgie South mechanical down distant approaching Craiglockhart was replaced by a new outer distant 2,029 yards out, motor operated from Gorgie Junction but rarely worked (other, it was rumoured, than for officers' specials), being only a relatively short distance from Morningside Road's down starter. The Outer Circle was track circuited from Morningside Road down starting signal to Gorgie Junction down main inner home, clearance of four track circuits allowing Gorgie Junction to give the 'Train Out of Section' for a 'down' train without seeing its tail lamp.

Gorgie South to Craiglockhart

Leaving Gorgie on a slight left-hand curve, the railway heads south-east and after about 70 yards passes beneath the stone bridge carrying Slateford Road over the line. The gradient, uphill since passing under the Wester Dalry branch, now starts climbing in earnest at an average of 1 in 80 to Morningside Road, 1 mile 200 yards away.

One of the last 'splitting distant' semaphore signals in Edinburgh was on the Outer Circle line 93 yards on the approach to the Slateford Road bridge. This had distant arms bracket mounted to left and right of the single home arm on a central post and applied to the Haymarket West and Haymarket Central routes respectively, the distant arms being controlled from these boxes through a Gorgie Junction (originally Gorgie South) 'slot'. This fine lattice post signal was replaced in the 1950s by a smaller 'slotted' single arm distant on a tubular post and Gorgie Junction down outer home was removed.

IN THE ABSENCE OF DEFINITIVE FRAME NUMBERING, CODE LETTERS HAVE BEEN APPLIED.

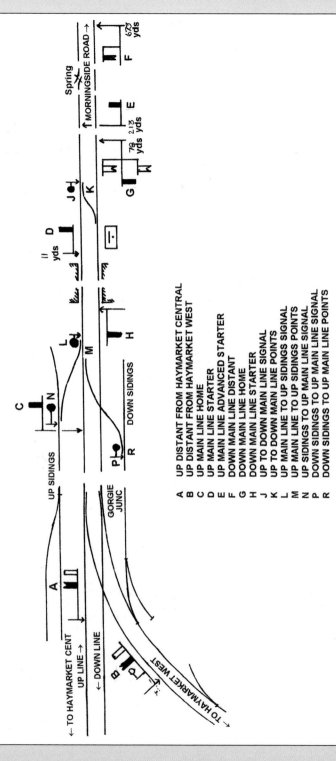

A   UP DISTANT FROM HAYMARKET CENTRAL
B   UP DISTANT FROM HAYMARKET WEST
C   UP MAIN LINE HOME
D   UP MAIN LINE STARTER
E   UP MAIN LINE ADVANCED STARTER
F   DOWN MAIN LINE DISTANT
G   DOWN MAIN LINE HOME
H   DOWN MAIN LINE STARTER
J   UP TO DOWN MAIN LINE SIGNAL
K   UP TO DOWN MAIN LINE POINTS
L   UP MAIN LINE TO UP SIDINGS SIGNAL
M   UP MAIN LINE TO UP SIDINGS POINTS
N   UP SIDINGS TO UP MAIN LINE SIGNAL
P   DOWN SIDINGS TO UP MAIN LINE SIGNAL
R   DOWN SIDINGS TO UP MAIN LINE POINTS

GORGIE SOUTH

10TH MAY 1930

A former War Department 2-8-0 locomotive pulls away from Gorgie heading a class 'E'
partially-fitted freight train and starts the climb towards Craiglockhart. To the rear is the
'splitting distant' signal with a single slotted home arm, but two distants, each controlled by
different signal boxes.   *Author*

From Slateford Road the line climbed towards Craiglockhart. The bridges over the Suburban in
the foreground conveyed the Caledonian Railway's Granton branch (now electrified and part of
the West Coast Main Line) and a few yards further on the Caledonian main line to Edinburgh
(now relegated to a service road bridge). In the middle distance is the embankment supporting
the Union Canal.   *Author*

One hundred and seventy yards from the road bridge, the Suburban passed under the Caledonian Railway's Leith and Granton branch and, 35 yards further on, the original Caledonian main line to and from Princes Street. When the Duff Street connection (now Haymarket East) opened on 5th September, 1964, the former branch became the main line (now electrified) and the former main line, the branch. On 5th September, 1965, Princes Street and Merchiston stations closed when their residual local passenger trains transferred to Waverley although limited freight continued as far as Morrison Street until 15th August, 1966, after which the rails were removed. The solum provided road access to Slateford yard, by then under the Civil Engineer, although whether by accident of design, one solitary colour light signal remained illuminated, but with no track to control!

The land above the cutting beyond the Caledonian main line bridge east of the Suburban had been developed as domestic housing by the Edinburgh Co-operative Building Society Ltd, between 1884 and 1894, streets being arranged in 'fishbone' style with back to back gable-ended houses in parallel terraces. All front doors were at ground level, arranged as two bay windows, four doors (two for upstairs) two bay windows, four doors, etc. Built on the Merchiston estate, the builders named the main street 'Shaftesbury Park' (possibly after the Earl of Shaftesbury), side streets bearing the names of wild plants such as Alder, Almond, Briar, Hazel, etc., all being suffixed 'Bank Terrace'.

The Caledonian Railway owned the land west of the cutting, between its main line and Union Canal. A small marshalling yard with 10 buffer-ended sidings was adjacent to its up main line from the late 1880s, the remainder of the land extending almost to Slateford station being later set out as playing fields until being partially used for domestic housing in the 1980s. A large water supply pipe supported on brick pillars (ostentatiously entitled an 'aqueduct' by Ordnance Survey), passed over the suburban line 130 yards beyond the Caledonian Railway main line bridge and 300 yards from the Union Canal tunnel entrance and this was duplicated on 19th October, 1947.

Craiglockhart (and Meggetland) District

District records exist from 1278 but the origin of the name is obscure, some sources claiming derivation from an ancient loch (in Gaelic, Craig-Loch-Ard = the high loch of the rocks), others linking it to the house of Alexander Lockhart of Covington built c.1780. However, the immediate locality (and Craiglockhart House) took the name from one of Edinburgh's seven hills nearby. The North British Railway named its then new station Craiglockhart in 1887 and the name spread over the intervening Meggetland estate (Meggetland House was only 200 yards away) and even part of Myreside. Much land in the area belonged to The Company of Merchants, formed in 1514 when Edinburgh Merchants drew up rules for their Guild to prevent illegal trading. They started to name streets in 1897 with Craiglockhart Terrace, part of which was parallel to, and overlooked, the cutting containing Craiglockhart station platforms.

Housing developed west of the station, at first mostly confined to the south of Colinton Road. Meggetland Terrace was for years the only commemoration of that estate, although playing fields north of the Union Canal were given that name that also leached to new housing beside the 1957 Craiglockhart and Slateford railway spur. Five minutes walk from Craiglockhart station was Waverley House (84

Colinton Road), which took its name from a writing instrument. The house was designed (some say over-designed) in 1884 by Sir James Gowans as a family residence for Duncan Cameron, head of the stationery firm responsible for the three types of pen nibs. They attained fame in the jingle, 'They come as a boon and a blessing to men, the Pickwick, The Owl and The Waverley Pen' which appeared on many vitreous enamelled advertising plates throughout the country. The firm's works in Blair Street were near Waverley station and when Craiglockhart opened in 1887, it is likely that Cameron was an early commuter. The house was sub-divided about 1970.

The last Edinburgh horse trams operated between Tollcross and the junction of Polwarth Terrace and Colinton Road until 24th August, 1907. After replacement by still relatively slow cable cars, trams were extended on 14th April, 1908 to near Craiglockhart Ponds, the area being known as 'Happy Valley'. Housing gradually spread towards Colinton village with a major army depot at Redford established before World War I *en route*, but public road transport only significantly improved when electric trams reached Craiglockhart station on 15th April, 1923, extending to Happy Valley shortly afterwards, and to Colinton in March 1926. Craiglockhart station was then largely by-passed and its importance declined.

Craiglockhart 1890 Exhibition and Stations

The 'International Exhibition of Electrical Engineering, General Inventions and Industry' opened on 1st May, 1890 and ran throughout that summer on land adjacent to the Caledonian marshalling yard and between the Co-operative Building Society houses and Union Canal on the east side of the cutting. Intended to demonstrate the then novel medium of electricity, it expanded to include other forms of engineering, even catering for those with an interest in fine arts although one cannot but feel that the latter was aimed at ladies accompanying their gentlemen! The machinery hall and adjacent 'Railway Court' were on the west side of the suburban railway cutting, a pedestrian bridge linking to the main site.

Both North British and Caledonian railways provided services to the exhibition. A joint station on the Caledonian Railway level was considered but unsurprisingly did not materialise. Eventually, both built temporary stations on their own lines, with direct site access, the Caledonian using a special section of track controlled by single line tablets. The North British merely built platforms on the gradient between Craiglockhart and Gorgie, temporarily replacing Craiglockhart station.

Although the suburban line station may have sufficed, the Union Canal interposed without a convenient crossing and pedestrian access to the main entrance in Polwarth Terrace was circuitous. This was also served by the Edinburgh and District Tramway Company, who altered and extended some routes to arrive at the gates using slow but frequent horse trams. The Union Canal on the south site boundary was used to demonstrate electrically-powered boats to a public who were invited to join in a short sail to Slateford and back for one half-penny. These were probably the last revenue earning passenger vessels to ply that particular stretch of water for the next hundred years! Some main line locomotives were on display in the Railway Court, the most interesting being the Great Western broad gauge single, *Lord of the Isles*. How it got there invites speculation! The NBR did not supply an engine, perhaps considering its new Forth Bridge to be a suitable engineering alternative.

The Edinburgh International Exhibition was held at Meggetland in 1890 on what was then open land on both sides of the suburban railway. The railway display included a number of items of rolling stock in the Machinery Hall on the west side of the suburban railway. In addition to locomotives from the North Eastern, Great Northern and (perhaps naturally) Caledonian railways, the old Great Western 4-2-2 *Lord of the Isles* was also on display. At that time, its 7 ft 0¼in. gauge from Paddington still had two years' life left before being converted to standard gauge. The NBR did not put rolling stock on display, but pointed the public towards its own recently opened engineering triumph, the Forth Bridge! The temporary NBR station on the suburban railway can be seen in the centre of the plan, with the Caledonian facility top left. The plan appears to indicate a single line siding with the connection near the site of today's Craiglockhart Junction into the exhibition area.

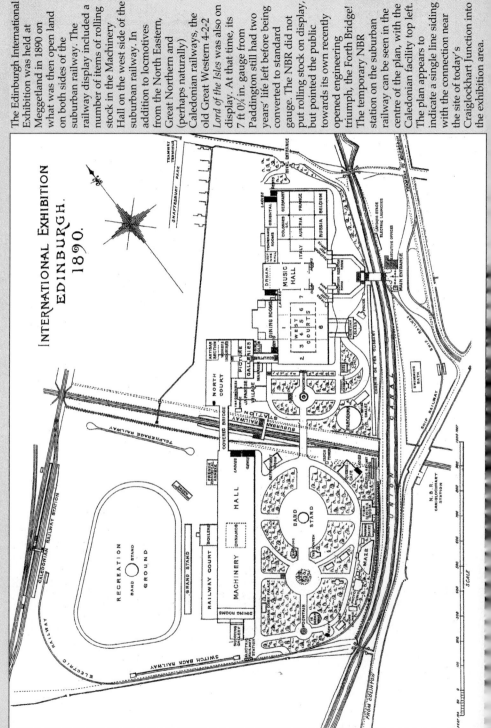

INTERNATIONAL EXHIBITION EDINBURGH. 1890.

For the International Exhibition of 1890, the NBR opened a temporary two-platform passenger station between Gorgie and Craiglockhart and during this period, Craiglockhart station was closed. Class 'V1' 2-6-2 tank No. 67617 is passing the Exhibition station site in August 1958 on its regular formation of two 1939 articulated twins flanking an older vehicle. The pipes across the cutting (colloquially termed as an 'Aqueduct') supply water to the houses on the right. *Author*

After the exhibition closed the railway facilities were dismantled, and domestic housing built above the east side of the cutting. Land west of the suburban line reverted to open fields (apart from more Caledonian sidings) until the mid-1950s when excavations started for the Craiglockhart and Slateford connecting spur line. The eastern end between curve and canal is now also a housing scheme, that further west dating from the 1930s. The central area, which includes the home of Boroughmuir Rugby Football Club, is still used for recreation, as is the now rejuvenated Union Canal.

Craiglockhart Junction and Spur

Although a connection between the North British suburban line and Caledonian Railway main line was mooted in 1880, this did not materialise until the mid-1950s under the British Railways modernisation plan. Finance became available for a double line connecting the Gorgie side of Craiglockhart tunnel on the suburban with Slateford station on the former LMS with the objective of improving freight movements from the Lothian coalfield to the west of Scotland. Sunday trains to and from Princes Street station were diverted around the Suburban into the east end of Edinburgh Waverley as the first stage of the closure of Princes Street station. Additional journey times involved did not seem to enter the equation.

A class '47' diesel locomotive leaves the Outer Circle suburban line at Craiglockhart Junction and heads for the Caledonian line with a rake of empty Freightliner wagons in September 2002. The short-lived Craiglockhart Junction signal box (in reality a large wooden garden shed) was to the left of the locomotive behind the buffer stops placed to stop runaways!   *Author*

Planning started during 1957, and construction works in the spring of 1958. To minimise main line disruption, the new line was built from the centre outwards and in October 1958 Slateford carriage sidings were closed, and the new line cut the connections to the goods sidings and small marshalling yard. Unfortunately this coincided with the biennial invasion of Welsh rugby supporters for the game at Murrayfield, and cleaning and servicing stock for the return journeys, hitherto a Slateford task, was carried out at Kingsknowe, Leith North and even Stepps, near Glasgow.

Double track from Craiglockhart Junction, the new line initially made a single lead junction at Slateford and after 15th February, 1959, trains to and from the suburban line passed through the westbound platform. Signalling there was by a 7-lever ground frame outside a grounded goods van body (a.k.a. signal box) at the east end of the westbound platform under Slateford (Caledonian Railway) signal box control. The double junction at Craiglockhart was scheduled for completion shortly afterwards and the new line was ready for opening on Monday 16th March, 1959. The first service train to use it was Edinburgh Area Trip Diagram E4 (Slateford - Granton) hauled perhaps appropriately by an LNER engine allocated to an LMS depot, namely class 'J39' 0-6-0 No. 64963 of Dalry Road. Three days later, the first 'passenger' train was a twin Craven diesel multiple unit conveying the Scottish Area Board of British Railways. The first diagrammed train was Edinburgh Area freight trip E46 (Portobello - Slateford), which officially started on Monday 30th March.

With most of the long Slateford sidings removed, shorter lines provided some compensation between the new spur and main Princes Street line. These were shared with the residual freight marshalling yard, and later transferred to the Civil Engineer who made adjustments to suit local requirements.

Craiglockhart Junction Signalling

Originally, Craiglockhart spur signalling was mechanical, controlled from a wooden ground level signal box (resembling a large garden shed) a few yards on the Gorgie side of the tunnel under the Union Canal. Sited a few feet behind a buffer stop-ended sand drag at the end of a short spur from catch points, had vehicles run away on the gradient from Slateford, the signalman would have had no chance, but fortunately the situation did not arise. The line from Slateford literally had a brick wall to stop runaways fouling the junction but that was to prove quite inadequate when put to the test. Both Craiglockhart Junction and Slateford Station 'boxes' were temporary until a new panel could be installed at Morningside Road and a new power signal box commissioned at Slateford Junction.

In Craiglockhart Junction box, the conventional lever frame had normal block instruments. On 27th November, 1960, the new Morningside Road panel was brought into operation with motor point operation and two, three or four aspect colour light signals. Craiglockhart Junction box was removed and the sand drag extended over its site. At Slateford, the new power box, commissioned on Sunday 18th December, 1960, took over from the 1888 Caledonian structure across the main line and the grounded van body at the junction to Craiglockhart. Concurrently, a double junction was installed at Slateford, as was power operation of the connections between both Craiglockhart lines and Slateford yard. Absolute Block working on the spur was replaced by Track Circuit Block.

These arrangements continued until under the Edinburgh resignalling, Morningside Road box closed on 26th June, 1977, and Slateford Junction power box on 17th August,

1981 the Craiglockhart line junction being altered to 'single lead'. Although Morningside Road box was removed, the Slateford structure was retained, being only 21 years old, later passing to 'First Engineering', the privatised successor to the railway's 'in house' civil engineering department. The area in front of the box, formerly occupied by a siding, was altered to feature several track and signalling items for staff training purposes.

The Edinburgh & Glasgow Union Canal Company

Edinburgh was something of a rarity, a pre-industrial age capital city without access to navigable water. The 35 mile-long Forth & Clyde Canal had linked Bowling in the west to Grangemouth in the east since 1790 and the idea of water communication throughout between Glasgow and Edinburgh was raised in 1793, and several surveys made. Some time after, the town council put these proposals to Mr Rennie, a London canal engineering authority for his opinion, but his response suggested a new single level link from Bruntsfield Links in Edinburgh to Hillhead in Glasgow. Nothing happened, however, until 1813 when the Forth & Clyde Canal proprietors suggested a collateral cut from their canal to Edinburgh on a line suggested by their architect, Mr Baird. Thomas Telford approved this in 1815 and a Bill was brought before Parliament, but being opposed by Edinburgh magistrates, was lost. Eventually, in 1817, after several other plans and meetings, Baird's plan was adopted and the Act of Parliament obtained.

Construction of the 31½ mile Glasgow & Edinburgh Union Canal linking Edinburgh to Falkirk, and by locks to the Forth & Clyde Canal, started in the Spring of 1818 and opened in May 1822 at the dawn of the railway era and at an estimated cost of £400,000. It gained the unofficial title of the 'Mathematical Canal' as it followed the 240 feet land contour, was 40 feet wide at the surface (apart from when it passed under some bridges), reducing to 22 feet at the bottom, yet was only 5 feet deep, its relatively narrow width restricting the size of the boats. Edinburgh had two terminals, the main one at Port Hopetoun, with coal being dealt with at Port Hamilton near Lothian Road. A whisky bond was near its Lochrin basin, and its infrastructure included three large aqueducts, a half-mile-long tunnel (to appease a local landowner) and 11 locks between the canals at the Falkirk end. A proposal made to extend it along the drained North Loch valley below Princes Street Gardens and terminate at Leith was never progressed.

Passenger facilities were not stinted. At one time, meals, music and even gaming tables were available, and even a night sleeper service between the two cities was claimed to have been popular with business, pleasure - and honeymooners!

The opening of the Edinburgh & Glasgow Railway in February 1842 marked a rapid decline in canal fortunes despite a vigorous but doomed price war. In 1848, it was sold to the Edinburgh & Glasgow Railway which commercialised its water, piping to breweries and distilleries as process water, and even supplying locomotives at Waverley station! Port Hopetoun basin was filled in during 1922 and the Lochrin Basin and Falkirk locks later although, for most of its route, it remained extant. Since the 1960s, under the British Waterways Board, the canal has been increasingly used for leisure pursuits, Edinburgh University, among others, using it for rowing training with a boathouse on the east bank, almost above the suburban railway tunnel at Craiglockhart, the public footpath being on the opposite bank.

The National Lottery granted finance in the late 20th century to redevelop and reinstate the Union Canal, and it was reopened throughout its length, albeit curtailed at the Edinburgh end. At Falkirk, it connected again with the Forth & Clyde Canal not by locks, but by the 'Falkirk Wheel', a massive engineering structure worthy of the 21st century. Once more, one can travel by water from Edinburgh to Glasgow and beyond across the central belt of the country, and in July 2003 a barge of road aggregate passed from Ratho along its length, its first commercial freight for nearly 70 years.

Proposed Union Canal Line to Tollcross

Drawings of 16th June, 1910 show that the North British Railway considered turning part of its Union Canal into a railway starting near Craiglockhart and terminating at Lochrin, near Tollcross in Edinburgh. Two railways were proposed, Railway No. 1 starting on the gradient after passing under the water supply pipe over the Suburban opposite the Caledonian Railway's Slateford Sidings. This would curve east in a cutting on a gradient of 1 in 70 and radius of 10 chains (220 yards) before easing to 1 in 100 and joining the (planned) drained bed of the Union Canal near Gray's Loan some 440 yards from its suburban junction. Railway No. 2 would start on the opposite side of Craiglockhart station, in the Myreside cutting near the playing fields pavilion on the west of the line. This line would then curve north-east in a cutting on a radius of 14 chains (260 yards), joining Railway No. 1 in a 'Y' junction when both attained the same level west of Harrison Road. From here the proposed branch was to head east towards the Lochrin district of Edinburgh terminating adjacent to the then Tollcross slaughterhouse where a major goods depot would be established next to the then cable car depot.

There is no indication on the North British plans whether the proposed lines would be single or double track, but it is probable that if it had gone ahead, all lines would have been double. The goods depot at Tollcross, had it been developed, would have involved significant upheaval to existing properties and included a new 60 ft-wide road from the corner of Morrison Street/Lothian Road, through Gillespie Crescent to Bruntsfield Place, being joined by a second road coming up Morrison Street from Haymarket. There is no reference to the scheme in the NBR minute books and nothing appears to have been developed beyond the preparation of plans. The reason for the scheme is also unclear, although the site for the proposed goods depot was available, as the slaughterhouse had moved out on 8th June, 1910 to the Gorgie cattle market. The 1 mile 660 yards canal branch would have given the North British a major goods depot in the west of the city, but only the drawings remain as a reminder of this potential period in Edinburgh's history.

Craiglockhart Tunnel

Craiglockhart Junction was a few yards from the mouth of the 65 yds-long tunnel that took the suburban railway under both Union Canal and Colinton Road. On at least one occasion during the excavations, the Union Canal burst through from above and work had to be suspended until it was repaired to the satisfaction of the North British Railway's Chief Engineer. Fortunately, the gradient towards Gorgie acted as a natural drain for errant water and indeed a canal overflow facility was provided nearby. After the station closed, the tunnel was lengthened to 78 yards by a concrete extension on the station side that occupied the site of the former wooden footbridge, supported a widened Colinton Road and eased a sharp and blind corner. However, by 2003, only the pavement was widened and fitted with 4 ft high wall.

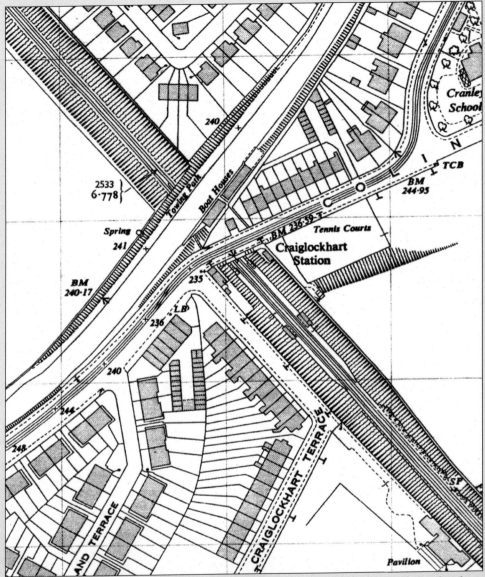

Opened on 1st June, 1887, Craiglockhart station had a brief early period of service, being closed on 1st May, 1890 when the Edinburgh International Exhibition opened on the north side of the Union Canal and an adjacent temporary station opened to cater for this event. After the exhibition closed, the station did not reopen again until 1st January, 1891, but was closed yet again as a wartime economy measure on 1st January, 1917, it being considered that adequate alternative public transport was available through the medium of the Edinburgh cable car system. It remained closed until February 1919, but thereafter maintained a very precarious commercial existence until final closure on 10th September, 1962 in line with the rest of the former Edinburgh Suburban & South Side Junction Railway. Ironically, it is now the most complete suburban line railway station, albeit only at platform level.

Reproduced from the 25", 1944 Ordnance Survey Map

Craiglockhart (Passenger) Station

Emerging from the tunnel, the line entered a cutting where over large areas, the nature of the soil dictated that the earth and stone sides be sheathed or supplemented by brickwork cladding with drainage holes. Although there was initial uncertainty regarding the station potential, the soil surrounding the excavations required stone retaining walls, and the opportunity was taken to set these 10 feet back from the line, providing space if a station was to be built at a later date. When the line opened, there was little traffic potential, and the horse tram terminus was only 150 yards to the east - in virtually open country. As Edinburgh expanded, passenger potential appeared and a basic passenger station was built.

This was a small single-storey rectangular stone building at street level on the corner of Colinton Road and after 1897 Craiglockhart Terrace and contained a booking hall, booking office (that doubled as staff room), ladies room and gentlemen's toilets. Evidence indicates that Craiglockhart had its own station master, and certainly in 1903 a Mr Underwood was in charge; it may well have been that the ladies room at street level was initially his accommodation. The building was relatively plain, the main street frontage having only a single window and wooden door into the booking hall. Waiting rooms on the platforms were timber fronted and inset into the cutting wall. A sturdy wooden footbridge straddled the line at the tunnel end of the platforms, with steps leading down from the station offices and the railway-owned footpath parallel with the line and along the top of the cutting on the opposite side of the line.

The station opened without ceremony on Wednesday 1st June, 1887 although it could by no means be classed as being in a populous area. Operationally, a heavy task was given to engines starting a train on the 1 in 70 Inner Circle rising gradient. Passenger potential was so sparse that, when the Duke and Duchess of Edinburgh opened the International Industrial Exhibition at Craiglockhart on 1st May, 1890, the NBR closed the station in favour of a temporary one nearer Gorgie, and it did not re-open until 1st January, 1891 some months after the exhibition closed.

Little changed over the years and during World War I the station was again temporarily closed from 1st January, 1917 until February 1919, one of 57 such North British stations. Although welcomed by traincrews, the closure criteria were actually based on the availability of alternative public transport services.

Nothing much changed over the next decade, but in trying to improve the building's appearance, the LNER invited tenders in August 1929 for replacing the booking hall wall on the Colinton Road frontage between sill and eaves by a timber and glass screen. The street wall was also lowered between booking hall and bridge over the line, to the new booking hall sill level, topped by iron railings, but retaining the drinking water fountain. All removed doors required to be reused! The drawing of the new frontage was dated 17th July, 1930, and the rebuilt structure remained thus until closure. A large wooden nameboard was affixed to the roof at street level, and this also lasted until the end.

There was no signal box, but Morningside Road up distant was located off the south end of the Inner Circle platform, the Gorgie South down distant being almost opposite it on the other side of the line between 1897 and 1931. The former survived, latterly with an upper quadrant arm, well into the British Railways period moving closer to the platform (and given intensified lighting) with the introduction of a new Morningside Road Inner Circle outer home in connection with the Craiglockhart and Slateford spur signalling. The Outer Circle distant was removed when Gorgie South

Craiglockhart station buildings on the corner of Craiglockhart Terrace and Colinton Road in its 1933 form when the large glazed areas were installed in place of the original stone walls with single door and small window. Just visible inside were handbills which were held in position by string passed through one corner and suspended from a nail!   *Author's Collection*

Craiglockhart platforms were connected (as were the station buildings and footpaths) by an attractive wooden footbridge of decidedly non-North British pattern. This succumbed to the need for adequate signal sighting for the semaphores initially installed for Craiglockhart Junction and was replaced by a utilitarian tubular steel structure. The original wooden footbridge is seem behind class 'J39' 0-6-0 No. 64794 on an engineer's train on 4th April, 1954.
G. M. Stadden

box closed, being replaced by a new motor distant out of sight of the station, but the Gorgie Junction outer home signal installed after 1931 on a right-hand bracket post, could be seen through the tunnel until the late 1950s.

On 22nd September, 1932, some 1,350 pupils and 70 teachers, of George Watson's (boys') College moved to new premises on Colinton Road. Previously Merchiston Castle School playing fields the new school lay about 715 yards from the station, offering welcome potential patronage. The LNER Advertising Manager got to work, and with the permission of the headmaster, supplied leaflets to all staff and pupils giving details of zone and season ticket rates, cheap day fares and a full Suburban Line timetable. This initially bore fruit, to judge by the number of maroon clad youngsters on the platforms, but the school was on a bus route, near other tram and bus services and the initial patronage gradually declined.

The wooden footbridge was replaced on 24th July, 1955 by a utilitarian steel structure a few yards along the platform, not on life expiry or for safety reasons, but to improve the sighting of semaphore signals that were to be temporarily installed for Craiglockhart Junction signal box. Actually, the footbridge was replaced at the second attempt as on the first, the crane positioned 'uphill' from the site ran away for a short distance on the 1 in 70 gradient, colliding with it. The semaphores were in turn replaced by colour light signals when a diagram in Morningside Road box replaced Craiglockhart Junction box. Maintenance costs of the waiting room fronts and canopies were considered too expensive, and they were replaced by a featureless corrugated iron roof projection over the now open stone-lined former waiting room recesses.

For administration, for most of its life Craiglockhart came under Morningside Road, whose clerical staff visited to check the books and deal with month end accountancy, daily booking and accounts work being undertaken by the porters. After the travelling cash box in a specified passenger train (popularly known as the 'Wells Fargo') was discontinued, one of the porters travelled to Morningside Road each lunchtime with the takings in a (small) padlocked leather bag. Latterly, manned by George Warren and David Campbell, they were opposites in personality and compatibility, and perhaps fortunately on opposite shifts! Boiling Brussels sprouts on the booking office open fire (the only cooking facility) was but one friction point. After the station closed, George moved to Waverley where he reluctantly drove a new mobile cleaning machine around the station concourse, but David just retired from the scene.

The street level buildings were later demolished, a new stone perimeter wall with curved coping was built along the edge, matching the original. The site was remodelled and a wider pavement 'landscaped' in paving stones. The footbridge was removed, apart from a section down to the Outer Circle platform from a gate in Craiglockhart Terrace. The platforms are still mostly intact, apart from the removal of their furniture and waiting sheds, but nature is trying to reclaim the surfaces.

Myreside Village

This district name combines the old Norse 'Myrr' or early Scots 'Mire' with the Anglo-Saxon 'side'. It was once near an expanse of water referred to by some as 'Jordanville Loch', near the source of the Jordan (or Pow) Burn. It was also the name of a farm on Merchiston Estate near today's George Watson's College and one of three villages (the others were Tipperlinn and Morningside) within the Morningside Estate when the Burgh Muir was divided in 1586. By the time that the suburban

Craiglockhart station from the Myreside Road end, looking towards the Union Canal tunnel in 1961. The old wooden bridge has been replaced and the junction for the line to Slateford lies just beyond the tunnel.   *J.F. McEwan Collection/East Dumbartonshire Library*

The Craiglockhart spur opening facilitated the closure of Edinburgh Princes Street station, and diversion of its services to the suburban line. Here, class '5MT' 4-6-0 No. 44956 heads a short train of three LMS pattern coaches and a BR full brake past Craiglockhart's Outer Circle platform. The distant signal beyond the end of the other platform now has intensified lighting, but was close to the repositioned trailing catch points.   *Author*

railway opened, loch and village were long gone, save for the small thatched 'Myreside Cottage' which stood in its own grounds next to the railway cutting on the east side east of Craighouse Road. Taken over by the Royal Edinburgh Hospital in 1860, it was destroyed by fire in the 1950s.

Myreside has been for long synonymous with playing fields of George Watson's College, a Merchant Company school founded in 1723 by the first accountant of the Bank of Scotland. The part of the land now known as 'Old Myreside' nearly achieved fame in early aviation days when £1,000 was offered to the first person to fly an aeroplane between Edinburgh and Glasgow, or £500 for a flight across the Firth of Forth. Several short flights were made from the playing fields by a machine exhibited at the 1910 Edinburgh Motor Show - but it could not manage the longer distances. This ground is mainly used in the summer for cricket, 'New Myreside' across Myreside Road containing the rugby pitches.

Craiglockhart to Craighouse Road Bridge

During the making of the railway cutting some 300,000 tons of spoil were removed and this provided geological evidence of the ancient loch at the west end of the Burgh Muir.

This section of the suburban railway passed through Merchant Company land in a cutting, the northern railway boundary being a low stone wall which formed the 1882 municipal boundary and the boundary of Watson's College recreation grounds. Edinburgh University used Merchant Company land south of the cutting as their Craiglockhart playing fields until they moved to Peffermill, near Duddingston in 1979. Their road access was from either Craiglockhart or Myreside ends, but when they vacated the site their buildings were removed and part of the ground given over to new housing. Craiglockhart remained unchanged, but a wide road was installed from Craighouse Road between the housing and south railway cutting wall. The field is still used, under the 'Craiglockhart' name, by George Watson's College.

Inside the railway boundary wall, a pumping shed was installed overlooking the cutting and accessed by a narrow stone wall lined footpath extending some 50 yards west from Craighouse Road bridge. The original building was later replaced by a more substantial brick structure, being renamed as the 'pumping station'. Its function is unclear and may have had some bearing on the course of the Jordan Burn, but after lying derelict for many years it was removed in early 2003. In general design and dimensions, it was similar to a stone structure in the Oxgangs area connected with Edinburgh's first drinking water supply, and appears to have had no bearing on the suburban line although on its land.

Down at rail level, Inner Circle trains starting from Craiglockhart faced a standing start on a 1 in 70 climb through the earth and rock cutting averaging 30 feet deep and reaching 45 feet in places for the next half-mile towards the summit. The station was also linked to Myreside Road by a 4 ft-wide railway-owned footpath between the playing fields boundary wall, and a 5 ft-high wooden palisade fence. Wooden gates at both ends restricted access to station opening hours, and were unlocked first thing in the morning and secured after the last train each day by Craiglockhart station staff. Not a popular duty, especially in inclement weather, but the footpath and footbridge also provided open access to the station platforms. Adjacent cast metal notices mounted on vertical bullhead rail sections intimated railway ownership of the path! Gates, plates and platform access were removed after the station closed, and the footpath is now a welcome public shortcut.

Most of the line from Craiglockhart to the summit at Morningside Road was on a curve in at first stone and later earth cuttings. To the left is the shell of the pumping station built around the time when the cutting was made and which is claimed to be linked with the start of the Jordan Burn.
Author

Craig House

This was initially a rectangular house built about 1565. Extended, by 1861 it was occupied by Dr John Hill Burton, the Queen's Historiographer Royal for Scotland who is said to have bought it as a birthday present for his wife, although he was doubtless relieved in getting somewhere to put his library of over 10,000 books! In 1878 the house and 60-acre Craighouse Estate were sold to the Commissioners of the Edinburgh Lunatic Asylum, who then decanted Dr Burton who died within a few years. An eminent psychiatrist of the day, Dr Thomas Smith Clouston drew up £150,000 development plans and a large building with interconnected satellite villas arose in the grounds near the original between 1890 and 1894. Named 'New Craig House', its orange sandstone exterior with green North of England slates dominated the hill above the railway. Opened on 26th October, 1894, it became a centre for well-heeled, privileged, often titled, society being treated for mental illness and which outrageously pandered to patients' whims. Suites of rooms were available and even servants could be engaged! Accessible from Craiglockhart station by the unpaved footpath along the top of the cutting, it was also served by horse cabs from Morningside Road station via Morningside Drive, more suitable to the clientele's lifestyle.

In 1948, the building came under the National Health Service and in 1972 was renamed as the 'Thomas Clouston Clinic'. However, its 'listed building' status made it difficult to alter to install lifts or modern equipment and it closed in 1993, its remaining patients, mostly elderly or long-stay, being dispersed into the community or to refurbished accommodation in the Royal Edinburgh Hospital at Morningside. Napier University bought the building in April 1994 and undertook a £10 million redevelopment, transforming it from lunatic asylum into university campus, although some folk claimed that a planning application for a change of use was not required! Reopened in its new guise on 9th June, 1997, a Lothian Buses service now terminates a few yards from the front door of the original Craig House, now Napier University's Careers Advisory Service. Nearby, the No. 38 bus follows the route of the suburban railway between Gorgie and Cameron Toll.

Craighouse (Myreside) Road

In 1880, Craighouse Road extended from Colinton Road past Myreside Cottage and between Plewlands Farm and Craig House estate. Asylum land lay north-east and south-west of the crossing, the Scottish Heritages Trust's Plewlands estate to the south-east and Merchant Company (George Watson's Hospital) land to the north-west. Before 1880 movement between the main Asylum and its 1878 acquisition just involved crossing Craighouse Road, but this was to change.

The railway acquired a triangle of land at the south-west corner of the Asylum grounds through which it created part of its cutting, Craighouse Road being carried over the gap by a stone bridge, breaking up the former through passage. Over the years this was addressed several times, and alternatives developed, but the original road bridge over the railway was unaltered. In 1936 the part of Craighouse Road north of the railway cutting and flanked by Myreside playing fields was renamed Myreside Road, the name of the road south of the bridge being unchanged. A different street nameplate at opposite ends of the bridge seems to indicate that it is in neither!

This bridge was the last original suburban stone railway bridge to be built. The 1880 Plewlands and Braidlands Plan shows a road width (*sans* pavements) over the

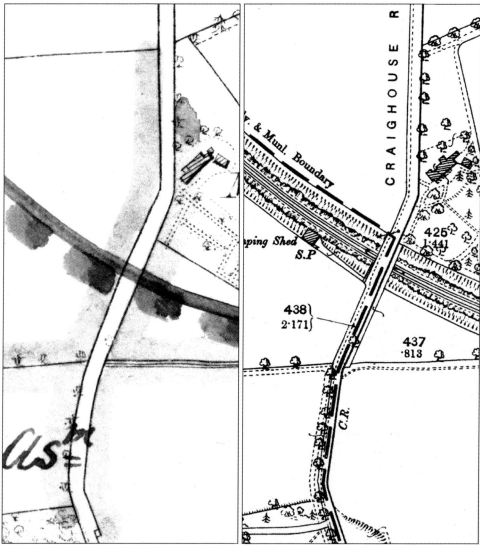

Craighouse (Myreside) Road Bridge 1855.
Prior to the coming of the suburban railway, Craighouse Road was a plain country road in the Myreside area.

Craighouse (Myreside) Road Bridge 1896.
The cutting for the suburban railway led to the provision of a separate path across to the railway bridge to link the two parts of the Royal Edinburgh Hospital grounds which now included land that was formerly Craig House grounds.

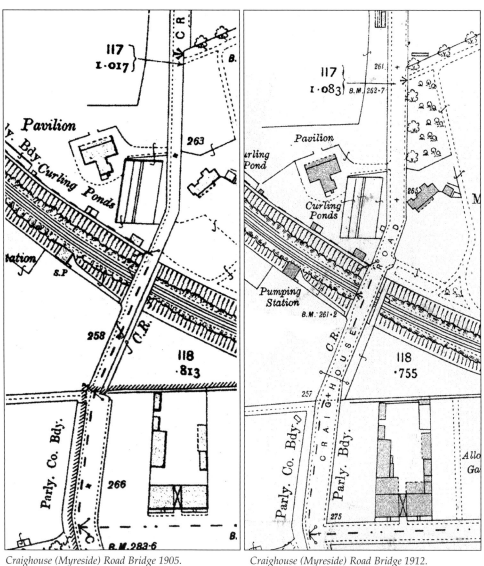

Craighouse (Myreside) Road Bridge 1905.
The approach to the bridge from the Scottish Heritages Company land to the south was widened but the bridge was unchanged.

Craighouse (Myreside) Road Bridge 1912.
By 1912, Craighouse Road had been widened throughout, and a separate bridge built over the cutting, to keep the link between both parts of the Royal Edinburgh Hospital grounds.

Passing under the eastern side of Myreside Road bridge is Dalry Road-allocated LNER class 'J39' 0-6-0 No. 64946 heading for Niddrie. Formerly a St Margarets engine, reorganisation of Edinburgh trip diagrams resulted in some former LNER engines being transferred to the LMS depot (and vice versa). *Author*

proposed bridge of 25 ft 0 in. and when the cutting was formed the street at the railway bridge was some 32 feet wide, with a pavement only on the western side. For the next 30 years it was narrowed on the eastern side by a separate walled path for inter-asylum movements. However, in 1911 it was decided that Craighouse Road be widened with pavements on both sides and the asylum wall moved back into its grounds, the discrete walled path over the bridge being dispensed with. To compensate for this, a separate steel footbridge was provided on stone abutments a few feet east of the original and was installed on Sunday 19th February, the contractors having full use of both lines between Haymarket Central and Morningside Road for the day. Concurrently, a new Asylum entrance was formed next to Myreside Cottage, and paths linked the new footbridge with others in the asylum grounds and with the new door in the Craighouse Road wall. The 1911 bridge, paths and gates still exist, disused and overgrown, as is the land triangle that was isolated when the cutting was made.

At street level, the east side of the bridge is a high blank straight stone wall and pavement, a relic of the former asylum pathway. On the west side, where the bridge wall is noticeably lower, a gate on the north end led to Craiglockhart station, that on the south end leading to the pumping station. Inside this latter gate, a ladder leads down the cutting sides to track level. Between the two the road forms a 'lay-by', which is also a bus stop.

The pumping station built above the railway cutting and accessed from the Myreside Road Bridge. The building was demolished in the spring of 2003 after a long period of disuse.   *Author*

Myreside Road bridge was one of the last major civil engineering works to be completed during the construction of the line. The original width was formed of a public road and separate path for the incumbents of the Edinburgh Lunatic Asylum, but when the road was widened, a separate girder foot bridge was provided to accommodate the latter on the eastern side.   *Author*

Elderly Caledonian Railway locomotives were used for cross-Edinburgh transfers via the Craiglockhart spur, and here the last of the famous Caledonian '812' class No. 661 (by then LMS '3F' No. 57645) of Dalry Road breasts the summit with a local freight from Niddrie to Slateford. *Author*

264

Chapter Seven

Craighouse to Morningside

Craighouse Road Bridge to Morningside Road

Two land packets flanked this section of line. To the north was the Edinburgh Lunatic Asylum, later retitled the Royal Edinburgh Hospital and to the south, the land of the Scottish Heritages Company Ltd, embracing Plewlands Estate. This name was derived from the Scots 'Plew land', a measure of (usually) arable land of 104 Scots Acres, or 8 Oxgangs, the area that could be worked by a team of eight oxen and a single plough. Apart from the triangle at Craighouse Road bridge, the land occupied by the railway company was formerly that of the Heritages Company. In contour, the line climbed towards its summit near Morningside Road signal box, stone cutting yielding to grass banking.

Apart from a set of catch points on the up line, both lines were plain track until the connection from the down line to the goods yard crossed the up line near the summit. The 1943 LNER wartime works programme proposed a facing connection from the up line to the goods headshunt although this could have been done by adding a single slip to the existing down main to yard headshunt crossover. This would have created a loop behind the box, but was not progressed although the catch points were moved further west to accommodate a new Morningside Road outer home under the Slateford spur signalling.

The Royal Edinburgh Hospital

When the 1880 Suburban Railway Act was passed, the Edinburgh Lunatic Asylum extended along the north side of the line from Craighouse Road Bridge to Morningside Road. Conceived in 1774 as the Edinburgh Lunatic Asylum, it opened in 1813 in rural countryside, just within Edinburgh's southern boundary - for those who could afford to pay. Finally completed in 1840, a second building, known as West House, opened in 1842, one year after the asylum had become The Royal Edinburgh Hospital, both main buildings being linked by a passageway under the lane between Tipperlinn village and, the Jordan Burn. Expanding west, Myreside Cottage and grounds were absorbed in 1860 and by 1884 further buildings added included a nurses' home and a second-hand small Gothic chapel with bell tower. A 12 ft-high stone wall enclosed the grounds, but this proved inadequate over the years to contain some inmates who met their ends under the wheels of trains. By 1890, grounds and perimeter wall bordered Craighouse Road and with the purchase of Craighouse Estate and construction of the new hospital in its grounds, East House was closed and demolished in 1896, the site being sold to James Miller for domestic tenements. West House expanded as mental illness facilities research developed over the years.

The southern Asylum boundary was the Jordan Burn, which parallels, runs close to, or intersects the suburban railway over much of its remaining course to Duddingston, and will be dealt with later. However, the 1880 Suburban Railway Act laid down that the asylum have its own private siding, a short buffer-ended line, just under 100 feet in length and capable of taking four wagons within the asylum gates. There being no loading bank, unloading was to a path on its west side and it connected with the northernmost siding in the Morningside Road goods yard. Although the track within the gate was later removed by the LNER, the points were left in place for some time afterwards.

Since it was built in 1924, a class 'N15' 0-6-2 tank engine No. 9125 (later No. 69220) of Haymarket regularly worked the 'sub goods' between Haymarket and Niddrie. After withdrawal, this duty was taken over, *inter alia*, by class LNER 2-6-2 tanks displaced by diesel railcars. No. 67620 heads back to Gorgie running bunker first.   *Author*

Scottish Heritages Company Limited

The Scottish Heritages Company was the land superior for the Plewlands Estate whose development plans would be significantly affected by the railway. Detailed 1880 drawings showed the general impact of the line between Craighouse Road and Morningside, then largely occupied by Plewlands Farm and tannery, and a fueing plan, showing the swathe of the railway, was produced two years later. Construction of the Maxwell Street tenements had started in 1877, it being speculated that it was named after Herbert Maxwell who owned and fued land north of the Jordan Burn in the 18th century.

Maxwell Street was planned to head south-west from where the railway goods yard gate was later sited to the corner of Morningside Cemetery wall, then along today's Balcarres Street and Craighouse Gardens to Craighouse Road. Belhaven Terrace had tenements planned for both sides with the gates of the Metropolitan Cemetery at the end, a side road leading to Maxwell Street on the route of today's footpath and bridge over the line. However, the Suburban literally drove a train through these proposals, its goods yard truncating Maxwell Street, space at the west end later hosting an electricity conversion station for the Corporation Tramways which was only demolished in August 2003 to make way for housing

As revised, the new road started, not from Maxwell Street but Belhaven Terrace. Building started in 1884 at the Morningside end, tenements lining the south side of the road between the cemetery gates and the corner of the cemetery wall. Baillie McKenzie, a partner in the heating engineering firm of Mackenzie & Moncur, had links with Balcarres House in Fife and is said to be responsible for naming this road,

'Balcarres Terrace Street'. West of the cemetery corner tenements first planned for the south side of the street were changed to be on the north side, house fronts facing the sun (when it shone). Space at the rear was later used for an approach to private railway sidings for the stoneworks and later extended to MacKenzie & Moncur Works.

Progress beyond the cemetery corner was slow. Tenements were not continuous, and at No. 21 commercial premises filled a gap, today a modern garage. Beyond No. 26 was the Bruce Street cul-de-sac of 1885, named after James Bruce of George Street who owned stables and houses on its west side which were replaced by tenements. A sleeper (now wire mesh) fence separated the street from the line. West of Bruce Street were more tenements, behind which was Buchan's small dairy farm. The farmhouse at No. 36, for a time the west end of the street, was separated from the tenements by a small covered pend through which the animals were driven to graze on pastures further west or in Plewlands farmland.

Beyond the farmhouse at that time was open ground leading to a boundary fence of railway sleepers which separated the street from Plewlands Farm. Here, Messrs W. & J. Kirkwood had their stoneyard and a private siding was laid for them. This impinged on the dairy ground and some buildings were removed, a small house being added beside the farmhouse. Later, both houses, ground and siding were taken over by Edinburgh Corporation for their cleansing department and today, with the siding lifted, it is a recycling reclamation site. Part of this area was also remodelled into a bus terminus.

By 1908, Plewlands Farm had gone and the area replaced by housing with some industrial premises, the largest two being McKenzie & Moncur's engineering works and the Craighouse Cabinet Works. Tenements were built on the railway side of the road between the Corporation depot and McKenzie and Moncur's, and in the rear of these houses laundry, smithy and sundry small firms existed alongside the railway siding but, as with the Craighouse Works, were not rail connected. A further tenement block was built on each side of the road, one opposite the factory on a short embankment, amidst semi-detached housing, and the other on the north side of the street near Craighouse Road amidst ubiquitous allotments. It took 15 years for Balcarres Street to extend from Morningside crossroads to Craighouse Road.

After the 1960s, the large industrial premises closed or moved away, MacKenzie and Moncur's works and the Craighouse Cabinet Works being replaced with housing. Beyond No. 50 was renumbered and renamed as 'Craighouse Gardens'. The triangle of asylum land near the Craighouse Road bridge, isolated when the railway was built, remains unkempt, contrasting with the well manicured grass around the modern homes.

In addition to allotments near Craighouse Road, land between the east end of Balcarres Street and the Outer Circle line was cultivated as allotments which still exist today, situated between the approach path to the Tipperlinn footbridge and the old corner smithy, now a motor vehicle repair shop.

The Metropolitan Cemetery Company opened Morningside Cemetery in 1878 to the rear of the future Balcarres Street, and appears in both 1880 and 1882 Scottish Heritages Company plans, although in the former its western end was merely 'Reserved for the Metropolitan Cemetery Coy'. This option was never taken up and it became 'Morningside Park' after 1932 with tennis courts, bowling greens and other leisure facilities bordered with hedges, shrubs and residential housing. After the cemetery closed to interments in 1981 its gates, fences and signs in Belhaven Terrace were removed, alternative pedestrian access being provided, the original entrance (never used for burials) being redeveloped for private housing.

The Jordan Burn (West)

The source of the streamlet known as the Pow Burn (it changes its name more than once during its journey) is unclear but Harrison's Map of 1850 shows two streams starting on the east side of Craiglockhart Hill. One heads more or less north towards the Water of Leith at Roseburn but the other east towards Craig House and Morningside. The burn's first sighting today is above the cutting just south of the bridge over the railway at Craighouse Road. Known throughout its course until about 1753 as the Pow Burn (a corruption of Scots Gaelic poll for 'mud, mire or bog water') its origin was close to the south boundary of the Burgh Muir from the 12th century and marked Edinburgh's south boundary until 1856. While passing through 'Canaan' and 'Egypt' farms in Morningside, it was locally called the 'Jordan Burn'.

During planning of the suburban railway, it was realised that it would have to cross the burn and a clause in the 1880 Act required the stream to be diverted along the south side of the line. At (precisely) 1 mile 1,320 yards from Haymarket Central Junction, it was to pass under the track before resuming its original course outside the asylum wall, opposite a curling pond (later stocked with trout) in the hospital grounds. In 1899, the new siding for Messrs McKenzie & Moncur's Works encroached on the waterway's path, so it was piped down the embankment and under the line, reappearing on the north side on its original course. It sluggishly flowed east through heavy undergrowth along the north of Morningside Road goods yard, past some crude poultry pens before reaching the railway weighbridge office at the goods yard entrance from Maxwell Street where it was joined by a watercourse from Comiston which had a more vicious flow. When foundations were being formed for a new telephone exchange in 1973-74, this was 'discovered' by flooding which had to be pumped out for several months before they became tame enough for building to continue.

Near the line summit where the railway passes over the Jordan Burn, Gateshead class 'V2' 2-6-2 No. 60812 heads an empty coaching stock train around the city *en route* to Craigentinny carriage sidings.   *Author*

Mackenzie & Moncur Siding

Messrs Mackenzie & Moncur, industrial engineers specialising in heating systems, had a private siding laid to serve their works under an 1899 agreement with the NBR with the railway installing track and signalling and the trader paying when completed. The siding connected from the Kirkwood Siding and had a 1 in 264 rising gradient to the works. The single approach line ran behind other industrial premises later including a smithy and laundry, and along an embankment before dividing into two parallel 140 feet lines, one entering the factory through a gate, the other continuing outside to a buffer stop which could have served the Craighouse Cabinet Works if extended.

Latterly the daily trip train from Duddingston that also shunted Newington and Morningside goods yards shunted the siding. This movement involved reversals and 'wrong line' working over the main line, the engine being 'shut in' until ready to return to the goods yard. Well into the 1950s, these moves were made under the vocal authority of the signalman, the points being only some 30 yards from the box. MacKenzie & Moncur's works became Balfour & Paul in the 1960s but was subsequently closed, being replaced by housing as an extension of Craighouse Gardens.

Kirkwood Stoneworks/Corporation Siding

A 245 ft-long single line siding was originally installed for Messrs W. & J. Kirkwood, building contractors who were involved at that time in several major projects, including Blackford Hill observatory and local domestic housing. Known as the Stone Siding, the stone works were next to the buffers and although adjacent to the Outer Circle line had access only from the Inner Circle by a trailing connection. Unfortunately, the proximity of the buildings to the west of Bruce Street severely curtailed the length and only about 70 feet was readily available. Details of the siding users are scarce, but by 1900 Kirkwood had vacated the site. James Moyes, a blacksmith also used the siding for ironwork, but he moved to new premises opposite the east cemetery wall corner in Balcarres Street about the time of Kirkwood's withdrawal.

The siding appears on a plan dated April 1899 for a proposed siding for McKenzie & Moncur but this was amended a month later and a new siding pencilled in 575 feet beyond Kirkwood's to serve the 'Town Depot', presumably referring the Cleansing Department of the Town Council. All connections were on railway land, with actual sidings on traders' property. When Kirkwood left, the land and siding was acquired by the council so the 'pencilled' siding was not required. Stoneworks buildings were removed, but some land at the east end continued to be tenanted by Buchan's dairy.

The 1901 agreement between the NBR and Edinburgh Corporation Cleansing Department noted that the siding would deal with manure traffic, the siding and surrounding land becoming the Balcarres Street Depot. The length of the new sidings on NBR land was 245 yards and the cost (£410) was borne by the Corporation who also bore the cost of materials, labour and maintenance. The siding opened on 15th July, 1901, leaving MacKenzie & Moncur's approach line (which was slightly lowered to accommodate it) and comprised of two loading bank-flanked buffer-ended sidings on Corporation land. Gates were provided which were normally closed across the railway, being opened only to shunt the sidings. A small dead-ended extension siding on MacKenzie & Moncur's line was also removed. LNER records confirm siding ownership transferred to Edinburgh Corporation in 1901 and as such it remained, albeit latterly mostly disused, into the second half of the 20th century, appearing in a 1959 resignalling plan as the 'Stone Works Siding'. Railway tradition dies hard!

Once the Great Northern Railway saloon for the Prince of Wales (later Edward VII), by 1925 it had gravitated to be used by Edinburgh's district operating superintendent after consideration as an observation saloon for the West Highland line. In its last days before becoming a church at Gatehouse of Fleet, it is passing the Corporation sidings at Balcarres Street behind St Margarets BR Standard 2-6-0 No. 78049.

Author

Tipperlinn Village and Pathways

The name probably derived from the Scots Gaelic 'Tobar' (well) and 'linne' (of the pond). The well still exists, albeit hidden, and the pond may have referred to Jordanville Loch. The village was on a north-west/south-east axis but the Royal Edinburgh Asylum expanded across its road, and the hand weaving industry for which it was famous ceased entirely in 1856. By 1880 the buildings had gone, the site having been absorbed into the hospital grounds. A new road outside the hospital wall was memorially named 'Tipperlinn Road', leading to a lodge at a new hospital entrance.

A new footpath linked the original path used by past generations of villagers to the Jordan Burn, passing above the internal link between East and West Houses. After East House was replaced by tenements in 1896, a new 'Morningside Terrace' paralleled the path down to the side of the goods yard. The old path had passed along the side of the burn, crossed a small footbridge into open land where the villagers could dig peat, but when the railway goods yard had been built it was extended along the side of the yard, turning south at the rear of the yard into Maxwell Street. A path forward to Plewlands was provided by a new passage along the rear of the goods yard. A standard NBR lattice pattern iron footbridge supported on standard metal pillars carried the path over the railway to Balcarres Street without access to the platforms, but none was intended. Part of this route closed in the 1950s when a fire in a nearby building made a wall unsafe, but in recent years new construction at the end of Morningside Terrace finally blocked the old direct right of way.

Morningside 'Village'

Some writers claim that the main street was on the line of a Roman road but the origin of the district name is obscure, one explanation being that it faced the morning sun. Another, based on myth, is that it was the 'Mourning side', linked to the Bore Stone, said to have held the Scottish standard before the 1513 disaster of Flodden. In 1850, Morningside was described as 'a secluded village, consisting of little more than a row of thatched cottages and a blacksmith's forge slumbering in rural solitude', large villas and fields of oats and barley separating the cottages from both Edinburgh and Newington and the more well-to-do Edinburgh citizenry spent holidays in the area. How times change!

Until the 1880s the road between Churchhill and Morningside comprised of several property groups (streets), not only individually named and numbered, but with different names on the east and west side of the road! The Scottish Heritages Company map of 1880 shows this as 'Morningside Road', but the 1884 Post Office map just calls it 'Morningside'. A single track for horse trams en route to Morningside Drive opened in 1883, but cars stopped at the toll house when the road elevation was changed for the new bridge over the railway, the truncated track acting as a 'headshunt'. The single line was doubled under an 1896 Act that also provided for cable or electric traction and a double line extension to Braid Burn.

When the railway opened, several roads converged within a short distance of each other and the station and these cross-roads became the 'hub of Morningside'. Horse trams terminated nearby and the busy post office dealt with many telegrams (no telephones) for the people in the 'big houses', telegraph boys jostling with delivery boys, 'fishwives' and their wares, and resting tramway, cartage and cab horses. Cabs and 'brakes' could be hired, the office later moving to the east side of the bridge, projecting over the cutting embankment.

Morningside Crossroads in the Edwardian era with horse traffic much in evidence. The imposing building in the centre was intended to be a hotel but finance was unavailable to complete the project. Supplementing the tall street lights, the station entrances have small conventional gas lamp posts. Cluny Gardens bears off to the left and Belhaven Terrace to the right. Ahead are Braid Road (*left*) and Comiston Road. Apart from vast intrusions of street furniture, the scene has altered little over the years.   *M. Cant Collection*

A contemporary postcard of the road in the opposite direction. The station is to the right of the cable car, but perish the thought today of standing holding a conversation like the two ladies with the pram!   *A.W. Brotchie Collection*

Belhaven Terrace tenements of 1880 lined the south of the road linking the cross-roads with the cemetery entrance. Had the 1880 Scottish Heritages Company plan been implemented there would have been tenements on both sides, but this never came to pass. Instead, between the cross-roads and footpath to the bridge to Maxwell Street was occupied by a monumental sculptor's yard, horse trough (for tram and cab), and public weighbridge (with common entrance to a gentlemen's convenience), with uncultivated ground to the west and rear. Two small shops, a newsagent and grocery, were later built and backed onto the wasteland. The sculptor (James MacDonald & Son) was originally at 426 Morningside Road, on the Outer Circle side of the line, his yard extending from the crossroads along the north side of the road opposite Belhaven Terrace. Access was down a slope into his works from Morningside Road. Being next to the station, he advertised that his wares could be sent anywhere, but in c.1910 a large shoe shop was built on the corner and his entrance moved round into Balcarres Street. Not to be outdone, he acquired a new postal address of 9 and 10 Belhaven Terrace, promotional material noting that this monumental sculptor was close to the cemetery gates! In the 1970s, 'progress' decreed that the land between cross-roads and footbridge path be redeveloped with a large branch of the Bank of Scotland and a public house restaurant, the former waste ground adjacent to the public house being turned into a car park for bank customers! The now redundant Outer Circle platform, buildings and gardens were removed and replaced by a vertical (now vandalised) plain concrete wall, although space exists for a platform should passenger trains be restored

On the corner of Belhaven Terrace and Comiston Road W.H. Torrance established a baker and confectioner's shop shortly before the railway arrived and created a tearoom in the tenement flat above, perhaps the equivalent of coffee-houses elsewhere. Later, this was converted to a domestic flat and his shop became a branch of the British Linen Bank. Each day, after the demise of the travelling cash box in specified passenger trains, station cash from Morningside Road and Craiglockhart was banked and wages cash withdrawn there, the British Linen being the NBR bankers before merging with the Bank of Scotland. Since moving across the road, the former bank has become an estate agent's office.

In 1884, plans were made for a hotel near the station which local businessmen intended to build in the fork of Braid Road and Comiston Road and to name either 'Pentland Hotel' (from the hills to the south) or 'Belhaven Hotel' after the nearby terrace. However, this became academic when the building was finished as there were inadequate funds to open and the three-storey building with attic staff quarters became residential flats with sundry street level shops.

By 1900 Morningside had a population larger than many small towns and an early 20th century census found an unusually large proportion of females in the district, many being in domestic service, perhaps illustrative of the district's affluence. Three Morningside Councillors donated a pedestal clock to the cross-roads in 1910, replacing a tall lamppost a few yards from the station. Some 88 years later, suitably refurbished, the clock was reinstated on a traffic island near its original site - with the unattractive ephemera of modern road furniture.

Rail traffic was seriously affected on 18th May, 1923, when fast electric tram services to and from the city replaced the old unreliable trundling cable cars. Three services terminated outside Plewlands Post Office, two others going forward to the Braids. On 31st January, 1927 service 5 was extended to Morningside Road station and when a siding opened in Belhaven Terrace on 28th July, 1929, service 23 arrived from Bruntsfield. The last Edinburgh tramcar (No. 217) left from this spur on the evening of 16th November, 1956 carrying councillors to an emotive ceremony at the

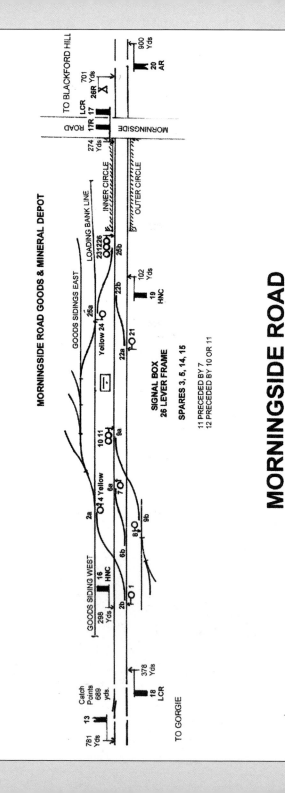

MORNINGSIDE ROAD

The original NBR lever frame was a Stevens pattern with 24 levers, with spares and spaces. Detonator placing was by stirrup mechanism as was signal wire tensioning. During the 1950s, a single disc shunting signal was changed to the tiered routeing ground disc signals Nos. 23, 12, and 26 on the same site at the end of the Inner Circle platform when a new frame was installed in preparation for the introduction of colour light signals. The control of some signals was also transferred to an illuminated diagram above the frame. This drawing represents the signal box diagram as at 27th October, 1960, its final fully semaphore layout. Shortly afterwards, the Outer Circle signals were altered to colour light to cater for the new spur from Craiglockhart to Slateford and a new semaphore outer home with a bracketed semaphore warning signal was installed on the Inner Circle, 535 yards from the signal box. These signals responded to levers Nos. 14 and 15 respectively. Distant signal No. 13 was repositioned 982 yards from the box and equipped with intensified electric light. Inner Circle catch points were also repositioned from 689 yards to 1,056 yards out from the signal box. Subsequently, the Inner Circle was also altered to colour light signalling.

foot of the Mound. Passenger trains were unsurprisingly withdrawn in September 1962 and the bus became omnipotent in Edinburgh. Other than a brief tram service from Morningside via the west end to Newington, and the bus to Blackford Hill, the train had provided the main public transport from Morningside around the southern suburbs. However, this was redressed by the Lothian Buses, creating a route that follows much of the route of the old suburban railway between Cameron Toll and Gorgie, albeit with longer journey times!

Morningside Road Signalling

Morningside Road signal box stood on the outside of the curve a few yards east of the line summit, with an excellent view in both directions. It was also near the throat of the goods yard and the connection from the Inner Circle, across the Outer Circle into the private sidings on the south side of the line. The signalman faced the frame and the trains. Eastwards, the box worked to Blackford Hill until this closed on 15th June, 1969 and then briefly to Niddrie West. Westwards, Morningside Road worked to Gorgie Station (1884-1897), Gorgie South (1897-1931), Gorgie Junction (1931-1959), Craiglockhart Junction (1959-thence Slateford Junction), Gorgie Junction again (1959-1975) then the Haymarket panel (1975 to 26th June, 1977) when the Edinburgh Signalling Centre took over its work.

The 1883 signal box drawing was produced for the Edinburgh Suburban & South Side Junction Railway, but of a typical North British hipped roof 'brick and timber' pattern with coal fire and gas light. However, the box that was built differed in height from that in the drawing. It had standard NBR internal fittings, block instruments and a Stevens' 24-lever frame with mechanical interlocking under the operating floor which also originally housed the oil store for the signal lamps. These were tended by the station staff and the lamps were filled and 'trimmed' there before being carried to the signals, where they were exchanged for those installed in the previous week. Lamps were raised into position and lowered by a windlass arrangement at the base of the signals, the provision of access ladders being of a much later date. Later (it was rumoured after a serious fire at Queensferry Junction), servicing was transferred to a custom-built flat-roofed brick lamp room with barrel cradle at one end and a metal-topped bench along one side under a single window, at the Gorgie end of the Inner Circle station platform.

The signals were to conventional North British 'Stevens' patterns and a trailing crossover between the two main lines was provided near the signal box. Goods yard access at the east end was by trailing connection from the Inner Circle line at the end of the station platform, the west end being linked directly by trailing points to the Outer Circle line. There was a small internal 'run-round loop' to assist in shunting. Its first recorded private siding opened in 1899 from the Inner Circle line across the Outer Circle for Messrs McKenzie and Moncur, the same main line trailing connection also giving access to the Edinburgh Corporation siding in 1901. Actually the latter pre-dated the former as it was in use as the 'Stoneworks Siding' for Messrs Kirkwood, but this was not listed in the Sidings Register. A second main line trailing crossover was later added between the west exit from the goods yard to the Outer Circle and the Inner Circle connection to the private sidings to simplify working between goods yard and private sidings.

On 6th September, 1911, a NBR 'open scissors' back shunt signal was installed about 200 yards from the points into the goods yard. Curvature, embankment and road bridge prevented the driver from seeing the points so the guard had to ensure

Morningside Road signal box with class 'J37' 0-6-0 No. 64569 passing on a mineral train. The wooden porch was a later addition, the plain wooden steps being rebuilt in brick and incorporating a coal store and toilet facilities in the mid-1950s. *Author*

Morningside Road box 'refuged' trains in the goods yard but, although no problem with ordinary freights, the combined weight of the 'A4' Pacific *Sparrow Hawk* and 'A3' Pacific No. 60077 *The White Knight* was a very different matter in 1956 and the elderly North British trackwork was unable to play such a supporting role. Surfacemen had to repair the track before normal service could be restored to the coal merchants in the yard. *Author*

that his train was clear of the points before advising the signalman to change the points and lower that signal. Concurrently, a disc signal for propelling from up main to down side sidings was removed, a single shunting signal sufficing for both moves as the small number of wagons able to be accommodated in the Corporation siding put the driver in hand-signalling sight of guard and signalman. Latterly, the 'scissors' arm was replaced by a banner signal, but the single disc at the yard entry points was triplicated - for routes into goods yard, private sidings and main line crossover!

Prior to the Craiglockhart and Slateford connection, Morningside Road signals were mechanical, the only major change over the years being replacement of lower quadrant arms by upper quadrants. Changes were made as traffic conditions determined, such as the removal on 20th May, 1930, of the down home signal without replacement. This resulted in renaming other Outer Circle signals, the starting signal off the end of the platform becoming the down home, and the former advanced starter, next to MacKenzie & Moncur's premises, as the down starter.

Before Craiglockhart Junction opened, the Inner Circle distant was off the end of Craiglockhart platform. The 'home' was near the summit and a co-acting starting signal at the end of the platform, between railway and stair up to street level. When this latter signal became upper quadrant in the late 1940's, the short arm had a piece removed to clear the steps. Outer Circle signals were unchanged since 1930, but a short distance beyond the Outer Circle down starter was the Gorgie Junction distant, installed after the closure of Gorgie South in September 1931. In view of its distance from Gorgie (and proximity to Morningside Road starter), it was motor operated, but usually functioned as a Gorgie 'fixed distant'.

The new Craiglockhart spur had a significant effect on Morningside Road signal box. The locking frame was replaced by a new one of 26 levers (24 working and 2 spare), equipment too distant for mechanical operation being worked electrically by switches on an illuminated diagram above the frame, the signalman now having his back to the trains. Some colour light signals were operated from the lever frame and these had shorter handles. Polished steel tops, carefully tended over the years with rags to avoid the rusting effect of skin contact were now covered in white plastic, and as the new set up blocked out the coal fire, electric heating was installed, but the biggest bone of contention was the lighting. During the engineering work, gas light was replaced by electric but after the work was finished, the electric light was removed and gas reinstated - until strong protests by the incumbent signalmen, Messrs Forbes, Brown and Lyon, restored electric light and heat.

The 'illuminated signalling diagram' included 10 thumb-switches for control of signals and points not worked from the frame. As an 'economy', the original three position LNER and NBR block instruments were 'rebuilt' by cutting off and mounting the dial of the 'receiving' instrument above the 'sending' unit, thus resembling a new British Railways double line block instrument (described as a 'BR block' on the diagram) but signalling to Slateford Junction was only by bell signals. Later, new instruments with standard dials formed part of the panel fascia.

On the Inner Circle, a new two aspect (red/green) colour light signal replaced Gorgie Junction's semaphore starter, and was jointly controlled by Morningside Road and Gorgie Junction some 1,743 yards from Craiglockhart Junction. Morningside Road's up distant remained semaphore but was moved 200 yards further out and fitted with intensified electric lighting. A new semaphore 'outer home', with bracketed 'warning' arm below was installed 300 yards from the existing home signal 535 yards from the box and being out of sight of the box it had a 150-yard approach track circuit.

A welcome sight in March 1959 was former Caledonian Railway 'Jumbo' 262 of 1883 (by then No. 57232 and allocated to Stirling) on a northbound freight at Morningside Road box. Drummond's similar North British engines became LNER class 'J32' and were regular visitors before withdrawal between 1921 and 1925. *Author*

It was not unusual for freight trains to be banked from either Duddingston or Gorgie to Morningside Road. There were no dedicated banking engines, but this was included in the duties of the yard pilots. Class 'C16' No. 67492, formerly NBR No. 448 of 1916, was employed as a Duddingston pilot and is seen here after having banked a freight train up the hill, bunker first, in 1958. Balcarres Street is over the wall at the rear. *Author*

The new signals required the Inner Circle catch points to be moved 376 yards further from the box. The tall co-acting twin arm signal at the Blackford Hill end of the station platform should have been replaced by a single arm signal 25 yards nearer the box, avoiding the stairway space constraint of the original, but when signal sighting was considered, was not pursued. The trailing connection to the 'Stonework's Sidings' over the down line was signalled, but then removed and 'plain lined'.

On the Outer Circle, colour lights replaced all Morningside Road semaphores. The distant became a three aspect signal (yellow/green/yellow) 800 yards out and the home, a four aspect colour light, 107 yards from the box, almost on the same site. A trailing connection was laid into the yard headshunt, west of the box crossover. The starter became a three-aspect colour light, 380 yards from the box, and the Gorgie motor distant was removed, being replaced by a four-aspect junction signal with route indicator and subsidiary 'warning' signal, 937 yards from Morningside Road. The warning signal had a 100-yard approach track circuit, and was cleared (only with route indicator) by Slateford Junction. Main line aspects were under the joint control of Morningside Road and Slateford or Gorgie Junctions as appropriate for the routes concerned.

From Slateford, a two-aspect colour light signal 1,399 yards from Morningside Road protected the junction. A three-aspect signal further back served as both Morningside Road branch distant and Slateford Junction 'branch starter'. Junction points were motor operated, both spur lines having sand drags at the junction, that facing trains from Slateford being motor-operated, the other being spring-worked although it could be manually-worked if required. Trains which were not fitted with continuous brakes such as ballast trains had to be 'topped and tailed' (a locomotive at each end) when working over the points, and this was one of nine such Scottish locations where this had to be undertaken.

When the spur opened, larger volumes of freight passed over the Suburban, particularly at night, and it was common for trains to follow each other at short intervals, under what is termed 'Regulation 5' (the train accepted with clearance only to the home signal, the normal clearing point for acceptance purposes not being clear). However, traffic declined dramatically after Millerhill yard opened in the 1960s, and Morningside Road was closed at weekends as traffic alternatively passed through Waverley. However, the Slateford spur lines were laid to passenger train standards and this proved invaluable. Although the Suburban was used for diversions these were mainly to allow planned engineering works elsewhere.

Morningside Road (Passenger) Station

The station site was outwith the city boundary when the Edinburgh Suburban & South Side Junction Railway Act was passed in 1880, but inside when the line opened in December 1884. Initially appearing in timetables as 'Morningside', in July 1885 it appeared as 'Morningside Road', coinciding with the NBR taking over the Suburban in accord with the 1880 Act. It also avoided confusion with the other NB 'Morningside' station on the former Wilsontown, Morningside and Coltness Railway in Lanarkshire. Contemporary directories and newspaper reports quote the Edinburgh name both with and without the suffix 'Road'. The station opened as 257 Morningside Road but with subsequent building, rebuilding and adjustments in street numbering, it was latterly No. 422. The station (master's) house was latterly a top flat in No. 6 Belhaven Terrace and being on the corner of Comiston Road gave an excellent view of his station and approaches.

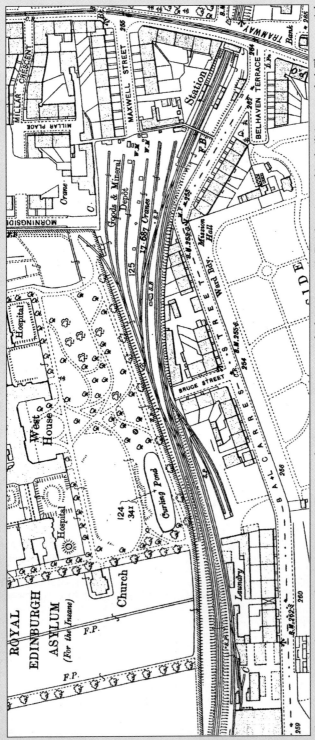

This view towards the end of the Edwardian era illustrates the maximum extent to which Morningside Road station and its facilities extended. The potential connection between Maxwell Street and Balcarres Street which was cut by the construction of the railway is clearly evident. The short private siding from the goods yard to the West House grounds of the Royal Edinburgh Hospital and the sidings on the down side of the line serving Edinburgh Corporation (two dock lines) and further to the left, into the engineering works of Messrs McKenzie & Moncur's engineering works are also evident.

Reproduced from the 25″, 1910 Ordnance Survey Map

The station offices were on street level at the crossroads, with platforms and passenger facilities below, the railway passing under the road (and booking office floor). The combined booking and parcel office was at one side of a booking hall, the other being planned as a large waiting room, before becoming a retail shop and small store. Linking the rear of the booking hall with the stairs down to the platforms was a covered, glazed veranda with three sets of double windows set into its 'tongue and groove' exterior extending the full length of the building. The booking office had a large sash window into this corridor, and on busy football or rugby match days it was not unusual for this to be opened as a supplementary booking window issuing pre-dated tickets. One set of veranda windows was opposite the booking office window, the central one opposite the booking hall passage and the third opposite a window in the original waiting room. Although the waiting room rear window was removed, its veranda windows remained until sheeted over after the station closed. Original plans show a large apex glazed roof canopy over each platform, supported on one side by the platform buildings and in the centre by pillars but this was never built. Indeed, there was no canopy at all until Edwardian days, when responding to complaints, a standard NBR pattern was provided projecting from each building without platform support.

Platform accommodation reflected the social aspirations of the district, being slightly more lavish than at other Suburban stations with separate ladies and general waiting rooms and toilets on each platform. Originally, the ladies waiting rooms were designated for first and second class ladies only (there was never second class accommodation on the Suburban trains), the other waiting room (presumably for third class passengers) being officially termed as the 'waiting shed'. One piece of equipment in the general waiting rooms in the 1890s was a 'Mutoscope' in which 212 card mounted prints were set on a wide revolving wheel and, after depositing a penny in a slot and turning a handle at the side, a 'moving picture' image was achieved. This could be a galloping horse or a strongman lifting weights, but unfortunately some devices in fairgrounds had more salacious pictures, and the machine became generally known as 'What the butler saw'. History does not record the theme in the waiting room! For many years, the Outer Circle general waiting room had a framed hand-coloured pictorial montage of Aberfoyle over the coal fireplace, with the trains in North British livery but this disappeared during a 1950s renovation. The Inner Circle general waiting room latterly had a large framed print from a 1930s LNER double royal poster, 'Teesdale', which had been previously brightened the wall in the goods weighbridge. Ladies waiting rooms (at the Craiglockhart end of both station buildings) had shaped wooden-slatted seats around the walls, designed with the Victorian period ladies outerwear in mind, and a large wooden table on four sturdy turned legs in the centre of the floor. Fittingly, entrance to the ladies toilets was only available from the ladies waiting room.

Staff accommodation was provided in the planned (but never used as such) Outer Circle booking office, a door to the platform replacing a window. It became the porters' room although some incumbents were more aptly designated as entrepreneurs! One such was Frank 'The Pie' Ramsay, his nickname attributable to the fact that with a wide circle of friends he had a finger in almost any pie. Nothing seemed impossible to acquire from a 'bookie' (before the days of betting shops) to a bicycle! In appreciation of his 23 years' work at the station, he received a 'wallet of notes' from the Suburban Travellers Association shortly before the station closed in 1962. Attractive gardens were cultivated by the staff on the slopes between both platform buildings and access stairs and on the Inner Circle platform between the

Morningside Road

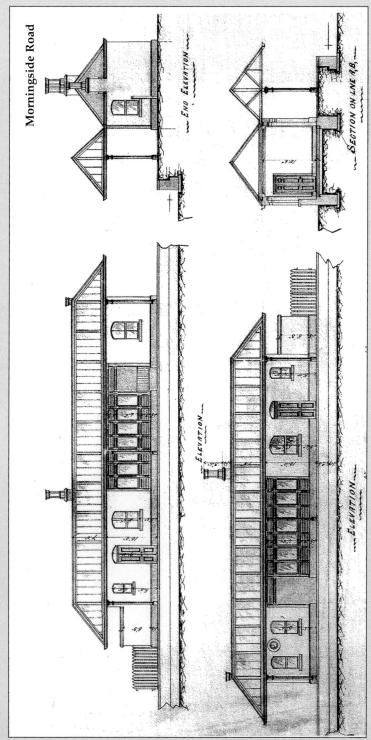

END ELEVATION

SECTION ON LNE A,B,

ELEVATION

ELEVATION

The original 1880 drawing prepared by the ESSJR for its proposed passenger station at Morningside which was not progressed as per drawing. Although provision was made for a booking office in Morningside Road proper and adjacent waiting room, each platform building was to have its own booking office, waiting rooms and conveniences. The large independent canopy was not developed, separate awnings being mounted from the platform building without platform pillar support.

Platform Buildings at Morningside Road

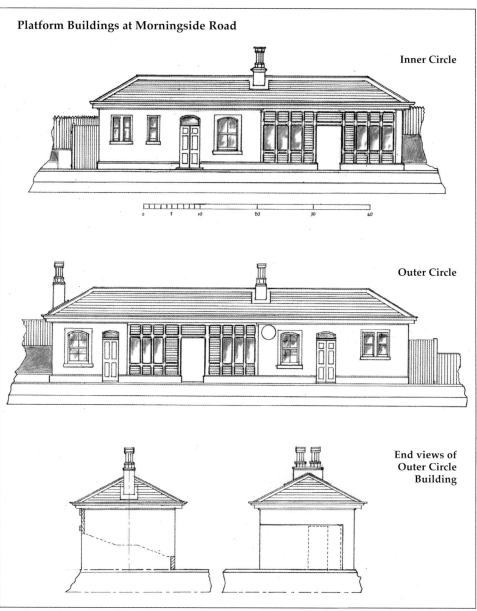

Inner Circle

Outer Circle

End views of
Outer Circle
Building

The left-hand plan shows the Outer Circle building from the east (Blackford) end, but also relates (in mirror image) to the Inner Circle building at the Blackford end. The right-hand plan shows the Craiglockhart end of both buildings (the Inner Circle one being in the form of mirror image). In all plans, the NBR platform canopy has been omitted for clarity, and the screen for the gentlemen's toilet does not show the vertical planking in the end view. Rear views of both buildings were of windowless plain brick.

Morningside Road Buildings at Street Level

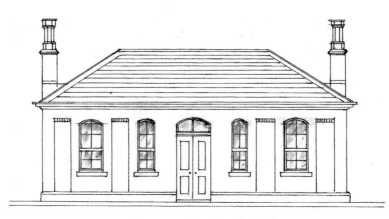

Frontage to Morningside Road

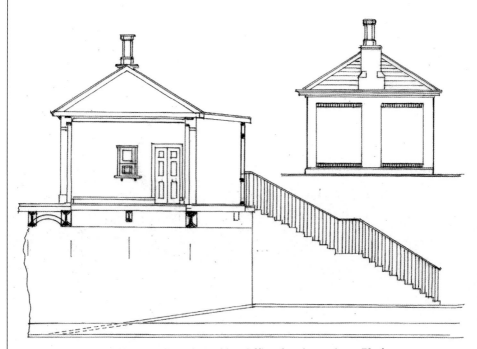

Side Elevation through Booking Office showing stairs to Platform

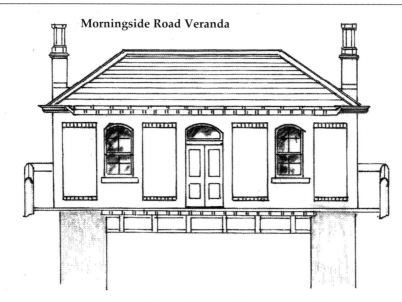

Morningside Road Veranda

Rear Street Office and Original Waiting Room Wall

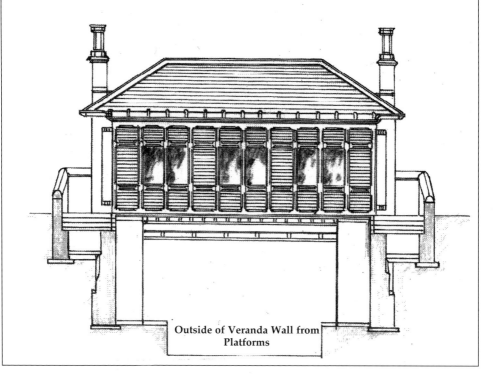

Outside of Veranda Wall from
Platforms

Edwardian fashions, lower quadrant signals and four-wheel passenger carriages headed by a small tender locomotive date this view of Morningside Road station at about 1910. As was usual at that time, copious advertisements adorn the fencing and station buildings, including the spaces between the platform building windows and even the veranda over the track.

Mrs L. Jenkins Collection

building and 'Tipperlinn footbridge'. All had wooden palisade fences at the rear and narrow terraces half way up each slope. In summer, the gardens presented an aromatic riot of colour from carefully planned layouts and when station gardens competitions started, prize money was ploughed back into plants for the next year, cultivation being the domain of the porters. 'Special Class' prizes were awarded so regularly that a first class prize was considered to be the equivalent of failure! After closure, the carefully tended plots returned to nature, those on the Outer Circle being removed.

A passageway linked the street with the veranda and platforms giving access to two shops that thus shared the same postal address. A series of coal merchants with premises in the goods yard occupied one shop for many years. In September 1889, one of these, a Mr J. Dawson of 320 Morningside Road (the station was then 318), applied to fit a letter box to the entrance gate, and although agreed at annual rental of 1s. it was only to last 'during the pleasure of the Directors'. The other shop was a small bookstall perched on a metal framework at the end of the passage next to the Outer Circle platform stairway, a wall-mounted glazed bookcase providing extra display space. In the late 1950s, the shop area that replaced the original waiting room was combined with the old storeroom as the new John Menzies bookstall and the original site was abandoned, to the delight of the two lady employees! The entrance was also changed from the street to the booking hall. A similar business still occupies the shop today.

Between the north end of the building and adjacent tenement, a wooden gate gave access to veranda or Inner Circle platform. After the station closed and the building changed to other occupiers, the gate was modernised and the one at the top of the steps leading down to the platforms was moved to the landing halfway down.

During the NBR and early LNER period, interior walls were lined with dark varnished vertical match boarding bearing a small black stencilled border at waist level but in LNER days this was painted green up to the waist and cream above, becoming brown and the cream under British Railways. The tongue and groove ceiling had a small hatch. Between the two street windows were two desks, the hinged centre tops of which sloped in the traditional manner. Here, station master (class 3) and clerk (class 4) sat facing each other, the latter with his back to ticket racks that extended from street wall to booking window. A counter projecting between booking window and door formed the parcels and enquiry office. A fixed sloping desk, the bottom of which was at standing waist height and which had cupboard space below, faced the door. On top of the desk was a rack with pigeonholes for collected tickets, segregated into originating stations and types. It was a daily clerical chore to cancel the tickets by clipping, sort into numerical order and tie with string before dispatch in a sealed bag to the audit office in Glasgow. A GPO telephone (MORningside 2828) was also on this desk, below a box with a four position dial that permitted calls to be transferred if required to and from the goods office by setting the knob and vigorously rotating a handle at the side. High tech indeed!

The large station reference 'library' rack was fixed to the wall above this desk and held equally large books. The most notable was the 'Coaching Arrangements Book', issued in the 1930s and constantly updated by sticking in paper amendment slips. By the 1960s its covers had long disappeared and the spine had become virtually circular - totally unmanageable, yet still officially functional! Other books dealt with rates, charges, station facilities and mileages.

Certificates from both stations and station gardens competitions were framed and hung above the coal fire in the booking office around a framed coloured print of the

Morningside Road station booking office and John Menzies shop frontages in this early 1961 view. The chalk blackboards are noteworthy, supplementing the official posters. Within two years the station had succumbed to new commercial tenant and today the bookstall has a new owner, although still a newsagent. Steele Allan's shop has gone completely, being replaced by a modernistic Bank of Scotland branch.

Author's Collection

The customary engine used for 'The Shunt' from Duddingston that latterly terminated at Morningside Road yard was a NBR 0-6-0 of class 'J36'. There were variations, however, such as LMS-designed 2-6-0 No. 46461, but its 'bacon slicer' reversing wheel was far from ideal in shunting. Passenger engines such as NBR 'Glens' were not common, but shunting with a big-wheeled 'Shire' was just too much for trainmen! *Author*

A new Matisa ballast cleaning machine was tried out at Morningside Road in 1959 and was parked between tests at the (otherwise disused) loading bank. When later used on the Edinburgh and Glasgow main line near Polmont, it literally ground to a halt and when stripped down, the problem was found to be caused by an early rail chair from the Edinburgh & Glasgow Railway. *Author*

Built in June 1944 by the Vulcan Foundry as War Department 78668, this engine became LNER class 'O7' No. 3151 in December 1945. Renumbered 63151 in May 1948, she became No. 90472 in June 1950. A Thornton Junction engine over her career, she is seen here shunted from the Outer to Inner Circle lines to allow another freight to pass at Morningside Road in 1957. No. 90472 was withdrawn in September 1962.   *Author*

Originally imported from the Great Northern section for express freight and fitted with new cabs for working on the West Highland line, class 'K2' 2-6-0 No. 61758, by then of Dunfermline shed, passes through the platforms at Morningside Road with a train of mineral wagons for the Niddrie yard. In the early spring of the year, the station gardens were in course of preparation, with the station 'greenhouse' next to the fence.   *Author*

Not an overpowered freight but class 'V1' No. 67617 returning to Duddingston after banking a freight train up to the summit. It was coupled to the regular 'shunt' headed by 'J36' 0-6-0 No. 65310 to minimise line occupancy. *Author*

Deputising for the class 'N15' No. 69220, a class 'J36' No. 65305 heads the Suburban goods train from Haymarket to Duddingston. There are six 'peak roof' 'L.G.W.' grain wagons in the formation. *Author*

Main line express locomotives were not uncommon over the Suburban on specials, reliefs and empty stock workings and No. 60083 *Sir Hugo* of Gateshead heads a rake of empty carriages around the Inner Circle line to Craigentinny sidings in 1957.   *Author*

An early form of ballast tamping machine much in use in the early days of British Railways was the 'Matisa', and one such example is seen scuttling through Morningside Road heading for Duddingston.   *Author*

Stopping passenger headcode indicates a not so urgent requirement for this class 'B1' heading the St Margarets breakdown crane and tool van passing through the Outer Circle platforms at Morningside Road on its journey around the suburban line.   *Author*

LNER 'V2' class 2-6-2 No. 60951 heads an unfitted freight train *en route* for Glasgow under clear signals. The leading mineral wagon contains one of the coal tubs used on the manual-coaling bank at St Margarets. Despite it huge allocation, the depot was never favoured by a mechanical coaling plant, probably due to space limitations.   *Author*

Successor to generations of six-coupled steam locomotives, six-coupled diesel shunter No. D3733 (later No. 08566) makes its slow, grinding and noisy way back to Duddingston on 'The Shunt'. Staff were none too happy about its 15 mph maximum speed, especially when completing their shift and returning to book off duty. *Author*

Diesel railcars used for the suburban service were provided either by Gloucester or Metropolitan-Cammell twin sets, but a stranger on the 1.42 pm to Musselburgh one day was this London Midland Region-allocated Derby twin unit. *Author*

LNER locomotive 4472 *Flying Scotsman*, bedecked for the Wembley Exhibition of 1925. When the number of certificates exceeded the number of frames, more than one certificate was put in one frame. Thus a full colour crested 1939 LNER Certificate for 'Best Kept Station' awarded to the then station master, Mr W. Anderson, survived, although the ink endorsement with date and name of station master have faded.

The parcel 'area' had a small weighing machine of the 'Avery' slide and bar type for relatively light parcel traffic, but great was the delight when the machine was replaced in the mid-1950s by one with a dial! Thereafter, the use of the large platform machine declined sharply. This was kept adjacent to a 'standard' North British unbraked three-wheeled barrow normally chained to the railings, but used almost daily to convey McKenzie & Moncur's 'Ledger Labelled' packages and castings from the foot of the steps to the brake van of the last Outer Circle passenger train to Waverley. 'Paid Parcels' had fixed value parcels stamps (latterly branded 'L.M.S. Railway' well into the 1950s) stuck to them with brush and heavy glue and were accounted for as tickets before 'Open Stamps' arrived whereon the clerks wrote the fee paid. .

Under the office counters were drawers and cupboards that contained anything from accountancy forms to custom-built drawer units for tickets and a standard NBR 'Milner' safe. The drawer below the booking office window held the till - removable wooden bowls suspended over the drawer base, banknotes going under the bowls, out of sight. To the right of the window and bolted to the counter was a vintage Edmonson ticket dating machine, which, judging from the groove worn in the counter, was an ESSJR original. As at most stations this also functioned as a store for loose (surplus) change, to assist in balancing the books, and was naturally the first target for a visiting Auditor!

Booking office heating was, until the mid-1950s, an open coal fire, much used by the 'head office clerks' awaiting their train but was replaced by two free standing gas fires, the one beside the desks providing an unofficial (and unhealthy) cold weather seat for staff! Over the right-hand end of the fireplace was the 'Control Circuit' telephone. Contact was made with that hallowed centre by pushing in plunger and operating a small switch lever. Right of the chimney breast were two wall-mounted internal circuit telephones linking local stations and signal boxes by depression of one of two buttons (one with a black top) in pre-selected 'Morse' codes. The 'ten o' clock' time signal (a series of short bell beats) was received on one phone, and repeated with gusto on the other which had mostly different recipients. Bemused counter customers watched this operation. A red-topped button was claimed to link with Edinburgh Control, but was rarely - if ever - used.

The booking office closed for the last time on Saturday 8th September, 1962 after the passage of the 2.14 pm Outer Circle train, the station master, Thomas Dagg, making sure that he definitely purchased the last ticket, albeit after the train had gone! He then transferred to the vacant station master's post at Currie, controlling the entire Balerno branch. However, the booking office was refurbished and reopened as a branch of the travel agents A.T. Mays, and was managed by a former station booking clerk who recognised the business potential cultivated by the railway over the years. Since then the old booking office has had several tenants, including a greengrocer, ladies' outfitter, and hairdresser.

Externally, an enamelled board was fitted beneath the eaves of the street building, in NB days showing railway and station name in dark blue letters on a white background. After 1923, this was altered for the LNER and, in the BR era, only the station name appeared in white on a light blue background. The sign is still there, but entirely overpainted blue.

Before Mark III carriages appeared in 1975, routes to Craigentinny were assessed for clearances and as a result, the Outer Circle platform copings and ramp edges at the east of the Inner Circle platform were removed. Later, all platform buildings and most of the platforms were removed although the base of the Inner Circle building still exists amidst undergrowth.

The area around the station acquired a (later unjustified) reputation for upper class residents, including several railway dignitaries. These included Mr George Mills, the Divisional General Manager of the LNER Scottish Area until his retiral, and Mr K.R.M. Cameron, the Scottish Region's motive power superintendent. In the mid-1950s, the latter sometimes used training runs of the then new Inter-City multiple units to get him to his office slightly later than usual.

Morningside Road Goods and Mineral Station

This was on the Inner Circle side, between Jordan Burn and the suburban line with road access from Maxwell Street and once contained a private siding for the Royal Edinburgh Asylum taken from the rear yard siding. A clause in the Suburban Railway Act stated that when the goods yard opened no sidings were to be laid opposite the Asylum property further west than 300 yards from the gable of the westernmost house on the north of Maxwell Street. This was adhered to, but had little effect on traffic handling. Only the yard headshunt extended beyond the specified distance.

The goods (weighbridge) office was a brick and timber hipped roof structure, on the north side of the road entrance just inside the yard boundary. Its last incumbent, John Fawcett, was a Northumbrian with a superb artistic talent that the booking office staff used to the full in promoting passenger train business by blackboards in the pre-electronic advertising age. The weighbridge was sited immediately in front.

When opened, farmers in the then mainly rural Comiston, Hunter's Tryst and Swanston districts south of the city used the yard, a major commodity being sheep that disrupted the area tranquillity by being driven loose along Maxwell Street and across the main road to holding fields. A double-sided loading bank in the yard facilitated transhipment between rail and road and, when the yard closed, memorials of these days were a single decaying cattle flake on the bank and a fixed crane of dubious reliability.

Although there were several small coal businesses before World War II, from the late 1940s the trend towards mergers left some, such as Bruce Lindsay Brothers and Waldie, as almost monopolistic. Some local firms, such as W. Steele Allan and Alexander Greig, still had small shops with large model wagons in their own livery in pride of place in their windows - and regular clients, but these dwindled as coal prices rose and quality declined nationally.

The railway's own store was a deteriorating old goods van body on original underframe but without wheels and ironwork set on the yard side of the fence bordering the lane between Maxwell Street and the footbridge over the station platforms. This had small vertical glass panes built into one side, the design being replicated at numerous other sites over the North British system. Latterly, the hut functioned (rather damply) mainly as a store for obsolete documents and materials, but during the war held materials for sawing up condemned wooden sleepers by railway staff for their own (legal) use.

Yard lighting was by a single tall square post-mounted gas lamp near the loading bank and which had access steps screwed into the side. Needless to say, it was only able to illuminate its immediate environs, the yard never aspiring to electric light. Adjacent to the lamp was a trough for the dray horses. A hand-operated loading bank crane was not mentioned in the 1891 Railway Clearing House *Handbook of Stations* but a later edition quotes a 5 ton capacity (and for the first time acknowledged the yard's ability to handle livestock and wheeled railborne traffic). However, it was rarely used in its last three or four decades as its mechanism was highly dangerous, the friction belt brake being likely to fail under load.

Most coal merchants were small family businesses with basic facilities. However, one or two had built more durable structures with railway approval and some small mobile cranes were used in the 1920s for unloading wagons. At least two firms built garages for their lorries, larger traders providing huts for their men along the boundary fence near the yard gate.

As goods and livestock traffic dwindled, the yard gradually became a purely mineral depot and even in the 1950s was served by two freight trains daily. The 'Sub Goods', from Haymarket and Gorgie was usually hauled by Haymarket 'N15' 0-6-2 tank locomotive No. 9125 (later 69220) between 1924 and 1962. The other train, 'The Shunt', came up from Duddingston, usually behind a St Margarets 'J36' 0-6-0 and undertook all yard and siding shunting and wagon placing, including those left by the 'Sub Goods'. Two of its regular mid-1950s drivers were Sandy Brady and Jock Rintoul and one of the guards, Alex Mann, achieved notoriety after painting one side of his ex-LNER 20 ton brake van with the words of a poem of his own composition. Sadly no photograph survives of this literary effort, perhaps unsurprising as officialdom took the view that it 'defaced' a perfectly good vehicle. On occasions unsuitable engines, such as 4-4-0 'Glen' or even 'Shire' classes, hauled 'The Shunt', the 'bacon slicer' type of reversing wheel being unpopular as frequent directional changes were required. Once, when a 'Shire' appeared on 'the Shunt', a second 'Shire' helped it up the hill to Morningside Road, although what happened at Blackford Hill while it shunted Newington yard, is not recorded!

Wagons normally arrived in the yard by conventional means, but during the World War II at least one came at the rear of an Inner Circle suburban passenger train, being detached in the station platform. Lacking another resource, station staff manhandled it into the yard, variations on conventional lexicography claimed to have been much in evidence.

The yard and loading bank hosted odd carriages, or complete trains, including occasionally the Royal Train, complete with noble incumbents. Once, while attending to the effluent tray under one coach, the designated platelayer felt a revolver placed in the small of his back by a Special Branch man who had not been appraised of the railwayman's duties. The physical reaction of the latter can only be assumed! In addition to Engineer's Department wagons, empty stock for rugby or football matches were temporarily stabled and once - only once - two large LNER Pacific engines coupled together were refuged behind the signal box to let another train pass. Although there was no contrary instruction, such was the track damage that it was never repeated! Trains could be 'refuged' but not 'looped', there being no main line facing points.

After the passenger train service was withdrawn, the goods yard became an 'unstaffed public siding' before the track was removed. The site lay derelict but was very valuable. The first intrusion was the large telephone exchange built inside the gate at Maxwell Street during 1974, perhaps recalling Morningside's first exchange with its 52 manual lines installed in the Swanson's domestic flat at 8 Maxwell Street in 1893. Plans were also considered for a branch of Marks & Spencer multiple store, but this did not materialise due, it was claimed, to inadequate car parking facilities in Maxwell

Street and the site developed as residential housing. These were numbered as an extension of Maxwell Street, perhaps partially reviving the 1880 Scottish Heritages Company scheme, so rudely interrupted by the arrival of the suburban railway.

Maxwell Street and the Toll House

East of the goods yard, the Jordan Burn passed between the rear of the Maxwell Street tenements and the wall of East House until the latter was closed and the ground sold for tenement housing at the end of the 19th century. Such was the power of the burn that a tenement on the west side of Morningside Road had its foundations eroded and was reduced to that of the street level shops. Nearby, at No. 366, a 1½ inches to the foot scale model of an RCH standard 12 ton coal wagon reposed for years in the window of local coal merchant, Alexander Greig, fully loaded and lettered in his livery. Research has failed to find a prototype and thus can be taken as imaginative, unless it was a 'leased' wagon, repainted during the merchant's temporary ownership.

Ecclesiastical Connections

Across Morningside Road, on the south bank of the Jordan Burn stood the Briggs o' Braid, the toll house guarding a southern entrance to Edinburgh (and restricting city expansion) from about 1852 until 1882 when the municipal boundary moved half a mile south towards the Braid Burn. The toll house fell into disuse, being removed and rebuilt stone by stone to the Hermitage of Braid.

On 27th January, 1883, Braid United Presbyterian Church congregation met in a very small iron church between Comiston and Braid Roads, overlooking Morningside cross-roads. In 1884, this church was replaced by a larger iron structure on the corner of Braid Road and Cluny Gardens, clearing the ground for the hotel planned for the cross-roads. In 1886, the foundation stone was laid (actually above the entrance portico) for a permanent building next to the old tollhouse. Taking the name of the estate on which it stood, the church was consecrated as Braid United Presbyterian Church on 10th July, 1887, the site on which the toll house had stood being incorporated into the area in front of the church. In 1929, it became Braid Parish Church and in 1990 united with Morningside Parish church as 'Morningside Braid'.

Meantime, St Matthew's parish church congregation built an iron church at 2 Cluny Avenue that opened in 1884, next to the railway cutting and was the only building then in the street. The foundation stone for their permanent building was laid in June 1888 on the site vacated by the Braid Iron Church, and this was consecrated on 4th May, 1890. In the 1950s, St Matthew's purchased a villa opposite the church at 3 Cluny Gardens, to cater for their burgeoning congregation, but in 1974 amalgamated with the 1892 South Morningside Parish Church, a few yards to the south, as Cluny Parish Church, worship continuing in the former St Matthew's building, the other being adapted as Cluny Church Centre, and enabling the villa to be sold into commercial use. Kirk Sessions and Deacon's Courts of all these churches included many railwaymen.

Chapter Eight

Morningside to Peffer Mill

Cluny and Mortonhall Estates

John Gordon was a successful 18th century merchant who had bought several Scottish Estates, including Cluny in Aberdeenshire that gave its name to this area of Edinburgh. His son had purchased the extensive Braid Estate north of the future suburban line in 1780 and when the town expanded Cluny's estates such as Midmar and Corrennie provided local street names. To build its line, the Edinburgh Suburban & South Side Junction Railway purchased a 700 yards-long strip of land between Morningside Crossroads and the boundary of John Gordon's Trustees land. They then continued eastwards for a similar distance through the Estate of Lt Col Henry Trotter of Mortonhall to the ancient road south from the city that had evolved into Blackford Avenue. The boundary between the two estates was more clearly marked when Oswald Road, named after General Sir John Oswald of Dunnikier, was formed after the railway opened.

Morningside to Blackford

The Post Office map of 1884 indicated little passenger potential. There were no buildings south of the line, although the city was expected to expand. Most land between Jordan Burn and the railway, once part of the extensive Egypt Farm, had by 1884 been 'zoned' for housing with back-to-back streets of spacious semi-detached houses having their own gardens.

Having passed under Morningside Road the line entered a 20 feet-deep earthen-sided cutting for some 370 yards, bordered to the north by land that was to form Cluny Avenue. Had the railway not been built, it is likely that there would have been villas on both sides, but in the event, the south side of the road became a narrow flat tree-lined strip above the cutting. South of the line was open land that would evolve into Cluny Gardens with the garden walls of the Victorian semi-detached villas overlooking the line. In November 1889, local resident Mr John Romanes, a Chartered Accountant, asked the North British Board for permission to plant shrubs on Cluny Gardens sides of the cutting. Permission was granted on the understanding that this would satisfy the Engineer, and 'continue only during the pleasure of the Board'. As Romanes was also land agent for Colonel Trotter of Mortonhall, he would not be unknown to the NBR Board. Cluny Avenue and Cluny Gardens were linked by Braid Avenue, its bridge over the line being narrower than the road approaches and parapet only 3 ft 6 in. high.

Meantime, the Jordan Burn, as municipal boundary, had followed a relatively straight course from the goods yard at Maxwell Street, passing behind the tenements and under Morningside Road at the tollhouse, to reach land where the cream of the Scottish Army was marshalled before Flodden. Railway and Burn were reunited halfway along Colonel Trotter's land and at the foot of a 12-hole Edinburgh Ladies Golf Course dating from about 1890. This extended down to the suburban line and had 'a number of hazards' - including the burn. The 1900 NBR Tourist Arrangements noted that ladies could join for 10s. and pay a 10s. annual subscription, but gentlemen had to pay double! Geographically nearer Morningside Road station, the winding

Approaching Morningside Road through the earth cutting from Cluny Road Bridge is class 'K3' 2-6-0 No. 61992 of St Margarets with a 'fitted head' of vacuum-braked mineral wagons in 1960. The engine was the last of the class to be built. It was on the right-hand side of this cutting that Mr Romanes was granted permission to plant shrubs in the early days of the line.

Author

route to the entrance (1,835 yards) meant Blackford Hill was the nearer station (1,007 yards). The large houses and grounds on the north bank of the burn later took on more utilitarian purposes and the golf course was incorporated into the Astley Ainslie convalescent and rehabilitation hospital after 1923.

At first, Cluny Gardens only extended as far as a bowling green and tennis courts which opened in 1892, but by the time of World War I had extended east, linking into Oswald Road *en route* to Blackford, flanked on the north by semi-detached houses and Blackford Hill public park (and pond) on the south.

Oswald Road crossed over the railway near the main entrance of the Blackford Hill Park, but although the abutments of the bridge were installed when the line was being built the final girders were not positioned until March 1892. Similarly, Cluny Gardens did not link Morningside with Blackford until the Edwardian era. East of the bridge, burn and railway ran side by side under Blackford Hill station and Blackford Avenue, the latter marking the boundary between Mortonhall Estate and that of Thomas Dick Lauder.

Blackford

In 1598, Edinburgh Magistrates passed an Act reserving a passage 'twelve ells* broad to and from the Pow Burn for the use of the town in times of pest and other times as has been of auld'. Indeed, in the 17th century the dead and dying from the last major Edinburgh plague were taken to that area for care, attention - and burial. This road became today's Blackford Avenue and, by 1884, headed past Blackford Farm, Blackford House and Blackfordhill Dairy to the slopes of Blackford Hill, passing over the Jordan Burn and new railway *en route*. Land was marked out for housing, but it was some years before this was realised, initially north of the line and later encroaching on the slopes of the hill itself. West Saville Terrace was extended west from Newington and from the east came Charterhall Road, linking Cluny Gardens to Blackford Avenue and forming the basis of today's busy crossroads near Blackford Hill station.

Blackford House and Farm were set in sylvan and rural surroundings, and were for many years the home of the Trotter of Mortonhall family although there were a few other buildings and the Jordan Burn, separating Blackford Farm house from Blackford House, was crossed by a little stone footbridge that still exists. This idyllic scene stopped when the railway arrived. Blackford House was later demolished (the main seat of the Trotters was at Charterhall in the borders), but the two-storey farmhouse was modernised and sub-divided, standing for many years in the middle of a modern housing scheme.

Seven months before the railway opened, Blackford Hill and some surrounding land south of the line was bought as a pleasure park by Edinburgh Corporation from the Trotters of Mortonhall for £8,000, although not without opposition as some councillors did not see it as value for money. Previously, for an annual outlay of £1, citizens could get a key to grant them access. A major feature is Blackford Pond, where, as Charles J. Smith recounts in his 'South Edinburgh' books, generations of children fed tons of breadcrumbs to a multitude of swans, ducks and other birdlife. Indeed, since 1848 it had played a part in leisure activities and, in severe winters when the pond froze over, curling and skating took place, the fact that it was 'bearing' being intimated in several shop windows in Morningside Road! In 1890, 3½ acres of ground on the east side of the hill were resold by the Corporation to the government for the location of a new Royal Observatory.

* In Scotland an 'ell' was 37 inches, in England 45 inches.

A class 'J36' 0-6-0 heads an eastbound empty mineral wagon train down the hill through Cluny towards Blackford Hill. On the right is Frank ('The Pie') Ramsay, porter at Morningside Road on his weekly trek to service the paraffin-lit signal lamp of the down distant signal operated by Morningside Road signal box.

Author

Golf Course Traffic

Mention has been made of the 12-hole ladies golf course on the site later occupied by the Astley Ainslie Hospital, accessed from Blackford Hill station. Golf had been played on Bruntsfield Links for several generations, but there was a growing demand for a larger municipal course free from an urban environment. The council considered the open expanses of Blackford Hill (which it owned) and Braid Hills (which it did not) in 1887, Blackford Hill being the chosen railway station for either. After much deliberation (and lobbying), it was decided to purchase the Braid Hills ground in November 1888, at a time when there was little public transport nearer than Morningside Drive or Blackford Hill station. The first course (there were two) opened in September 1889, and proved extremely popular although it was not until 1896 that an Act of Parliament provided for a double line extension of the trams from Morningside Drive to a terminus at Braid Hills Road. The Blackford Hill station access option then quickly faded. The new tram route passed up Comiston Road, parallel with Braid Road, whereon lay the private Mortonhall Golf Course, opened in 1892 with an entrance fee of 10 guineas and an annual subscription of 1 guinea. The North British Railway Tourist Arrangements booklet of 1900 noted that the 5,345 yards-long 18-hole Braid Hills golf course was 'about a mile from Morningside Road station and greatly patronised by all classes of players' with perhaps the only cost being a regulation ticket at 1*d*. assisting its popularity! The nearby Prince's course of 9 holes was free. A horse 'brake' ran from the station when there was sufficient demand to Braid Hills, Mortonhall or the private Lothianburn course one mile beyond the Braids. Braid Hills Hotel, opened in 1881, met the needs of the golfing fraternity and perhaps adversely affected the potential of the proposed 1884 hotel at Morningside Crossroads. East of Blackford Hill, a new private Craigmillar Park course moved from the Newington area and had its clubhouse some 500 yards from the station.

Blackford Hill (Passenger) Station

The railway initially planned a passenger station where Blackford Avenue crossed over the Jordan Burn. This set the station in the grounds of Blackford Farm with the main building on the Inner Circle platform, a wide and level 'drive' extending from Blackford Avenue to the booking office which was level with the street. The Jordan Burn was contained in a brick-lined culvert under the platform and main building. The single level Outer Circle building contained waiting rooms and shared a common approach road, or rather track, with Blackford House. The surrounding area was then largely undeveloped and in the cold light of finance and prospects, construction was cancelled.

In 1883 this decision was reversed and work started, anticipating the April 1884 designation of the hill as a public park but with a more modest station. The main building was still on the Inner Circle side, nearest to its customers, with the booking office in the upper storey some distance from the road, but accessed by an elevated wooden veranda. A wooden stairway led down to the Inner Circle platform and a footbridge passed over the line to the Outer Circle but the latter was replaced on 25th August, 1895 by a conventional iron lattice footbridge by Arrol of Leith. The single-storey brick and timber Outer Circle building was more modest, only containing waiting rooms. The station was gas lit from the outset, and the growth of the surrounding area raised its revenue potential, but also attracted road competition.

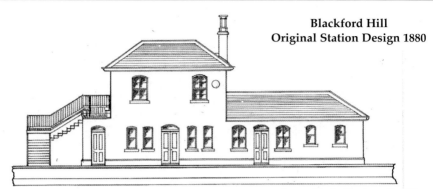

**Blackford Hill
Original Station Design 1880**

Inner Circle Platform Buildings

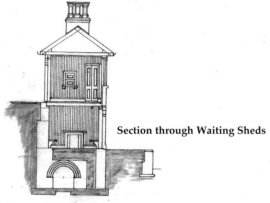

Section through Waiting Sheds

Plan of Inner Circle Building Upper Storey

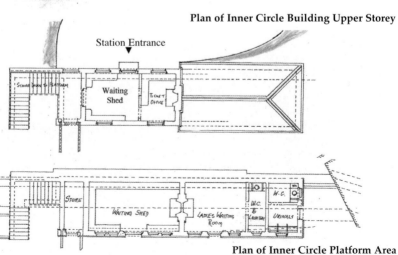

Station Entrance

Waiting Shed

Ticket Office

Stairs Down to Platform

Store

Waiting Shed

Ladies Waiting Room

W.C.
to Cleaners

Urinals

W.C.

Plan of Inner Circle Platform Area

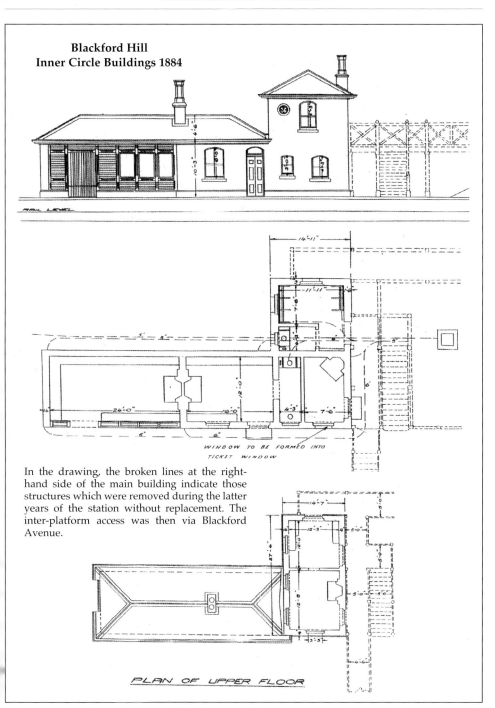

**Blackford Hill
Inner Circle Buildings 1884**

In the drawing, the broken lines at the right-hand side of the main building indicate those structures which were removed during the latter years of the station without replacement. The inter-platform access was then via Blackford Avenue.

WINDOW TO BE FORMED INTO
TICKET WINDOW

PLAN OF UPPER FLOOR

Blackford Hill station in rural and sylvan surroundings about 1890. The city has yet to encroach on its solitude, and the main alternatives in buildings are Blackford House and Farm.

Author's Collection

Horse buses started in 1896 on a 15-minute interval frequency from the Mound via Causewayside. However, at the end of 1904, the operators, the Edinburgh Street Tramways Company, was wound up and the service ceased. Thereafter, until 1923, the railway provided the only convenient local public transport, but its circuitous route and street access at Waverley was counterproductive. On 18th January, 1923, the Corporation restored the bus service between Blackford and the Mound, making serious inroads into railway revenue. In June 1923, this was extended to Morningside cross-roads and within a year to Morningside Drive. Both railway and bus lost out to the private car from the 1950s, but today buses operate over much the same route to the city centre as in 1923.

Initially, the station had a station master, two clerks and two porters, but by 1903 came under Newington. Clerical staff were later withdrawn, 'wages grade' staff undertaking all booking and basic accountancy, major accounts being undertaken by Newington staff. Although the goods yard extended between Blackford Hill and Newington, with the points near Blackford Avenue overbridge, 100 yards from the signal box, both also came under Newington, and the station only dealt with passenger and parcels traffics and proved a popular venue for family and leisure excursions to Blackford Hill.

On 3rd April, 1916, a Zeppelin bombed parts of Edinburgh and train movements were suspended. Before things got back to normal, one goods train is said to have spent the night at the platform, the traincrew being victualled by a local family.

To reduce maintenance costs, the veranda, footbridge and inter-platform links were removed in 1954, isolating and abandoning the upper storey. Outer Circle passengers reached the platform by the old road to Blackford Farm, but Inner Circle passengers used a new metal stairway from street to platform, the only way between the platforms being by Blackford Avenue. Provision was made for a booking office on each platform, the Inner Circle one being created by altering a window in a then disused room at the corner next to Blackford Avenue. For the Outer Circle a partition with a door was built across the interior of the former 'general waiting room', the resultant two rooms being redesignated as 'booking hall' and 'booking office', the latter doubling as staff accommodation. The ladies waiting room was reclassified as a 'general waiting room', but falling patronage produced no real problem. If the new Inner Circle booking office was used, it was only briefly, as latterly booking and parcels work took place from the more accessible Outer Circle building, which had most originating journeys. Needless to say the normal staff path between platforms was across the rails!

When the station closed in September 1962, buildings and platforms, remained but the Inner Circle buildings were removed in July 1966, a sad time for 80-year-old Mrs Norrie who had lived alongside the station for 54 years and got to know many of the trainmen. The Outer Circle buildings and platform remained for a few more years until they too were removed.

Today, little remains with modern domestic housing encroaching on the site. Some space remains, however, to reinstate the platforms if it is decided to restore the passenger service. It certainly has a much greater catchment area than when it closed, but whether the local population could be persuaded to forsake their cars is a different matter!

Blackford Hill station from track level near the end of its operational life in August 1961. The signal box can be seen through the arch of the bridge under Blackford Avenue.   *Author*

Blackford Hill station viewed in August 1961 from almost under the Blackford Avenue bridge at the eastern end. The two-storey booking hall on the Inner Circle platform is on the right, the top storey being disused and isolated after the removal of its access stairway and footbridge.

J.F. McEwan Collection/East Dumbartonshire Library

Above: Modern housing surrounds the station in this 1964 photograph, two years after closure and railway ephemera had been removed. The area is now well built up, with the motor car the predominant form of transport.

Author

Left: An example of the use of the suburban line for special passenger traffic is the six-car set of Derby 'High Density' diesel multiple units used to convey participants to the rehearsal of the opening ceremony for the Commonwealth Games at Meadowbank. The train is passing through the site of Blackford Hill station and shows how complete was the removal of the suburban station.

Bill Roberton

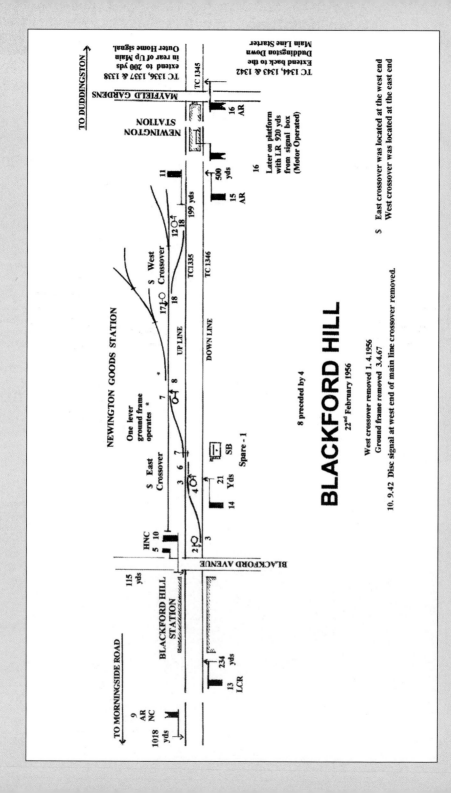

BLACKFORD HILL

22nd February 1956

West crossover removed 1.4.1956
Ground frame removed 3.4.67
10.9.42 Disc signal at west end of main line crossover removed.

8 preceded by 4

$ East crossover was located at the west end
West crossover was located at the east end

Blackford Hill Signal Box

Blackford Hill signal box was located on the Outer Circle side of the line, east of Blackford Avenue overbridge opposite the goods yard entry points and had an 18-lever Stevens mechanical locking frame. Line nomenclature and geography conflicted as the 'up' line was downhill to Newington, and the 'down' line was on the uphill grade to Morningside Road. Conventional signals was employed, with distant, home and starting signals on both lines with an additional outer home on the down line. Internally, the box retained its NBR pattern instruments until closure, supplemented by fittings on its block shelf for the automatic searchlight signals introduced at Cameron Toll between Blackford Hill and Duddingston Junction by the LNER in 1942.

A trailing main line crossover was provided, facing points from the up line gave entry to the goods yard and a crossover from the southernmost siding of the yard later trailed into the up main line. The latter, known as the 'west crossover', (albeit at the east end) was removed on 1st April, 1956. At one time some Inner Circle trains terminated at Blackford Hill, where the engine ran round using the main line and the southernmost goods yard siding, an alternative being an internal goods yard loop. A single-lever ground frame giving access from the yard loop to the yard sidings was removed on 3rd April, 1967. Thereafter, the box merely became an intermediate block post between Duddingston Junction and Morningside Road. It closed, together with Duddingston Junction, on 15th June, 1969 after track and signalling rationalisation and when the Cameron Toll colour light signals were also taken out of service. The structure remained until it was removed on 13th April, 1970.

Looking from Blackford Avenue towards Newington in 1966, with the signal box on the right overseeing the goods yard connections on the inside of the curve.   *Author*

The other LNER No. 4472, (formerly NBR No. 185) was a vacuum-braked former North British Railway 'J35' class 0-6-0, and here heads a Sunday School 'express passenger' excursion from Duddingston to Aberdour up the gradient towards Blackford Hill signal box in June 1956. This engine was withdrawn in March 1962.   *Author*

The Royal Observatory Siding

Astronomy had been taught in Edinburgh since 1583, initially in the 'Tounis College', later Edinburgh University. A bid to set up an observatory in 1776 ran out of funds and it was not until 1792 that it opened on Calton Hill as a joint venture between University and City. A new building opened in 1818 and, when George IV visited the city in 1822, the observatory acquired 'Royal' status, opening in 1824. However, in 1880, the Government proposed that it be closed due to atmospheric pollution which donated the nickname of 'Auld Reekie' to the city. Lord Lindsay, 26th Earl of Crawford and Balcarres, then offered his library of astronomy books, one of the finest in the world, to the state providing that a new observatory was built in the city. This offer was too good to miss and several locations were surveyed before an investigating committee unanimously agreed to a site on Blackford Hill. The prevailing wind blew towards the city, and the 539 feet summit was as high as possible above Edinburgh's 'reek'. Opened in 1896, stellar observations started in January 1897 with instruments brought from Calton Hill and Dunecht. Today it includes the Institute of Astronomy for the University of Edinburgh and still forms an important research facility and includes the original library, but stellar observations ceased some years ago.

Work on the building started in 1893, materials, such as the sandstone from Doddington Hill in Northumberland, arriving via the suburban line. A siding, laid at the railway expense, appears in the NBR Siding Register at Blackford Hill for 'Messrs W. & J. Kirkwood, contractors for the new Observatory', although it was also to be available 'for other traffic if required'. The firm also had premises (and stone works siding) near Morningside Road station, but there was then no direct road between the two places. Costing £292 17s. 0d., Blackford Hill siding opened on 8th August, 1892 but was removed, or ceased to be regarded as a private siding, on 17th May, 1895 when the observatory was almost complete. The siding is not shown on plans or maps, but may have been the group at the Blackford Hill station end of Newington goods yard as photographs show that this was laid after the main yard was operational. As the later West Relugas Road had not been built, the contractor would have required to make a detour to access the observatory site. In the late 1930s, a new stone works opened adjacent to these sidings which had a loading bank and was probably on the original Kirkwood site, but, as far as is known, rail traffic was minimal, if any at all.

Newington Goods Station

East of Blackford Avenue, the Jordan Burn reverted to its original name of Pow Burn. When the railway was surveyed, the burn meandered over the site of the proposed railway goods yard and so had to be realigned. The land for the railway and goods yard was acquired from the estate of Sir Thomas N. Dick Lauder, the main line curvature following the land boundary. South of the line, the land belonged to the estate of Mr W.J. Little Gilmour and on this, light industry developed on the top of the cutting but this was not rail connected and has now been replaced by domestic housing

Operationally it would have been logical to name the goods yard as 'Blackford Hill', but as it extended east to Mayfield Road where the goods office was situated it was decided to use 'Newington'. Five main and two short loading bank buffer-ended sidings (one with capacity to deal with end loading) were installed, opening shortly after the passenger service started and a small goods shed was built near the centre of the rearmost line. A second group, extending to five smaller lines was laid at the west end when the new Royal Observatory was being built, but these later gravitated to handle coal. Most building materials such as slate from Easdale, the Western Isles and Wales, stone from several quarries and imported timber for the extending surrounding suburbia passed through the yard gates into Mayfield Road. These were off-loaded into bays rented by the tradesmen and transferred to iron-tyred two-wheeled carts hauled by Clydesdale horses that noisily clattered to their destinations over the causey stanes* of the street. Carters, sucking on battered tin-lidded 'cutties', perched on grubby sacking draped over the cart shafts. Regardless of their opinions, it was their horses that determined the delivery speed as the carts swayed or slid on the uneven road surfaces.

Newington Goods was the North British railhead for the International Exhibition of Industry, Science and Art held in the Meadows between 6th May and 30th October, 1886 and the railway exhibited a one-month-old, 7 ft driving wheel 4-4-0 express passenger locomotive (No. 592) and new six-wheel first class carriage. These were moved to the eastern end of the goods yard where the wall bordering the north side was taken down. The rolling stock was placed on roller-mounted low platforms dragged by teams of horses, the journey from the goods yard to the exhibition site taking all of two days. This was reversed after the exhibition closed. Neilson & Co. of Glasgow provided a 4-2-2 tender locomotive for display that was subsequently taken over by the Caledonian Railway - the preserved Caledonian 123 - but this

---

* An established Scottish word for what in England are called cobble or paving stones.

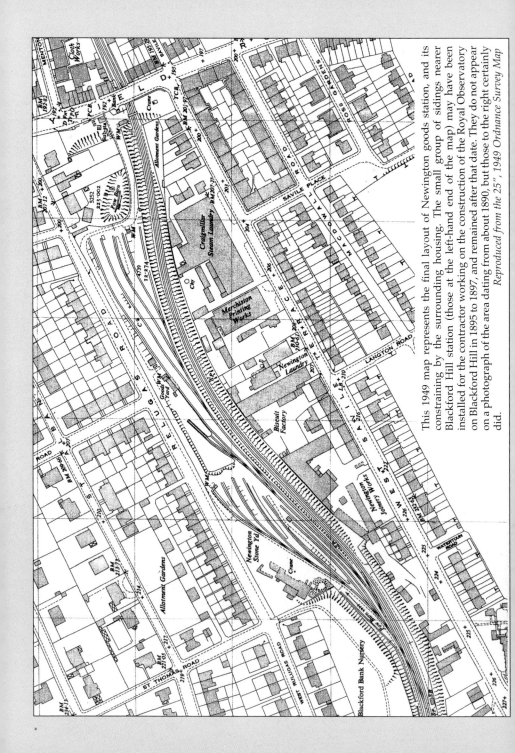

This 1949 map represents the final layout of Newington goods station, and its constraining by the surrounding housing. The small group of sidings nearer Blackford Hill station (those at the left-hand end of the map) may have been installed for the contractor working on the construction of the Royal Observatory on Blackford Hill in 1895 to 1897, and remained after that date. They do not appear on a photograph of the area dating from about 1890, but those to the right certainly did.

Reproduced from the 25", 1949 Ordnance Survey Map

A 1930 aerial view of the east end of Newington Goods yard and the surrounding land. *J. Jones Collection*

Above: Goods yard lighting in the suburban line goods yards was primitive to say the least. At Newington, for example, the structure on the foreground was the base of the solitary gas lamp for the entire depot!   *Author*

Right: Close up view of the lamp supports above the wooden pole which served as the base. Similar structures of varying lengths were provided at the other goods yards on the line.   *Author*

arrived via Lothian Road goods station and used (for the tender at least) the horse tram rails. After the exhibition closed, Newington Goods resumed its everyday but essential existence, ruffled again only by freight for the Highlands and Agricultural Show that was held in the Meadows in 1919.

In mid-September 1905, Newington Goods briefly took on the status of a passenger terminal when the final Review of the Scottish Volunteers was held in Holyrood Park, special trains arriving in the early hours crammed with tired, cramped, cold soldiers, many having travelling all night in unheated four- and six- wheel carriages. The loading bank was used for disembarking and return embarking, but many soldiers still had to climb in and out at ground level, using vehicle footboards. With dress uniforms under greatcoats, they marched out through the goods yard gates towards breakfast in local halls and schools before parading. Shortly after, the Volunteer force was replaced by the Territorial Army.

Most coal arrived in open wagons, not so much owned by the colliery or traders but leased or rented from a central source and painted in distinctive local liveries. When damaged or defective, it was more expedient (and economical) to repair locally, often with primitive equipment (and a general disregard of today's health and safety regulations), to meet the operational requirements of railway (and owner's) inspectors. In practice, the local firm acted as a 'corner garage' as they undertook what could be regarded as light repairs. These sidings were leased in an otherwise public area of goods yards and referred to as 'allocated', not 'private' sidings.

One such 'allocated' siding area was at the Newington station end of the yard. On 31st December, 1933 Mr F.J. Henderson, who already rented 447 square yards of ground in the yard, applied to rent two wagon lengths for repairing and painting wagons. He was granted one wagon length at the buffer ends of both Nos. 4 and 5 sidings (those nearest to Relugas Road) at £5 per annum, the let of which was taken over from Messrs Horace Caldwell & Co., coal merchants, of which Henderson was also the sole proprietor!

In common with most other small depots, Newington gradually lost most of its 'goods' traffic and gravitated to a coal receiving depot with ground rents, excess space and demurrage charges becoming the main, if not sole, freight revenue. In assessing their 'competitive' rates, it was common for road hauliers to telephone the railway and obtain rates that the railway legally had to apply, and then undercut this to prospective customers and secure the traffic.

Although the Newington station master had an office at the passenger station, railway operation economics (a.k.a. staff economies) led to him moving from his small cramped office on the platform to the larger goods office in Mayfield Road which also had its own 'steelyard' (cart weighing machine) outside. In the early 1960s, when passenger carriage condemnation was gathering momentum, Newington Goods hosted a number of old (and not so old) main line carriages, including several redundant catering vehicles awaiting their final journey.

After the suburban passenger train service was withdrawn, Newington Goods became an unstaffed public siding for wagonload traffic. With the coal industry in decline, expansion of smokeless zones and coal depot concentrations, many local coal merchants ceased trading and the yard finally closed on 2nd January, 1967. The area is now covered by residential housing, the site of the goods office now being occupied by a motor car showroom.

An early view of Newington station, taken shortly after the line was opened. The restrictions of space imposed by the island platform gave little scope for a station garden, but the staff compensated in the early days by making and installing window boxes!

Author's Collection

Newington District and Powburn

While Edinburgh's 18th century new town attracted professional and upper classes, the building of the South Bridge attracted the mercantile classes to create their big houses in the Newington district. In his 1879 *Edinburgh - Picturesque Notes* Robert Louis Stevenson was somewhat scathing in his description of these houses, stating that, 'they were not designed for human habitation, and the internal arrangements are, ... fantastically unsuited to the needs of man. They belong to no style of art, only to a form of business much to be regretted'.

Three main roads from Edinburgh to the south passed through Newington, that on the east becoming Dalkeith Road and the west, Causewayside. Minto Street was built between them in the 1820s to ease growing congestion on the others and all were interconnected by self-contained houses giving privacy and seclusion. By 1880, Newington was the most densely populated of Edinburgh's southern suburbs, having a large Jewish mercantile element from the Low Countries. It had been served since 1872 by horse trams down Minto Street (extended as Mayfield Gardens) to the Pow Burn, although by then Powburn village had virtually disappeared, extending into Craigmillar Park in 1877. When the railway opened, a half-hourly tram service was operating to Leith, and beyond Haymarket to Coltbridge and (via Dalry) to Polwarth Gardens near Craiglockhart. The relatively slow horse trams and buses offered no real competition to the trains, nor did the later cable cars, but when electric trams were introduced in June 1922, without the inconvenience of the pedestrian climb out of Waverley (or later traffic congestion), rail passenger traffic to the city centre dwindled.

Powburn village existed before the 18th century where the road to Liberton passed over the Pow Burn, some research also indicating that the ancient Roman Deer Street had also crossed the burn in the vicinity. At one time Powburn had its own baronet and Powburn House next to the railway north east of Mayfield Road bridge was only demolished in 1898. This was replaced by tenements and back greens between railway and Mentone Terrace, which was later extended, and tenements built on land backing on to the line. Local street names were attributed to the local landowner Duncan McLaren, Edinburgh Lord Provost and MP.

Immediately north of Powburn village was Causewayside village, the name being derived from the road's 'causey stanes'. In the 19th century this was a small community of artists and handloom weavers, many of the latter succumbing to the industrial revolution. The villages were separated by Grange Tollbar but, as Edinburgh's boundary moved south, so did this, which became Powburn Toll. The tollhouse was on the west of the road and although it made money, it created a financial inhibition to southern suburb expansion. Abolition of road tolls in 1883 would have made it redundant anyway, but as the railway had to excavate the land on which it stood to take its line under Mayfield Road, it had a slightly earlier demise! A tannery and some dwellings were also removed concurrently, being later replaced by other small businesses.

Newington Passenger Station

Newington passenger station was east of Mayfield Road where Mayfield Gardens joined Craigmillar Park. When the line was planned, as it was the only place with an immediate catchment area, Newington was to be the main station. Great patronage was anticipated, particularly from the prosperous merchants residing locally who

Carrying express passenger train headcode, Corkerhill-based class '5MT' 4-6-0 No. 45053 approaches Newington station on a special of non-corridor coaching stock. The fence separates the footpath to the rear from the line and, despite appearances, was too far from the track to be a station platform.   *Author*

A 1961 view of the pedestrian approach to Newington station from the west was by this footpath alongside the railway line and thence across the wooden footbridge of a similar style to that at Craiglockhart. The distant signal on the platform was relocated from the approach to the Mayfield Gardens bridge at the east end of the station in the late 1950s.

J.F. McEwan Collection/East Dumbartonshire Library

The Suburban was well used as a diversionary route for out-of gauge loads and LNER class 'V1' 2-6-2 No. 2919 takes this stator *en route* from Parsons of Newcastle to Glasgow Corporation gingerly through the Outer Circle platform at Newington on Sunday 25th July, 1937. The operation seems to have attracted some little local attraction as the station was officially closed on Sundays! *Author's Collection*

In August 1956, class 'V3' 2-6-2 tank locomotive No. 67668 heads the 12.37 pm Outer Circle passenger train into Newington. The leading coach is a BR standard non-corridor brake third, a type that only rarely worked in Edinburgh services as 1939 twin sets and pre- and post-war LNER-designed stock was in good supply.

Author

Allocated to Haymarket depot in April 1957, 'Clan' class Pacific 72000 *Clan Buchanan* heads a troop special through the Outer Circle platforms in August of that year bound for the west of Scotland. *Author*

Station staff at Newington in April 1955 comprised of one booking clerk and two porters who undertook the bookings before and after the clerk was on duty (thus covered most trains!). On the right is Duncan Marshall in porter's uniform of the period and the clerk on the right is Douglas Wight, clerks being expected to provide and wear their own clothes at their own expense. The LNER pattern nameboard which replaced the original NBR vitreous enamelled one has individual letters later covered by a vitreous enamelled sheet. Below the nameboard was the nearest that the station got to having a station garden. *Author*

The main Newington passenger station entrance in Mayfield Gardens. Apart from the disappearance of the station buildings in the hollow, the removal of the overhead lamp supports and securing the gates, this view is little changed today.   *Author*

The entrance to the station from Mayfield Gardens is the gate on the right. Next is the driveway to the Royal Blind School with gate lodge, both of which were moved a few yards to the south when the railway was built in 1884. Beyond the lodge is Mayfield Church of Scotland.   *Author*

worked in Edinburgh and Leith, but these were never realised, probably due to trams giving a straight and direct (albeit slower) route. The poor access to the city centre from Waverley contributed then - and still does today!

The line initially passed through land obtained from the Female Blind Asylum, established in 1874 to the south and was flanked on the north by the then Parliamentary and Municipal boundary of the Pow Burn. To minimise land requirement (and expense), the station was of the island type in the cutting below street level with all buildings on the platform. The sylvan entrance and approach driveway from Craigmillar Park to the Asylum were rebuilt to allow excavations for the railway. The gate lodge adjacent to a timber yard was also rebuilt, before the yard was sold to build Mayfield (now Craigmillar Park) Church. The Asylum acquired 'Royal' status in 1893 and now houses the Blind Press Publishers as well as the Royal Blind School for people between 3 and 19. A fairly common duty of the station staff was the retrieval of the special balls with internal bell that had strayed over the wall on to the line. The dressed stone cutting retaining wall alongside the Outer Circle platform sported commercial advertising, as did the lower boundary wall beside the Pow Burn.

Pedestrian access from Mayfield Road was by steps down to a cinder path at about normal platform height parallel with the line, although set back from it, thence by a wooden footbridge over the line. Stone steps connected the east end to Mayfield Gardens. On the opposite side of the steps was a 'standard' NBR three-wheeled platform barrow which, having no brakes, was chained to the railings. The station coal store and dust bin repository was under the stairs but as the prospect of lugging loaded metal dustbins up two flights of steps to street level was daunting, the normal practice was to strengthen the ballast in that area - when nobody was looking!

The station had no proper garden, although the soil surrounding the large enamelled station nameboard (dark blue letters on white background) was 'cultivated' to give a small splash of colour. However, window boxes were also made for several window sills, particularly around the booking and station master's offices. Recesses under the sills were also occupied by commercial advertising boards in North British days.

The station building was of brick, with wooden platform canopies over the central part of its length but no drawings seem to have survived. The booking/parcels office at the east end of the building also served as staff accommodation and was protected from the elements by a wooden 'lean-to'. This also gave shelter to the large and cumbersome 'slide-bar' parcels weighing machine which was rarely used and 'laid off' in the mid-1950s when a smaller dial type was installed on the parcels counter. The booking window was in a transverse passage between booking and station master's office, the latter becoming a store when the incumbent transferred to the goods office on Mayfield Road. The adjacent general waiting room, like Morningside Road, briefly had a 'Mutoscope' machine for the entertainment of waiting passengers. The telegraph office was next, but its equipment was later moved into the booking office. Next was the 'Third Class Ladies Room' with 'en suite' toilet and at the west end the gent's toilet had its open entrance shielded by a large vertical tongue and groove screen, which bore commercial posters until the passenger service was withdrawn.

The main passenger destinations were latterly to Gorgie and Morningside Road as there was no competitive public transport and, despite low revenue yield, in the middle 1950s the station had a booking clerk and two porters. Most bookings were

A loaded train of coal hoppers passes the site of Newington station in October 2002, headed by Canadian-built class '66/0' locomotive No. 66246 in the livery of the English, Welsh and Scottish Railways. This was the fourth last engine of the class and at that time was allocated to Toton Maintenance Depot. *Author*

Across the main road are the Newington Cemetery entrance gates and approach road which were provided by the railway company in compensation for the originals which had to be removed to enable excavation of the railway cutting when the line was built. *Author*

made by the porters on opposite shifts who compiled the 'Train Account Book' at the end of their turns, the mid-shift clerk compiling more detailed accounts, parcels documentation and the cumbersome 'Account Current' at the end of each four-weekly period. The station master dealt with these aspects on behalf of Blackford Hill, as well as paybills, goods documentation and general accountancy, stores and operating matters, and was also in charge of Blackford Hill signal box. His other duties included goods checker, number-taker and measuring and invoicing for wagon demurrage and excess ground occupied by traders, leading to meetings (sometimes heated) with traders. All this for a class 3 salary!

One of the last Newington porters was James Mercer, an Edwardian who was a familiar figure taking a Sunday stroll along Portobello Promenade in an olive green suit and matching bowler hat, his equally elderly sister on his arm. He joined the railway in 1940s when his previous employment with Edinburgh Corporation as a street light extinguisher closed with the blackout and thus Adolf Hitler could be said to have made him redundant! His religious background came to the fore in his dispatch of the Post Office telegrams, dictated in a loud voice over the booking office 'candlestick' telephone using his own phonetic alphabet, such as 'A' for 'Aaron', 'I' for 'Isaiah', 'Z' for 'Zebediah', etc. He was also intense in his belief that there would be an interim interdict from the Town Council to stop the line being closed but none was forthcoming. Indeed the Council voted in those pre-Beeching days to give no financial assistance, thus promoting its closure. It was perhaps ironical that he was on duty for the passage of the last passenger train in September 1962.

The Halls of Residence for female students at Edinburgh University opened in 1914 in nearby East Suffolk Road to a 17th century Scottish country house style. At the close of each term, this generated significant amounts of 'Passengers Luggage in Advance' traffic, although the 'passengers' invariably travelled from the Princes Street or Waverley, usually on the return portions of tickets. Newington could issue long distance tickets, but this was rare, and the only revenue the station achieved was the fee for the luggage (and insurance when students could be persuaded to part with their money).

The station remained relatively intact, after closure, but the buildings were demolished in 1966. The platform was removed in 1983, enabling track realignment and easing the speed restricting 'dog leg' on both lines. Steps from Mayfield Gardens were fitted with a wooden extension to track level, and the former platform area used by the civil engineer but space still exists for an island platform if passenger trains are reinstated. The gate and steps from Mayfield Road exist only to the intermediate landing. Most of the now overgrown fenceless path beside the line also remains.

Newington Station 'Signal Box' and Signals

The station was 1,020 yards from Blackford Hill signal box and 833 yards from Cameron Toll when the latter was open between 1900 and 1925. At 12 noon on Sunday 17th September, 1905, a (very) temporary 'Signal Box' opened on Newington station platform, dividing the Blackford Hill and Cameron Toll section with the sole purpose of helping with train working for the Royal Review of Volunteers in Edinburgh on the following day. It seems that it was just a platform-mounted ground frame that remained operational until 10 pm on the 18th when normal block working was resumed. Circulars indicate that it was a block post in its own right, with the Cameron

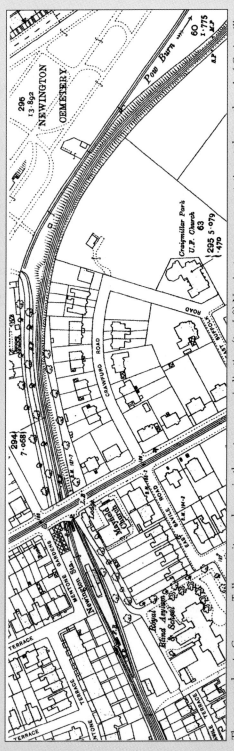

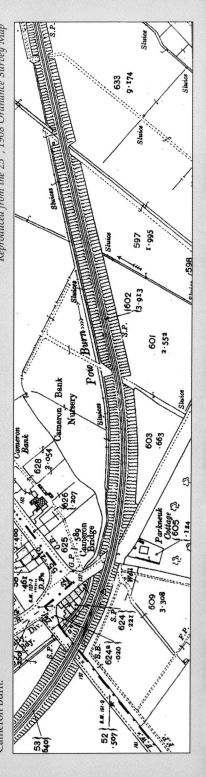

The approaches to Cameron Toll summit are shown in these two maps indicating (*top left*) Newington passenger station at the south end of Craigmillar Park. The relatively short-lived Cameron Toll signal box (1900-1925) is immediately to the right of the bridge over Lady Road, which enters the diagram at the left-hand side of the lower diagram. Also shown running close to the railway line is the Pow Burn, which in this area is sometimes referred to as the Cameron Burn.

Reproduced from the 25", 1908 Ordnance Survey Map

Toll - Newington and Newington - Blackford Hill sections working under double line Absolute Block regulations. Only two signals were provided - a down starting signal at the Blackford Hill end of the platform and an up starting signal at the Duddingston end.

'Newington Station signal box' was resurrected on 8th July, 1907 for an identical purpose - a military review, and appeared from contemporary circulars to be the 1905 platform-mounted ground frame supplemented by a two-lever dwarf ground frame alongside. Again two 'stop' signals were provided, the up and down line starting signals being 90 yards and 86 yards respectively from the dwarf frame. Cameron Toll up distant was temporarily removed and replaced by a bracket arm on the Newington station up starting signal. The block post opened at 10 am on Monday 8th July, 1907, remaining 'in circuit' until 10 am on Saturday 13th July.

Although Newington had no other signal boxes, apart from that at Cameron Toll, visible Blackford Hill signals gave the staff an indication of the approach of Outer Circle trains. In the late 1950s, at the east end of the station, the then motor-operated Blackford Hill down distant of 1942 was moved from east of the Mayfield Gardens road bridge to the west end of the station platform, bracket mounted for visibility and positioned near where a former Cameron Toll signal had stood. Although theoretically shortening the braking distance, the rising gradient probably had more effect. Duddingston down starting signal was also converted to colour light about that time.

Newington and Cameron Toll

Immediately east of the platform, twin single line tunnels carried the Suburban (and parallel Pow Burn) under Mayfield Gardens. Steel girders on stone abutments support the east side of the roadway, as at Morningside Road.

Newington Cemetery, originally laid out in 1846, was north of the line and had a long tree-lined approach road linking it to Mayfield Gardens, opposite the asylum gate. However, as with the asylum, this required to be excavated to form the railway. A new road was built on the opposite side of the Pow Burn 'of at least equal width and gradient to the original'. It also had to be fenced and lined with 'good and sufficient walls' to separate the cemetery road from the railway and of sufficient height to keep the 'engines and trains out of view of horses and persons riding carriages along the new access road'. The railway met these requirements, but the road was later superseded by a new access on the opposite side of the cemetery direct from the adjacent Dalkeith Road. Today the suburban railway gates are in disrepair and their road is now disused and largely overgrown.

The line, separated from the cemetery wall by the Pow Burn, continues in shallow cutting until it reaches the east end of the cemetery, when it starts a short climb on a sharp curve towards the bridge over Lady Road and Cameron Toll where a signal box existed between 1900 and 1925. About 100 yards beyond, a second bridge carried the line over the Old Dalkeith Road before heading east towards Duddingston. The Pow Burn meantime was renamed as the Cameron Burn after passing under Dalkeith Road at Cameron Bridge. It then passed along the south side of Cameron Bank and headed north again under Peffermill Road, then by Closeburn House to join a tail burn from Duddingston Loch at Bowsinch (saved as a nature reserve from a housing development), before entering the Braid (or Peffer) Burn at Forkenford.

Left: Leaving Newington, the line passes under the main road and almost immediately starts climbing on the curve towards a mini-summit at Cameron Toll. The cemetery path, built by the suburban railway is on the left, and housing occupies the space behind the shrubbery on the right. *Author*

Below: Class 'V1' 2-6-2 tank No. 67608 heads a five-coach typical Suburban train of two 1939-built twin sets and single centre vehicle around the curve from Cameron Toll on the approach to Newington. *Author*

Land in this area was owned by Sir Robert Murray of Camrone but the area name may derive from the common, or Cameron Myre through which the Cameron Burn flowed - or just from a corruption of Murray's title. When the line was built, it was some 300 yards from Cameron House, which dated from 1770. Initially in its own grounds, the three-storey house was divided into flats in 1973. Now succumbed to surrounding urbanisation it is now much less prominent.

Cameron Toll was originally known as Cameron Bank Toll and operated at the foot of Lady Road near the junction of Old Dalkeith Road and Peffermill Road from 1820 to 1878. Initially there was a simple road junction with Lady Road coming in from the west a few yards north of the junction of the Musselburgh road (now Peffermill Road) and Dalkeith Road. The suburban line later crossed both Lady Road and the Old Dalkeith Road by separate bridges, but these were strengthened in April 1906 and in the latter part of the 20th century. The road junction was rebuilt as a roundabout. Alongside Lady Road is the site of Craigmillar Gardens leisure area where Cameron Toll shopping centre was opened in 1984 as Edinburgh's first suburban covered shopping mall and was sold to an Irish investor for £75 million in 2002. A further expansion is planned. A short distance from the railway embankment, the centre is seen as an element in the plan for reopening of the suburban line to passengers. The Braid Burn, which crossed the site, was channelled underground and superstores and a collection of smaller shops were built above. Lady Road was realigned and the original formation with its residential housing was truncated as a parallel cul-de-sac. Where old and new roads met (and where there was an outlet from the shopping complex) a further roundabout was created. Some late 18th century houses and outbuildings near the old junction, formerly 2 and 4 Peffermill Road, succumbed to the developers, modern housing now occupying the site.

Cameron Toll Signal Box and later Automatic Searchlight Signals

This first appears in Working Time Tables for October 1900 and was located on top of the embankment on the Outer Circle line immediately south of the bridge over Lady Road, near the 'mini-summit' of the climb from Newington, with an excellent view of the line towards Duddingston. The structure appears to have been built of brick. It had a conventional trailing crossover outside and the usual range of signals on each line but no sidings, its main function being to break up the 2 miles 230 yards-long section between Duddingston Junction and Blackford Hill. Although the actual signals diagram appears no longer to exist, signal and points probably worked from its lever frame can be identified from interpretation of contemporary maps. Operationally and administratively, the box came under the station master at Newington.

The temporary creation of the ground frame 'signal boxes' at Newington affected Cameron Toll signalling, but not to any degree. In 1905, additional stop signals were provided, one on each line at the departure end of the station platform and controlled from Newington station. In 1907, the original Cameron Toll up distant was removed, and a new distant arm provided on a bracket post below the Newington station up starting signal.

The after-effects of the miners' strike in the autumn of 1920 led to a reappraisal of the need for the box, and it was deemed surplus to requirements. Hitherto manned continuously from 6am on Mondays until 5am on the following Sunday, it closed as a block post on 1st August, 1921, although its equipment remained in position. However, the box, its locking frame, all signals worked from it and the crossover road were to be removed on Sunday 4th April, 1925, the opportunity being taken

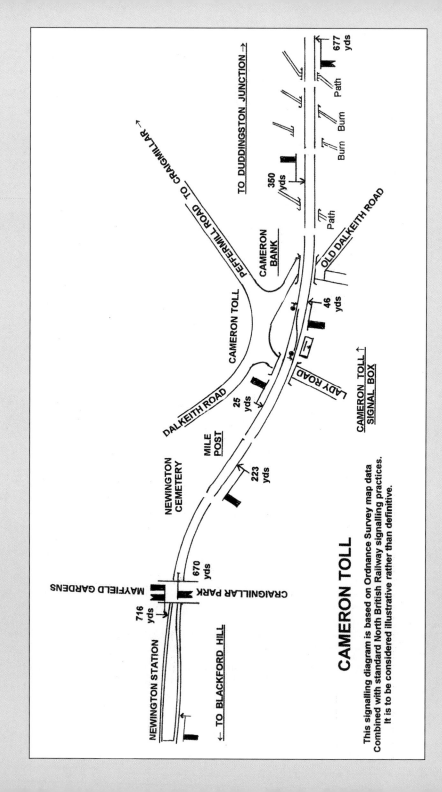

CAMERON TOLL

This signalling diagram is based on Ordnance Survey map data
Combined with standard North British Railway signalling practices.
It is to be considered illustrative rather than definitive.

when the line was closed for this work to be done to repaint several suburban line bridges. A large advertising hoarding at the approach to a busy road junction now hides the site of the box.

With the massive increase in traffic using the Suburban during World War II, automatic colour light signals were installed between Blackford Hill and Duddingston Junction boxes on 13th September, 1942. Concurrently, some changes were made to existing signals. At Blackford Hill, a new down main outer home (semaphore) signal was provided 429 yards east of the box, and a motor-operated distant signal immediately east of the Mayfield Gardens bridge at Newington station, 1,093 yards out. This was later replaced under a 1950s maintenance programme by a motor-operated arm on a bracket 173 yards nearer the box. At Duddingston, a new track-circuited up main outer home was provided, 743 yards west of the box. The up main (semaphore) distant and down main starting signal at the end of the Outer Circle platform were removed, the latter being replaced by a new signal with telephone 'D' plate, approaching overbridge 23, some 688 yards west of the box.

As normal LNER practice, the new colour light signals were identified by the initial of the line to which they referred, 'U(p)' or 'D(own)' and the miles from the main junction, in this case Gorgie Junction, distant signals being prefixed 'R' (for Repeater). Four automatic searchlight signals were provided. Towards Duddingston on the Inner Circle, U4 was a three aspect (red/yellow/green) at 4 miles 576 yards, (1,502 yards from Duddingston) with a telephone 60 feet before the signal post. Lever 55 in Duddingston Junction enabled the signal to show a green aspect in place of the normal yellow. This was preceded by a two-aspect automatic searchlight distant signal (RU4) 700 yards nearer Newington. On the Outer Circle, D3, was a two aspect automatic searchlight signal (red/green) at 3 miles 1,628 yards, (1,535 yards from Blackford Hill) and had a telephone 60 feet on the approach side linked to Duddingston box and was preceded by a two-aspect automatic searchlight distant signal (RD3) 600 yards east. Advance track circuits replaced all four signals to their most restrictive aspects, but RD3 was restored by occupancy of the track circuit ahead of signal D3. Catch points were 500 yards in rear of D3, between D3 and RD3 protecting against runaways on the gradient. A switch in Duddingston Junction box enabled the light intensity to be dimmed in the event of a threatened air raid, but this was discontinued on 17th July, 1945. All four signals were removed when the 'controlling' Blackford Hill and Duddingston Junction signal boxes closed in 1969.

Proposed Cameron Toll Station

The continuing southern expansion of Edinburgh and the presence of the massive Cameron Toll shopping centre would appear to indicate that the reinstatement of the closed Newington station, should the line ever reopen to passenger trains, may prove uneconomic. Certainly, when that station was open, patronage from the locality was poor, and although it is claimed that the station could benefit from today's city traffic congestion, the number of buses now operating is greatly increased over that of the 1960s. If the shorter station to station journey time is offset by the time taken to access city streets from the depths of Waverley, unassisted by escalators or lifts, this advantage diminishes. On the other hand, a station near Cameron Toll built on what might be termed a 'green field' with potential for scratch installation of 21st century facilities and direct access with the shopping centre, could have potential. Only time will tell.

Cameron Toll and Peffermill

The Cameron Toll signal box overlooked Cameron Bank, as the first section of Peffermill Road is known, and on which were situated nurseries and dairies. The former were part of market gardens serving the city, and the latter claim to have been moved to the suburbs to meet the demands of Dr Littlejohn, Edinburgh's first Environmental Health Officer as part of his campaign to eradicate tuberculosis and other cattle related diseases from the city. On 3rd April, 1916, one of several bombs dropped from the marauding Zeppelins fell on the Cameron Bank Dairy, only 400 yards from the railway. Suffice to say that the accuracy of the drop and the size of the bomb caused damage in total estimated at only £1 - or two broken windows.

After passing the box, the line descended towards Duddingston at 1 in 100 for almost ¾ mile, largely through meadowland, and passing over the Braid Burn *en route*. The course of this waterway was changed after it passed under the Old Dalkeith Road, and instead of meandering across open meadow, was channelled straight through land used by Edinburgh University as playing fields, enhanced in the 1970s by the transfer of facilities from Craighouse. Near here, the NBR proposed to create a triangular junction in 1865 on a stillborn suburban line scheme, which had branches to Lasswade, etc.

Peffer Mill means 'a mill on a dark and muddy stream', the stream being the Braid Burn. Peffermill House of 1636 is said to be where the Laird of Dumbiedykes lived in the Scott novel *Heart of Midlothian*, but has little historical pedigree. Restored in 1980, with a 17th century interior style, it is still occupied although surrounded by Peffermill Industrial Estate. The originally water-powered threshing mill was removed in the late 1970s, some 80 years after its pond and lade.

Before the line was built, the road between Cameron Toll and Cairntows Toll followed a 'dog leg' formation along the boundary between two landowners and this road was crossed on the level by a single track railway between Craigmillar Quarry and Cairntows on the St Leonards branch. This North British line, termed as a 'tramway' by Ordnance Survey, had originally opened in March 1859 but was later closed and lifted. Reinstated again in October 1874, for a different contractor, it was closed and lifted again in 1882 when the suburban railway was under construction. When the suburban line was built, the main road was straightened and carried over the line by a skew bridge although part of the original course was retained to serve as access to Peffermill House and today forms the entrance to the Industrial Estate.

Chapter Nine

Duddingston

Duddingston Village

Duddingston village is some 2 miles from the centre of Edinburgh on the south-east slopes of Arthur's Seat and may have taken its name from the Dodin (Dodington) family who settled there in the 11th century. There was certainly a settlement there in the 12th century, when the Norman church was built on a rocky knoll overlooking Duddingston Loch. Modified, it is still essentially Norman, with carved door and original arches over the south doorway and chancel. Near the entrance is a 'Loupin-on Stane' by which corpulent or elderly parishioners mounted their horses and at the churchyard entrance is an iron collar chained to the wall, which was used in the 16th and 17th century for restraining and publicly humiliating members of the community judged guilty of adultery or other offences against the laws of God (and for scolding women!) The manse dates from 1805, a visitor being Sir Walter Scott who wrote part of the *Heart of Midlothian* there and became a Kirk Elder in 1806. The then minister was an accomplished landscape artist, John Thompson, who painted in a small round hut near the loch, which he named 'Edinburgh'. When in his retreat, his wife could quite honestly say that he was 'away in Edinburgh!' At one end of the main street is the 18th century successor of the 16th century 'Sheep's Heid Inn', one of Scotland's oldest hostelries, the name deriving from a culinary delicacy served to the Stuart dynasty on hunting pursuits. At the other end is a white house where Princes Charles Edward Stuart is said to have lodged before and after the battle of Prestonpans. By the early 19th century, almost every village house had its own weaving loom and some 40 of these produced a cloth called 'Duddingston Hardings'. Known for the coal carriers and labourers in its small population, the brewing industry that dominated the area for almost a century was of the future, directly resulting from improved transport brought about by the suburban railway.

The village remained outwith Edinburgh's boundary until 1901 and Duddingston Loch south of the village (now much smaller) became a bird sanctuary in 1923 with its surrounds a nature reserve. This loch is partly fed from the 'Wells o' Wearie' next to the Edinburgh & Dalkeith Railway at the foot of the Cairntows and St Leonards incline.

West of the village lies today's Duddingston Road West and some half a mile south was Cairntows with its level crossing over the Edinburgh & Dalkeith Railway, a bridge carrying the road over the suburban railway a few yards further on. Duddingston's goods and passenger stations were between Dalkeith and suburban lines, east of the road.

Duddingston Brewing

The first brewery was built half a mile south of Duddingston Kirk. A foremost pre-requisite for quality beer is a good clear water supply and Artesian bores beside the railway proved that this existed in abundance, aided by geographical subterranean layers. Water quality resulted in several rail-connected breweries being established, the first being the Craigmillar Brewery of William Murray in 1886 followed by Drybrough's in 1892. To these were added the North British, Castle,

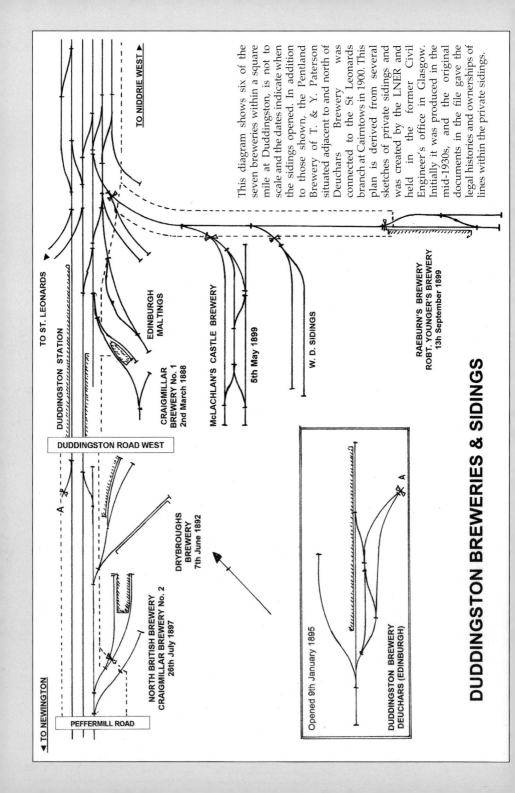

This diagram shows six of the seven breweries within a square mile at Duddingston, is not to scale and the dates indicate when the sidings opened. In addition to those shown, the Pentland Brewery of T. & Y. Paterson situated adjacent to and north of Deuchars Brewery was connected to the St Leonards branch at Cairntows in 1900. This plan is derived from several sketches of private sidings and was created by the LNER and held in the former Civil Engineer's office in Glasgow. Initially it was produced in the mid-1930s, and the original documents in the file gave the legal histories and ownerships of lines within the private sidings.

TO NIDDRIE WEST ►

TO ST. LEONARDS

DUDDINGSTON STATION

EDINBURGH MALTINGS

CRAIGMILLAR BREWERY No. 1
2nd March 1888

McLACHLAN'S CASTLE BREWERY

5th May 1899

W. D. SIDINGS

RAEBURN'S BREWERY
ROBT. YOUNGER'S BREWERY
13h September 1899

DUDDINGSTON ROAD WEST

◄ TO NEWINGTON

DRYBROUGHS BREWERY
7th June 1892

NORTH BRITISH BREWERY
CRAIGMILLAR BREWERY No. 2
26th July 1897

PEFFERMILL ROAD

Opened 9th January 1895

A

DUDDINGSTON BREWERY
DEUCHARS (EDINBURGH)

DUDDINGSTON BREWERIES & SIDINGS

Aerial view of the Duddingston breweries surrounding the railway station, taken about August 1930. The open terrain to the south (*top of the picture*) has much changed over the intervening years.   *Bill Roberton Collection*

Raeburns (later Robert Younger's) and Pentland, as well as several maltsters. The railway derived revenue from brewery workers (most did not live locally), inward raw materials, and outward brewing produce. Indeed on occasions it had to concede passenger train 'political points' to some brewers in view of the volume of their freight business.

Good malting barley initially came from the surrounding agricultural land in the Lothians, although as the industry expanded, grain was imported through Leith Docks from Australia, America and Canada. This arrived either in sacks or in special grain wagons from which the grain was gravity discharged through hoppers in the wagon floor. Brewing hops came from the south of England, primarily Kent, again most arriving by rail. A clean atmosphere was also available, despite Edinburgh's reputation, as the prevailing wind came from the south-west.

Beer casks were loaded in the brewery sidings as 'full wagon loads' direct to destinations, but smaller consignments went into separate wagons which only ran to Duddingston goods yard loading banks where 'bank' wagons from several breweries were combined into full wagon loads. By the late 1930s, almost all the output was destined for Scotland and North East England and a regular express freight left Duddingston around midnight for Newcastle (Forth) loaded almost entirely with cask ale in railway-owned wagons, the empties returning in specially built or adapted railway-owned vehicles.

Although brewing of cask beer dated from 1886, bottled beer really only developed during and after the Great War. Industry by-products also generated significant traffic such as 'Yeastrel', which was yeast left over from beer making, its high vitamin content being used for many culinary purposes such as sandwich spreads and soup flavouring. Collected as 'Draff' from the breweries, large quantities were also sent out as cattle fodder after drying.

Duddingston Sidings (West)

All breweries were east of Peffermill Road bridge. Drybrough's and the North British Breweries were next to each other on the down side of the suburban line with Duddingston Brewery on the up side and the smaller Pentland behind. However, industry technical developments, rationalisation, mergers and 'take-overs' mean that all have now closed, their sites forming 'business parks' or 'industrial estates' - or still awaiting exploitation.

Access to Drybrough's Brewery came from a shunting siding which trailed into the down suburban. When Blyth & Cameron's (later North British) Brewery opened in 1897, the west end of this line was extended under Peffermill Road bridge to provide a down side headshunt, Duddingston Brewery trailing into the up suburban line. All had internal private sidings, Pentland Brewery being served from the St Leonards branch.

Drybrough's Brewery Siding

Andrew Drybrough was brewing before 1750 and was succeeded by James Drybrough at the Tolbooth Wynd in Edinburgh's old town. The firm moved to the south side of the North Back of the Canongate, in 1782 as 'Andrew Drybrough & Co.' and in 1874 expanded into the Craigend Brewery on the same side of the street. In 1892 they wanted to expand again but had no space. However, the North British Railway wanted their site for its Waverley station rebuilding and the brewery gratefully moved to a 'green field' site at Craigmillar, with the suburban railway literally on its doorstep. Drybrough & Company registered as a limited company in December 1895, formally acquiring the business.

The brewery siding came from an agreement between the NBR and Drybrough & Co. of 1st December, 1891. The railway agreed to make and maintain at its expense the 22 yard link from the shunting line to its boundary, the brewery continuing it into their premises and maintaining these internal lines at their own expense. Opened on 7th June, 1892, the siding had a connection from the shunting line, a single buffer-ended railway-owned siding between brewery and Suburban which made a trailing connection with the down main. Inside the brewery premises, the siding divided into two small groups, one of which had a small 'rounding loop', although this was later removed. The whole internal brewery layout was repaired in 1943 at brewery expense.

Most of Drybrough's output for many years went to South West Scotland and North East England, beer being supplied to the Alnwick Brewery in Northumberland in 1963, expanding in 1964 to Dundee. Messrs Watney Mann acquired the firm in 1965 and the railway connection and sidings closed on 2nd October, 1967, the 1891 agreement being considered as terminated from that date. The brewery continued with road transport until it closed on 23rd January, 1987, 15 days after being sold to Allied Lyons, on behalf of the Alloa Brewery. The site now contains light industrial units.

North British (Craigmillar No. 2) Brewery Siding

On 17th July, 1896, a drain was provided for Messrs Blyth and Cameron's North British Brewery and the Outer Circle was closed for the day to allow this work. In 1897, a siding was opened for the firm, later Messrs J. Somerville & Co., with 33 yards on NBR land and another 393 yards beyond, costs being estimated as £320, with the NBR bearing the cost of the portion on its land and the trader paying the balance. Siding materials belonged to the railway but the trader had the responsibility for maintenance outwith the railway boundary. Opened on 26th July, 1897, a second siding was also laid on railway land, 22 yards from the main line, with a loading bank between. A turntable from the siding nearest the brewery let wagons move at right angles into the brewery and a steelyard (weighbridge) was installed at the trader's expense in April 1898. A separate siding, the property of the brewery although on railway land and accessed by a ground frame, was later added towards Peffermill Road bridge. Initially, a signalled trailing connection was laid from Peffermill Bridge end into the siding, but this was removed on 18th November, 1901 when a new facing connection with appropriate signalling was installed at the Duddingston station end and the shunting siding made buffer-ended and extended under Peffermill Road bridge. Both North British and Drybrough's premises were then served by trailing points from the shunting siding. In 1922, William Murray and Company, owners of Craigmillar Brewery east of the station, took over the North British Brewery and renamed it as 'Craigmillar Brewery No. 2'.

When the North British Brewery opened literally next door to Drybrough's in 1897, a new working arrangement came into operation. The original short 'shunting line' outside Drybrough's was extended west, requiring a new bore underneath the Peffermill Road Bridge and for 100 yards beyond. New trailing connections were taken from the extended 'shunting line' instead of the down suburban line into both breweries.

Breweries lined the approach to Duddingston from the west. In this 1930 view from Peffermill Road, a six-coupled tender engine is shunting the premises of the North British Brewery, with Craigmillar No. 2 beyond and Deuchars across the suburban main line. *Author's Collection*

Having concluded its shunting operations at the breweries west of Duddingston station, an 'N15' class 0-6-2 tank engine propels its van back towards Duddingston Junction. The 'seamless' extension to the Outer Circle platform to deal with departing troop trains during and after World War I is clearly seen almost as far out as the signal box. *Author*

Entry to the shunting line was by ground frame released by Annett's Key interlocked with Duddingston Junction signals. Only one locomotive was allowed on the shunting line at any one time and before the Key was handed to the guard or shunter, the signalman had to set the points. The Key was then shown to the driver as authority to pass the Duddingston down starting signal at 'danger'. When the movement was completely on the shunting line and the ground frame controlled points reversed and locked 'normal', the Key was returned to the signalman who replaced it into his frame to resume normal Suburban working. When shunting was finished, the guard or shunter returned to the signal box for the Key to unlock the ground frame and the engine could return to Duddingston. Wagons were hauled into the shunting line and set back into the appropriate brewery sidings, and on exit, propelled 'wrong line' through Duddingston Outer Circle platform to Duddingston Junction.

Brewing ceased at the original Craigmillar Brewery in 1950, but continued at the North British site before Murray's were taken in over in May 1960 by Northern Breweries of Great Britain Ltd, later United Breweries Ltd. Passing to Charrington & Co. via a Charrington group holding company in 1962, resource rationalisation led to the North British ceasing brewing in May 1962, residual work moving to the old Aitchison Jeffrey Ltd 'Heriot Brewery' in Roseburn Terrace, near Haymarket engine sheds. For the next two years, the North British building continued with bottling and malting, until that was also discontinued and the premises finally closed. Sidings remained in position until 9th October, 1967, the formal agreement with the brewery having terminated in the previous week. 35 years on, some buildings still await their fate in the 'Holyrood Business Park'.

Duddingston (Pattison's and later Deuchar's Edinburgh) Brewery

Pattison, Elder & Company's brewery was across the suburban line from Drybrough's and was built for the two Pattison brothers, perhaps better known in whisky production circles. It was served by a trailing connection from the Inner Circle (up) line close to the bridge carrying Duddingston Road West over the suburban line. Under an 1895 agreement between the NBR and the brewery, the railway paid for the main line connection and track up to the trader's gate (including the trap points) at the railway boundary, but other costs were borne by the trader. The siding initially comprised of a single line from the NBR points to a brewery headshunt and a trailing connection from this to a buffer-ended loading bank and opened on 9th January, 1895 resulting in some signalling changes including the control of the connection by Annett's Key. Extended by 35 ft at the trader's expense in September 1896, Pattison's provided a crossover road in March 1897.

Unfortunately, the business acumen and accountancy methods of the brothers were questionable and both served terms in prison for fraud. In 1899, the firm went into voluntary liquidation. In 1900, the Newcastle-based firm of Robert Deuchar Ltd (registered 1897 to acquire the Newcastle brewery of John Arnison Simson), took over the nearly new building at an extremely favourable price together with St Mary's Canongate Brewery of Simson and Matheson Ltd. This had ceased brewing in 1898 but continued as maltings until 1967.

At the end of 1911, a further siding extension to the brewery (by then renamed Deuchar's Edinburgh Brewery) lines was authorised at a cost of only £29. A further extension in 1919 cost the brewery £3,893, well within the agreed estimate of £5,000.

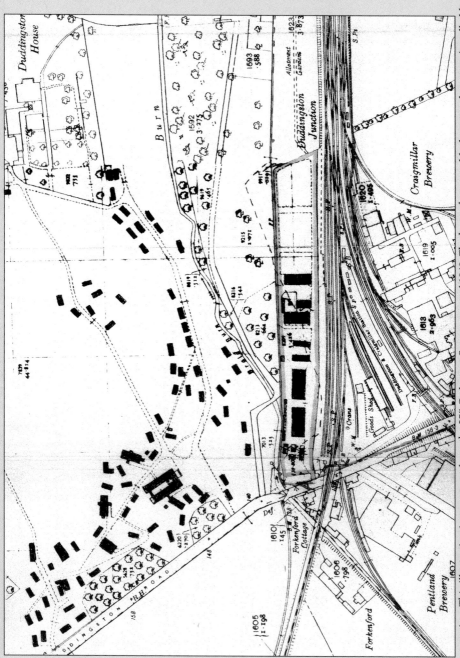

Duddingston station. This illustration is an extract from the 25" Ordnance Survey map of 1948. The huts, shown as black rectangles, were installed by the army during World War II. Abandoned after the war they were 'taken over' by civilians. Eventually the area was cleared by land sale.

In 1941, Steel, Coulson & Co. acquired Deuchar's of Edinburgh and the entire siding was overhauled in November 1945, costing the trader £1,310. Deuchar's Edinburgh Brewery and some 360 tied houses were taken over by Newcastle Breweries in 1954. Newcastle Breweries merged with the Scottish Brewers consortium in 1960, forming Scottish and Newcastle, but a survey of the new concern indicated surplus capacity and brewing at Duddingston ceased in 1961 although the premises continued as maltings until about 1970. Meantime, after termination of the agreement with Deuchar's on 6th May, 1968, the siding connection was removed. The building, largest of the Duddingston area breweries, was demolished in the early 1970 and the site remained empty for nearly 30 years. Meantime, ground to the west had been transformed into Peffermill Industrial Estate.

Railway siding working arrangements were similar to Drybrough's, although the ground frame released by the Annett's Key worked main line points. When an engine or train required to work the siding, the Key was obtained from the signalman, allowing the driver to propel 'wrong line' to the siding points. Once inside, main line points were reset at the ground frame and the key returned to the signalman, who could then unlock the protecting main line signal. The shunting engine propelled its van, and any other wagons, to Duddingston Junction, but on the 'right line'.

Duddingston Station

The south end of Duddingston Road passed above the Suburban on an overbridge. To the east, the line curved to join the St Leonards branch at Duddingston Junction, the passenger station being on this curve. Cairntows was where Duddingston Road crossed Peffermill Road, the level crossing being about midway to Duddingston Village. The station served the village, albeit some distance away, but additional patronage was anticipated from the extensive golf course that was being created in the grounds of nearby Duddingston House. Members of the Edinburgh Insurance and Banking Golf Club are believed to have made a contribution towards the station cost.

The station buildings were similar to Gorgie, using red brick, with timber fronts to the general waiting rooms and no canopies were provided. Both platforms had independent road access, the Outer Circle platform being level with Station Road, the Inner Circle by a slope down from Duddingston Road West. A lattice footbridge connected the platforms at the Newington end of the buildings. Two booking offices were provided, one on each platform, although as elsewhere, one was later adapted to other uses. Gentlemen's toilets were accessed from behind a screened doorway at the east end of the building, but ladies accessed their toilets through the ladies waiting rooms.

The suburban line passed midway between Duddingston village and Craigmillar Castle, both being incorporated in the station name. There was little passenger potential until the brewing industry developed and a substantial Victorian tenement was built beside the Outer Circle platform. Initially 'Duddingston and Craigmillar' in public timetables, Craigmillar Castle was perhaps the most significant landmark. The extensive Craigmillar housing schemes which were to dominate the district were still decades away. The original name was still used in 1940, but by the time British Railways was formed in 1948, it was merely 'Duddingston', the 'and Craigmillar' being restored in the early 1950s.

Station Buildings at Duddingston and Craigmillar

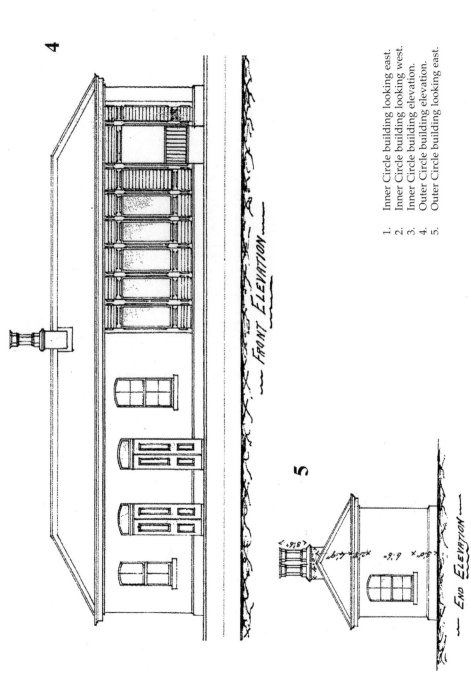

4

~ FRONT ELEVATION ~

5

~ END ELEVATION ~

1. Inner Circle building looking east.
2. Inner Circle building looking west.
3. Inner Circle building elevation.
4. Outer Circle building elevation.
5. Outer Circle building looking east.

Duddingston and Craigmillar station from the road bridge over the line at the west end of the platforms and retaining at that time the LNER fittings and long name-board. This was replaced by a shorter Scottish Region blue vitreous enamelled sign with the name in white on two lines.

W. Lynn Collection

Former War Department 2-8-0 No. 90182 passing Duddingston on the last lap of its run from Fife to Niddrie in September 1960. Built by the North British Locomotive Company at its Hyde Park Works, Glasgow, it was initially equipped with an air brake pump on the smokebox side when loaned to the LNER as WD 7206 from September 1943 to December 1944. It returned to the LNER on loan in March 1947 as WD 77206 and when taken over by British Railways was renumbered 90182. *Author*

If an 1896 NBR scheme had been developed, the original station would have been replaced by an island platform. The then Outer Circle (down) line was to become a shunting siding with its buildings becoming goods offices. The Inner Circle (up) line and platform would have become the Outer Circle line, and a new Inner Circle line taken through a new tunnel under Duddingston Road and around the rear of the original, which would have got a new platform face. Pedestrian access to the island platform would have been from Duddingston Road, the booking office remaining at the road bridge end. The new Inner Circle platform would have been 600 ft long and the Outer Circle 570 ft, but the scheme was abandoned after drawings were prepared on 20th August, 1896. The island platform scheme would have almost eliminated the goods station between suburban and St Leonards lines and Deuchars brewery would have been required to yield land.

In 1910, Duddingston was the scene of another stillborn North British proposal, this time for a carriage cleaning and storage depot. Land between the sidings adjacent to the St Leonards branch and Duddingston House grounds was earmarked for a nine-road carriage servicing depot, three being equipped with low platforms for exterior washing. Original estimates quoted a holding figure of 314 carriages, a nominal average figure of 35 on each line. The sidings were, as would be expected, on level ground, and the cost estimated at £9,139, with cleaning platforms accounting for £650. In addition to standage sidings, a 34 vehicle-long run-round loop was envisaged between the St Leonards sidings and the carriage sidings. Buffer stops of all sidings were close to Duddingston Road, the access requiring all trains to set back from the suburban line, with existing track being adjusted to suit. Siding access would have been controlled by Duddingston Junction box, which then had a separate adjacent lamp room.

At the end of World War I, a camp was set up for military demobilisation in the grounds of Duddingston House and special trains were run to and from the station until the requirement ceased. When the camp closed on 4th March, 1919, it was estimated that some 52,206 officers and men had translated to civilian life. Discounting administrative staff, it appears that, allowing for an inward and outward journey for each serviceman, some 104,412 journeys were made through its platforms. To deal with this, the Inner Circle (Newington to Niddrie direction) platform was extended eastward using timber built on and from the ramp of the original and trains arrived and departed from here to destinations all over Britain those going south being routed either by the East Coast or Carlisle. The lengthened platform extended almost to Duddingston Junction signal box and remained long after it was required. No changes were possible to the Outer Circle platform which lay between siding points and Duddingston Road West overbridge. The station was well used by the military during the two world wars - and also by Italian PoWs during World War II when paroled to make trips to Edinburgh.

Duddingston Goods

Duddingston Goods lay in the fork of the suburban and St Leonards lines, much of its work being associated with the private siding traffics although a temporary livestock loading bank was installed on 4th July, 1907. Little changed in the goods office, however, and even in the 1950s, clerks worked at high sloping desks in parallel lines where they could either stand or sit on high stools in Victorian fashion. Heating was by a circular coal stove in the centre of the rectangular office. In

Duddingston Junction signalling diagram

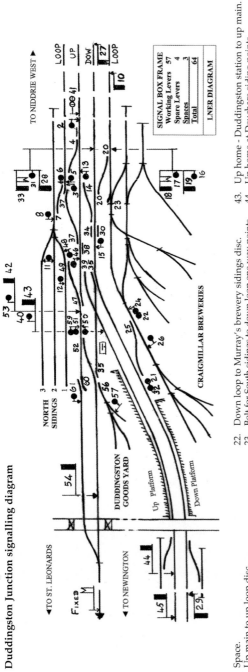

1. Space.
2. Up main to up loop disc.
3. Up loop to up main disc.
4. Up main to up loop points.
5. Up loop to up main disc.
6. Up loop to Niddrie West disc.
7. Up sidings to up loop points.
8. Up sidings to up loop or headshunt disc.
9. Spare.
10. Down home.
11. North sidings 2 and 3 to No. 8 disc.
12. North sidings No. 1 to No. 8 disc.
13. Up main to down main crossover disc.
14. Up main to down main crossover points.
15. Down main to up main crossover disc.
16. Down loop to down line sidings disc.
17. Down loop to St Leonards branch disc.
18. Down loop to St Leonards branch home.
19. Down loop to down suburban home.
20. Down loop to down main points.
21. Down suburban to down loop disc.
22. Down loop to Murray's brewery sidings disc.
23. Bolt for South sidings to down loop one way points.
24. Down loop to down suburban disc.
25. Down loop to down suburban points.
26. Brewery sidings to down loop disc.
27. Down distant from Niddrie West.
28. Down main to down suburban home signal.
29. Down advanced starter to Blackford Hill.
30. Facing point lock, down main to Sub line.
31. Down main to Duddingston goods yard disc.
32. Down suburban to down main disc.
33. Down main to down St Leonards branch.
34. Facing point lock, down main to up main.
35. Down main to Sub or St Leonards branch points.
36. Spare.
37. Up loop to up main points.
38. Facing point lock for No. 37 points.
39. Up suburban or St Leonards branch points.
40. Up Duddingston station to up main disc.
41. Up starter to Niddrie West.
42. Up home - St Leonards branch to up main.
43. Up home - Duddingston station to up main.
44. Up home at Deuchars siding points.
45. Up outer home.
46. Up main to up Sub or up St Leonards branch disc.
47. St Leonards branch or up Sub to up main point.
48. North sidings to St Leonards branch sidings disc.
49. North sidings to St Leonards branch sidings points.
50. St Leonards branch sidings to St Leonards branch disc.
51. Up main to goods yard disc.
52. Up main to goods yard or St Leonards branch points.
53. St Leonards branch to up loop disc.
54. Home from St Leonards.
55. Automatic signal U4 to set lever at green.
56. Points for entry to Duddingston goods yard.
57. Exit from Duddingston goods yard disc.
58. Spare.
59. Up main to St Leonards branch trailing disc.
60. Trap points from St Leonards branch.
61. Trap points disc.
62. Spare.

documentation, Scottish brewing terminology was used for the differing sizes of casks, much to the bewilderment of relief clerks where the pronunciation differed from the spelling!

One customer of the goods station was the Craigmillar Creamery which had been established in 1855 and daily sent out vanloads of 'Apple Blossom Margarine'. Across the main road from Raeburn's Brewery, it was never rail connected, and closed in the 1960s.

Most sidings near the goods office had loading banks, simplifying cask and barrel handling and a goods shed provided cover for traffic requiring weather protection. The goods station survived the passenger station by almost six years, mostly handling beer traffic, and it closed on 5th February, 1968 but all traces were subsequently removed and the site still remains a wasteland 35 years on. Although passenger trains were withdrawn, parcels traffic continued to be dealt with at the Inner Circle booking office. The former Outer Circle platform was removed completely, but the overgrown Inner Circle platform still remains. The short street from Duddingston Road West to the Outer Circle platform was named 'Station Road', but changed to 'Peffer Street' in 1967, avoiding confliction with an identically named Corstorphine street. Similarly, Mitchell Street at the south end of Station Road became 'Peffer Place' in 1966, avoiding duplication with an identically named street in Leith. The demolished Craigmillar Brewery and Maltings site was redeveloped as 'Castlebrae Business Centre' and Peffer Place extended to meet Harewood Road in the Niddrie housing scheme.

When Edinburgh Corporation created their Niddrie/Craigmillar housing schemes their bus service was adequate, but has since been vastly improved by Lothian Buses (successor to Edinburgh Corporation Transport) and it is doubtful if there is a future for a reopened station, at least on the original site. The area is not high in private transport, but the convenience of the bus is a major factor and with the disposition of population to the east, there may be scope for a station in Niddrie.

Duddingston Junction Signal Box

East of the passenger station, the Suburban joined the former Edinburgh & Dalkeith Railway at Duddingston Junction, also known as St Leonards Junction, Duddingston goods station connecting into the St Leonards branch. The original 30 ft signal box was overwhelmed by railway expansion and private siding connections and when the line between Duddingston and Niddrie West was quadrupled, it was replaced by a larger structure but the actual date is unclear. This may have been on 5th October, 1899 when significant signalling alterations were completed. A larger Niddrie West Junction box opened at the opposite end of the quadrupling on 17th June, 1900 and further signalling was added at Duddingston on 18th November, 1901. The Duddingston and Niddrie West quadrupling officially opened on 3rd August, 1902.

In the late LNER period Duddingston Junction box had a 64-lever frame, 57 of which were operational, with 4 spare and 3 spaces. The decline of the brewing industry and wagon-load traffic together with the opening of Millerhill yards led to the closures of the Niddrie yards which were inconvenient and in excess of requirements. Duddingston Junction had been connected to Cairntows (*en route* to St Leonards) by a bi-directional single line with parallel loop but closure of the branch in 1968 virtually eliminated the need for the box and it closed on 15th June, 1969, being demolished on 13th April, 1970.

In addition to working to Niddrie West and Blackford Hill (Cameron Toll from 1900 to 1925) Duddingston Junction box also worked to Cairntows, a small elevated ground frame in a brick and timber building resembling a small hipped roof North British Railway signal box at the east end of the St Leonards branch. Before the arrival of the suburban railway, a branch line left the St Leonards line on Duddingston Road at Cairntows and headed south to the Craigmillar Quarry but this was closed and lifted when the suburban line cut across its path at Peffermill Road. Cairntows had a 'Stevens' 9-lever ground frame, no block instruments, and the level crossing gates across Duddingston Road were manually operated without gate locks or wheels. Creature comforts for the occupant comprised of a dilapidated wooden chair and open coal fire. The St Leonards branch Train Staff custodian was the Duddingston Junction signalman, the branch being worked by 'Staff and Ticket' regulations, the staff having an Annett's Key to operate the points at each end of a loop on the branch before the 1 in 30 climb for 1,208 yards to St Leonards. Certain Duddingston Junction signals were 'slotted' with Cairntows signals to protect the two level crossings (one for the branch and one for Gilmour's siding) at Cairntows. Originally the speed over the crossings was 3 mph, but this was later raised to 5 mph. After Duddingston Junction box closed, all equipment was removed and the building demolished on 13th June, 1970.

Duddingston ('Wet Review') Station

Troops attending the Volunteer Review in Holyrood Park in 1881 and who arrived by rail from the south and east were dealt with at what was termed 'Duddingston Station' in formal North British Railway documents. Although the suburban railway was under construction at that time, there was no station, or even platforms, at Duddingston and the official documents actually refer to a platformless halt on the level portion of the St Leonards branch where the soldiers were expected to disembark from the trains, reversing the process for the return journey. As trains were predominantly of four- and six-wheelers with no corridors, the troops were presumably expected to clamber down from their carriages either by using carriage footboards, or simply jump down, carrying their equipment. The weather was atrocious and the review acquired the title of the 'Wet Review'. One must feel sorry for the men on their return journey, soaking wet and travelling in cold, unheated compartments, sometimes for hours. It is ironical that in view of the absence of platforms it was noted on the NBR circulars relating to the workings that, 'Enginemen, Guards, Signalmen and all others are earnestly requested to use the utmost caution and remember that SAFETY, not speed is the first consideration'.

Duddingston Locomotive Servicing Facilities

Apart from the need to assist trains up the gradient to Morningside Road, Duddingston also had a number of pilots for local trips and shunting. Supplied by St Margarets, rudimentary crew facilities were provided in the form of an old grounded NBR six-wheel carriage body, which was considered adequate. With most of the doors sealed up and the interior gutted, it had been refitted with benches along the sides, mandatory locomotive department notice cases, a primitive writing desk and that most welcome of accessories, a coal fire. The locomotives were catered for by suitably positioned water columns.

At the end of the 19th century, North British Working Time Tables quoted that a double-shifted pilot for Duddingston came down from Niddrie West at 6.00 am and undertook shunting until 9.30 am. It then proceeded to Newington, calling at the Drybrough and Somerville brewery sidings *en route*. It departed for Morningside Road at 12.30 pm and remained there until 2.00 pm. It then returned to Niddrie West, with empty wagons calling at Blackford Hill. Continuing on to Duddingston it shunted as required until 5.30 pm, after which it assisted trains up the hill to the summit. A second pilot locomotive was booked on duty at 9.30 am working as required and assisting until 8.00 am the next day.

At the end of the NBR era, Duddingston had five pilots. Two were treble-shifted, undertaking goods shunting, local trip work and banking to Morningside. Another two were only double-shifted and there was one single-shifted shunting and assisting engine that only operated from Mondays to Wednesdays between 9.00 am and 4.30 pm.

In 1943, Duddingston acquired an engine servicing pit, but by 1953 had been reduced to two pilots, both of which shunted, made trip runs and assisted in banking freights as required. One was double-shifted on weekdays, single shifted on Saturdays, and departed from St Margarets at 5.30 am calling at Niddrie West and, on arrival at Duddingston, shunted as required until its return to the shed at 8.00 pm. The other engine, also double-shifted, worked from 6.00 am until 9.00 pm and was booked to service the intermediate yards to Morningside Road, extending to Gorgie or Niddrie West if required.

Craigmillar 'Non-Station'

'Craigmillar' may be traced to the Scots Gaelic 'Craig Mol Aird', or 'Big High Cliff', the district taking its name many centuries later from 14th century Craigmillar Castle, one of Scotland's most impressive medieval remains which was some distance from the line. The area between Peffermill Road, Craigmillar Castle and Niddrie developed as a slum clearance scheme for the St Leonards area of the City between 1930 and 1934, to the City Architect's designs. Most houses were of the three-storey Scottish tenement style but their somewhat spartan frontages were described by one leading architect as 'barracks for the deserving poor'. Although eventually having a population similar to Dumfries, it seemed to lack a soul and community focus, although conventional schools, etc., were included and, from the outset, the housing scheme was well served by Edinburgh Corporation (now Lothian) buses. The suburban line passed through the centre of the development, but it never had a railway station although there were several proposals.

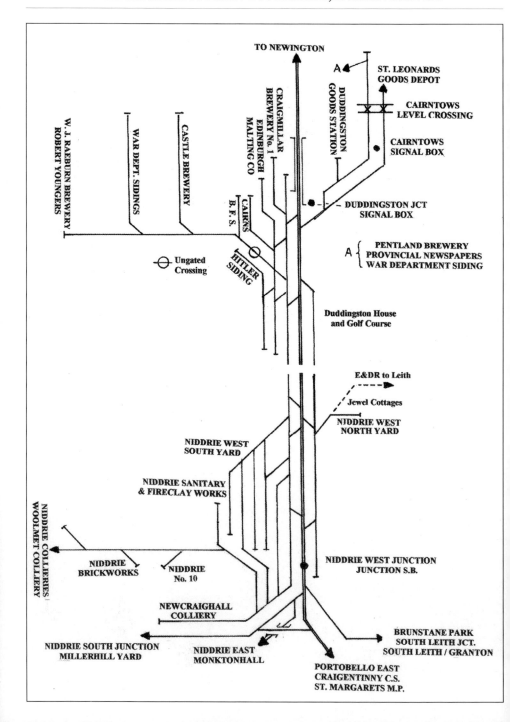

Chapter Ten

Duddingston to Niddrie

Duddingston Sidings (East)

Apart from the small goods station, the siding laid for Murray's Craigmillar Brewery in 1886 (Ordnance Survey cartographers of 1892 omitted a connection) was the first of many sidings at Duddingston both private and railway owned. These included a short branch line as well as main line quadrupling. Buffer-ended 'Refuge Sidings' were installed after the quadrupling on the down side although these could also be used as 'headshunts' for brewery sidings and Gilmour's branch. There were also mostly buffer-ended sidings on the north side of the line alongside the St Leonards branch.

Craigmillar Brewery Sidings

This siding was originally laid for Messrs Graham & Co., but later taken over by William Murray who had established brewing and farming businesses at Ednam, near Kelso in 1880. When fire destroyed this brewery, he moved to Edinburgh, establishing Craigmillar Brewery on Cairntows land in 1886, and a limited liability company formed in 1897 acquired the business for £75,000. The NBR leased a triangular portion of ground for a connection between the brewery and suburban railway from Henry Wobridge Gordon, trustees of Mr Walter James Little Gilmour's Estate, and Colonel Wauchope, in July 1887. The railway laid and maintained the brewery connection, which opened on 2nd March, 1888.

Traffic developed and the loading bank at the brewery line was extended by 90 ft at the railway's expense in May 1894. The brewery paid for an additional siding in March 1898 on the opposite side of the loading bank. One siding was extended in May 1898 at a cost of £47 to the brewery and after the firm established a bottling store, a further siding for this opened on 9th October, 1924. In 1922, Murray's had taken over the North British Brewery of John Somerville & Company, the original Craigmillar Brewery became Craigmillar Brewery No. 1 and the North British plant near Peffermill Road Bridge, Craigmillar No. 2.

The substantial growth in road transport after 1945 led to a decline in rail traffic. William Murray & Company and Aitchison Jeffrey Breweries merged to form United Caledonian Breweries and in 1950 brewing ceased at Craigmillar No. 1, the building being converted into a distribution and storage depot, and box-making unit. In 1960, the firm was taken over by Northern Breweries, part of United Breweries, and its product range reduced. With the further fall in rail traffic, the sidings were closed and removed on 20th October, 1965, although the brewery building remained until 1987.

Edinburgh Malting Co. Siding

Another parcel of land was fued from Walter James Little Gilmour on 6th July, 1887 through Henry Wobridge Gordon as Trustees, and a siding connection was laid over this for the Edinburgh Malting Company. The firm had fued ground at Duddingston station immediately west of Craigmillar Brewery to erect Malt Barns and requested a siding to be laid into their premises. The NBR agreed, and the cost of construction and maintenance to the boundary of the trader's land (including 44 yards on land fued by the NBR in July 1887 for Craigmillar Brewery siding), was borne by the NBR, that on the firm's land by the trader. The siding opened on 27th August, 1892, before the agreement was finalised and was a short buffer-ended siding with even shorter loop. The 1892 agreement was later assigned to Wm McEwan & Co. Ltd, of Fountain Brewery, Edinburgh on 28th November, 1928 but expired on 6th May, 1968 after which the siding was removed.

Cairns (later Brewers Food Supply) Siding

Land for the Edinburgh Malting Company siding connection was also used for a connection to a single buffer-ended siding for Messrs W.G. Cairns under a 1903 siding agreement with the NBR, which also started on the land fued by the NBR in 1887 from H.W. Gordon. The Cairns siding left Refuge Siding No. 1, immediately south of the down goods loop at Duddingston station, and was entirely the property of Cairns, later a part of the Brewers Food Supply Co.

A second buffer-ended siding was laid in 1921 under an agreement between the NBR and the Brewers Food Supply Company Ltd (BFS) from Gilmour's branch into Cairns' premises. BFS owned, provided and laid all the track and the railway estimated the total cost at £700. The firm also paid for the fencing and the siding opened in January 1922. This appeared to have a loading bank with faces on its own line and on Gilmour's branch. Starting on the branch just outwith the railway boundary but with a short length on railway land, a gate was just inside the firm's premises the rails terminating in a new building outside which was a 30 ton wagon weighbridge, on the firm's land.

A third Brewers Food Supply single line siding was laid under a 1942 agreement with the LNER, although it was actually laid three years previously! This was an extension of the headshunt for 'Refuge Siding No. 2' and appears to have been a holding rather than an operational siding, situated on the east side of Gilmour's branch behind the water tank at the junction. Laid entirely by the LNER at the firm's expense, only the plain track from the former buffer stop site on the refuge siding was considered as the trader's property. A level crossing was also provided over Gilmour's branch, it being stipulated that this was to be built and maintained in good repair and working order, entirely at the trader's expense. In view of when it was built, it acquired the name of 'Hitler's Siding' remaining until 5th January, 1966 when, having been declared redundant, it was lifted by British Railways without cost to the trader, although he received a proportion of the sleepers on his ground.

Gilmour's Branch (later Liberton and Craigmillar Estates Siding)

Land leased to the NBR on 6th July, 1887 was used for a branch from the siding throat near Duddingston station to serve McLachlan's Castle Brewery and the later W. & J. Raeburn's brewery (subsequently renamed 'Robert Younger's Edinburgh Brewery'). Under an 1898 agreement between NBR and the landowner Robert Gordon Gordon Gilmour (subsequently Liberton and Craigmillar Estates), the NB laid the line at Gilmour's expense, the railway being assigned to 'make, maintain and work in perpetuity a railway siding on a plan of the lands of Cairntows'. Apart from the first 44 yards, the branch belonged to R.G.G. Gilmour, but was maintained by the railway company at railway expense. The NBR also had to 'maintain the said railway siding so long as any work connected therewith receives and forwards traffic thereby'.

MacLaughlan's Castle Brewery Siding

George and John MacLaughlan, two brothers from Strathallan started in the wine and spirit trade in the 1870s and built Castle Brewery at Maryhill, Glasgow in 1889. The 30,000 barrels a year produced did not meet demand and so they opened a larger establishment at Craigmillar in 1901 with an annual capacity of 104,000 barrels, and also bought Auchentoshan Distillery. John died in 1903, and his brother took over. McLaughlan's developed a good export trade, especially with India and South Africa, but went into voluntary liquidation in 1923, reforming as McLaughlan's Ltd, and becoming a public company in 1947. J. & R. Tennant acquired the business in 1960, but ceased brewing at the Castle Brewery in 1967, the year that its name changed to Kenneth MacKenzie (Wines).

On 9th February, 1899, an agreement was made with Messrs G. & J. McLachlan to lay a siding at their Craigmillar brewery at an estimated cost to the firm of £858. McLaughlan's would own the materials and maintain the line beyond Gilmour's branch land. Length outwith the NBR property (which also included the Gilmour's branch portion) was 1,050 yards and it opened to traffic on 5th May, 1899, a severe curvature restricting shunting speed to 4 miles per hour. The siding was a single line spur from Gilmour's line, dividing into three within the brewery, the centre one forming a 'run round' facility and an old photograph shows the sidings containing empty NBR cask wagons. A loop was also laid from the centre of the southernmost line to a small headshunt with a radius of 150 feet. In 1940, the LNER took over the maintenance of the sidings at the request of the War Office (*see below*).

According to the NBR Sidings Register, the points for the line into McLachlan's Brewery were near the corner of the Edinburgh Malting Company premises at the east end of Mitchell Street, the siding agreement being terminated in September 1966, the track being then removed. Brewing also ceased in 1966 and the buildings were later demolished, the site now forming part of a 'business park' with Peffer Place (Mitchell Street before 1966) extending over the former branch.

W. & J. Raeburn (later Robert Younger Ltd) Brewer Siding

The NBR Siding Register entry shows a continuation of Gilmour's branch made under an 1898 agreement with Messrs W. & J. Raeburn's brewery and states that when the NBR obtained possession of the land, they would make the sidings. On completion, Messrs Raeburn would pay costs incurred, the siding length beyond the NBR land (and Gilmour's branch) being quoted as 262 yards. The NBR Board Minute Book on 9th February, 1899 reported that arrangements had been made with Raeburn for making the sidings, the cost being borne by the trader who then owned and maintained the track. On 11th August, 1898, the NBR Engineer estimated costs as £247, excluding ground formation, walls, fences, gates and loading platforms, which the firm was to undertake. The siding opened on 13th September, 1899 as an extension of Gilmour's branch and took a 'Y' formation, a loading bank being placed between the two roads at the north end and also alongside the line nearest Cairntows. The line on the Niddrie side continued almost to the main road (now Niddrie Mains Road) serving the coal and coke store *en route*. A turnout beyond the loading bank accessed the middle of a further double buffer-ended siding almost in line with the loading bank siding, but separated from it by the loading bank 'bridge'. Alongside the loading bank, from north to south, were the ale store, brew house and maltings.

Robert Younger Ltd took over Raeburn's brewery in 1913 and paid £439 for changes in December 1920 to simplify the layout. The Cairntows siding line was extended to the main road and the other shortened but the intermediate points were retained. In 1943, repairs were also carried out at Younger's expense. The siding agreement ended on 6th May, 1968 and the rails were removed.

War Department Sidings

After the outbreak of World War II, the War Department laid sidings from Gilmour's branch, by then renamed, 'Liberton and Craigmillar Estates Siding', between McLachlan's and Younger's Breweries. A single connection was laid and after leaving the branch, and crossing over the railway boundary, this divided into two parallel buffer-ended lines. Their use is unclear but the LNER Divisional General Manager wrote to the Scottish Area Director of (Army) Transportation on 30th September, 1940 stating that if the railway took over maintenance of McLachlan's Brewery Sidings, other army sidings and the Pentland Brewery Sidings, an extra man would be required. They would provide the man if the War Office paid for maintenance of the Royal Engineers Dump and a suitable sum for the Estates private siding, costs being assessed pro-rata on traffic volume. The War Office agreed to pay costs for the RE Dump, but the LNER raised maintenance charges on a pro-rata basis for the others - and billed the War Office! The date for the removal of the siding is only quoted as being 'after the war'.

Duddingston and Niddrie West

The 4 ft 6 in. gauge double track Edinburgh & Dalkeith Railway opened on 4th July, 1831, its route following an almost straight line between the later sites of Duddingston and Niddrie West Junctions. The North British bought the E&D in 1845 and converted it to 'standard' gauge in 1847, but when Edinburgh traffic was diverted from Niddrie by Portobello to the North Bridge station it was singled and the Niddrie - St Leonards line closed to passengers on 1st November, 1847.

The E&DR had laid this part of its line on a level grade (and slight embankment) to suit horse haulage. The 1880 Edinburgh Suburban & South Side Junction Railway Act proposed a separate double line alongside the then single line of the old E&D, passing under it before heading north-east to Portobello. However, in the 1882 Act, this was changed to a single line beside the E&D one, restoring the latter to its original double track form before going from Niddrie West to Niddrie North and Niddrie East to connect with the NBR main lines. The route passed over the Niddrie Burn, the main road between Niddrie and Portobello (then Niddrie Road) and several culverts and streams. Under the 1901-02 quadrupling, the culvert containing the burn was lengthened to accommodate the entrance to Niddrie West (South) marshalling yards and now flows through a large concrete duct under the (now) double track plain line.

In the late 19th century, freight traffic through Niddrie stretched capacity and it became inevitable that action was required. The existing headshunts for Duddingston and Niddrie yards were linked to form a quadruple section, the new goods lines having no signalling, trains simply following each other. The widening was included in the North British Railway Act of 1900 and additional sidings provided at both ends, including a new Niddrie West yard headshunt and bridge over Niddrie Road. Given the nature of the land, engineering work was fairly straightforward, most difficulties being in widening bridges over intermediate burns, culverts and tracks.

New signal boxes opened at Duddingston Junction and Niddrie West in 1899 and 1900 respectively and the engineer began to build up embankments for the new lines on 17th November, 1901, being undertaken with the minimum of disturbance to other lines. The new 'Goods Loop Lines' opened on 3rd August, 1902 with a speed restriction of 5 miles per hour, drivers exercising caution and being ready to stop short of any train ahead, especially after dusk and in reduced visibility.

As both ends of the new lines were controlled by separate signal boxes, in the late LNER era they were briefly termed as 'Up and Down Independents'. The closure of many small Edinburgh marshalling yards after Millerhill Marshalling yards opened in 1962-63, geographical factors and a reduction in the number of trains, enabled many freights to run through Waverley, by-passing the suburban line. The quadruple track was reduced to double line later in the decade and with the removals of private sidings, other connections, and St Leonards branch closure in 1968, the section became plain line.

Duddingston House

This two-storey house in its extensive grounds adjoining the north side of the line dates from 1763. The 8th Earl of Abercorn commissioned the designer of Somerset House in London, to make a suitable residence and it was accorded the district name. The surrounding parkland, in the style of 'Capability' Brown, later became Duddingston Golf Course, the clubhouse being next to the railway. It is said that at one time King Edward VII considered the property as a royal residence, but bought Sandringham instead. One wonders what effect that would have had on the area, station or later council housing schemes! Spacious grounds and proximity to the station made the site attractive to the military and they used it in both world wars, their peripheral huts lingering on for years afterwards. During the army occupation from 1939 the house deteriorated, but it was later restored as a hotel (The Milton House Hotel) and is now a scheduled monument - golf still being played in its grounds, and Holy Rood High School opened in the north-west corner of the grounds in 1971.

Proposed 'Craigmillar' Marshalling Yards

At the end of 1922, the North British management planned a large gravitational marshalling yard with a capacity of 3,100 wagons on the south side of the Suburban between Duddingston and Niddrie West, modelled on Feltham yard of the London & South Western Railway. Two separate yards were envisaged, each with four reception sidings, the up yard comprising of 15 sidings and the down yard 18, each holding between 60 and 70 wagons. Humps for gravitation shunting were planned midway between reception sidings entrance and sorting sidings. A transit shed provided for crippled wagons and a small adjacent locomotive depot was also incorporated. The scheme envisaged savings of 26 staff and five locomotives (two from Portobello, one from Hardengreen, one from the Smeaton branch and one from a Berwick working). These were estimated at £4,044 6s. 0d. from Operating and £21,255 6s. 2d. from Locomotive Departments, a total of £25,299 12s. 2d., but the main benefit was seen as improving train working. However, before it came to fruition, Edinburgh Corporation acquired the ground for housing and the marshalling yard plans were shelved.

The 1922 plan was revived in 1929, but for a yard on the north side of the Suburban between Duddingston and Niddrie West. This was to have up and down 'hump' yards and a locomotive depot for 30 tender locomotives. In 1930, the proposed locomotive depot was deleted and provision made for five down and four up reception sidings with a total yard capacity of 2,792 wagons. Estimated savings of £9,137 represented only 1.73 per cent of the work, the cost of which was put at £528,519 and the scheme was again shelved. The 1929 scheme, with locomotive depot, was estimated at £600,000 excluding land, legal expenses and compensation, the modified one costing £494,219 for the works and £34,300 for land and compensation. Unfortunately, the Wall Street Crash and subsequent depression put paid to the scheme.

Niddrie (or Niddry)

East of Duddingston, the district south of the line was called 'Niddrie', said to be derived from 'Nodrof' (1166), 'Nudrie' (1329), and 'Nordry' (1421), becoming 'Niddrie' about 1603 although there are several other spellings. It may also derive from the Welsh, 'Newydd' (new) and 'Dref' (a farm). An alternative spelling is 'Niddry', and this interchanges regularly. Lairds of Niddrie were hereditary Bailies to the Keiths, Earls Merschell (Marischal) and Marischal deputes in Midlothian.

The village grew round the mansion house occupied by the Wauchopes, a powerful Scottish Lowlands family. Originally in an agricultural environment, the estate extended along both sides of a stream from the Pentland Hills to the Forth of Forth (the Niddry Burn) where a mill and mill lade took water. Coal was mined from the 16th century and collier housing was provided near the mill, away from the mansion but this had faded out by the 1850s. In 1792, the village had 300 houses, three breweries and 14 houses dispensing liquor! Wauchopes' opposed the Edinburgh & Dalkeith Railway as they had their own mineral line from their Newton Parish Collieries to the main road into Edinburgh near Little France and saw the new railway as a threat. Their opposition to the first Bill caused the railway to be resurveyed avoiding their estate, but when they realised that they could make money from granting mineral rights, way-leaves, and rent and also sell land to the railway, they quickly reversed this opposition and a Wauchope was on the E&D Committee of Management in 1826! Indeed, by the late 19th century, the family was making at least £20,000 a year from these with no effort on their part!

The Leith branch of the E&DR left its main line ½ mile west of the junction for Fisherrow, facing to trains from the port. Passing under the NBR line west of Portobello, from 1847 and 1859 a spur at Craigentinny let Musselburgh trains (extended from Fisherrow) run direct to the North Bridge (Waverley) station. The spur closed when a link was made into the Hawick branch and a separate station at Portobello was built for the Leith service. Earthworks at the Niddrie end remained, later being widened to accommodate the 14 buffer-ended sidings of Niddrie West (North) yard.

Between Duddingston and Niddrie West signal boxes, land for this 1 mile 220 yards section was once in Wauchope's Estate. To the west was the Craigmillar Estate of W. Little Gilmour and to the north, the Duke of Abercorn. In 1874, Wauchope sold land to the Niddrie Colliery Company, between 1875 and 1880 to the Benhar Coal Company and in 1880 to the Edinburgh Suburban & South Side Junction Railway. In 1882, the Niddrie and the Benhar Coal companies merged into the Niddrie & Benhar Coal Company (Wauchope was a minor shareholder), and local industries which were to use the suburban railway were collieries (from the outset), a creamery (1885) and several breweries (after 1886).

The Wauchope dynasty ended in 1899 when Major-General Andrew Gilbert Wauchope of the Black Watch was killed in the Boer War and, having no children, his widow stayed in the mansion on her own for the next 40 years. In 1928 the estate was sold to Edinburgh Corporation, the year when council houses were built on the neighbouring Craigmillar Castle estate. Former Wauchope land that the NBR had considered for its 1922 marshalling yard was used for council housing between 1929 and 1933. Land north of the line belonging to the Duke of Abercorn, considered for the LNER 1929 marshalling yard, was not acquired and instead was sold for housing in 1942. When Niddrie West marshalling yards closed after the Millerhill yards opened, their site was absorbed by light industry and housing in the 1960s and 1970s. Niddry House, a Civil Defence Centre during World War II was by then in considerable disrepair and was demolished despite local opposition. The last relics of the Wauchopes of Niddry Marischal are a graveyard, Pavilion, street names, a monument near the site of the mansion house and the family tomb in among the council houses off Niddrie Marischal Terrace.

'The Jewel' and local Pit Siding

The area north of the railway was named after a type of coal that outcropped nearby and the colliery which closed c.1892. 'Jewel Cottages' were small collier houses built from 1890 beside the main Niddrie and Portobello road (then named Niddrie Road) near the then Fever Hospital to replace Niddry Village. The first houses were on the east side of the road, backing onto the embankment supporting the stub of the one-time E&D Leith branch. More houses were then built on the west of the road (which was also widened over that part), and most survived into the 1960s, their site now absorbed into the Jewel Public Park. The part of Niddrie Road under the railway and southwards was unwidened, but, in early 1966 after the marshalling yards closed, the Secretary of State for Scotland approved the total replacement of this bridge to allow road widening which also swept away the last of the cottages. The cost was estimated to be in excess of £100,000 and a 75 per cent grant was made to the Corporation. The old 19 ft wide (across the road) bridge with its 13 ft 9 in. headroom was replaced by one 44 ft wide with 16 ft 6 in. headroom and a 9 ft wide footpath on each side. 'Niddrie Road' was renamed 'Duddingston Park South' and in later years, a new road between the suburban line and the Niddry Burn was named 'The Jewel', a large supermarket at its east end occupying some former railway land near Niddrie North Junction.

Niddrie Coal Company's Jewel Pit Siding was served by a buffer-ended siding which the Siding Register noted was situated between St Leonards and Niddrie, the then single track St Leonards branch being worked by a Train Staff. Belonging to the Niddrie Coal Company, the connection was laid in for £284 10s. 1d. at the trader's expense but although it opened on 15th April, 1875, it is said to have closed in May

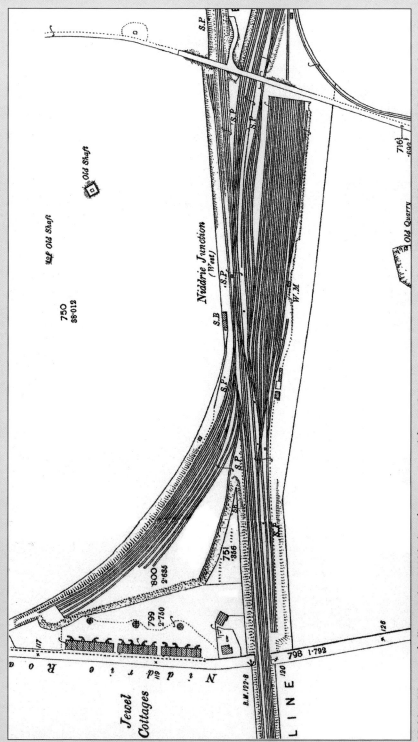

Niddrie West marshalling yard in 1893 before the expansion of the yard.

Reproduced from the 25", 1893 Ordnance Survey Map

1877. Unfortunately, no records survive to show its location or when the rails were removed and it may well have survived into the suburban railway era, as the pit apparently did not close until about 1892. Lothian colliery operations and dates were notoriously fickle and transient.

On the same day as the Jewel Pit siding opened, another single line Train Staff-worked double-ended siding opened for the Benhar Coal Company's No. 1 and 7 Pits. This cost the coal company £531 8s. 1d., with the additional proviso that they would need to provide a locking frame if and when requested by the NBR. The plan was dated 3rd July, 1875 (nearly three months after it opened) but before the official opening date the NB were charging 2d. per ton to work its traffic!

Niddrie West Junction Signal Box

The first signal box at Niddrie West Jn dated from the opening of the line in 1884, but with the expansion of the yards and the quadrupling between Niddrie West and Duddingston, it was replaced by a larger structure almost on the same site in June 1900 and in the then North British architectural style. It was later able to absorb the additional workload created by the 'Lothian Railways' scheme opened in 1915. In connection with the 1970s Edinburgh resignalling, the line to Niddrie North Junction was singled in May 1973 and the box finally closed on 26th June, 1976 when its work was transferred to a panel at Portobello prior to incorporation in the new Edinburgh Signalling Centre.

Niddrie West Marshalling Yards

The Edinburgh Suburban & South Side Junction Railway planned to create a marshalling yard at Niddrie in 1882 alongside its main through line from Niddrie East to Haymarket. Primarily dealing with local Lothian coal traffic, it was also intended to deal with general freight to relieve Portobello yard. In the spring of 1884, the NBR put forward an alternative proposal requiring more land than originally envisaged and there was some delay while this was sorted out. Eventually the suburban concern took land as specified in its Parliamentary estimates, but also with a five-year option on the additional adjacent land on behalf of the North British at the same price.

Two siding groups formed the initial layout, one on each side of the suburban line. At first, these were adequate but as traffic increased, particularly in minerals, more accommodation was needed, exacerbated after New Craighall Colliery opened and which directly connected into the south (or down) yard. Niddrie West down yard then became two separate siding groups on the south side of the suburban line, and with the single up yard, all were used for goods train marshalling until displaced when Millerhill yard came 'on stream' in the 1960s.

In planning their 'Lothian Railways' scheme, the Directors proposed on 19th October, 1911 to increase accommodation at Niddrie West at a cost of £6,436, £250 being charged to Revenue. They also agreed to lay in an extra connection to the Niddrie & Benhar Coal Company's network, estimated at £1,216. On 12th December, 1912, the Directors recommended that this £1,216 and a further £253 for improving the occupation crossing and an additional siding be charged to Capital, the rails being the property of the NBR. Five days before, the Engineer had been asked to supply a valuation plan of all lines in Niddrie West yards, railway boundaries and private sidings and this was presented to the Board on the 5th September, 1913. On

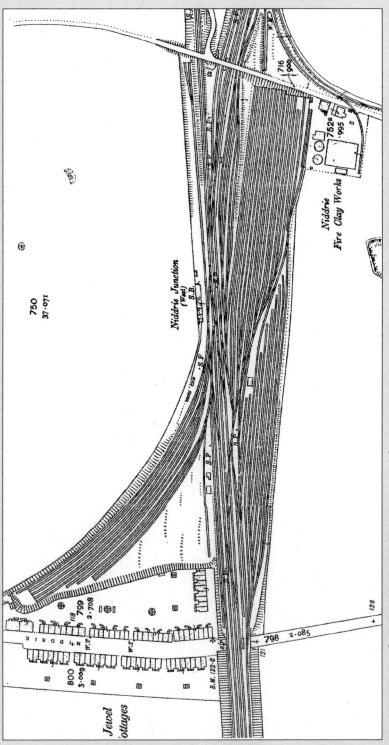

Niddrie West marshalling yard in 1914 after expansion of the yard as a result of development of the Lothian coalfields and general merchandise traffic before World War I. The only industry near the yard was the Niddrie Fire Clay Works, this firm having a siding from the self-contained mineral branch line which linked the Niddrie & Benhar Company's pits to the south of the yard. Out of sight to the right of this map was Newcraighall Colliery. The single line of Jewel Cottages on the 1893 map have doubled and the public road passing between them has been widened on the northern approach to the suburban railway bridge. The curved sidings on the northern side of the line were partially built on the solum of the Edinburgh & Dalkeith Railway link from Niddrie to Portobello and these have increased in length over the intervening period.

Reproduced from the 25", 1914 Ordnance Survey Map

This sturdy modern six-coupled saddle tank was built by Andrew Barclay of Kilmarnock for the Lothian Area of the NCB in 1957. Initially it was allocated to Niddrie and Newcraighall Collieries, and carried the number 25. In 1959 it was transferred to Newbattle, returning to Niddrie in the following year where it remained until locomotives ceased to be used on the colliery line. It moved to Polkemmet Colliery in West Lothian in December 1972. It is depicted in the exchange sidings between Newcraighall Colliery and Niddrie West Yard, the line in the rear linked Niddrie West with Niddrie South and Monktonhall. *Bill Roberton*

A general view of the east end of the yard at Niddrie West from the overbridge about 1931. The lines in the foreground are from the exchange sidings at Newcraighall Colliery. *Author's Collection*

24th November, 1913 the Engineer questioned maintenance responsibility for the lines authorised on 12th December, 1912 that were completed in August 1913 and was advised that all were to be maintained by the NBR.

Electric lighting came to the yards under a scheme of 27th January, 1934, when it was proposed to install 10 x 500 watt bulbs and 1 x 200 watt to 'floodlight' the yard complex, as well as supplying several offices and bothies.

The closure of Berwick marshalling yard in March 1940, placed additional work on Niddrie yards. Consequently, marshalling and departure of east coast freights was transferred to Meadows yard on the Portobello and South Leith branch, hitherto only a staging point for shipment coal traffic from the Lothian (and other) coalfields through Leith Docks - traffic which had measurably declined since the outbreak of war. Meadows had no regular pilot at that time but then acquired three, usually class 'J36' 0-6-0 tender engines. Two shunted the yard with the third also assisting goods trains up the hill past Baileyfield to Portobello and the main line as well as over the single Lothian Railways spur to Niddrie West.

Under the LNER '5 year plan' published in 1946, a new marshalling yard and 'other improvements' were mooted for the Edinburgh Area, the cost being estimated at £3,267,000, but was not progressed in the post-war financial climate.

Shunting and inter-yard trips declined sharply when Millerhill opened in 1962 and 1963, the Niddrie yards closing in 1963, most track being removed by 1965. The sites lay derelict for a time, although some use was made of them by the Civil Engineer before moving to Slateford, but the site gradually assumed the mantle of light industry and domestic housing.

Carlisle Waterproofing Company (Niddrie Sanitary & Fireclay Works) Siding

An 1898 agreement between the NBR and Carlisle Waterproofing Company stated that for the sidings, the trader had to pay the cost of lines outwith the NBR boundary and half the cost of those on NBR land. Two sidings were involved, one, jointly owned by trader and NBR lay between Niddrie West (South) yard and railway boundary, thereafter entirely on the trader's land, including the loading bank in the works. A second, entirely trader-owned siding entered the works from the private Niddrie Colliery branch line on the opposite side of what was termed as the occupation roadway. The Carlisle Waterproofing Company became Messrs Steele Brothers & Sons, trading as the 'Niddrie Sanitary and Fireclay Works'. At least one siding appears to have been worked by the Niddrie and Benhar Coal Company engines from their branch.

Niddrie Stations

It is not clear how many stations were in the Niddrie area, or indeed their actual locations. As the Edinburgh & Dalkeith Railway did not issue tickets, and appears to have had no station-based accountancy, the provision of passenger facilities did not appear to be too critical. Passengers could enter and alight from vehicles in the traditional manner of stage coaches (i.e. from ground level). All that was required was somewhere 'trains' could arrive and depart in rough accordance with the timetable, and perhaps where the horses could pause and take on food or water according to the service requirements.

The first passenger 'station' appeared to be near the junction between the Edinburgh & Dalkeith main line and Fisherrow branch, which opened in October 1831. A second station may have been at the Leith branch junction half a mile to the west. Although this branch officially opened in October 1838, there are references to it being at Leith in 1830 and also on an 1835 map. The Leith 'junction' station may have displaced or supplemented the first, but neither appears on maps. The branch from Leith later ran to and from a separate station at Portobello and the Niddrie and Portobello line was lifted. When the St Leonards passenger service was withdrawn in 1847, Niddrie (E&DR) and St Leonards closed to passengers.

A third passenger station opened on the Edinburgh and Hawick line on 1st September, 1848, with conventional platforms and buildings a short distance before the divergence of the Fisherrow branch near Niddrie North Junction, there being no need for this to serve the St Leonards line. Served by Musselburgh and Hawick line trains, the station was in rural countryside although there was some colliery activity nearby and unsurprisingly it closed on 1st February, 1869.

A goods station existed east of where the former Fisherrow branch passed under the main line from Edinburgh to Hawick, although the opening date is indistinct. The North British Railway Sidings Register notes that a double-ended connection was provided from the St Leonards branch (presumably to delineate from the main Hawick and Carlisle line) on 14th May, 1876 at the railway company's expense. A later map showed facilities including buildings, but no rails! Niddrie Goods was, however, responsible for the invoicing of coal from the several collieries in the area and the site may have translated from a goods depot to a convenient goods documentation office.

In March 1986, Edinburgh's Napier College suggested, in a report on a proposal to reopen the suburban line to passengers, a station that they termed as Niddrie/Bingham. This was to be above 'Granny's Bridge', at the end of Hay Drive on the underpass linking Niddrie, south of the line, with Bingham, a housing scheme on the north. Stairs from the underpass could access both platforms built on the solum of the then removed up and down 'independent' lines between Duddingston and Niddrie West. This station could have replaced the old Duddingston and Craigmillar station, ¾ mile west.

Niddrie Coal Company Branch

This was a complete mineral line with its own workshops, locomotives, engine shed and sidings. Connection with the NBR was authorised under an agreement of 1875 between the NBR and the Niddrie Coal Company (the NB Siding Register stated Benhar Coal Company) to serve Niddrie Collieries Nos. 9 to 13 and later, Woolmet Colliery some 1½ miles to the south and Newcraighall Colliery at the north end. Sidings for Nos. 1, 2 and later No. 3 (Newcraighall) Pits were parallel to the line between Niddrie West and Niddrie Junction (South), but were not on railway land. The rail connection with the main line railway was at Niddrie West. The Niddrie Coal Company merged with the Lanarkshire-based Benhar Coal Company in 1882 as the Niddrie & Benhar Coal Company Ltd and this incorporated John Wauchope's Edmonstone Colliery near Danderhall to the south. Gradually, the big coal companies replaced the empires of the old coal owners. By 1892, the north end of the branch terminated in a group of three loops, and after reversing, a single line passed under a road bridge into the rear lines of the NBR Niddrie West sidings.

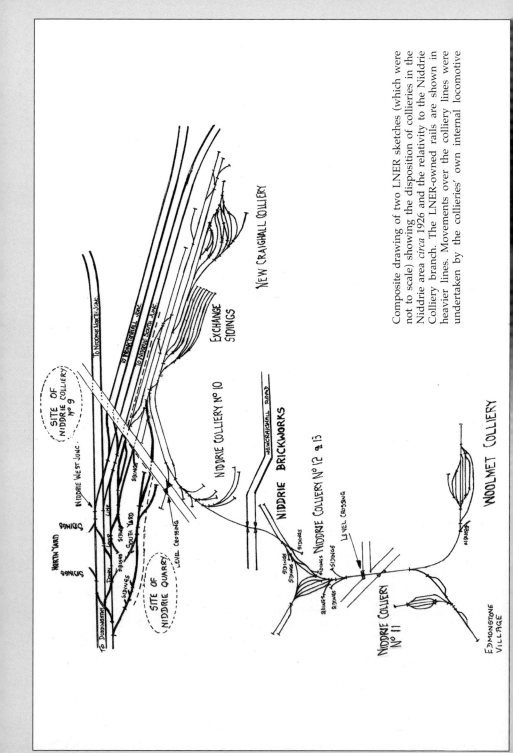

NORTH YARD SIDINGS

SIDINGS

To DUDDINGSTON

NIDDRIE WEST JUNC.

DOCK

LOOP

SIDINGS

SIDINGS

SOUTH YARD

LEVEL CROSSING

SITE OF NIDDRIE QUARRY

SITE OF NIDDRIE COLLIERY Nº 9

To NIDDRIE NORTH JUNC.

To NEWCRAIGHALL JUNC.

To NIDDRIE SOUTH JUNC.

EXCHANGE SIDINGS

NEW CRAIGHALL COLLIERY

NIDDRIE COLLIERY Nº 10

NIDDRIE BRICKWORKS

NEWCRAIGHALL ROAD

NIDDRIE COLLIERY Nº 12 & 13

SIDINGS

SIDINGS

SIDINGS

LEVEL CROSSING

WOOLMET COLLIERY

SIDINGS

SIDINGS

SIDINGS

NIDDRIE COLLIERY Nº 11

SIDINGS

EDMONSTONE VILLAGE

Composite drawing of two LNER sketches (which were not to scale) showing the disposition of collieries in the Niddrie area *circa* 1926 and the relativity to the Niddrie Colliery branch. The LNER-owned rails are shown in heavier lines. Movements over the colliery lines were undertaken by the collieries' own internal locomotive

On Whitsunday 1889 the Niddrie & Benhar Coal Company started to reduce its interests in the west of Scotland, finally pulling out in 1897, although the name did not change. They then concentrated attention in Midlothian, particularly at Newcraighall where a new deep mine was being developed (it opened in 1910) and Woolmet, built from 1898 to 1904.

The branch also served Niddrie Brickworks, which opened in 1924 immediately south of Niddrie No. 10 Pit which was then in its final years, and the Niddrie Fireclay Company works. Both sites now part of Fort Kinnaird Retail Park.

Edmonstone Colliery closed before 1926 and other Niddrie pits by September 1927 (some did not reopen after the 1926 General Strike). However, Newcraighall and Woolmet Collieries, the workshops, engine sheds and offices remained being connected to the LNER network through Newcraighall Colliery exchange sidings. Locomotives for the branch were maintained and based at Niddrie, west of the line between the Fireclay Works and New Craighall Road, but Newcraighall engines had a small shed within that colliery. Woolmet had a washer added in the 1920s.

On 1st January, 1947, New Craighall and Woolmet Collieries, the surviving locomotives, their engine shed and workshops became part of the National Coal Board Area No. 2, together with a sizeable fleet of open wagons.

The workshops closed c.1959, the locomotives becoming part of the NCB Lothians Area fleet in 1962 and Scottish Area fleet in 1967. The part of the branch from the land-sale depot to Woolmet Colliery closed in the autumn of 1966 and the Newcraighall Colliery link in May 1968. Engines were not used after the end of 1972.

Former North British Railway 0-6-2 tank No. 69135 heads a short transfer freight along the single line linking Lothian Lines to Suburban at Niddrie West. Immediately to the right is the suburban double track line between Niddrie West and the Carlisle line at Niddrie North. The other lines to the right connect the Sub east to Wanton Walls and south to Millerhill. Newcraighall Colliery and sidings are on the extreme right.   *G.M. Stadden*

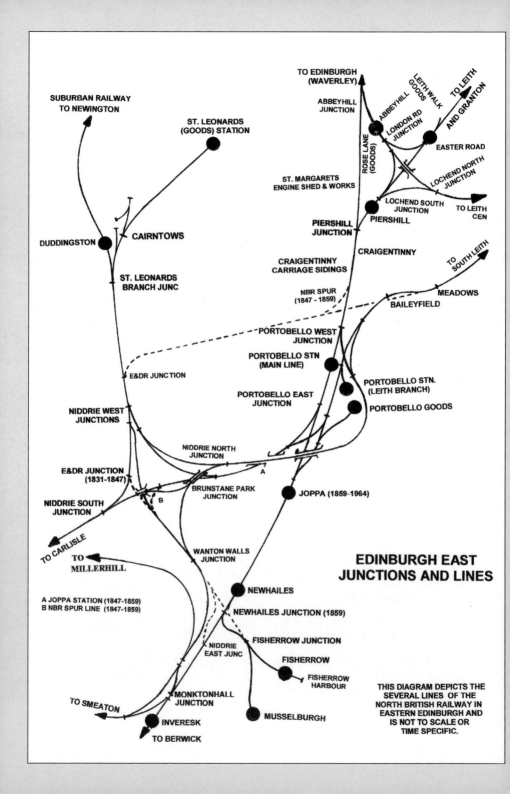

EDINBURGH EAST
JUNCTIONS AND LINES

THIS DIAGRAM DEPICTS THE
SEVERAL LINES OF THE
NORTH BRITISH RAILWAY IN
EASTERN EDINBURGH AND
IS NOT TO SCALE OR
TIME SPECIFIC.

Chapter Eleven

East of Niddrie

Niddrie's Eastern Connections

Untouched by the first (1880) Edinburgh Suburban & South Side Junction Railway Act, the only railways in the Niddrie area in 1882, other than some small mineral lines, were the 'Waverley Route' between Edinburgh and Carlisle and the single line remnant of the Edinburgh & Dalkeith Railway. The latter curved south to join the Carlisle line near the bridge over today's Newcraighall Road, a few yards from Niddrie Junction (South) and the present single platform Newcraighall station. The easy gradients of this section (level to 1 in 2000) had suited the original (literally) horse power. Other Niddrie junctions (those to Leith and Fisherrow) had long disappeared.

Once the works authorised under the 1882 Edinburgh Suburban & South Side Junction Railway Act were complete, four double track lines left Niddrie, literally heading north, south, east and west. At their hub was Niddrie West Junction, west of the original Edinburgh & Dalkeith Railway Fisherrow branch junction.

To the west, the suburban railway had restored the E&D line to double track between Duddingston and Niddrie South. Northwards, a new line from Niddrie West trailed into the line from Carlisle at Niddrie North. To the east, the Edinburgh and Dalkeith Railway single line branch of 1831 via New Craighall, Wanton Walls Farm and Newhailes to Fisherrow, near Musselburgh started back at Niddrie West and a new eastbound line descended a gradient and passed under, instead of across, the Carlisle line. Emerging, it passed through Niddrie Goods station site before joining the solum of the double line spur from Edinburgh to Musselburgh (1848-1859). Near Wanton Walls Farm it turned right before descending to join the Berwick line at Niddrie Junction (East).

Lothian Railway Connections

Heavy actual and anticipated mineral traffic from the several pits of the Lothians coalfield before World War I (and not least the threat of a separate independent colliery owned and operated line) led to the passing of the North British Railway Act of 1913, creating the freight-only mostly single line 'Lothian Railways'. Six of these made connections with the suburban railway lines east of Edinburgh.

The lines concerned were:

South Leith Branch to Smeaton Branch 'main line'	(Railway No. 7)
Portobello West to South Leith Junction	(Railway No. 8)
Niddrie West Junction to Brunstane Park Junction	(Railway No. 9)
Niddrie South Junction to Brunstane Park Junction.	(Railway No. 10)
Niddrie West Junction to Wanton Walls Junction	(Railway No. 11)
Connection to East Coast Main Line at Monktonhall	(Railway No. 12)

The main line of the 'Lothian Railways' (Railway No. 7) extended from a junction with the old South Leith branch and Railway No. 8 at Portobello, passing around the

Above: With Newcraighall Colliery behind, Holmes 0-6-0 No. 65234 hurries a mixed train of mostly coal wagons from Hardengreen on the Hawick line to Niddrie West yard. This vacuum-fitted engine was one of the last of the class to remain in service, latterly working several railtours before being condemned in April 1967. The tender lives on, being paired with the preserved 'J36', formerly No. 65243 and now NBR No. 673 *Maude*.

Henry Watson

Right: Two English Electric type '1' locomotives double-head this 1972 train of coal hoppers along the Monktonhall Junction and Niddrie West line, probably from Cockenzie power station. The lines to the right connected Niddrie West to Niddrie South and the pit bing is from Newcraighall Colliery, closed four years before.

Bill Roberton

north of Portobello yard and over the main East Coast and Waverley Routes. At Brunstane Park signal box, before crossing over the Hawick main line, a single line headed south to join the suburban railway at Niddrie West signal box (Railway No. 9) and a short distance beyond another headed south to join the Hawick line near Niddrie South Junction (Railway No. 10). Railway No. 7 continued east to trail into the 1884 suburban line a short distance east of the bridge over Newcraighall Road, the short connection being known as Railway No. 11, the actual junction taking its name from the nearby Wanton Walls Farm. To ease the curve and gradient down to Niddrie East, a new double track alignment was laid on a widened embankment clear of the old suburban main line connecting directly with the Smeaton branch at Monktonhall, some 1 mile 45 yards east. The Lothian Lines connected directly into the Smeaton branch at Monktonhall and into the East Coast Main Line by a crossover (Railway No. 12). The old Suburban route to Niddrie East remained in use while the new was built alongside, and when the latter was commissioned, the Wanton Walls connection to Niddrie East Junction was removed. Although authorised for lifting in Clause 18 of the 1913 Act, much of this old double line link was retained as sidings from the down loop at Niddrie East signal box.

Niddrie North Junction box closed on 28th November, 1926, its function (and name) being transferred to the Brunstane Park box on the Lothian Lines which overlooked the junction. The lines between Wanton Walls and Niddrie North (part Railway No. 7) closed on 8th April, 1963, followed by Railway No. 9 between Niddrie West Junction and Niddrie North) on 23rd December, 1963. Track and bridges were removed and also in the case of No. 9 the embankment, the route later being incorporated into a supermarket and car park.

Apart from the line between Wanton Walls and Monktonhall, the remainder of the Lothian Lines (between Niddrie South and South Leith Junction) closed on 9th January, 1967, after which track, bridges and some earthworks were removed.

On 5th May, 1973 as part of the Edinburgh resignalling, the double track Suburban curve between Niddrie North and West was singled. In 1986, an authorised survey by Edinburgh's Napier College suggested that a single platform be created on the solum of the lifted line to serve the adjacent supermarket, housing scheme and Jewel & Esk college if the Suburban reopened to passengers. Although this came to naught, the single platform Brunstane station opened in 2002 on the former Waverley Route at Niddrie North Junction *en route* to Newcraighall (and Millerhill).

The Niddrie East/Monktonhall line through Niddrie and south Edinburgh suburbia to Haymarket Central and West Junctions gave well used, congestion reducing lines in Edinburgh's rail network. Unfortunately, lying on an east-west axis, it lost significance when Millerhill yard opened in 1962 and was largely replaced by a new line from Monktonhall to Millerhill that provided an alternative north-south facility. The line between the new Millerhill line junction (reusing the name 'Wanton Walls Junction') and Niddrie West was lifted in the latter part of 1984.

New Craighall Colliery

Coal had been worked locally for many years before colliery sidings originated in an agreement of 1875 with the Niddrie Coal Company. This referred to a simple colliery owned siding next to the Niddrie West-Niddrie South Junction line and east of an occupation road. The Niddrie and the Benhar Coal Companies merged to form the Niddrie & Benhar Coal Company in 1882 and work started on a new colliery in

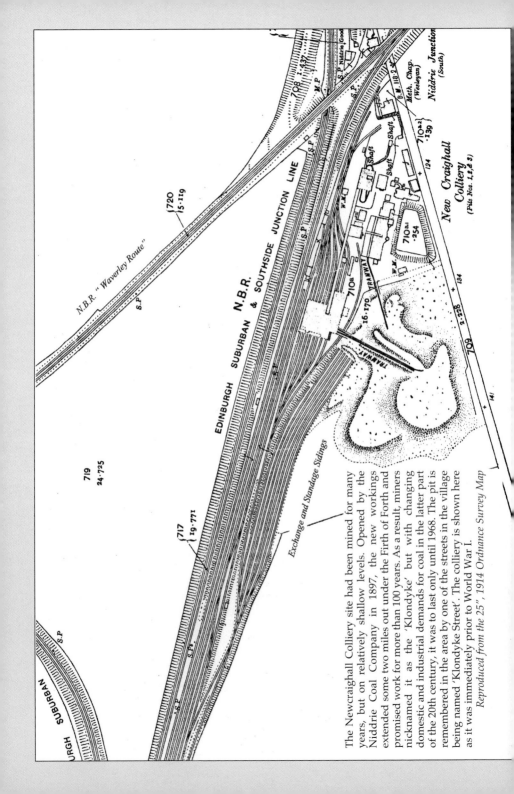

The Newcraighall Colliery site had been mined for many years, but on relatively shallow levels. Opened by the Niddrie Coal Company in 1897, the new workings extended some two miles out under the Firth of Forth and promised work for more than 100 years. As a result, miners nicknamed it as the 'Klondyke' but with changing domestic and industrial demands for coal in the latter part of the 20th century, it was to last only until 1968. The pit is remembered in the area by one of the streets in the village being named 'Klondyke Street'. The colliery is shown here as it was immediately prior to World War I.

Reproduced from the 25", 1914 Ordnance Survey Map

1897. With the promise of regular work and wages for years to come, the miners dubbed it 'The Klondyke'. Initially this comprised of two inclined mines driven at a four-foot seam outcropping in the area. Cannel coal had been in great demand for making coal gas, but with the introduction of incandescent gas mantles, gas could be obtained from 'ordinary' or 'bituminous' coals and demand for Cannel fell. When the shallow coal had been worked out, it was decided in 1910 that a vertical shaft (No. 3) be sunk to exploit depths where substantial coal reserves were known to exist. The shaft was brick-lined, 811 feet deep and 16 ft in diameter and from the bottom, a 'level horizon' mine was driven out to the coal face heading north under the Firth of Forth, 3,000 feet below Fisherrow Harbour, the distance to the coal face exceeding 2 miles. At the pithead screening and wash plants controlled quality and size, domestic markets absorbing the large coal and industry used the smaller sizes. Waste was taken to a hopper at the bing top by conveyors.

When output increased with the new shaft, the coal company laid many additional colliery sidings and new connections with the NBR. The latter provided additional accommodation at Niddrie West, as mentioned in Chapter Ten under 'Niddrie West Marshalling Yards'. Work undertaken by the railway was maintained by it at its own expense. Niddrie Colliery closed in 1927 and later developments at New Craighall included an underground link to Woolmet Colliery in 1936. Graded as Category 'A' in 1962, Woolmet was downgraded to 'B' in 1965, and closed in September 1966, it being hinted that this was due to the opening of Monktonhall pit in 1965.

Once, New Craighall pit had employed 1,000 miners producing 250,000 tons of coal per annum, most of which went by rail, but with the availability of cheaper alternative power sources and decline of the coal industry, it was reduced to single-shifted in 1962 when the NCB Lothians Area decided to concentrate on high grade house coal. Underground loading was mechanised and centralised, further reducing the coalface workforce, and by 1963 only about 700 were employed. The last coal was hewn on 26th May, 1968.

New Craighall Road and Village

New Craighall Road was initially a cart track extension of Niddrie Mains Road, 350 yards south-west of the later Niddrie marshalling yard. The road continued in largely open country, passing the Niddrie Quarry Cottages before reaching a level crossing over the Niddrie Coal Company's mineral railway. North of the road were the workshops and locomotive sheds of the Niddrie Coal Company and on the opposite side were the now closed Niddrie Brick Works dating from 1924. The landscape was dominated by buildings and bings of Newcraighall Colliery and beyond the road passed under the railway to Hawick by a still narrow stone bridge almost under Niddrie South Junction and then enters Newcraighall village, becoming 'Whitehill Street', claimed to be a corruption of Scots Gaelic 'Baile Chruthail' ('elegant village'), an old local name.

Sir Alexander Hope, Bart came from Fife in 1768, bringing the name of Craighall with him. He started mining in Inveresk Parish and founded the village in 1827 as a string of single-storey colliers' cottages, near the future Edinburgh and Dalkeith Railway's Fisherrow branch of 1831, the village being in the fork of main and branch lines. In 1848, a spur from the Hawick line to Musselburgh joined the old Fisherrow branch north of the village, but this closed on 16th May, 1859 when a new route to Musselburgh opened from Newhailes on the main Berwick line. Newhailes station

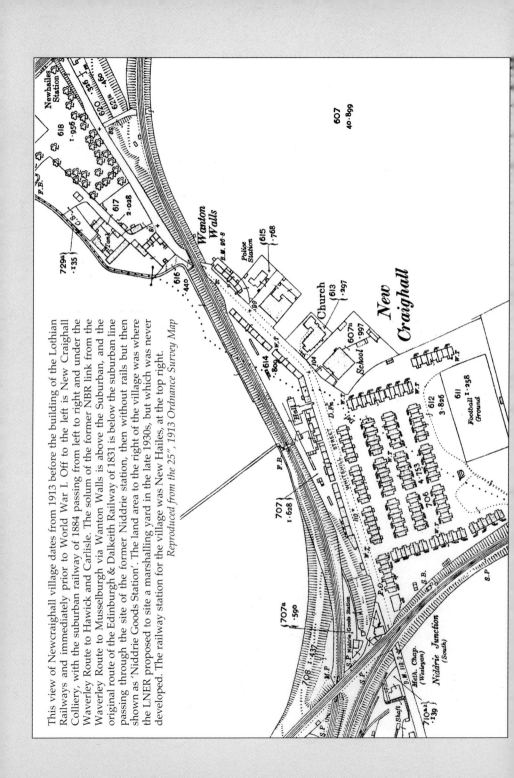

This view of Newcraighall village dates from 1913 before the building of the Lothian Railways and immediately prior to World War I. Off to the left is New Craighall Colliery, with the suburban railway of 1884 passing from left to right and under the Waverley Route to Hawick and Carlisle. The solum of the former NBR link from the Waverley Route to Musselburgh via Wanton Walls is above the Suburban, and the original route of the Edinburgh & Dalkeith Railway of 1831 is below the suburban line passing through the site of the former Niddrie station, then without rails but then shown as 'Niddrie Goods Station'. The land area to the right of the village was where the LNER proposed to site a marshalling yard in the late 1930s, but which was never developed. The railway station for the village was New Hailes, at the top right.

Reproduced from the 25", 1913 Ordnance Survey Map

Newhailes Station

Wanton Walls

Police Station

Church

New Craighall

School

Football Ground

Niddrie Junction (South)

S.P. Niddrie Goods Station

Meth. Chap. (Wesleyan)

WHITEHILL STREET

was about 350 yards west of the village, but at that time colliers and their families were legally bonded to their coalmasters with arguably the worst working conditions and lowest pay in Europe, no education, spare time or money and could not afford to travel.

As demand for coal (and colliers) increased, the village expanded with rows of two-storey brick houses with dry toilets, unmade roads and outdoor pumps to supply water and, by the late 19th century, the 'usual appointments' of church, school, police station and recreation grounds were added, new houses being laid out in a square grid south of Whitehill Street. Newcraighall became a Parish in its own right in 1897.

Boundary changes brought Newcraighall within Edinburgh in 1920 and in 1925 more new streets and houses were added although the village remained a close knit community. Corporation buses reached Newcraighall in February 1921 with a service to the city via Craigmillar at peak times, and after July 1933 passed the St Leonards terminus of the Edinburgh & Dalkeith Railway. Losing out to bus and car, Newhailes station (it had no goods yard) closed on 4th February, 1950.

After the colliery closed, the village future became uncertain as many buildings were a good age, and lacked modern facilities. Edinburgh Corporation recommended that it be razed and notice was served on the residents, but with people power pressure, it was reprieved and redeveloped, retaining its sense of community. 'Klondyke Street' at the east reflected past glory days, but only some of the older houses, now refurbished internally, on the north side of Whitehill Street survive. The Scottish Special Housing Association built two-storey houses south of the road, mingling with the Victorian church, Edwardian school and small retail outlets. The 1925 Newcraighall Miners Welfare Society building still stands witness to the past glory days, but the police station has gone and the village is now just another Edinburgh suburb.

East of the village, the road reverts to being Newcraighall Road, passing under the old Edinburgh and Dalkeith Railway Fisherrow route, its bridge being widened to double track when the line was relaid under the 1882 Suburban Act. When the up line was put out of use on 7th February, 1971 and later lifted, the part of the deck that supported it was also removed. A few yards beyond, the road was crossed by a now removed single line bridge linking the 'Lothian Railways' junctions at Brunstane Park with Wanton Walls. A short distance beyond, the road passes over the East Coast Main Line at the site of Newhailes station before heading north to Fisherrow and Musselburgh.

Today, Newcraighall Road is replete with roundabouts and trappings of modern road infrastructure. Collieries and works have gone, replaced by Industrial Estates, Retail and Business 'parks'. A new single platform station opened at Newcraighall with 'park and ride' facilities on the stub of the 'Waverley Route' to Millerhill together with Brunstane on 4th June, 2002. However, car parking took priority, the station entrance being on the opposite side of the embankment from the village, with the platform some (uncovered) distance from the car park! Trains from Bathgate to Waverley extended to Newcraighall (calling at Brunstane) before returning to Edinburgh *en route* to Dunblane, and there was talk of routeing these diesel units by a reopened suburban line, and including a dieselised North Berwick service, but nothing has yet come of this. Cynics claim that these plans were to ease the growing congestion at Waverley. Shades of 1890!

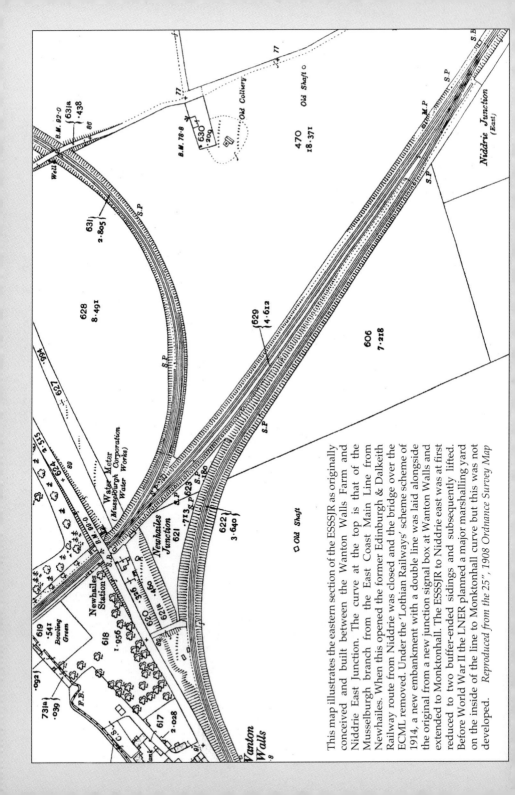

This map illustrates the eastern section of the ESSJR as originally conceived and built between the Wanton Walls Farm and Niddrie East Junction. The curve at the top is that of the Musselburgh branch from the East Coast Main Line from Newhailes. When this opened the former Edinburgh & Dalkeith Railway route from Niddrie was closed and the bridge over the ECML removed. Under the 'Lothian Railways' scheme scheme of 1914, a new embankment with a double line was laid alongside the original from a new junction signal box at Wanton Walls and extended to Monktonhall. The ESSJR to Niddrie east was at first reduced to two buffer-ended sidings and subsequently lifted. Before World War II the LNER planned a major marshalling yard on the inside of the line to Monktonhall curve but this was not developed. *Reproduced from the 25″, 1908 Ordnance Survey Map*

Niddrie East Junction

Niddrie East signal box was on the north side of the main East Coast route some 550 yards from Newhailes Junction where the Musselburgh (1859) branch left the main line in a sharply curved double line connection. The box was opened in 1884 as part of the 1882 Edinburgh Suburban & South Side Junction Railway scheme, and conforms to the suburban line brick signal box drawings. In 1910, a new box was proposed south of the main line between the suburban line junction to Wanton Walls and western end of a proposed marshalling yard at Monktonhall Junction, but this was not developed.

Under the 'Lothian Railways' scheme, a separate parallel double track line was taken from a new junction near Wanton Walls Farm to Monktonhall Junction, and this opened on 9th August, 1915 by-passing Niddrie East. This made the original through line redundant and at Wanton Walls a new signal box opened and the suburban route to the East Coast Main Line was extended east to Monktonhall. The original running lines between Wanton Walls and Niddrie East were converted into buffer-ended sidings with trap points clear of the down goods loop to Newhailes and at Niddrie East the double junction was removed. In pursuit of economies, both curtailed sidings and their relevant signalling was removed on 28th October, 1924. Niddrie East main line crossover was removed on 18th November, 1924 and on 31st December, 1924, an unusual bracket signal was commissioned. At the top of the main post was Niddrie East down main line home, with a co-acting semaphore on a left-hand bracket. Below the main arm, was Newhailes down distant, 'slotted' on the post with the Niddrie East home. Below the distant was the down loop entry signal. On Sunday 3rd May, 1925, Niddrie East box closed, its loop entry points becoming electrically worked from Newhailes Junction. However, it was not demolished for a further 40 years, being used for departmental purposes.

To deal with the increased 1939 wartime traffic, the down loop was extended (after excavations) at the end of November 1941, and a second loop laid, each with a capacity of 80 wagons, engines and brake van. Opened on Sunday 15th March, 1942, Newhailes Junction box locking frame was concurrently renewed. On 31st October, 1971 Newhailes Junction box closed and both loops were removed. The original Musselburgh branch had closed in 1964, but a new Musselburgh station opened on 3rd October, 1988 just west of the former Mucklets Road (now Whitehill Road) bridge some 140 yards east of the site of Niddrie East signal box.

Wanton Walls Junction

The junction dates from the 'Lothian Railways' Act of 1913, and opened on 9th August, 1915 when the suburban line was realigned between Newcraighall Road bridge and Monktonhall and a junction laid between Suburban and single goods line from Brunstane Park Junction. When the new alignment was being made, a new 24-lever signal box was built at Wanton Walls between old and new lines, on the outside of the new curve. When the new lines opened, the connection to Niddrie East was severed. Wanton Walls Junction box was 1,315 yards from Brunstane Park Junction (renamed Niddrie North Junction in 1926) on the Lothian Lines, 1 mile 687 yards from Monktonhall and 1 mile 66 yards from Niddrie West.

On 4th March, 1927, a proposal was made to remotely work Wanton Walls junction from Niddrie South Junction box, but this was not progressed. Basically, the Lothian

Newhailes East Junction signal box closed in 1926, but was of the pattern created for the Edinburgh Suburban & South Side Junction Railway Company and was the last survivor of the type. Photographed in the early 1960s, it had been disused for many years.   *W.S. Sellar*

'J37' class 0-6-0 No. 64572 passes the eastern entry points to the loops at Newhailes. That adjacent to the main line dated from the early days of the suburban railway, the other being installed during World War II. *D. Yuill Collection*

Reawakening memories, former NBR 'Intermediate' class 4-4-0 No. 62451 hustles along the East Coast Main Line, its exhaust concealing Niddrie East signal box. The six-coach train comprises of two matching three-car sets of LNER vehicles, (BT3, CKL, T) with one post-war steel coach in the front portion. The engine, built in 1907 as North British No. 890 was first used on express goods work before moving to passenger duties which included the Edinburgh suburban circle. As part of LNER class 'D32' in 1923, it was the only member of its class to acquire British Railways numbering, before being withdrawn in March 1951. *D. Yuill Collection*

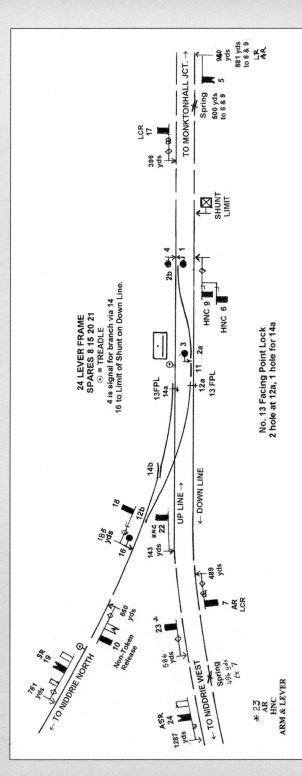

24 LEVER FRAME
SPARES 8 15 20 21
⊙ = TREADLE
4 is signal for branch via 14
16 to Limit of Shunt on Down Line.

No. 13 Facing Point Lock
2 hole at 12a, 1 hole for 14a

13FPL
14a
12a 11 2a
13 FPL
14b
18
12b
16
HNC 22
185 yds
143 yds
UP LINE →
← DOWN LINE
2b 4
1
HNC 9
HNC 6
SHUNT LIMIT
396 yds
LCR 17
Spring
600 yds to 6 & 9
5
881 yds to 6 & 9
960 yds
LR AR
→ TO MONKTONHALL JCT. →

← TO NIDDRIE NORTH
761 yds
SR 19
10
Non-Token Release
860 yds
23 *
586 yds
Spring
4⁹⅜ yds ex 7
→ TO NIDDRIE WEST
489 yds
7 AR LCR
ASR 24
1287 yds

* 23
AR
HNC
ARM & LEVER

Treadle frees Wanton Walls non-token instrument allowing clearing back of train
Only operates when 14 points are reversed and instrument slide "in" for train from Niddrie North.

WANTON WALLS

13ᵀᴴ FEBRUARY 1954

The bridge carrying Mucklets Road over the East Coast Main Line was duplicated with the opening of the Lothian Lines in 1915. This train of empty mineral wagons is passing underneath the new bridge headed by class 'J37' 0-6-0 No. 64566, still bearing its former owner's legend on the tender on 18th June, 1949. The two signals on the bracket to the main post granted entry to the Newhailes loops. The new Musselburgh station now lies immediately beyond the old bridge, the Lothian Lines beyond the new bridge now forming the station car park.

D. Yuill Collection

Proposed (1937) LNER Marshalling Yard between Wanton Walls and Monktonhall

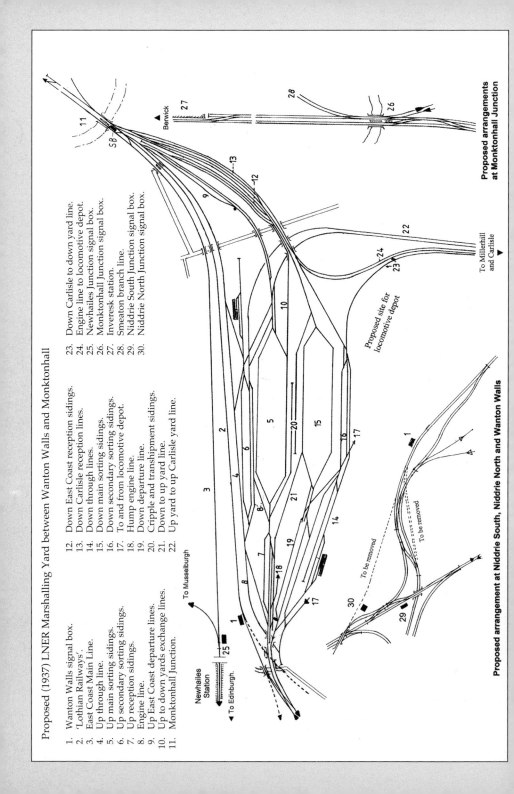

1. Wanton Walls signal box.
2. 'Lothian Railways'.
3. East Coast Main Line.
4. Up through line.
5. Up main sorting sidings.
6. Up secondary sorting sidings.
7. Up reception sidings.
8. Engine line.
9. Up East Coast departure lines.
10. Up to down yards exchange lines.
11. Monktonhall Junction.

12. Down East Coast reception sidings.
13. Down Carlisle reception lines.
14. Down through lines.
15. Down main sorting sidings.
16. Down secondary sorting sidings.
17. To and from locomotive depot.
18. Hump engine line.
19. Down departure line.
20. Cripple and transhipment sidings.
21. Down to up yard line.
22. Up yard to up Carlisle yard line.

23. Down Carlisle to down yard line.
24. Engine line to locomotive depot.
25. Newhailes Junction signal box.
26. Monktonhall Junction signal box.
27. Inveresk station.
28. Smeaton branch line.
29. Niddrie South Junction signal box.
30. Niddrie North Junction signal box.

Proposed arrangements at Monktonhall Junction

Proposed arrangement at Niddrie South, Niddrie North and Wanton Walls

Lines Junction would have had electrically-detected motor-operated points, existing Wanton Walls distant signals would be fixed and the box crossover removed. Wanton Walls down starter and Niddrie West down distant were to be removed, the latter's up inner home becoming the up starter.

On 28th February, 1928, the Engineer opened a single line coup* siding on part of the 1884 line solum, the points 145 yards north of the signal box on the line from Niddrie North being worked from an adjacent two-lever ground frame. The siding was removed on 1st June, 1933 but, on 14th November, 1941, an up siding opened at Wanton Walls, 24 feet on the approach side of the starting signal for Monktonhall Junction, 396 yards from the box. Created for coal storage, entry was controlled by a one-lever ground frame with Annett's Key release interlocked with the up starting signal, crossover points, inner and outer home signals from Niddrie West and the Niddrie North home signal. The siding was removed after the war.

On 8th April, 1963, the single goods line of the Lothian Railways from Niddrie North (formerly Brunstane Park) Junction closed and was lifted, its bridge over Newcraighall Road being removed. Wanton Walls box became a simple block post between Niddrie West and Monktonhall. However, the Monktonhall to Millerhill yard spur line seriously reduced its requirement and it was no surprise when the box closed on 8th January, 1967.

Proposed Wanton Walls Marshalling Yard

With the failure of the 1920s schemes for marshalling yards in the Duddingston/Niddrie areas, the LNER drew up plans in 1937 for an alternative site between Wanton Walls and Monktonhall Junction on the south side of the line. The land was (and still is) mainly agricultural the railway being on an embankment with descending gradient towards Monktonhall.

At the Niddrie End, considerable alterations were to be made to the existing lines. The former Lothian Railways single line between Brunstane Park (then Niddrie North) and Wanton Walls and the 1882 suburban railway route from the rear of Newcraighall village and Wanton Walls would be removed and replaced by new connecting lines providing alternative routes either to the Lothian Lines beyond Wanton Walls or directly into or out of the new proposed yard.

At Monktonhall Junction, further layout modifications were envisaged. The connection from main line to the Smeaton branch would be removed, branch trains crossing to the Lothian Lines before gaining the branch. However, there was a direct main line connection with the proposed marshalling yard similar to that employed some 25 years later for Millerhill. Down Carlisle trains arrived from the Waverley Route in sidings adjacent to the down East Coast sidings for sorting.

Within the yard, the up and down sorting sidings were alongside each other, separated by buffer-ended cripple sidings and each main group had secondary sidings alongside. There were direct departure lines to both East Coast and Hawick lines. As in the aborted Niddrie schemes, a locomotive depot was envisaged on land between the yard and Hawick line south east of the village. As before, plans were never finalised and the single Edinburgh area yard concept was left to the British Railways Modernisation plan of 1955 to develop. Unfortunately, the era of significant colliery output and small wagonload traffic was drawing to a close and the new Millerhill yards had only a relatively short life span.

---

* Coup - Scottish for rubbish tip, dirty or untidy place.

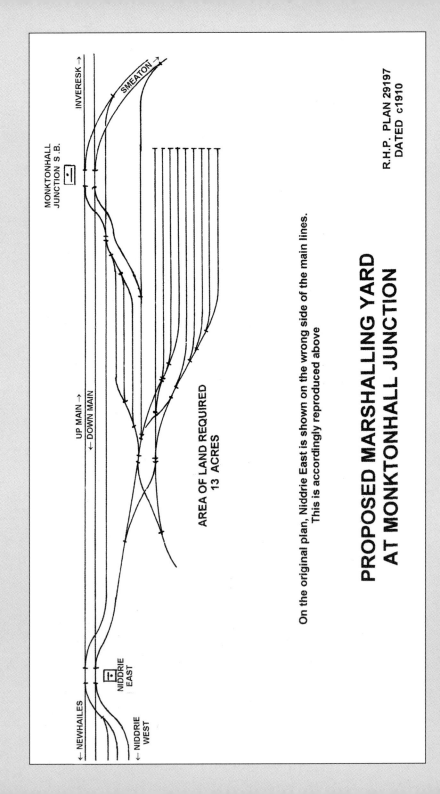

NEWHAILES →

NIDDRIE EAST

NIDDRIE WEST →

UP MAIN →
← DOWN MAIN

MONKTONHALL
JUNCTION S.B.

INVERESK →

SMEATON →

AREA OF LAND REQUIRED
13 ACRES

On the original plan, Niddrie East is shown on the wrong side of the main lines.
This is accordingly reproduced above

PROPOSED MARSHALLING YARD
AT MONKTONHALL JUNCTION

R.H.P. PLAN 29197
DATED c1910

Monktonhall Junction

Monktonhall took its name from the Monks of Newbattle Abbey whose interests involved coal mining, vital to the community (and centuries later to the North British Railway). When the NBR opened, Monktonhall was a small group of buildings between the River Eden and the Berwick main line. This changed when the North British Railway (Branches) Act of 1862 authorised a branch south towards Smeaton whence other lines radiated to Macmerry and Gifford and the Waverley Route at Hardengreen. A junction was installed at Monktonhall and a signal box opened on the north side of the line 1 mile 572 yards from Newhailes Junction, controlling the double junction into the single line branch, its main line crossover being on the bridge over the River Esk. The branch officially opened to goods and mineral traffic on Sunday 22nd December, 1866, and this is taken as the date the signal box officially opened, although it had been in use beforehand.

In 1884, the Edinburgh Suburban & South Side Junction Railway junction at Niddrie East, 1 mile 110 yards west of Monktonhall Junction and dividing the section from Newhailes, opened enabling East Coast freight to go direct to the then new Niddrie yards, and via the suburban line to bypass Waverley.

About 1910, consideration was given for a small marshalling yard at Monktonhall with nine buffer-ended sidings and four reception lines. Linked with the proposed doubling of the line to Smeaton this was to occupy some 13 acres of land, the layout plan suggesting a new signal box at Niddrie East on the south side of the main line. This was not progressed, being overtaken by the construction of the 'Lothian Lines' from Monktonhall to the marshalling yard at Niddrie West.

On 12th December, 1912 the Monktonhall and Smeaton line was doubled, abstracting traffic from the Hardengreen line, although creating a potential minor bottleneck between Monktonhall and Niddrie East Junctions. To match the increased workload, a larger signal box opened on 15th December, 1912 at Monktonhall Junction on the south of the line, three days *after* the new track arrangements and 65 yards nearer Niddrie East.

Under the North British Railway Act of 1913, the extended suburban line connected at Monktonhall link directly into either the Smeaton branch or the East Coast Main Line. Trains between the Smeaton branch and Niddrie West marshalling yards could then pass behind the signal box, without encroaching on the main line. During the construction work for this line, one road bridge over the main line was demolished, several dwellings were removed and the course of public paths were altered. Steel decks and stone abutments carried the new lines over roads, tracks and culverts.

After the Great War, traffic via Smeaton declined in the face of road competition and industrial retraction, but the section of the Lothian Lines between Monktonhall and Niddrie West remained relatively buoyant. The work of Inveresk Station signal box, 637 yards to the east, was absorbed into Monktonhall Junction on 12th June, 1922, and it formally closed on 15th April, 1924. Inveresk goods yard headshunt on the up side was extended and a new facing connection provided from the up main at Monktonhall. Inveresk passenger station, the nearest to Monktonhall, lasted until 4th May, 1964.

In 1953, the Coal Board built Scotland's first central preparation plant near Dalkeith No. 9 pit and the output from all the nearby collieries was sent there, with the initial 1,500 tons per day capacity expected to rise to 3,000 tons per day. Considerable economies were effected, even the shunting being undertaken by

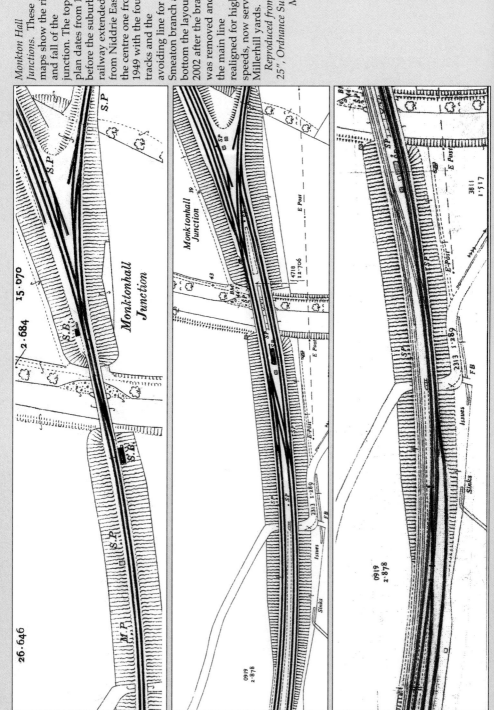

Monkton Hall Junctions. These maps show the rise and fall of the junction. The top plan dates from 1914 before the suburban railway extended from Niddrie East, the centre one from 1949 with the four tracks and the avoiding line for the Smeaton branch and bottom the layout in 2002 after the branch was removed and the main line realigned for higher speeds, now serving Millerhill yards.

Reproduced from the 25", Ordnance Survey Maps

Monktonhall Junction

Monktonhall Junction

traversers instead of locomotives. In 1954, test bores adjacent to Dalkeith No. 9 showed seams of good coal, and exploitation was planned, but Council planning restrictions hampered the development and the Board cancelled the scheme by the end of 1956.

Abortive NBR and LNER plans for a major marshalling yard in the Edinburgh District eventually bore fruit at Millerhill under the 1955 British Railway Modernisation plan. A substantially-engineered double line link was provided from the Monktonhall - Niddrie West line by April 1961 and although Monktonhall was resignalled on 11th November, 1961, the new spur did not open until 23rd April, 1962, with the up yard officially opening on 10th June, 1962. Trains could then run between Monktonhall and Millerhill, avoiding Niddrie West or Edinburgh. The Monktonhall and Niddrie West link remained, albeit reducing in importance after the opening of Millerhill down yard on 8th April, 1963, but continued to be useful for planned (and unplanned) passenger diversions, although not for regular passenger services.

Economics inevitably reared their head and the up line between Niddrie West and the Millerhill line junction was removed on 7th February, 1971, the double line between Monktonhall and Smeaton being singled on 1st February, 1973. On 26th June, 1976 the surviving Monktonhall to Niddrie West line was bi-directionally signalled.

Monktonhall Junction was remodelled again on 12th June, 1977 and as the control area of the Edinburgh Signalling Centre expanded, the box became a 'fringe' box when Edinburgh absorbed the Portobello Panel 13 days later. Some colour light signals were installed but did not become operational until 1st August when Edinburgh took over from Monktonhall, the latter box closing on that date. On 12th March, 1978, the Edinburgh and Berwick resignalling was completed, and although the singled Smeaton branch officially survived until 31st December, 1980, rail traffic had ceased at the end of 1978, with the closure of Dalkeith Colliery. By September 1979 the track was considered unsafe, and was removed.

After the final junction remodelling, the main line, now devoid of flanking refuge sidings and branch junction, crossed the River Esk by the Lothian Lines bridge, the older one alongside being abandoned. Passing behind the site of the signal box, it crossed over the delightfully named Cowpitsford Road, 65 feet to the west of which is the facing down line connection to Millerhill. Sixty yards beyond is a high speed trailing main line crossover and 400 feet further on is another down line facing connection, this time used by trains from Millerhill yard using the crossover to gain the up main line. For a time, the name 'Wanton Walls Junction' was applied to the Millerhill lines junction to differentiate from Monktonhall Junction before the 'Lothian Lines' forward to Niddrie West were lifted.

In the final years of the North British Railway, Edinburgh suburban line coaching stock could at times present a very mixed formation. In this view, 'Yorkie' tank No. 134, a regular Suburban engine, heads an Inner Circle train under the gantry supporting the Portobello East Junction signal box with a motley six-coach rake of Holmes coaches, including six-wheel and bogie first class carriages in the centre of the formation. Both brake thirds had five passenger compartments. Latterly British Railways No. 67459, the engine lasted until October 1955 finally allocated to Polmont.   *J.F. McEwan Collection/Kirkintilloch Library*

'C15' 4-4-2 tank No. 9133 eases past the signal box at Craigentinny on an Inner Circle service of 1924 stock, built to NBR specifications, but with York LNER exteriors. The engine bears NBR destination board and Edinburgh Suburban headlamp code, but the neat formations were soon to be displaced by 'N2' tanks and Group Standard carriages and moved to lighter duties. No. 9133 was withdrawn in February 1956 as BR No. 67481, about the same time as the carriages. Sister Suburban engine No. 9135 achieved fame after 1940 on the Arrochar-Craigendoran push-pull service, latterly as No. 67460.   *R.W. Lynn Collection*

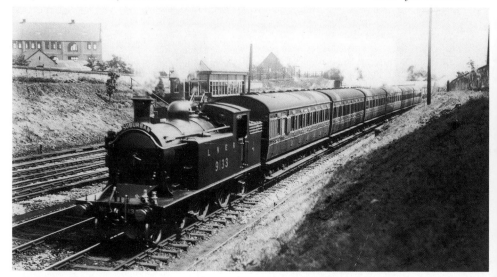

Chapter Twelve

Accidents and Incidents

Over the years, there were few significant accidents involving trains on the Edinburgh Suburban line proper, although there were incidents involving suburban circle trains elsewhere on this service.

On 20th November, 1915, NBR 4-4-2 tank locomotive No. 39 (latterly class 'C15' No. 67477) at the head of the 8.14 am Outer Circle collided at Edinburgh Waverley with a light engine, 4-4-0 No. 737 (later LNER class 'D31'), but without fatalities.

On Monday 28th July, 1924, when the 6.41 pm Inner Circle service from Leith Central (6.50 pm from Edinburgh Waverley), was standing in Haymarket station platform, it was struck in the rear by the 6.54 pm from Edinburgh to Port Edgar (the public timetable shows to South Queensferry) via Kirkliston at an estimated speed of only 10 mph. However, due to the incidence of the Edinburgh Trades Holiday, the regular robust Suburban bogie stock had been replaced for the day by eight Victorian four-wheelers and six-wheel brake weighing only 98 tons tare. Telescoping resulted in five fatalities and 54 injuries. The Suburban train was headed by 'C15' class 4-4-2T No. 133 (latterly No. 67481) and the four-coach (102 tons) Port Edgar train by ex-works class 'D29' 4-4-0 No. 9338 *Helen McGregor* of Haymarket running tender-first. The Queensferry train driver misread signals at the entrance to the Haymarket tunnel and also missed the tunnel entrance warning bell. Unfortunately, tunnel visibility was hindered by exhausts from previous trains and damp weather conditions. The Suburban train had been held at Haymarket for a few minutes to enable a Polytechnic party to join and these passengers obligingly joined the rear carriages which were nearest the steps down to the platform and took the brunt of the impact.

On Sunday 24th April, 1938, a goods train which had left Stirling at 10.35 pm on the Saturday night for Niddrie West reached Gorgie at about 5.15 am and called to detach some wagons. When the train came to a stand clear of the points, the Gorgie Junction signalman reset the points from Haymarket West Junction for another move to Haymarket Central. Eight wagons loaded with coal next to the brake van were uncoupled from the Stirling train, but started to run back down the gradient picking up speed before passing under the Caledonian Wester Dalry branch. Sadly, a set of catch points was open on the north side of the bridge and the brake van led the wagons through these and down an embankment. Unfortunately, the guard was still in his van and was fatally crushed as it disintegrated around him. His body was extricated three hours later and it was noticed that his watch had stopped at 5.25, three minutes after the incident.

On Friday 21st December, 1951, the 5.00 pm Outer Circle train from Leith Central to Leith Central via Duddingston, headed by class 'V1' 2-6-2 tank locomotive No. 67630, collided with a stationary A4 Pacific No. 60018 *Sparrow Hawk* between Lochend Junction and Piershill Junction. The passenger train had the customary five-coach formation, the leading two being 1939-built articulated twin brake third/first (80295/4). The other three carriages were a post-war third (82732), a 1927 third (82305), and post-war brake third (87144). No. 67630 was withdrawn for repairs, exacerbating a shortages of locomotives of its type at St Margarets, where two others (Nos. 67659 and 67666) were similarly 'crocked'.

Of course, in addition to the incidents that resulted in damage to stock or injuries to passengers, there were countless instances of goods trains coming to a stand on

Scene of the fatal accident between Gorgie Junction and Haymarket Central Junction on Sunday 24th April, 1938 when the uncoupled rear portion of a freight train ran away from Gorgie, passed under the Caledonian Railway bridge and derailed at catch points, crushing the unfortunate guard. *Author's Collection*

the gradients up to Morningside Road from both Gorgie and Duddingston. On one occasion, a freight train on the Inner Circle failed on the curve at the Myreside Road bridge. Assistance came in from the rear in the form of a class 'V1' 2-6-2 tank which ended up assisting the failed train *and* hauling its own train load of passengers at the same time up the 1 in 70 gradient! The same goods train failed at the same place on the following night but this time the passenger train remained firmly anchored at Gorgie until the freight had been split and taken forward to the summit in two parts. Perhaps officialdom took a dim view of the previous day's escapade!

On 26th October, 1964, a Clayton diesel locomotive (later class '17') on the 2.30 pm Mossend to Leith freight train of steel coil derailed after hitting the buffers at the trap points on the spur from Slateford at Craiglockhart Junction. Fourteen of the 21 wagons were also derailed and breakdown cranes from St Margarets in Edinburgh and Thornton in Fife worked throughout the night to clear the wreckage. All four lines were blocked, but no one was seriously injured. The fireman and guard had jumped clear, but the driver remained in the cab.

On 22nd May, 1969, class '40' diesel No. 359 on an eastbound freight train bound for Millerhill via the Inner Circle line came to a stand on the bridge over the main road at Cameron Toll with smoke and fire coming from the centre axle on one bogie. However, this was dealt with by the train crew, with only a 10 minute delay.

An entire passenger train derailed about 8 am whilst moving at 40 mph between Niddrie West and Craiglockhart Junction on 24th January, 1987. This was the Inter-City 'raspberry ripple' set of Mark I FOs, 2 x RBK, a BFK and an observation saloon at the rear. All vehicles except the locomotive, No. 37405 *Strathclyde Region*, and the saloon were derailed, blocking both lines. Breakfast ended up on the kitchen floors, but no one was hurt and the carriages remained upright. Passengers transferred to a three-car dmu that pulled up in front, having run wrong line from the Haymarket direction. It took until Saturday evening to re-rail the train and, after lifting and examining, the set, except for the leading two vehicles which had taken most of the strain, was used back to London St Pancras together with six sleeping cars.

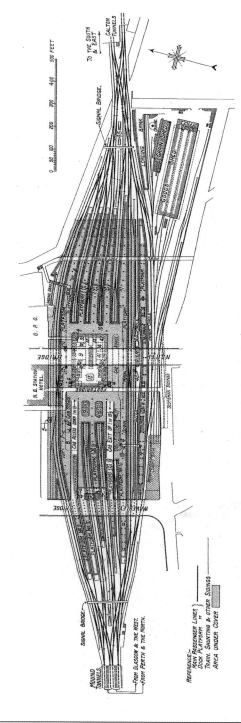

PLAN OF WAVERLEY STATION, SHOWING PLATFORMS, LINES, APPROACHES AND PRINCIPAL OFFICES, ETC.

(Covered Area shown Stippled.)

1. West Signal Cabin.
2. Parcel Office.
3. Parcel Yard.
4. Hoist.
5. North Signal Cabin.
6. Carted Luggage, Parcels, &c.
7. Ticket Collectors.
8. Ambulance.
9. Left Luggage Room.
10. Bookstall.
11. Bar (West End).
12. Train Letters.
13. Booking Office.
14. Staff.
15. Kitchen and Canteen.
16. Parcels Store.
17. Cab Office.
18. Luggage Bridge.
19. Waiting Rooms.
20. Suburban Signal Cabin.
21. Booking Office.
22. Tobaccos.
23. Passage.
24. L.M.S. Office.
25. Offices.
26. Gentlemen's 1st Class Waiting Room.
27. Ladies' 1st Class Waiting Room.
28. Ladies' Lavatory.
29. Entrance to Upper Floors.
30. Gentlemen's Lavatory.
31. Tea Room and 3rd Class Bar.
32. Telegraph Office.
33. Post Office.
34. Service Room.
35. 1st Class Refreshment Room.
36. Enquiry Office.
37. Seats and Sleepers.
38. Season Ticket Office.
39. Ladies' 3rd Class Waiting Room.
40. Ladies' 3rd Class Lavatory.
41. Station Masters' Dept.
42. Dining Room.
43. South Signal Box.
44. Water Tank, &c.
45. East Signal Cabin.

Plan of Edinburgh Waverley station *circa* 1926. This plan highlights the peak of Waverley as a passenger station.

Appendix One

Waverley Suburban Station

In 1880, Waverley was an island platform with eight bay platforms at the east end but only two at the west. The sides of the 'island' platform gave two long through platforms that on the north (up) side being divisible into two of 980 feet and 340 feet respectively, whereas the 'down' platform was only 930 feet long. At the east end, which catered for much short distance traffic to Granton (for the ferry to Fife and the north), Leith, Carlisle and local East Lothian services the dock platforms were short, varying between 190 and 470 feet in length from ramp to buffers, the average being 337 feet. The west end pair were only 280 feet and 360 feet long. Not at all suitable for a major city terminal, let alone a major capital city! Of course, all goods trains passing through Edinburgh on the North British also had to navigate the Waverley complex - and this was the period of the 'industrial revolution'. To complicate matters, all trains shared only double track through Princes Street Gardens going west and to Abbeyhill in the opposite direction, and passenger trains shared this with freights, light engines, empty coaching stock and trains running out of their booked 'slots'. This was the era of through carriages requiring train remarshalling in the platforms and the adjacent goods yard had to be serviced.

In the next few years, endeavouring to relieve this congestion, an additional island platform some 753 feet long and not wide enough to carry buildings was squeezed in west of the North bridge pillars between the station wall and the main island platforms. Of course track had to be sacrificed to provide the required space.

The service pattern for the suburban circle meant that trains had to stand for up to 20 minutes in each hour throughout the day at an 'up' or 'down' main line or through island platform. To avoid this, a goods shed and most sidings on the south of the station between North Bridge and Waverley Bridge outside the main station wall were removed and a new island platform built. However, its 750 feet length was constrained by the North Bridge piers that forced the station to extend under Waverley bridge towards the Mound tunnel and it was also partially isolated by a wall that supported the main station roof between the two bridges. In effect this suburban station was a station within a station with its own accesses and exits yet linked with the main station by footbridges, but is actually on the site of today's Platform 11. As perhaps befits a station of a railway that was (formally) not then part of the North British, it had its own characteristics.

The 1880 drawings for the building on the suburban platform show typical NBR period architecture. Access to the platform was by a double door in the east side of Waverley bridge, thence by an 8 ft wide covered stairway of 56 steps in four groups of 14 with intermediate landings. Arches underneath were available as stores. From the foot of the steps, a glazed canopy with valance side and end boards extended across the width of the platform, and was supported on independent pillars. The 80 ft-long building had a 13 ft- long booking office at the west end, the booking window facing the steps. At the rear of the booking office was a 24 ft-long general waiting room, a 10 ft-long gents' urinal area, a 14 ft-long waiting room for the first class passengers, a 4 ft 6 in. WC space in two sections with a partition parallel to the railway and, at the east end, a 14 ft-long 'First Class Ladies Waiting Room'. The platform canopy continued for a further 42 ft. Glazing started 3 ft above platform level, the area above the windows being glazed or tongue and groove wood-boarded. West of Waverley bridge the platform was uncovered. The platform and buildings lasted for only a decade.

After the Edinburgh Suburban & South Side Junction Railway officially became part of the North British in 1885, it was considered as part of the Waverley 'package' in redevelopments which were not long in coming. The opening of the Forth bridge in 1890 totally changed the traffic flow, the west end becoming the more important as the east end lost its north traffic. The North British embarked on a major reconstruction, not only of the station but also of the line on both sides, quadrupling out to Saughton in the west and to Abbeyhill and thence, taking the Piershill loop to Portobello in the east. Acquiring land formerly occupied by decrepit tenements south and east of the station and reconstructing the North Bridge and the Waverley Bridge enabled the station area to be widened. A new Waverley station for the 20th century appeared gradually (it took some 10 years as the old one had to be kept going in the meantime) and with it a new 'suburban' station - complete with booking office, stores, waiting rooms and signal box. However, it had its own separate entrance from Waverley Bridge and was still only connected to the main station by footbridges and hydraulic hoists. The new suburban station opened officially on 17th April, 1898 and remains operational today, still separated by the station wall, although most buildings and the steps to Waverley bridge have gone. Platforms 20 and 21 were known as the 'Sub' platforms by generations of railway staff, as indeed did by the LNER 1930s signalling equipment, the formal numbering being of relatively recent date.

Ironically at 1,129 feet, they are the longest platforms in Waverley today, and were considered ideal for the 'Eurostar' services when they were first mooted, but the perhaps arrogant Anglophobic mentality meant that this never came to pass. However, they still perform a valuable service in dealing with Anglo-Scottish services acting as an 'overflow' when the main station, drastically reduced in scope and facilities during government inspired cutbacks of the 1960s, cannot cope.

The footbridge to main station and to Market Street opened to the public on 19th March, 1899, the painting operation of the outside being carried out by contractors standing on the roof of old Ashbury carriages provided for the purpose!

Signalling the Suburban Platform

In the early days of the suburban railway, the island platform that was used by the train service formed part of the general Waverley complex, but it appears that it had its own dedicated signal box, or at least signalmen. From 26th November, 1897, as part of the resignalling and station reconstruction, Waverley signal box was closed and all the signals connected with it were removed. A new temporary signal box immediately to the west of the North Bridge opened and the signalmen with the telegraph instruments transferred from the Suburban signal box.

Two paragraphs in the instructions related to the instructions regarding the Train Regulators' areas of control. They performed similar duties to the 'Operating Department Representative' of later years for 'on site' signalling of trains and were distinguished by a red cap by day and carried a hand lamp after dark capable of displaying either red or green aspects. They had to ensure that all unconnected points were safe for the passage of trains within their own geographical areas of responsibility. On 17th April, 1898, when the new suburban platforms were commissioned, so was a new Train Regulator's Section. The individuals responsible controlled, over the 24 hour period, the working of the new down suburban line, i.e. between the fouling point of the down suburban line and east end of the up goods line, and the fouling point of the down suburban line and west end engine siding.

On 19th June, with the opening of the Waverley South Central signal box situated in the station wall between suburban platforms and main station, the temporary signal arrangements were withdrawn and the signalmen transferred to the new box. Consequently, train regulators on the down suburban line (and down main line) were withdrawn.

A new signal box exclusively controlling the suburban platforms, was opened on 28th November, 1897, but closed on 18th November, 1900 when replaced by a new box on the platform. On 7th December, 1930, this was closed and converted to a store, its former work being taken over by the Waverley East and West mechanical boxes, although some suburban signals were altered to colour lights at that time anticipating the 1935 and 1937 resignalling schemes.

Appendix Two

Early Timetables and Tourists

Suburban Timetables

The Suburban line was shown in the North British Railway Timetables from 1st November, 1884, although the service did not commence until the following month.

The service was shown in the North British Railway timetables from the start, and the public timetable for 3rd July, 1885 showed the first Outer Circle train leaving Waverley, via Duddingston and Gorgie, at 8.15 am, and thence at 15 minutes past each hour until 7.15 pm. In the reverse direction, via Gorgie and Duddingston, the Inner Circle, the first departure was at 9 45 am, thence at 45 minutes past each hour until 10 45 pm. All trains conveyed first and third class accommodation only and called at all stations with connections at Portobello with some trains for the eight minute trip to South Leith, albeit with substantial delays in the connecting service departure times and requiring a change of platform.

Timings were	Waverley	XX 15	X1 25
	Portobello	XX 23	X1 15
	Duddingston	XX 30	X1 06
	Newington	XX 34	X1 02
	Blackford Hill	XX 36	X1 00
	Morningside Road	XX 39	XX 57
	Gorgie	XX 43	XX 53
	Haymarket	XX 47	XX 49
	Waverley	XX 55	XX 45

Note the extra times at Haymarket (going to Waverley) and at Portobello (also going to Waverley). It is not clear if this was for ticket collection purposes or to allow for the known growing congestion delays before arrival in the city centre!

Morningside did not acquire the suffix 'Road' until 1885 and Duddingston was shown as Duddingston and Craigmillar from the outset, although periodically curtailed to just 'Duddingston'. Similarly, Blackford Hill was also periodically referred to as 'Blackfordhill'.

North British Railway Tourist Arrangements for September 1895

Morningside Road is shown as having three golf courses in the neighbourhood:

Greenhills about a mile distant of 18 holes and 'greatly patronised by all classes of players'. It was free to all.
Princess, a course of 9 holes.
Mortonhall was a private course of 18 holes with an entrance fee of £10 10s. 0d. with annual subscription of £1 11s. 6d. The membership was then 350.
In addition, *Lothianburn* was about 2½ miles from the station and had nine holes at that time, with a further nine due to be added within a short space of time. The course was a private one.

A 'brake' ran from Morningside Road station to each of the golf courses when sufficiently patronised.

Blackford Hill was the station for the Edinburgh Ladies Golf Club which was a new course of 12 holes, including a number of hazards including a wall and a burn. It had 450 members and the entrance was 10s. with an annual subscription also 10s. Gentlemen paid double!

Craiglockhart station had the Edinburgh Hydropathic Golf Course with 9 holes and cover 34 acres of ground. Annual Subscription was 25s. and had a membership of 90.

At Duddingston, a new course of 18 holes was then planned on the estate of Easter Duddingston, belonging to the Duke of Abercorn. It was close to the railway station and the presence of the water hazard presented by the Braid Burn was a source of interest as it had to be crossed no fewer than eight times. Leased to the Insurance and Banking Golf Club for £500 per annum rent, members alone had the privilege of introducing strangers.

Appendix Three

Summary of Daily Average Passenger Journeys, 1960

	1	2	3	4	5	6	7	8	9	10	11
1 Edinburgh Waverley	-	*	130	60	165	80	25	30	*	*	*
2 Haymarket	*	-	80	30	60	15	15	-	*	*	*
3 Gorgie East	175	40	-	5	50	25	30	25	15	10	5
4 Craiglockhart	45	20	5	-	5	15	15	10	5	-	-
5 Morningside Road	145	40	40	5	-	10	15	15	10	-	-
6 Blackford Hill	70	20	25	15	15	-	5	10	-	-	-
7 Newington	25	15	25	20	15	5	-	10	10	5	-
8 Duddingston	30	-	25	10	15	10	10	-	25	10	5
9 Portobello	*	*	15	5	5	-	10	10	-	*	*
10 Piershill	*	*	15	-	-	-	5	15	*	-	*
11 Abbeyhill	*	*	10	-	-	-	-	5	*	*	-

* Railway passenger train services were to continue between these stations, and data was not included.

Numeric codes along the top of the table relate to the numbers against the station on the left of the table.

The statistics above relate to aggregated passenger journeys and not to passengers, and are also not related to revenue.

The suburban railway provided an extra 'out and back' lunch-time service for business people whose work permitted.

There was no differentiation between single, return or season ticket holders or railway staff holding residential tickets.

These statistics were also used in determining line viability.

Appendix Four

Particulars of Traffic (excluding Private Sidings), 1961

	Passengers Daily		Annual Parcels Traffic 1961		Wagon Load Traffic	
	Joining	Alighting	Forwarded	Received	Forwarded	Received
Duddingston & C'millar	140	130	602	88	not quoted*	
Newington	130	130	127	7	1	1292
Blackford Hill	160	160	27	2	not applicable	
Morningside Road	280	330	1,485	288	48	1227
Craiglockhart	120	150	165	114	not applicable	
Gorgie (East)	380	410	350	169	not quoted*	
Bonnyrigg	170	170	6,908	11,320	799	105
Rosewell & H'den	85	85	819	384	12	-

* Due to incidence of private siding traffic which would continue.

Appendix Five

Summary of Revenue and Expenditure Comparisons, 1961

(This data also incorporated the separate Rosewell & Hawthornden line)

	£	£	£
Immediate and Short Term Savings:			
Staffing costs	54,614		
Repair of Rolling Stock	8,870		
Movement Costs	4,300		
Day-to-day Costs	2,491	70,275	
Provision for renewals saved:			
Rolling Stock and Plant	7,455	7,455	
Total Savings		77,730	
Deduct:			
Estimates Gross Receipts loss:			
Passenger	19,000		
Freight	511		
Miscellaneous	0	19,511	
Provide alternative road services		1,334	
Total deductions from Savings		20,845	

Net estimated annual savings on combined Suburban and Rosewell Withdrawals   £56,885

Unspecified savings expected to be made in avoiding renewals between 1962 and 1966 amounted to a further £13,049.

Appendix Six

Passenger Timetable Survey

Timetable Date		Apr. 1900	Apr. 1910	Jul. 1922	Sep. 1931	Oct. 1939	Dec. 1939	Apr. 1940	Oct. 1947	Sep. 1950	Jun. 1962
Outer Circle	SX	20	20	18	19	17	12	12	8	8	13
	SO	20	17	18	16	9	11	11	7	7	8
Inner Circle	SX	19	20	21	17	10	14	14	10	10	19
	SO	19	19	20	14	10	12	12	5	5	7

SO = Saturdays only.   SX = Saturdays excepted.

Acknowledgements

The core of this book is that derived from files of the former British Railways (Scottish Region) to which I had relatively free access, direct and indirect, during a railway career spanning several decades and departments, and from documents in the National Archives of Scotland (formerly the Scottish Record Office). Having worked at all bar one station on the line, I have also been able to draw on personal reminiscences. Locomotive and train workings are derived largely from the railway press, particularly the contemporary enthusiast journals, such as those of the *Railway Magazine*, Railway Correspondence and Travel Society and the Stephenson Locomotive Society, and from the personal remembrances of railway staff.

On the more general historical front, it would be an impertinence to try and appraise the work previously undertaken by local historians Charles J. Smith and Malcolm Cant. Alan Brotchie also supplied - knowingly or otherwise - many details of other local public transport and particular thanks are due to the staff of the Edinburgh Room at Edinburgh Public Libraries and to staff in the Map Library of the Scottish National Library of Scotland in Edinburgh, for whom nothing seems to be too much trouble. Thanks are also due to Harry Jack, Bill Roberton, and John Jones for access to the aerial photographs that date from 1930 and to John Smith of Bearsden for his continuous support.

Bibliography

Minute Books of the Edinburgh Suburban & South Side Junction Railway.
Minute Books of the North British Railway.
Minutes and correspondence of several railway committees.
Official correspondence of the ESSSJR, NBR, LNER, BR (Scottish Region) and its successors.
Operating, civil and signalling engineering circulars of the ESSSJR, NBR, LNER and British Railways.
ESSJR, NBR, LNER and BR maps, plans and diagrams.
Timetables, circulars, correspondence and other documents of the railways concerned.

The several editions of Ordnance Survey Maps of Edinburghshire and Midlothian

Scotsman, Edinburgh Evening News, Evening Dispatch and various other Scottish newspaper files.

Historic South Edinburgh, C. J. Smith (Birlinn Press, 2000).
South Edinburgh in Pictures, C.J. Smith (Albyn Press, 1992).
Morningside, C.J. Smith (John Donald Publishers, 1992).
Gorgie & Dalry, M. Cant (M. Cant Publicatons, 1997).
Villages of Edinburgh, 1 North, M. Cant (M. Cant Publications, 1995).
Villages of Edinburgh, 2 South, M. Cant (M. Cant Publications, 1997).
Scotland's Newspaper 1817-1992, Albert Morris (Scotsman Publications, 1992).
Old Tollcross, Morningside and Swanston, M. Cant (Stenlake Publishing, 2001).
Old Gorgie, M. Cant (Stenlake Publishing, 2002).
Edinburgh from the Air, John A. Jones (Stenlake Publishing, 2002).
Lost Railways of the Lothians, Gordon Stansfield (Stenlake Publishing, 2003).
Old Newington, Grange, Liberton and Gilmerton, Robin Sherman (Stenlake Publishing, 2000).
Mining the Lothians, Guthrie Hutton (Stenlake Publishing, 1998).
Edinburgh's Transport, D.L.G. Hunter (Advertiser Press, 1964).
Edinburgh's Transport - 'The Early Years', D.L.G. Hunter (Mercat Press, 1992).
Edinburgh's Transport - 'The Corporation Years', D.L.G. Hunter (Adam Gordon, 1999).
Edinburgh - Picturesque Notes, R.L. Stevenson (Rupert Hart-Davis, 1954).
Locomotives of the LNER, (RCTS, various).
Locomotives of the NBR 1846-1882, Stephenson Locomotive Society (SLS, 1970).
Edinburgh, an Illustrated architectural History, Charles McKean (RIBA (Scotland) 1992).
LNER Footplate Memories, Charlie Meacher (D. Bradford Barton).
Living with Locos, Charlie Meacher (D. Bradford Barton, 1980).
Edinburgh Curiosities Vol. 2, J.U. Thompson (Birlinn Press, 2004).
Morningside Memories Vol. 2, Morningside Association (MHA, 2003).
Lost Railways of Midlothian, W.S. Garden Hays (W. & E.A. Munro 1985).
Scottish Beer Guide, Gavin Smith (Mercat Press 2001).
Scotch Missed, Brian Townsend (Neil Wilson Publishing 2000).
Between the Streamlet and the Town, Charles Smith (Astley Ainslie Hospital 1988).
From SMT to Eastern Scottish, D.L.G. Hunter (John Donald Publishers 1987).
Illustrated History of Edinburgh Railways, W.A.C. Smith and Paul Anderson (Irwell Press 1995).

As the initial work on this book started over 40 years ago, I crave the indulgence of those who have assisted and are not included in the above.

Index

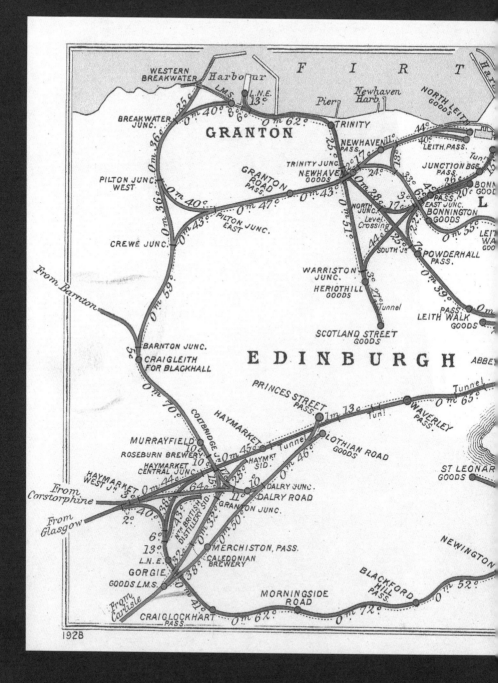

FIRT

WESTERN BREAKWATER
Harbour
LMS
L.N.E. 13°

Pier
Newhaven Harb.
NORTH LEITH GOODS

BREAKWATER JUNC.
25°
0 m 40°
0 6°
0 m 62°
TRINITY
NEWHAVEN 11°
44°
LEITH. PASS.

GRANTON

NEWHAVEN PASS.
25°
17°
18°
33°
JUNCTION BGE. PASS.
26°
BONN GOOD

TRINITY JUNC.
NEWHAVEN GOODS
24°
0 m 28°
3°
PASS. 20°
EAST JUNC.
BONNINGTON GOODS

PILTON JUNC. WEST
0 m 36°
0 m 40°
GRANTON ROAD PASS.
0 m 47°
0 m 43°
17°
0 m 55°
LEIT WA GOO

NORTH JUNC.
Level Crossing
0 m 51°

CREWE JUNC.
0 m 43°
PILTON JUNC. EAST
44°
SOUTH JN.
POWDERHALL PASS.
0 m 39°
PASS.
0 m

WARRISTON JUNC.
3°
0 m
LEITH WALK GOODS

0 m 59°
HERIOTHILL GOODS
27°
Tunnel

From Barnton

SCOTLAND STREET GOODS

EDINBURGH
ABBEY

BARNTON JUNC.
5°
CRAIGLEITH FOR BLACKHALL

PRINCES STREET PASS.
Tunnel
0 m 65°

0 m 70°
HAYMARKET
1 m 13°
Tun!
WAVERLEY PASS.

MURRAYFIELD
10°
COLTBRIDGE JN.
Tunnel
LOTHIAN ROAD
GOODS

ROSEBURN BREWERY
10°
0 m 45°
0 m 46°

HAYMARKET CENTRAL JUNC.
0 m 44°
HAYMKT. SID.
28°
10°

From Corstorphine
3°
15°
DALRY JUNC.

HAYMARKET WEST JN.
0 64°
11°
DALRY ROAD

From Glasgow
2°
40°
53°
GRANTON JUNC.

6°
0 m 43°
0 m 50°

13°
L.N.E.
Nth BRITISH DISTILLERY SID.
0 m 32°
MERCHISTON. PASS.

CALEDONIAN BREWERY

GORGIE
GOODS L.M.S.
38°

ST LEONAR GOODS

NEWINGTON

BLACKFORD HILL PASS.
0 m 52°

From Carlisle
MORNINGSIDE ROAD

CRAIGLOCKHART PASS.
0 m 62°
0 m 72°

1928